Why We Venerate the Saints

Why We Venerate the Saints

Patricia A. Sullivan

A Herder & Herder Book
The Crossroad Publishing Company
New York

This printing 2019

The Crossroad Publishing Company
www.crossroadpublishing.com

© 2012 by Patricia A. Sullivan

ISBN (13-digit): 978-0-8245-2436-4

The stylized crossed letter C logo is a registered trademark of The Crossroad Publishing Company.

In continuation of our 200-year tradition of independent publishing, The Crossroad Publishing Company proudly offers a variety of books with strong, original voices and diverse perspectives. The viewpoints expressed in our books are not necessarily those of The Crossroad Publishing Company, any of its imprints or of its employees. No claims are made or responsibility assumed for any health or other benefit.

Printed in the United States of America.

Cataloging-in-Publication Data is available from the Library of Congress

Books published by The Crossroad Publishing Company may be purchased at special quantity discount rates for classes and institutional use. For information, please e-mail sales@crossroadpublishing.com.

For

my Mother, Mary Ellen Sullivan,

and

my Father, Daniel Stephen Sullivan.

He loves each one of us as if there were only one of us.
— Saint Augustine

Contents

Acknowledgements

My thanks for valuable input and support are due to a diverse group of individuals who were of assistance professionally and personally during my work on this project. Reviewing the entire manuscript were two admirable colleagues at Saint Anselm College. Dr. Kevin A. McMahon, Professor of Theology, generously made time in a busy schedule to read the chapters and provide perceptive notations as I finalized the manuscript; his validation of my work was a boon in its completion. Dr. Montague Brown, Professor of Philosophy and Chair of the Philosophy Department, kindly took time from a sabbatical to read through the document and offer helpful comments. Several other esteemed colleagues, from my own institution and elsewhere, read portions of my manuscript dealing with their areas of expertise and offered useful remarks: Dr. Kenneth Hagen, Professor Emeritus of Theology of Marquette University, reviewed sections dealing with the Protestant Reformation and with Protestant history and theology generally; Dr. Demetrios S. Katos, Associate Professor of Religious Studies and Dean of Hellenic College, reviewed sections dealing with Orthodox and Eastern thought and history; and Rev. Peter J. Guerin, O.S.B., Assistant Professor of Theology at Saint Anselm College, reviewed the chapter dealing with liturgical history and theology. Also among those contributing directly to this project, I owe special gratitude to John Jones, Editorial Director of The Crossroad Publishing Company, whose interest in my manuscript proposal made this volume possible, and to his assistant, Nancy Neal. For indirect contributions, I would be remiss if I did not recognize Rev. David Coffey, Professor Emeritus of Theology of Marquette University, my dissertation director under whom my work on the saints, some of which is reflected in this examination, began a decade ago in a study of invocation and intercession. For their enthusiasm and genuine theological interest in the subject of the saints, I am also grateful to my students at Saint Anselm College, especially those who have taken my Christian Saints course, source of inspiration for this book. Finally, I give thanks to and for my family, especially my parents to whom I dedicate the book, for their patience and love in all of my good pursuits, of which I hope that this work will prove to be one.

Preface

Eminent Catholic theologian Karl Rahner, allowing that veneration of the saints "is not in itself laid as an absolute duty upon the individual Christian" and that the tendency toward silence on the matter on the part of many Christians of his time (the middle of the last century) might have a positive function, wrote: "In the silence of death, in the silent presence of God precisely as the inexpressible mystery, God is actually closer and more 'present' than in much talking." But he also suggested that Christian hope might develop individual Christians' love of living neighbors into their love of the neighbors who are saints. As he wrote with Johann Baptist Metz in their small but great book, *The Courage to Pray*, "Christians should openly admit and even seriously question their inability to venerate the saints. They should not see this as inevitable or self-justifying. Instead, they must ask themselves if they can or should try to overcome it."[1] But it is difficult to overcome if the obstacle is not lack of desire but lack of information about the ancient tradition of veneration of martyrs and then of other saints.

Today's younger generations of Catholics, especially, have much curiosity yet little knowledge about the rich tradition of veneration of those recognized by the Catholic Church as models, companions, and intercessors. Indeed, any Catholic born during or after the Second Vatican Council is likely to have had little contact with the saints. This is a pity, for, even if one's spirituality would not be helped by private veneration of the saints, certainly one should understand that and how one is engaged in the Church's corporate and liturgical veneration of the saints. This longstanding practice, which arose in the early Church, is integral to the Catholic Church's doctrine of the communion of saints that touches upon critical issues of Christology, ecclesiology, theological anthropology, and pneumatology. Until lately, it factored significantly in the consciousness and lived faith life of individual members of the Church. Absent instruction in the theology of the communion of saints and veneration of its canonized members, there is danger of misunderstandings and aberrations on the part of those who are interested in the saints—and on the part of any who are intrigued by spiritualities involving the dead without realizing that some of these promoted by the larger culture can be the antithesis of Catholic and even all Christian thought and practice.

Although plenty of books about saints have been published in recent years, their intent has not been to provide a sustained biblical, historical, and theological review of veneration of saints. This work aims to offer that, to the extent possible given its modest length and its target audience and yet the vastness of the subject. It marshals basic critical biblical and historical information, and it offers extended systematic explanations that explore the Catholic Christian teaching on veneration of saints and that serve as signposts for continued reflection. Inspired by my need for a comprehensive theological source for my Christian Saints course at Saint Anselm College in Manchester, New Hampshire, it attempts—in fifteen chapters, corresponding to a traditional undergraduate semester— to address the questions and concerns expressed to me by my students. It also explores issues that have occupied my own thoughts. Therefore, grounded in the Catholic tradition, it presents Catholic teaching, but it also reflects upon doctrine and interprets it with a view to the circumstances, concerns, and sensibilities of our time. One happy fact of our age is the ecumenical movement, so, in working on this project, I had in mind Christians in other traditions, too, whether or not they validate veneration of saints, and even non-Christians inquisitive about the tradition of veneration of saints especially in its Catholic form. In a sense, then, this book is in some part a modern exercise in apologetics in its intent to explain veneration of the saints (and even to defend it, since there are people today who discourage it not only without but within churches that recommend it) in a manner meaningful for the contemporary person.

Because the book is meant for a diverse audience, in the case of reference works, where there was opportunity I consulted those that might be readily available on the shelves of local libraries or even in homes. For the same reason, and because veneration of saints has not only the public, corporate dimension encountered in the liturgy and articulated in official Church documents but also the individual dimension of private devotion, among the suggested readings at the end of chapters are some of popular piety, along with those of academic concern. Foreign terms are used in the text minimally and only in cases in which definitions, which are provided, can be found in standard translation dictionaries. For primary documents, readers are directed to worthy online sources, not only to promote familiarity with the wealth of history and theology about the saints readily available, but, because in the matter of the saints, Church documents and news reports are often most abundantly, accurately, and swiftly obtained at Church websites. Even though this latter choice will have the inevitable effect of dating parts of the book more quickly, particularly where website addresses change, and although this may introduce the risk of discouraging readers to seek the much greater wealth of information about the saints that exists beyond the Internet, the decision will have been profitable if readers are encouraged to follow the lead to reputable online sources and to search on their own for additional information both on and off the Internet. Despite these few concessions to custom of and for convenience of readers, the requisite academic sources of a depth considerably greater than usually assigned to undergraduate students are the rule in the research, so all readers will not be able to follow the footnotes to sources that will be easily accessible to them or congenial to their interests. My concern that this disjunction would make for a confused presentation was allayed by my conviction that such an approach is in keeping with the matter of veneration of saints, because of its residence in both the private devotional life of Christians and in the official theology and corporate life of the Church. And it is in continuity with a justifiable method in undergraduate instruction—on the one hand, distilling complex thought to provide students with points of access to the subject matter, and, on the other hand, sustaining some discussion just beyond immediate comprehension to entice students into serious reflection and to provide pathways for such reflection in the hint of the riches of theological exposition that already has occurred. I am no longer surprised at how many students take the initiative to follow such pathways.

In the Catholic Church, some medieval practices of the cult of the saints have been left behind for good reasons noted in the pages that follow. Others have been reinterpreted for fuller integration into the theology and practice of the Church as it has developed in time. But the recession from prominence in the last half-century of the saints generally, rather than only some practices related to them, is, despite many plausible suggestions, not fully explicable. In his ample canonizations, Blessed Pope John Paul II certainly presented plentifully opportunities for notice of the saints and their importance to the Church, as has Pope Benedict XVI. The fact of the canonized saints among us in the communion of saints attests, indispensably, to the inherently communal reality of the Church—the Body of Christ—and of all of human life. The saints are symbols, icons, or sacraments, that disclose and mediate grace to us because of their definitive unity with Christ. Now at rest in him, in their holiness, saints are evidence of Christ's enduring salvific presence in the world for people in every place and day. And this incarnational reality gifted by God is the essence of Christianity, as Catholics and many other Christians believe.

Abbreviations for Biblical Books

New Testament

Acts	Acts of the Apostles
Col.	Letter to the Colossians
1-2 Cor.	Letter(s) to the Corinthians
Eph.	Letter to the Ephesians
Gal.	Letter to the Galatians
Heb.	Letter to the Hebrews
Jas.	Letter of James
Jn.	Gospel According to John
1-3 Jn.	Letter(s) of John
Jude	Letter of Jude
Lk.	Gospel According to Luke
Mk.	Gospel According to Mark
Mt.	Gospel According to Matthew
1-2 Pet.	Letter(s) of Peter
Phil.	Letter to the Philippians
Philem.	Letter to Philemon
Rev.	Revelation to John (The Apocalypse)
Rom.	Letter to the Romans
1-2 Th.	Letter(s) to the Thessalonians
1-2 Tim.	Letter(s) to Timothy
Tit.	Letter to Titus

Old Testament
(Books Referenced in this Text)

Dan.	Book of Daniel
Dt.	Book of Deuteronomy
Ex.	Book of Exodus
Gen.	Book of Genesis
Is.	Book of Isaiah
Job	Book of Job
1-2 Kg.	Book(s) of Kings
Lev.	Book of Leviticus
1-2 Macc.	Book(s) of the Maccabees
Num.	Book of Numbers
Pr.	Book of Proverbs
Ps.	Book of Psalms
1-2 Sam.	Book(s) of Samuel
S. of S.	Song of Songs

One

VENERATION OF SAINTS:
PAST AND PRESENT

For centuries, a parade of the Catholic faithful has sought the blessing of priests who cross two candles upon recipients' throats and offer the prayer, often followed by the Sign of the Cross: "May God at the intercession of Saint Blaise preserve you from throat troubles and every other evil." This ritual commemorates the holy life of one who died seventeen centuries ago but whom the faithful sense to remain pertinent to their own lives. A fourth-century martyr and bishop of Sebaste about whom other historical details were long ago lost, Saint Blaise himself is not thought to have blessed throats, although legends identify him as a doctor who once extracted the bone of a fish from the throat of choking boy. Probably for the reputation of healing that developed about him, he became one of the most famous saints in the medieval world. Appearing by the ninth century in European martyrologies (martyr lists that included brief histories), in the latter Middle Ages he was counted among the "Fourteen Holy Helpers" around whom enthusiastic devotions arose.[1] While some of these Helpers have not retained great popularity into the present, Saint Blaise has remained notable in the Church's catalogue of saints, likely due in large part to the blessing of throats that occurs on February 3 of the current liturgical calendar of the Roman Catholic Church (and on February 11 of liturgical calendars of Eastern churches) or, for the convenience of local parishioners, on the Sunday immediately following. Recipients of the blessing engage in one of the Church's major acts of "veneration of saints"—that of invocation for intercession of a saint. In invocation of saints, we ask saints to pray for us, we ask that God will help us through the intercession of saints who do pray for us, and thereby we recognize and praise God as the source of all good that comes to us in the communion of those who believe in Christ and his ongoing activity among us.

Imitation of saints, too, is a profound form of veneration of saints. While, like invocation of saints, this is today not always a prevalent focus of spiritual instruction or exercise, many do engage in it, even if sometimes unintentionally in observation of popular customs inspired by the memory of particular saints. One example, unusual and perhaps

1

glaring for some, is the practice in the United States and elsewhere of giving gifts at Christmas under the name of Santa Claus, following a tradition of a December 6 feast of the fourth-century martyr and bishop Saint Nicholas of Myra that in some quarters of the Church is still enacted on the standing memorial date. As in the case of Blaise, memory of this saint survives mostly in legends. Nicholas's reputed generosity during his life, as well as many miracles associated with him in his life and death, became the source of the now standard role adopted by many Christian parents at Christmastime in imitation of him that, at its best, teaches children about God's benevolence in providing undeserved favors to us through the charity of those who are open to his work in them. In the West, Saint Nicholas's fame rose dramatically in the eleventh century, when his relics were moved (translated) to Bari, Italy, and his shrine became one of the most frequented by medieval pilgrims. In the East, devotion to him was already well-established by the sixth century, when a church was dedicated to him at Constantinople.[2]

Anciently, serving as both a Christian model and an intercessor is, prominently, the Blessed Virgin Mary. Catholics and other Christians most deliberately engage in imitation of her, exemplar of Christian faith, hope, and love. And confidently do Catholics and many other Christians invoke her for prayers, she among human beings who is closest to her Son, Jesus Christ, but still companion to us. In churches throughout Christian history, she, with Christ's many saints, has been honored in icons and other images that have inspired and instructed countless faithful. The impression that these images made upon those living among or visiting them was described by the late Trappist monk and author Thomas Merton. ". . . [I]f I just knelt where I was, everywhere I turned my eye I saw saints in wood or plaster or those who seemed to be saints in flesh and blood—and even those who were probably not saints, were new enough and picturesque enough to stimulate my mind with many meanings and my heart with prayers," wrote Merton near the middle of the twentieth century as he recounted a visit as a young man to Cuba and its many Catholic churches.[3] How different his experience was from that of many Catholics since then, who might have come into contact with images and stories and devotional traditions of the saints only through such popular customs as those connected to Saint Blaise and Saint Nicholas. And since these traditions are not always encountered or presented in the full context of the Catholic Church's veneration of saints, their deepest theological meaning has not always been made clear. Given the history of the Church's attention to the saints, this development is, in ways to be considered, surprising.

If one lacking great familiarity with contemporary Catholicism were to read the documents of the Second Vatican Council and the papal documents issued in its wake, or to have noticed from afar the frequent news of canonizations from the late Pope John Paul II, popularly deemed the "saint maker" and now himself beatified, as well as from Pope Benedict XVI, keeping pace with a growing list of "blesseds" and "saints" under his pontificate, one might logically assume that members of the Catholic Church are individually, actively invested in the traditional cult of the saints. But viewed more closely, it would seem that, at the beginning of Christianity's third millennium, those privately engaged in veneration of saints are not the majority. In fact, other than through senior family members whose devotion to the saints was nurtured in the first half of the twentieth century, most people growing up since Vatican II would seem to have had little contact with the saints. Except in the liturgy and in the naming of parishes, activities traditionally connected with the cult of the saints—veneration of relics and icons or other images, pilgrimages to holy sites, and novenas and other private devotions—have largely disappeared from popular Catholic experience in the most developed countries. Perhaps especially in the United States, where there are none of the medieval churches that still stand in European countries with their elaborate interior walls offering scenes from the lives of the saints, as well as their massive domes depicting the saints and angels in their heavenly home, there is little even in the way of aesthetics to remind believers of the ways in which grace has successfully transformed the lives of those who have gone before us. Even the Stations of the Cross—in which, along with Jesus, are depicted those saints who lived nearest, historically, to his saving mission—are often relegated to inconspicuous locations except in the nation's oldest churches. And familiarity with the saints' stories is scarcer than in the past, likely due in part to the hagiographical style of some traditional accounts—such as those of Saint Blaise and Saint Nicholas—that a more mature Merton saw as "a chain of fantastic miracles interspersed with pious platitudes."[4] Elements of legend frequently render such tales of saintly lives inaccessible to modern sensibilities.

There are various possible reasons for the decrease in individual attention to the saints in the last couple of generations. One suggestion is that the decline is a result of Vatican II's intent to direct attention squarely onto Christ.[5] Vatican II's alteration of the liturgical calendar excluded many of the feast days of saints that had filled the calendar for centuries, in order to move the faithful to more fervent reflection upon Christ himself, the events of his earthly life, and the lives of his apostles and disciples in the early Church. At the same time that the changes to the calendar were made, so, too, were changes made in the recommendations for church architecture and the interior configuration of worship spaces. This resulted in the near disappearance of the Baroque walls and ceilings filled with the saints of Christ, which had been a fixture in Catholic churches the world over for centuries. But there is much to suggest that the Council's refocus of liturgical interests is not the sole reason for decline in private attention to the saints on the part of today's Catholics. In other chapters it will be shown that Vatican II firmly held to the tradition of veneration of the saints, if anything giving the cult of the saints more solid grounding in the Church's eschatological mission. So other reasons, too, are offered for the decline in private attention to the saints:

— a contemporary emphasis on the humanity of Christ has turned our attention to social justice concerns sometimes aimed at a Utopia rather than at our supernatural destiny;[6]
— contemporary people are unable to separate the subject of the saints from medieval literalistic and materialistic theologies of resurrection (often involving beliefs connected to saintly relics as well as stories of saints that reflect preoccupations with the material continuity of bodies) that can seem bizarre from a modern standpoint;[7]
— the idea of saints acting from faith and emotion rather than from autonomy or independence, and the idea of their venerators acting from a hierarchical notion of the goodness of human beings, are antithetical to postmodern and democratic ideas;[8] and
— amidst the great problems of our time, Christians have less confidence than ever in the power of petitionary prayer,[9] the type of prayer traditionally associated with veneration of the saints.

A particular issue for North America is that it has few centers for private devotion to and public celebration of saints, in contrast to Europe or to South America, where pilgrimage sites still can draw the religious imagination if not the physical presence of the faithful.[10]

Shortly after Vatican II, the influential twentieth-century Catholic theologian Karl Rahner observed that God and all who rest in him seemed obscure and indistinct in the perception of people in his time. Many Christians no longer felt any contact with the dead, including dear family members who seemed to exist only in the memory of those they left behind rather than as living relatives in another realm. The person of his day had a profound sense of the incomprehensibility and remoteness of God, even while he or she knew that God is equally profoundly present. "God is, to a large extent, experienced as the silent mystery, infinite in his ineffability and inconceivability. And the more man advances in his religious life the more *these* aspects of God come consistently to the fore (instead of diminishing). Into this silent, unfathomable, and ineffable mystery the dead disappear," he wrote.[11] But Rahner's description of the attitude toward the dead in the 1960s may not offer an accurate assessment of today's situation. And this makes for a curious anomaly where private veneration of the saints is concerned.

At least in the developed nations today, there appears to be a rise in interest in spiritualities that exhibit a curious fixation on matters of life after death, along with a startling level of confidence in our ability to communicate with the dead. This is easily evidenced, in the United States and elsewhere, by a proliferation of television and radio programs and Internet sites with hosts or occasional guests acting as modern shamans who communicate with the particular dead of audience members. At the same time, there still is avid interest in traditionally popular saints. Even since Vatican II, for example, sales of Saint Christopher medals are strong, despite the fact that this saint was expunged from the liturgical calendar in 1969 because his existence most certainly is only legendary. From a Christian point of view, not all such spiritualities are helpful or even correct. Certainly spiritualistic dalliances on the part of Christians such as those propagated by television, radio, and Internet psychics are questionable, spurious occupations. But the attention to such in our culture today suggests that interest in and, indeed, belief in "communication" between the "pilgrim church"[12] on Earth and the "heavenly church"[13] is more attuned to contemporary sensibilities than might be supposed by many of those who have noted the marked decline in private veneration of the saints. Generally speaking, there is no evidence of reduced belief in the enduring significance of the dead, especially when their lives as a whole or noble final moments represent an ideal and thereby capture the admiration of others. Current events have perhaps awakened a new consciousness in this regard, one that is not antithetical to the ancient Christian impulse toward the veneration of saints and their relics. As one example, intensification of conflict in our world, including that from terrorist activity leading to such tragedies as September 11, has resulted in new discussions of the concept of "sacred space" as it applies to the locations where those have been killed who are effectively symbols of a particular way of life. Also, the usually impromptu practice of marking highways with crosses or other symbols of respect at the places of death of motorists appears to be growing. And the adornment with flowers and gifts of the sites of the death or life of deceased individuals particularly admired by a populace is a seemingly expanding worldwide custom.

Specifically with regard to the Church, as people the world over become more global in their perspective, exposure to particularized cultural sensibilities regarding death may be shown to reveal important insights consonant with Christian beliefs and practices. Some theologians have noted the possible affinity between the cult of the ancestors that is part of the cultural heritage of African members of the Church and the cult of the saints, one aspect of the Catholic Christian understanding of the communion between the living and the dead.[14] That the doctrine of the communion of saints retains at minimum subconscious extra-liturgical currency in the lives of Catholics "universally" is evident in the preserved custom of giving Christian names to children at birth as well as having children choose to take a saint name at Confirmation. And in parts of Europe, any Catholic Christian's special day—as in religious orders—still is more often celebrated on the feast of one's patron saint than on one's birthday. So the demise of private recognition and celebration of the communion of saints in which the "official" saints function as models, companions, and intercessors, as Vatican II affirmed,[15] should not be announced too loudly or definitively, for it might not be permanent, and it might even now be exaggerated. Even while Rahner wrote of the decline of many traditional practices associated with the cult of the saints, he acknowledged the evidence of feelings of communion with the dead that can readily be found in some quarters of the Church where "many ages live side by side with one another." It might be expected, he observed, that a flux in interest in the saints may be experienced as the pilgrim church moves through different layers of consciousness and understanding on its way to full participation in "the liturgy of perfect glory."[16]

Why should people today concern themselves with the communion of saints as expressed in veneration of the saints, though, if many do not find private practices of veneration compelling? There are several reasons.

First, Catholic generations reared since Vatican II have a better understanding of their faith when they are acquainted with a tradition that compelled most Christians for two thousand years, that still compels large numbers of Christians, and that remains perhaps the boldest statement of Catholic belief in the eschatological communion of all of the faithful in Christ. Although private veneration is not required of any Catholic Christian, all Catholic individuals must share in the Church's corporate veneration of the saints, and they cannot fully do so without understanding it.

Second, related to this, without the examples of the saints, there is the danger that Catholics will turn to models that do not inspire attention to the supernatural destiny of human beings. Loss of the eschatological sensibility of Christian life is a loss of the gospel message.

Third, veneration of the saints is a tradition that Catholics share with their Orthodox brothers and sisters. And, in this age of ecumenism in which Protestants and Catholics have engaged in substantial and valuable conversation about this practice and its theology, one largely opposed by the Protestant reformers, there is some irony that there are individual Catholics who feel as experientially disconnected from the tradition as their Protestant brothers and sisters.

Fourth, in the absence of a proper understanding of the dynamism of relationships among those in the communion of saints, the living and the dead, a seemingly natural human need to connect with the dead could lead Catholics to fall prey to types of spiritualism that are counter to Christianity.[17]

Fifth, there is a theological truth proclaimed perhaps more loudly than anywhere else in the tradition of veneration of the saints: Christ's victory over sin and death is manifest in all times and places; his grace is present and transformative wherever it is accepted.

Sixth, since the saints are signs of Christ's victory and our hope, they are equally invitations to all to seek a fulfilled humanity. Christ's love, tangible in the lives of the saints, can be catalytic of transformation in us, if we have eyes to see it.

Seventh and finally, the theological truth residing in veneration of the saints can perhaps be grasped fully only through an individual's participation in it. After all, as other chapters will show, it is the experience of union with Christ through devotion to the saints that gave rise to the developed notion of the communion of saints that included veneration of its holiest members. Rahner and Johann Baptist Metz suggested that a cultivated "solidarity" with and "loving veneration" of the dead is "essential if humanity is to be able to give itself up to God. Only those who can love always and everywhere can achieve this final submission."[18]

Guiding Terms and Concepts

In description of the state of veneration of the saints today, as well as the sensitivities of contemporary people in the wider culture to matters of the afterlife, a number of terms and concepts have been introduced that should be briefly clarified here: the communion of saints, saints, veneration of saints, the cult of the saints, and tradition.

The "communion of saints" refers to all of the faithful, living and dead. The Catholic sense of sacramentality—that all of reality may be permeated by God's presence—includes a strong consciousness of God mediating himself through earthly realities, preeminently so through human beings, who have the unique capacity among God's earthly creatures to respond to his grace and thereby to become more or less fully signs of his activity in the world. Those who have been canonized saints are those the Church deems to have been revealed to be the most dramatic signs in human persons of God's presence to the world, those who have been most fully transformed by his grace, those who most fully image Christ. This does not mean that those who have not been declared saints have not been touched and transformed by grace; it does not mean that others are not in Heaven. It means that some have been revealed to be not only our companions in faith as are all Christians, but also models and intercessors for the living who have not yet completed the journey to God.

The term "saints" is used in Christianity in several different but related senses. Again, in speaking of the communion of saints, reference is to the general sense of the term as all of the Christian faithful, living and dead. The New Testament speaks often of saints in this regard (e.g., 2 Cor. 13:12; Eph. 1:1).[19] More particularly, the term is used in the tradition to refer to the Christian faithful who have completed their earthly journey and now have eternal life with Christ as the "Church Triumphant" in Heaven, which is distinct from the "Church Militant" of those on Earth and the "Church Suffering" of those in Purgatory. In another particular sense, the term refers to certain persons within the community regarded as exemplarily holy. The Book of Revelation used it in reference to the martyrs (e.g., Rev. 16:6, 17:6, 18:24) around whom devotional customs later grew because of the martyrs' dramatic witness to Christ. Such devotions led to one final particular sense of the term, the sense that will be the primary concern of this study about veneration of the saints. Holy persons such as the martyrs, as well as those who were deemed models of virtue, were eventually given official recognition in the Church. They were "canonized" saints—included in the Catholic Church's official list or canon (from the Greek *kanon*[20]) of those declared to be worthy of public veneration. The Church's inclusion of an individual in the list of saints is a declaration that this person has been revealed to be in Heaven and is a worthy companion, model, and intercessor. The process for this determination will be reviewed in future chapters.

"Veneration" of the saints is respect and honor given to the saints. Saints are not worshipped. (Confusing to readers today are works of the past that occasionally used the term "worship" to refer both to worship properly speaking and to veneration of saints; fortunately, study of the context of such usages reveals the distinct intended meanings). A careful and important distinction made by Church Fathers between *dulia* (or *douleia*, as *proskunêsis*), a Greek term meaning "veneration," "honor," or "service," and *latria* (or *latreia*), a Greek term meaning "worship" or "adoration," was ratified at the Second Council of Nicaea in 787, before the separation of the Catholic and the Orthodox Churches. Religious images are given *dulia*; God is due, and he alone is given, *latria*. This council is an "ecumenical council," an assembly of bishops representing the whole Church who gather to make decisions about doctrine and governance of the Church. As such, and because this council occurred before the schisms that resulted in the present three major Christian communities, it is considered authoritative by Catholic and Orthodox Christians and by some Protestant Christians. The first seven ecumenical councils also are called "Christological councils," because they dealt with matters that led to precise theological articulations about the person and work of Jesus Christ. The Second Council of Nicaea, then, was supremely conscious of the unique role of Christ, affirming the value of religious images or "icons" in light of their relationship to him. It condemned iconoclasm (the banning of icons and other images used in the liturgy and in devotions), recognizing that the holiness depicted in religious images is possible only through grace. In honoring the images, including the saints, we are honoring and indeed worshipping God to whom all images of holiness point. More will be said in chapter 7 about this important council and the critical distinction yet unity that it emphasized between *dulia* and *latria*.

The term "cult" is an uncomfortable one for many today, given the movements of our time, often destructive, that are sometimes associated with it. In contemporary common usage, it refers to many types of groups that have an exclusive, secretive nature designed for cohesiveness of members and their separation from the larger world. Although such movements are not necessarily religious, they may be so. Often they are initiated by a charismatic leader espousing syncretistic, esoteric doctrines. But the term in its basic sense refers simply to a body of people and its variety of worship and/or ritual.[21] So in the context of early practices connected to the saints, it meant public and private worship of God, and the collective of people engaged in this, through a particular type of devotion. This community was inspired by and responded in ritual to images of the divine glimpsed in the lives and deaths of those who imitated Christ perfectly by surrendering themselves totally to God. The word itself is derived from the Latin *cultus*, which means "reverence" or "cultivation." To be sure, some of the practices connected with the early cult of the saints, and especially those that developed in the medieval Church, are uneasy for the contemporary religious sensibility even of Catholics. But behind the development of the cult in its various historical-cultural contexts are basic motivations affirming the union of all the faithful, living and dead, in and as the communion of saints. The Catholic Church today allows public cultic acts of veneration, which occur in the liturgy and are performed by ecclesiastical authorities in the name of the Church, only for "Servants of God" who are listed in the Church's calendar as "Blessed" or "Saint."[22] Early activities of the cult of the saints, initially "the cult of the martyrs," will be highlighted in chapter 3.

The term "tradition" has several senses, all of which are relevant to discussion of the communion of saints and veneration of the Church's official saints. In Catholicism, tradition is a theological category, not simply an historical one. It refers to the process of preserving faithfully and transmitting to each new generation the revelation of Christ and the Holy Spirit as given to the apostles, contemplated by believers, and preached by the bishops who are the successors to the apostles. This occurs through the Church's "doctrine, life, and worship," through which the Church "perpetuates and transmits to every generation all that it itself is, all that it believes," as *Dei Verbum*, Vatican II's Dogmatic Constitution on Divine Revelation, explains.[23] That which is preserved and handed on, "everything that serves to make the people of God live their lives in holiness and increase their faith,"[24] also is referred to as "tradition." This, the understanding of which progresses in time "with the help of the Holy Spirit," includes revelation and the Church's resulting beliefs and doctrines, rituals, and Scriptures that comprise the life of the Church.[25] Both of these senses of the word are distinct from "tradition" as a "custom" that may be useful to the Church in a particular time and place but is not binding on all generations. From this brief description, it will be clear that it is paramount that the Catholic Church determines to what sense of "tradition" a given matter belongs, since that will dictate whether a particular tradition is an element of the essential content of Christian revelation and its transmission or simply a custom consistent with revelation but not essential to its preservation. Veneration of the saints is considered by Catholics to be a legitimate element of the life of the Church, expressing a critical theological truth about Christ's person and work and therefore belonging properly to the classes of tradition that refer to the content of faith that must be preserved and the process by which that content is preserved. But there are traditions that have been connected with veneration of the saints that may have been useful to the spirituality of people in earlier places and times, yet are not binding practices on Catholics today or in the future. This will be made clear as the development of the cult of the saints is reviewed in succeeding chapters.

Conclusion

The aim of this book is to provide for the contemporary person a thorough but accessible theology of the communion of saints, particularly as it manifests itself in veneration of the saints, in the full tradition of the

Church, inclusive of Vatican II. But the basic theology of veneration of the saints is unchanged in the history of the Church. It was expressed concisely but beautifully by the unknown author who gave us the final words of *The Martyrdom of Perpetua* more than eighteen hundred years ago:

> O brave and fortunate martyrs, truly called and chosen to give honor to our Lord Jesus Christ! And anyone who is elaborating upon, or who reverences or worships that honor, should read these more recent examples, along with the ancient, as sources of encouragement for the Christian community. In this way, there will be new examples of courage witnessing to the fact that even in our day the same Holy Spirit is still efficaciously present, along with the all powerful God the Father and Jesus Christ our Lord, to whom there will always be glory and endless power. Amen.[26]

These words convey critical insight, as a quick dissection of them reveals. It is not only in the final actions of the martyrs who would be saints, but in their reverencing and "worshipping" by those in the Christian community, that we witness to the presence of the Holy Spirit, love of the Father and the Son, "even in our day," as ever. By the witness of the martyrs, *and* by the witness of those who "elaborate" upon their actions or read about and reflect upon the grace-filled actions of the saints, we present "new examples of courage" testifying to the power of God in our own time. The stories of the saints are "sources of encouragement." The ongoing telling of these stories, the honoring of those to whom the stories refer, also is doxological; it is praise of God whose grace makes such realities possible. As *Lumen Gentium*, Vatican II's Dogmatic Constitution on the Church, asserted, "Our relationship with the saints in heaven, provided that it is understood in the full light of faith, in no way diminishes the worship of adoration given to God the Father, through Christ, in the Spirit; on the contrary, it greatly enriches it."[27] For it is God "who is wonderful in his saints and is glorified in them."[28] This is why the Catholic Church canonizes saints, why it venerates them liturgically, and why it recommends their private veneration by the faithful.

From the perspective of third millennium Christians, perhaps the story of the young Christian martyr Perpetua's death at the end of a gladiator's sword so many years ago seems remote. Yet is it striking that, written less than two full centuries after the death and resurrection of Jesus Christ, the account of her martyrdom with fellow Christians was presented in contradistinction to "ancient" martyrs' stories; Perpetua was already distant enough from the foundation of Christian faith that new theologizing on the meaning of martyrdom was necessary. Since the gospel message that we see lived in the actions of saints must ever be appropriated in the time and place in which it is encountered so that it reaches each person in a way in which it can be heard and understood, new theologizing is no less necessary today.

Terms for Study

Apostolic Succession

Bishop

Canon

Canonization

Church Father

Church Militant

Church Suffering

Church Triumphant

Communion of Saints

Cult of the Saints

Doctrine

Doxology

Dulia/Douleia

Ecumenical Council

Eschaton

Hagiography

Heaven

Heavenly Church

Iconoclasm

Latria/Latreia

Liturgy

Martyr

Martyrology

Pilgrim Church

Purgatory

Sacramentality

Saint

Schism

Second Vatican Council

Tradition

Veneration

Suggested Readings

Dei Verbum. In *Vatican Council II: The Basic Sixteen Documents; Constitutions Decrees Declarations*, rev. trans. Edited by Austin Flannery. Northport, New York: Costello Publishing, 1996:97–115.

The Second Vatican Council's Dogmatic Constitution on Divine Revelation, this document describes the character of revelation and its interpretation and preservation by the Church. Of particular importance for study of veneration of the saints, the Constitution outlines the relationship between Scripture and tradition. "Flowing from the same divine well-spring" (paragraph 9), Scripture emerged from, is preserved by, and is interpreted by the tradition from which it sprang when early Christians committed to writing the words and actions of Jesus that initially had been transmitted orally.

Lumen Gentium. In *Vatican Council II: The Basic Sixteen Documents; Constitutions Decrees Declarations*, rev. trans. Edited by Austin Flannery. Northport, New York: Costello Publishing, 1996:1–95.

The Second Vatican Council's Dogmatic Constitution on the Church, this document describes the nature of the Church as mystery, as well as the common call to holiness of all of the "People of God" and the distinctive roles of clergy and laity. Chapters seven and eight have especial relevance for understanding veneration of the saints, dealing with the "pilgrim church" in journey toward its final goal in which the saints and Mary rest.

The Martyrdom of Perpetua. At New Advent [online]. Available from http://www.newadvent.org/fathers/0324.htm. Accessed 1 September 2011.

Arguably the most widely-read martyrdom account, this document appears in many published sources. It is a "passion," recounting the final days and death of the young North African martyr Perpetua and her companions, including Felicitas.

Rahner, Karl, and Johann Baptist Metz. *The Courage to Pray.* Translated by Sarah O'Brien Twohig. London: Burns & Oates and Search Press, 1980. Original edition, *Ermutigung zum Gebet*, Freiburg im Breisgau: Verlag Herder, 1977.

A small but rich reflection on prayer, one of the matters explored is veneration of the saints, including prayer to the saints. The co-authors challenge readers to examine the reasons for a lack of "solidarity" with the dead and to invest in the tradition of veneration that recognizes the unity in grace of the living and the dead.

Two

THE SAINTS IN THE BIBLE: COMPANIONS, MODELS, INTERCESSORS

The charge sometimes is made that veneration of saints is unbiblical. Although it is true that veneration of the saints in the developed form that it has taken in the Catholic Church (and, for that matter, in the Orthodox Church and in some Protestant communities) does not exist explicitly in the Bible, from a Catholic view this form is not inconsistent with the Bible, and this is the critical issue. As the Gospel of John concludes, its writer tells readers that "there are also many other things which Jesus did; were every one of them to be written, I suppose that the world itself could not contain the books that would be written" (Jn. 21:25).[1] The New Testament does not claim, then, even that every minutia of the earthly life of Jesus has been recorded, let alone every detail of the practices of the early Church as they are to be replicated for all ages. Preserved in Scripture is the revelation of Christ, not a detailed plan for the development of the Church. But nothing that develops in the Church can contradict the Bible, for that would be to depart from revelation. Any Christian practice must adhere to and flow from the message and meaning of the mission of Jesus as we have received it from Christ through the apostles. As explained in chapter 1, in Catholicism, it is tradition that ensures that the revelation of Jesus Christ will be preserved faithfully. Catholics stress that Scripture emerged from the tradition. Jesus himself did not write or dictate the Bible. Rather, his words and actions were preserved orally by those who witnessed them and later by those who remembered the stories about him. Eventually, as the Christian community grew, and as time passed, taking some of the apostles and other of Jesus' closest disciples with it, the stories were committed to writing so that they could be shared in their full integrity with Christians present and future. But the faith that was recorded in the Bible was a living faith, and it did not cease living for appearing in print. It has manifested itself in varied ways and degrees consistent with the biblical record wherever Christ has been accepted—most dramatically in the lives of the saints who have so fully followed him that to see them has seemed to Christians to be a glimpse of Christ himself, reminding all that his victory over evil was complete, for all times and all places.

The possibility of saints in the particular sense that validates veneration is grounded in the one reality of Christ as savior for all, for the saints' difference from other human beings is of degree, not of kind. Therefore, biblical passages that are relevant to the Catholic Church's understanding of the function of the saints who are venerated deal not only with the relationship that certain special people have had vis-à-vis God and their fellow human beings, but also with the relationship of any and all persons to God and to fellow human beings. However, since the canonized saints are the final focus of this study, it will be useful to consider the biblical material according to their three roles—model, companion, and intercessor—validated by the Second Vatican Council.[2] It will be left to later chapters to study the long history of Christian beliefs and practices associated with these roles, as well as the roles' proper theological interpretation.

Saintly Companions

As later chapters will show, from a theological standpoint, the canonized saints' role as companion is most basic; it is our shared humanity and faith that make it possible for any human person to serve effectively and worthily as a model and as an intercessor for another. The venerated saints' close proximity to Christ accounts for the unique character of their companionship to others in the communion of saints. The special communion of all who are in Christ is a constant theme in the New Testament, a theme communicated in ways implicit or subtle and in ways explicit and dramatic. The Christian communion is borne not by natural human affection alone, but by supernatural grace operating in and through all who have faith in Jesus as the Christ (Gk. *christos*, "the anointed one"), the Messiah. This is apparent in the New Testament, first, in basic attestations to the fellowship that exists among Christians, as well as in Jesus' commandment compelling Christian fellowship, and, second, in the theological explanation of the Christian communal reality, as well as in claims of the depth of necessary commitment to this reality on the part of all Christians.

Christian Fellowship

It is perhaps in the epistles that the simplest evidence is found of the early Christians' understanding of themselves as existing in a communion with each other in Christ and the Holy Spirit. Here, writers offer warm greetings and farewells from and to Christian communities of "brethren" (1 Cor. 16:20; 2 Cor. 13:11; Gal. 1:2, 6:6; Eph. 6:23; Phil. 4:21; Col. 1:2; 2 Tim. 4:21; Heb. 13:22)[3] with whom all Christians have "fellowship" (2 Cor. 13:14) through Christ (1 Jn. 1:6–7).[4] The openings and closings of epistles explain that "those sanctified in Christ Jesus" are "called to be saints together with all those who in every place call on the name of our Lord Jesus Christ . . ." (1 Cor. 1:2). They should "[g]reet one another with a holy kiss" (2 Cor. 13:12).[5] The faithful in Christ are "brother" (2 Cor. 1:1; Eph. 6:21; Col. 1:1, 4:7, 9; Philem. 1; Heb. 13:23; 1 Pet. 5:12), "sister" (Philem. 2), and "child[ren]" (1 Tim. 1:2; 2 Tim. 1:2; Tit. 1:4; 3 Jn. 1:4) to each other.[6] The body of the epistles explains: "For all who are led by the Spirit of God are sons [and daughters] of God" (Rom. 8:14).[7] Christians share "spiritual blessings" and are bidden to share "material blessings" as well (Rom. 15:27),[8] living in "harmony with one another" (Rom. 15:5) with "one voice" (Rom. 5:6) and with "the same mind and the same judgment" (1 Cor. 1:10), "in one spirit" (Phil. 1:27) and "having the same love" (Phil. 2:2),[9] "to die together and to live together" (2 Cor. 7:3). Paul, "apostle to the Gentiles" (Rom. 11:13), told the Galatians: ". . . [D]o good to all men [and women], and especially to those who are of the household of faith" (Gal. 6:10).[10] And the earliest Christians followed this advice of Paul's epistles: the Acts of the Apostles records the earliest days of the religion when ". . . all who believed were together and had all things in common; and they sold their possessions and goods and distributed them to all, as any had need" (Acts 2:44–45).[11]

In the gospels, there is an explicit mandate for unity among Christians—Jesus' commandment to love: "A new commandment I give to you, that you love one another; even as I have loved you, that you also love one another. By this all men will know that you are my disciples, if you have love for one another" (Jn. 14:34–35).[12] This second greatest commandment is related to the first, in a way that will be considered in detail in later chapters. For now, it should be noted that the synoptic gospels (i.e., Matthew, Mark, and Luke, which share much material about Jesus and order it similarly) record Jesus teaching at once the importance of the two commandments on love : ". . . 'You shall love the Lord your God with all your heart, and with all your soul, and with all your strength, and with all your mind; and your neighbor as yourself'" (Lk. 10:27).[13] In the Gospel of Mark, Jesus affirms a scribe's understanding of the teaching, that "to love him [God] with all the heart, and with all the understanding, and with all the strength, and to love one's neighbor as oneself, is much more than all whole burnt offerings and sacrifices" (Mk. 12:33).

Communion of Grace

New Testament writers referred abundantly to the gift and power of grace, as in the closing benediction of 2 Cor. 13:14, notable for its explicitly Trinitarian structure: "The grace of the Lord Jesus Christ and the love of God and the fellowship of the Holy Spirit be with you all."[14] Such passages show consciousness that the profoundly communal relationship enjoyed by Christians is possible only through the grace of Christ. A preeminent metaphor explaining the ontological nexus of believers in Christ is that of the "Body of Christ": "For as in one body we have many members, and all the members do not have the same function, so we, though many, are one body in Christ, and individually members one of another" (Rom. 12:4–5). This is a Eucharistic reality, of which Paul writes to the Corinthians: ". . . The bread which we break, is it not a participation in the Body of Christ? Because there is one bread, we who are many are one body, for we all partake of the one bread" (1 Cor. 10:17). The gifts of this participation are for the sustenance and increase of the Body of Christ, which is the Church (Eph. 5:23). ". . . [S]trive to excel in building up the church" (1 Cor. 14:12),[15] Paul wrote to the Corinthians. ". . . Let all things be done for edification" (1 Cor. 14:26). He told the Romans: "Having gifts that differ according to the grace given to us, let us use them: if prophecy, in proportion to our faith; if service, in our serving; he who teaches, in his teaching; he who exhorts, in his exhortation; he who contributes, in liberality; he who gives aid, with zeal; he who does acts of mercy, with cheerfulness" (Rom. 12:6–8).[16] The Ephesians were instructed: ". . . [W]e are to grow up in every way into him who is the head, into Christ, from whom the whole body, joined and knit together by every joint with which it is supplied, when each part is working properly, makes bodily growth and upbuilds itself in love" (Eph. 4:15–16).

Because we are one body in Christ, we must share each other's sufferings, as Christ bore suffering on our behalf. "If one member suffers, all suffer together; if one member is honored, all rejoice together" (1 Cor. 12:26), Paul told the Corinthians. "Bear one another's burdens, and so fulfil the law of Christ" (Gal. 6:2), he told the Galatians. Love is the "more excellent way" (1 Cor. 12:31) of using the gifts of Christ for the building up of the Body of Christ.[17] "[H]e who loves his neighbor has fulfilled the law" (Rom. 13:8), the Romans were told. "The commandments, . . , are summed up in this sentence, 'You shall love your neighbor as yourself.' Love does no wrong to a neighbor; therefore love is the fulfilling of the law" (Rom. 13:9–10).[18] Early Christians, persecuted, understood that such suffering has purpose. And so the First Letter of Peter encouraged:

. . . Be sober, be watchful. Your adversary the devil prowls around like a roaring lion, seeking some one to devour. Resist him, firm in your faith, knowing that the same experience of suffering is required of your brotherhood throughout the world. And after you have suffered a little while, the God of all grace, who has called you to his eternal glory in Christ, will himself restore, establish, and strengthen you. . . . (1 Pet. 5:8–10).

In Paul's suffering for the gospel, he "endure[d] everything for the sake of the elect, that they also may obtain salvation in Christ Jesus with its eternal glory" (2 Tim. 2:9–10). For the sake of the gospel, others, too, must "[s]hare in suffering as a good soldier of Christ Jesus" (2 Tim. 2:3). This is so that, by faith, Paul, and other Christians, "may know him and the power of his resurrection, and may share his sufferings, becoming like him in his death" to "attain the resurrection from the dead" (Phil. 3:10–11). To become like Christ in the communion formed by him, with the Holy Spirit, is to become a model for others.

Saintly Models

The importance of models in Christian living can be considered according to three areas of focus in the New Testament: Christ as *the* exemplar, exemplary Christians as instructors in imitation of Christ, and the transformative power of Christian "modeling."

Christ *the* Model

The model for Christian life is, of course, Christ himself. As the writer of the First Letter of John explained, "He who says 'I know him' but disobeys his commandments is a liar, and the truth is not in him; but whoever keeps his word, in him truly love for God is perfected. By this we may be sure that we are in him: he who says he abides in him ought to walk in the same way in which he walked" (1 Jn. 2:4–6). Jesus taught his followers to "walk" as servants. In the Johannine account of the Last Supper, Jesus washes the feet of his disciples, and he then instructs them to follow his example:

If I then, your Lord and Teacher, have washed your feet, you also ought to wash one another's feet. For I have given you an example, that you also should do as I have done to you. Truly, truly, I say to you, a servant is not greater than his master; nor is he who is sent greater than he who sent him. If you know these things, blessed are you if you do them (Jn. 13:14–17).[19]

In the Gospel of Matthew, too, Jesus instructs the apostles to imitate him in his servanthood:

> . . . , 'You know that the rulers of the Gentiles lord it over them, and their great men exercise authority over them. It shall not be so among you; but whoever would be great among you must be your servant, and whoever would be first among you must be your slave; even as the Son of man came not to be served but to serve, and to give his life as a ransom for many' (Mt. 20:25–28).

With slight variations in language, this speech appears elsewhere in this gospel and in the other synoptic gospels, with the clear implication that it is necessary to imitate Christ if we wish to follow him truly. "He who is greatest among you shall be your servant; . . ," (Mt. 23:11). ". . . [L]et the greatest among you become as the youngest, and the leader as one who serves. For which is the greater, one who sits at table, or one who serves? Is it not the one who sits at table? But I am among you as one who serves" (Lk. 22:26–27).[20] ". . . [W]hoever would be great among you must be your servant, and whoever would be first among you must be slave of all. For the Son of man also came not to be served but to serve, and to give his life as a ransom for many" (Mk. 10:43–45).[21] ". . . 'If any man would come after me, let him deny himself and take up his cross and follow me'" (Mt. 16:24).[22]

Christ's injunction to imitation of him in his posture of servanthood is echoed by his early followers who wrote the New Testament epistles. The First Letter to the Ephesians enjoins: "Therefore be imitators of God, as beloved children. And walk in love, as Christ loved us and gave himself up for us, a fragrant offering and sacrifice to God" (Eph. 5:1–2). The Philippians are told: "Let each of you look not only to his own interests, but also to the interests of others. Have this mind among yourselves, which is yours in Christ Jesus, who, though he was in the form of God, did not count equality with God a thing to be grasped, but emptied himself, taking the form of a servant, . . ." (1 Phil. 2:4–7). In the context of a discussion of "domestic codes" (outlines of proper attitudes and behavior of persons toward each other based upon their social roles), the First Letter of Peter calls Christians to "live as servants of God" (1 Pet. 2:16), to imitate the example of Christ in patient endurance even of unjust suffering (1 Pet. 2:18–20):

> For to this you have been called, because Christ also suffered for you, leaving you an example, that you should follow in his

steps. He committed no sin; no guile was found on his lips. When he was reviled, he did not revile in return; when he suffered, he did not threaten; but he trusted to him who judges justly. He himself bore our sins in his body on the tree, that we might die to sin and live to righteousness. By his wounds you have been healed. For you were straying like sheep, but have now returned to the Shepherd and Guardian of your souls (1 Pet. 2:21–25).[23]

These words bolstered the resolve of Christians to be steadfast in faith despite persecution and general pagan opposition.[24] And those who followed Christ's example became models for other Christians.

Christian Models of Imitation of Christ

In the developing Church structure of the first century, exemplary leadership was seen as a buttress to the faith of oppressed Christians. Elders of the early Christian community were exhorted to "[t]end the flock of God that is your charge, not by constraint but willingly, not for shameful gain but eagerly, not as domineering over those in your charge but being examples to the flock" (1 Pet. 5:2–3).[25] The source of such humility "under the mighty hand of God" (1 Pet. 5:6) is ". . . the God of all grace, who has called you to his eternal glory in Christ . . ." (1 Pet. 5:10). All of those serving in leadership positions in the Church are to be examples. The First Letter to Timothy insists that a bishop "must be above reproach" (1 Tim. 3:2) and "well thought of by outsiders" (1 Tim. 3:7). Deacons "who serve well" will "gain . . . great confidence in the faith which is in Christ Jesus" (1 Tim. 3:13). "[G]ood minister[s] of Christ Jesus" (1 Tim. 4:6) are to "set the believers an example in speech and conduct, in love, in faith, in purity" (1 Tim. 4:12). In the Letter to Titus, this "partner and fellow worker" of Paul (2 Cor. 8:23) is advised: "Show yourself in all respects a model of good deeds, and in your teaching show integrity, gravity, and sound speech that cannot be censured, so that an opponent may be put to shame, having nothing evil to say of us" (Tit. 2:7–8). Early Christians were bidden to observe the example of those strong in the faith and in the life of the faith. The author of the Letter to the Hebrews urged his readers to "[r]emember your leaders, those who spoke to you the word of God; consider the outcome of their life, and imitate their faith" (Heb. 13:7).[26] Christians must ". . . not be sluggish, but imitators of those who through faith and patience inherit the promises" (Heb. 6:12). The author of the Letter of James exhorted Christians to patience in expectation of the "Parousia," the second coming of the Lord in glory,[27] by appealing to a model from the Old Testament: "As an example of suffering and patience, brethren, take the prophets who spoke in the name of the Lord" (Jas. 5:10). Faith of such power was originally modeled by Abraham. ". . . [F]ollow the example of the faith which our father Abraham had . . ." (Rom. 4:12), wrote Paul to the Romans. "He [Abraham] received circumcision as a sign or seal of the righteousness which he had by faith while he was still uncircumcised. . . . to make him the father of all who believe without being circumcised and who thus have righteousness reckoned to them, . . ." (Rom. 4:11).[28] The Letter to the Hebrews contains a litany of Old Testament figures exemplary in faith: Abel, Enoch, Noah, Abraham, Sarah, Isaac, Jacob, Joseph, Moses, Rahab, Gideon, Barak, Samson, Jephthah, David, Samuel and the prophets, and others (Heb. 11). And wrote the author of the Letter of James: "Behold, we call those happy who were steadfast. You have heard of the steadfastness of Job, and you have seen the purpose of the Lord, how the Lord is compassionate and merciful" (Jas. 5:11).

Of exemplary figures among the early Christians, Timothy was given the leadership model of his senior colleague, Paul: "Now you have observed my teaching, my conduct, my aim in life, my faith, my patience, my love, my steadfastness, my persecutions, my sufferings, . . . what persecutions I endured; . . . Indeed all who desire to live a godly life in Christ Jesus will be persecuted, . . ." (2 Tim. 3:10–12). Speaking on behalf of Timothy, as well as of missionary companion Silvanus, and for himself (2 Th. 1:1), Paul told the Thessalonians:

> For you yourselves know how you ought to imitate us; we were not idle when we were with you, we did not eat any one's bread without paying, but with toil and labor we worked night and day, that we might not burden any of you. It was not because we have not that right, but to give you in our conduct an example to imitate (2 Th. 3:7–9).[29]

Paul also urged the Philippians: "Brethren, join in imitating me, and mark those who so live as you have an example in us" (Phil. 3:17).

Transformation from Imitation

In conjunction with exhortations to imitation of Christ and of those who imitate him, the New Testament writings contain a critical emphasis in explanation of the function and meaning of Christian models: a fruit of observing and imitating good models of faith is transformation, by grace, of the imitator—into a model of faith for yet others. The possibility of this exponential spread of faith through imitation of those who imitate Christ is expressed especially in the writings of Paul. Paul commended the Thessalonians for being "imitators of us [Paul and his missionary companions]" (1 Th. 1:6) and thereby becoming "an example to all the believers in Macedonia and in Achaia. . . . [Y]our faith in God has gone forth everywhere, so that we need not say anything" (1 Th. 1:7–8).[30] The Thessalonians had become ". . . imitators of the churches of God in Christ Jesus in Judea; for you suffered the same things [persecution]. . ." (1 Th. 2:14) but were unshakeable in accepting and adhering to "the word of God, which is at work in you believers" (1 Th. 2:13).

⌈The likeness to Christ of those who follow him and thereby lead others to do the same is dramatically apparent in the case of Paul, who presented himself as an unlikely example chosen for his role in spreading the gospel precisely to convince others of the power and love of Christ.⌉ In words attributed to the one known formerly as Saul of Tarsus,[31]

> [T]hough I formerly blasphemed and persecuted and insulted him [Jesus Christ]; but I received mercy because I had acted ignorantly in unbelief, and the grace of our Lord overflowed for me with the faith and love that are in Christ Jesus. The saying is sure and worthy of full acceptance, that Christ Jesus came into the world to save sinners. And I am the foremost of sinners; but I received mercy for this reason, that in me, as the foremost, Jesus Christ might display his perfect patience for an example to those who were to believe in him for eternal life (1 Tim. 1:13–16).

Now as one of the "servants of Christ and stewards of the mysteries of God" (1 Cor. 4:1), Paul told the Corinthians: "For though you have countless guides in Christ, you do not have many fathers. For I became your father in Christ Jesus through the gospel. I urge you, then, be imitators of me" (1 Cor. 4:15–16). "Be imitators of me, as I am of Christ" (1 Cor. 11:1). Indeed, Paul implied that in imitating Christ well, one manifests him for others; Christians are "always carrying in the body the death of Jesus, so that the life of Jesus may also be manifested in our bodies. For while we live we are always being given up to death for Jesus' sake, so that the life of Jesus may be manifested in our mortal flesh" (2 Cor. 4:10–11).[32] It is such exemplary imitation of Christ, truly disclosing him to others and thereby rendering the imitators conduits of his grace, that makes the saintly models worthy and effective intercessors.

Saintly Intercessors

The Letter of James recalls that rain was withheld or given as a result of prayer of Elijah (Jas. 5:17–18), for "[t]he prayer of a righteous man has great power in its effects" (Jas. 5:16).[33] The prayer of this righteous man even brought to life the dead son of a widow who had cared for Elijah at the direction of God (1 Kg. 17). In both of these cases, Elijah petitioned God. Petitionary prayer is an entreaty, a plea to God for divine assistance. But Elijah petitioned God for the sake of others: he functioned as an intercessor. Intercessory prayer, then, also is an appeal to God; it is a type of petitionary prayer given consciously by or for the "mediation" of another. All Christian prayer, explicitly or implicitly, is through *the* Mediator, Jesus Christ, the second person of the Trinity who became incarnate. But, through the grace of Christ, human beings can serve as intercessors, too, a belief that is attested amply in the New Testament.

Since petitionary prayer and intercessory prayer are related, scriptural instances of each must be considered for a thorough understanding of the way in which saints can function as intercessors. Scriptural references to petitionary prayer can be divided into three categories: Jesus' instruction in the practice of petitionary prayer, the Spirit's assistance in petitionary prayer, and "saints'" practice of petitionary prayer. References to intercessory prayer also can be studied under three related groupings: Jesus as *the* Mediator and Intercessor, the Spirit as intercessor, and "saints" as intercessors.

Petitionary Prayer: Jesus' Instruction

Jesus' most explicit instruction on prayer involves petition. "When you pray, say: 'Father, hallowed be thy name. Thy kingdom come. Give us each day our daily bread; and forgive us our sins, for we ourselves forgive every one who is indebted to us; and lead us not into temptation'" (Lk. 11:2–4).[34] His further instruction regarding petitionary prayer is that we *should* make request of God the Father.

> Ask, and it will be given you; seek, and you will find; knock, and it will be opened to you. For every one who asks receives, and he who seeks finds, and to him who knocks it will be opened. Or what man of you, if his son asks him for bread, will give him a stone? Or if he asks for a fish, will give him a serpent? If you then, who are evil, know how to give good gifts to your children, how much more will your Father who is in heaven give good things to those who ask him (Mt. 7:7–11)![35]

Faith renders such prayers efficacious. Jesus told Peter and the other apostles as they questioned him about the fig tree withered at his curse that "whatever you ask in prayer, believe that you have received it, and it will be yours" (Mk. 11:24).[36]

Jesus taught not only the form of petitionary prayer and confidence in offering it, but persistence. The Lukan story of the importunate friend who, precisely because of an insistent request, will be successful in rousing from sleep a friend to feed him, makes it plain that the Father is persuaded not only by our faith, our friendship with him, or our needs, but by our persistence in petition: "I tell you, though he will not get up and give him anything because he is his friend, yet because of his importunity he will rise and give him whatever he needs," said the Lord (Lk. 11:8). So, too, in the parable of the unjust judge in Luke 18 which the evangelist presented as Jesus' lesson that disciples "ought always to pray and not lose heart" (Lk. 18:1), the judge decides finally for the widow against her adversary "because this widow bothers me, [so] I will vindicate her, or she will wear me out by her continual coming" (Lk. 18:5). Such prayer may be part of the very process of God bringing to fruition that which he has planned, for when Jesus instructed the disciples about the Kingdom of God via a metaphor about the need for laborers to harvest, he told them to "pray therefore the Lord of the harvest to send out laborers into his harvest" (Mt. 9:38; Lk. 10:2).[37] The New Testament teaches, then, that it is God's will that we come to him with our requests, which should be in correspondence to the divine will. The supreme example of prayerful submission to the will of God was given by Jesus himself at the Mount of Olives as he uttered his fateful words: "Father, if thou art willing, remove this cup from me; nevertheless not my will, but thine, be done" (Lk. 22:42).[38] At this same time, he told the disciples: "Pray that you may not enter into temptation" (Lk. 22:40, 46).[39]

Petitionary Prayer: The Spirit's Assistance

Scripture suggests that prayer reveals to us our real needs and therefore readies us to understand when and how God has fulfilled them. As 1 Cor. 2:10–13 proclaims,

> God has revealed to us through the Spirit. For the Spirit searches everything, even the depths of God. For what person knows a man's thoughts except the spirit of the man which is in him? So also no one comprehends the thoughts of God except the Spirit of God. Now we have received not the spirit of the world, but the Spirit which is from God, that we might understand the gifts bestowed on us by God. And we impart this in words not taught by human wisdom but taught by the Spirit, interpreting spiritual truths to those who possess the Spirit.

The Holy Spirit is given if we ask. In the Gospel of Luke, it is not simply "good things" (Mt. 7:11) that the Lord will give to us in answer to our pleas, but this very gift of grace: "If you, then, who are evil, know how to give good gifts to your children, how much more will the heavenly Father give the Holy Spirit to those who ask him!" (Lk. 11:13).

Petitionary Prayer: 'Saints" Practice

The will of God for our confidence and persistence in prayer would seem to be manifested amply in Jesus' followers featured in the New Testament. The Philippians were instructed by Paul: "Have no anxiety about anything, but in everything by prayer and supplication with thanksgiving let your requests be made known to God" (Phil. 4:6). Paul urged the Thessalonians to "pray constantly" (1 Th. 5:17), while they "[r]ejoice always" (1 Th. 5:16), and to "give thanks in all circumstances; for this is the will of God in Christ Jesus for you" (1 Th. 5:18). The Letter of James echoes this, recommending petitionary prayer when one is suffering (Jas. 5:13). But, although God generously gives wisdom to all who request it, we must "ask in faith, with no doubting, for he who doubts is like a wave of the sea that is driven and tossed by the wind. For that person must not suppose that a double-minded man, unstable in all his ways, will receive anything from the Lord" (Jas. 1:6–8). The same writer reprimanded: "You ask and do not receive, because you ask wrongly, to spend it on your passions" (Jas. 4:3). To do this is to make oneself a "friend of the world" which is "an enemy of God" (Jas. 4:4).

During the earthly life of Christ, those who believed in him as the Messiah displayed the faith and fervor of petition recommended by the later epistle writers. The gospel accounts record occasion after occasion on which Jesus was approached for healings, exorcisms, or other miraculous events, from that of the leper who appears in the synoptic gospels to tell Jesus that "if you will, you can make me clean" and is commanded by Jesus to "be clean" (Mk. 1:40; Mt. 8:2; Lk. 5:12) to a paralytic who appears in each of the four gospels under a variety of circumstances but always with the result that he picks up the pallet on which he had lain before meeting Jesus and walks away (Mt. 9:1–8; Mk. 2:1–12; Lk. 5:17–26; Jn. 5:1–18).[40] In the Acts of the Apostles, it is recorded that after the resurrection and ascension of Jesus, the apostles offered a prayer of petition that the correct disciple would be chosen by them to fulfill the role of the twelfth apostle vacated by the death of Judas Iscariot (Acts 1:15–26).[41]

Intercessory Prayer:
Jesus *the* Mediator and Intercessor

The clear statement of the Christian Scriptures is that Jesus is *the* Mediator or Intercessor, so there can be no sense in which understanding the saints as intercessors supplants in our minds the role of Christ. In fact, the only possibility of any human person becoming a saint and/or intercessor is through Christ. "If you abide in me, and my words abide in you, ask whatever you will, and it shall be done for you" (Jn. 15:7), as Jesus' words to his disciples are recorded in the Gospel of John. ". . . [I]f you ask anything of the Father, he will give it to you in my name. . . ; ask, and you will receive, that your joy may be full" (Jn. 16:23–24).[42]

Confidence in the absolute power of Jesus Christ to mediate or intercede for us is the very point of the New Testament. The Letter to the Hebrews exclaims that "he is able for all time to save those who draw near to God through him, since he always lives to make intercession for them" (Heb. 7:25). This is so because "Christ has obtained a ministry which is as much more excellent than the old as the covenant he mediates is better, since it is enacted on better promises" (Heb. 8:6). "[H]e is the mediator of a new covenant, so that those who are called may receive the promised eternal inheritance, since a death has occurred which redeems them from the transgressions under the first covenant" (Heb. 9:15).[43] As the First Letter of John exclaims, ". . . [W]e have an advocate with the Father, Jesus Christ the righteous; and he is the expiation for our sins, and not for ours only but also for the sins of the whole world" (1 Jn. 2:1–2). Christ Jesus "who died, yes, who was raised from the dead, . . . is at the right hand of God" and "intercedes for us" (Rom. 8:34), Paul told the Romans. "[I]f you confess with your lips that Jesus is Lord and believe in your heart that God raised him from the dead, you will be saved" (Rom. 10:9). For, as proclaimed emphatically in the First Letter to Timothy, ". . . [T]here is one God, and there is one mediator between God and men, the man Christ Jesus, who gave himself as a ransom for all, the testimony to which was borne at the proper time" (1 Tim. 2:5).

In the gospels, Jesus Christ *the* Mediator is recorded as having prayed for others. In other words, Jesus engaged in intercessory prayer. It is his prayer that keeps Peter from losing his faith and betraying him, as did Judas, and that prepares Peter for his coming role as leader of his "brethren" (Lk. 22:31–32).[44] Jesus prays for the forgiveness of those who crucify him (Lk. 23:34). In the Gospel of John, Jesus promises at the Last Supper: ". . . I will pray the Father, and he will give you another Counselor . . ." (Jn. 14:16). As he anticipates and welcomes his glorification in death at the end of his mission, he prays "for those whom thou [the Father] hast given me, for they are thine; . ." (Jn. 17:9).

". . . [K]eep them from the evil one," he asks (Jn. 17:15), that they "may be consecrated in truth" (Jn. 17:19). "I do not pray for these only, but also for those who believe in me through their word, . . , so that the world may believe that thou hast sent me" (Jn. 17:20). Jesus' eloquent petitionary prayer to the Father in chapter 17 of the Gospel of John also includes "those who believe in me through their [believers'] word, that they may all be one; even as thou, Father, art in me, and I in thee, that they also may be in us, so that the world may believe that thou hast sent me" (Jn. 17:20–21). But this reality is not to be realized only in his earthly ministry, for, as Jesus is to be "no more in the world" (Jn. 17:11), he asked that "they also, whom thou hast given me, may be with me where I am, to behold my glory which thou hast given me in thy love for me before the foundation of the world" (Jn. 17:24).[45]

Intercessory Prayer: The Spirit as Intercessor

Despite the fact that Jesus is *the* Mediator or Intercessor, others also are mentioned in Scripture as intercessors, including the Spirit who was present at significant moments of Jesus' ministry. As written in the fourth gospel account, Jesus' own prayer of intercession requested that the Father provide for us ". . . another Counselor, to be with you for ever, even the Spirit of truth, whom the world cannot receive, because it neither sees him nor knows him; you know him, for he dwells with you, and will be in you" (Jn. 14:16–17). Paul explained to the Romans that the Spirit guides our prayer: "[T]he Spirit helps us in our weakness; for we do not know how to pray as we ought, but the Spirit himself intercedes for us with sighs too deep for words. And, he who searches the hearts of men knows what is the mind of the Spirit, because the Spirit intercedes for the saints according to the will of God" (Rom. 8:26–27). Paul urged the Ephesians to rely on the mediation of the Spirit for the benefit of others: "Pray at all times in the Spirit, with all prayer and supplication. To that end keep alert with all perseverance, making supplication for all the saints, and also for me, that utterance may be given me in opening my mouth boldly to proclaim the mystery of the gospel, . . ." (Eph. 6:18–19).

Intercessory Prayer: 'Saints' as Intercessors

The New Testament encourages human beings to intercede for each other, a possibility precisely because of the mediation or intercession of Christ. It is *not* that we *instead of* Christ can intercede for our fellow human beings, but that, *in* Christ, whether this is explicitly recognized or not, we are joined to him in petition. We have been "called into the fellowship of his [God's] Son, Jesus Christ our Lord" (1 Cor. 1:9), explained Paul to the Corinthians. "I have been crucified with Christ; it is no longer I who live, but Christ who lives in me; . . ," (Gal. 2:20), he preached to the Galatians. "For as many of you as were baptized into Christ have put on Christ" (Gal. 3:27). And so the insistence in the First Letter to Timothy that Jesus Christ is the one Mediator between God and human beings (1 Tim. 2:5) is prefaced with an entreaty for the intercessions of Christians for fellow human beings: "I urge that supplications, prayers, intercessions, and thanksgivings be made for all men, for kings and all who are in high positions, that we may lead a quiet and peaceable life, godly and respectful in every way. This is good, and it is acceptable in the sight of God our Savior, who desires all men to be saved and to come to the knowledge of the truth" (1 Tim. 2:1–4). The First Letter of John would seem to present intercessory prayer as a mutual responsibility of Christians for one another: ". . . [I]f we ask anything according to his [God's] will he hears us. And if we know that he hears us in whatever we ask, we know that we have obtained the requests made of him. If any one sees his brother committing what is not a mortal sin, he will ask, and God will give him life for those whose sin is not mortal" (1 Jn. 5:14–16).[46] The final words of the first Christian martyr Stephen at his stoning, as recorded in chapters 6 and 7 of the Acts of the Apostles, echo the intercessory words of Jesus on the Cross: "Lord, do not hold this sin against them" (Acts 7:60).

Requests of Christians for the prayers of other Christians appear throughout the New Testament. The Romans (Rom. 15:30), the Thessalonians (1 Th. 5:25; 2 Th. 3:1–2), the Philippians (Phil. 1:19–20), the Colossians (Col 4:2–3), and Philemon (Philem. 22) are all asked to pray for Paul, and often for his missionary colleagues; alternately, these communities are thanked for their prayers. In Paul's Second Letter to the Corinthians, as he recounted a recent divine deliverance from a death sentence during a missionary journey in Asia and expressed hope that "he [God] will deliver us again" (2 Cor. 1:10), he urged the community to join him in giving a prayerful thanks that included a perhaps implicit petition: "You also must help us by prayer, so that many will give thanks on our behalf for the blessing granted us in answer to many prayers" (2 Cor. 1:11). Other early Christians also asked for prayers, as well as recommended them. "Pray for us, . ." (Heb. 13:18), the Letter to the Hebrews requests. "Is any among you sick? Let him call for the elders of the church, and let them pray over him, . . ." (Jas. 5:14), wrote the author of the Letter of James. ". . . [P]ray for one another, that you may be healed" (Jas. 5:16). The necessity of praying even for one's enemies or persecutors is a key theme in the New Testament: ". . . Love your enemies and pray for those who persecute you, . . ." (Mt. 5:44), Jesus taught.[47]

Paul prayed for elders of the churches he founded in Christ.[48] He was consistent in opening his letters and sometimes dotting them elsewhere with assurances of his prayers and those of his entourage for the communities addressed.[49] The efficacy of his prayers and of those of other Christians is attested in Acts, where stories are recounted of Paul's answered prayers for his shipmates during a perilous voyage to Malta and of a successful community prayer gathering at the home of one Mary and her son John Mark to effect the release of Peter from prison.[50] While on the island of Malta, Paul healed the father of a high official, as well as many others (Acts 28:7–9). When Paul and Silas were imprisoned in Rome, after prayer and song to God an earthquake opened the doors of the prison, as well as the heart of the jailor, who took the disciples from the jail to his home, where he was baptized with his entire family (Acts 16:25–34). Many miracles occurred through Paul on a visit to Ephesus: "[H]andkerchiefs or aprons were carried away from his body to the sick, and diseases left them and the evil spirits came out of them" (Acts 19:11–12). Elsewhere, in Jesus Christ's name, Peter healed a lame man at the gate of the Temple (Acts 3:1–9). He raised Tabitha when he arrived at Joppa too late to cure her of the deathly illness that caused disciples to summon him (Acts 9:36–43). Peter and other apostles performed many "signs and wonders," including healings of multitudes carried to them (Acts 5:12–16).[51] After Peter and John were released from arrest and questioning by the Sanhedrin in Jerusalem, their friends prayed "through the name of thy holy servant Jesus" and ". . . the place in which they were gathered together was shaken; and they were all filled with the Holy Spirit and spoke the word of God with boldness" (Acts 4:23–31).

Also not to be ignored are the numerous instances recorded in the gospels in which, during his earthly life, Jesus' believers acted as intercessors, receiving assistance from him for others: an official's servant or son is cured from a deathly illness (Mt. 8:5–13; Lk. 7:1–10; Jn. 4:46–54); Jairus's daughter is raised after being declared dead (Mt. 9:18–19, 23–26; Mk. 5:21–24, 35–43; Lk. 8:40–42a, 49–56); a man's son is cured of epilepsy or of a spirit that "seizes him" (Mt. 17:14–21; Mk. 9:14–29; Lk. 9:37–43a); a demon is cast out of a Canaanite woman's daughter (Mt. 15:21–28; Mk. 7:24–30); Peter's mother–in–law is rid of a fever (Mk. 1:29–31; Lk. 4:38–39);[52] and Lazarus is raised after his sisters, Martha and Mary, send for Jesus when their brother falls ill (Jn. 11:1–44). Strikingly, "the first of his signs"—the water turned to wine at the wedding at Cana— occurs at the intercession of Jesus' mother, Mary (Jn. 2:1–11).

The clear implication of gospel stories of Jesus—or, through him, Jesus' disciples—raising from dead those for whom others had requested help is that our petitions for others can be efficacious in life and in death. Yet it will not have gone unnoticed that explicit scriptural exhortations to intercessory prayer in the New Testament do not deal with prayer of the living for the dead, or of the dead for the living.[53] But they do not prohibit it either. And, although challenging to interpret, there are a few pericopes in Christian Scriptures that might suggest early Christian belief in this.[54] Some have noted an implicit suggestion of the possibility of effective intercessory prayer of the dead for the living, and vice versa, in the Lukan parable of the rich man and Abraham. The rich man, dead and suffering in Hades, begs Abraham for the mercy shown the also now dead poor man Lazarus or, failing that, for Lazarus to warn the rich man's living and sinning family members of their fate failing conversion (Lk. 16:19–31). Also of interest are two passages in the Book of Revelation (5:8 and 8:3–4) that refer to the inclusion of "the prayers of the saints" and "the prayers of all the saints" in the worship of the Lamb by angels and other creatures in Heaven.

Conclusion

This chapter's survey of passages in Christian Scriptures shows that references to companions, models, and intercessors are sometimes to Christians in general and sometimes to special members of the Christian community. All Christians are companions in faith, members of a communion borne by the grace of Christ and on the same journey toward eschatological fulfillment in Christ. Bidden to love others, Christians are to bear each others' burdens. Suffering has meaning in light of the suffering of Christ on our behalf. Jesus Christ is *the* model for Christians, revealing and by grace empowering the full possibilities for human living. Christians, therefore, are to imitate him. Those who imitate him most fully are models of imitation of Christ; so, too, are those transformed who follow their example, and so on. Christians were engaged in intercessory activity from the religion's early days. They prayed for each other and requested prayers for each other, following the example of Jesus who instructed his disciples to petition God the Father for their needs and who himself prayed to his Father for his disciples' needs. One of these needs was for "another Counselor" (Jn. 14:16), the Spirit who assists in prayer, helping to align the will of the one who prays with the will of God. Early Christians had especial confidence that prayer would be answered of one with a will so aligned. Christians, companions all, then, found in the Body of Christ some who were particularly good models and especially worthy and effective intercessors. The Catholic understanding of the relationship between nature and grace validates this conviction. Fallen human nature is perfected by grace. Grace is offered to all but not forced upon any, so the mysterious workings of the love of

God upon human free will can produce cases of sanctification that are inspiring for others. And these may be efficacious for others precisely because of the communal reality, in grace, of Christians. This subject will be discussed more fully in chapters 10, 11, and 12, which provide systematic theological reflection upon the roles of the saints. Chapter 3 will turn to the Middle Ages, during which consciousness of the Christian communal reality was as strong as in the early Church and keen of that reality's encompassment of the living and the dead both.

Terms for Study

Acts of the Apostles
Apocrypha
Apophaticism
Apostle
Benediction
Cataphaticism
Christos
Deuterocanonical Literature
Disciple
Eucharist
Gospel(s)
Incarnation, The

Intercession
Messiah
New Testament Epistles
Ontology
Parousia
Revelation, Book of
Sanhedrin
Septuagint
Supernatural
Synoptic Gospels
Theodicy

Suggested Readings

The New Testament.
      Various recent English translations exist and are readily accessible. The New American Bible (NAB), prepared by the Catholic Biblical Association of America, is the version used in English-language Catholic liturgies. The Revised Standard Version (RSV), originally produced under the direction of the Division of Christian Education of the National Council of the Churches of Christ in the United States of America, has been validated for Catholics in the edition known as *The New Oxford Annotated Bible with the Apocrypha*. As "an ecumenical study bible," it has been valuable in Protestant-Catholic dialogue. Also validated for Catholics in the *New Oxford* edition is the New Revised Standard Version (NRSV).

Three

THE CULT OF THE MARTYRS:
THE SAINTS IN THE EARLY CHURCH

After the close of the biblical period, the Christian consciousness reflected in the Bible of the relationships among persons within the "communion of saints," as it will come to be called, led to development in practices connected with those deemed particularly holy, those who will become the Church's "official" saints. Development does not equal discontinuity. Again, it is from tradition that Scripture emerged. Not every practice in history connected to veneration of the saints, and certainly none that would contradict Scripture, is validated by the Church; some practices have been expressly condemned, as will be explained in chapters 6 and 7. But others have been deemed "orthodox," a term from the Greek *orthos doxa* meaning "right belief" or "right praise," and are integral to the faith of the Church because they witness to the revelation that gave birth to the Church.

In the practices that will be described in the pages of this chapter, the saints will be glimpsed in their defined "saintly" roles of companion, model, and intercessor. The theoretical task—applying the history and spirituality of the communion of saints reflected here to Catholic thinking on each of the saints' roles—will be left to later chapters. Initial Christian cultic activity involving the saints will be studied for now, showing that belief in an ecclesial communion of living and dead is ancient. Veneration of the martyrs and then of other saints was part of the corporate and private consciousness of the Christian faithful from early on, having precedent in Judaism.

Early Christian Cult of Martyrs and Saints

It is the age of the martyrs that gave rise to the cult of the saints, for the concept of sainthood itself is derived from the exemplary "witness" (the meaning of the Greek term *martys*) of these early followers of Christ who came to be called "Christians" (a name derived from the Greek term *christos* meaning "the anointed one" and the Latin *–ianus* meaning "belonging to"). As the New Testament writings show, after the death of Jesus, tensions developed between Jews who believed in him as the expected Messiah and those who did not. Christian martyrdoms occurred as a consequence of the separation from Judaism of the followers of Jesus. The martyrdom of Stephen in the middle of the first century was likely the work of a mob incensed over his exceptionally "Hellenist" Christian view of Jewish worship and laws—that these were unimportant after Jesus Christ. Eventually all Jewish Christians were expelled from synagogues; Christian sensitivity about this probably is reflected in the gospels, in such as chapter 23 of Matthew and chapters 5 through 8 of John, wherein recounted are Jesus' authoritative words and actions aimed at relativizing Jewish law. The Christian communities that at first had been considered part of Judaism became increasingly Gentile in the 40s through the 60s, due in large part to the missionary journeys of Paul who was called to preach the gospel to Gentiles (Gal. 1:13–17). A particularly definitive moment in the break of Christians from the Jewish religion occurred in 48 or 49 A.D. at an assembly in Jerusalem described in Acts 15:1–35 and in Galatians 2:1–10. After a representative from one of the Jewish-Christian groups in Jerusalem visited the largely Gentile-Christian community in Antioch with the message that the salvation for which Christians hoped could not be had without circumcision as required by the law of Moses, Paul and Barnabas, with Titus and others, traveled to Jerusalem to discuss this claim with other notable early Christian leaders Peter, John, and James. The decision was made that Gentile converts need not be circumcised. In other words, Gentiles were not required to become Jewish for admittance into the Christian community. Perhaps the determinative moment for exclusion of Christians from the Jewish community occurred in the Palestinian city of Jamnia at the end of the first century. Although the Gospel of Mark, the first gospel to be written, may reflect that tumultuous time, many scholars believe that it shows the already growing distance in the mid- to late-60s of Christians from Jews, during the emperor Nero's brutal persecution of Christians in Rome, as well as the rising conflict between Jews and Romans that would ignite the Jewish War ending in the Romans' destruction of the Temple in Jerusalem in 70 A.D. The significance for Christianity of the demise of the Temple is reflected in the later three canonical gospels, during a time in which Jamnia became a new center of Jewish life, with the Torah and its interpretation by the rabbis in the synagogue filling for Jews the void of the lost Temple where priestly ritual had been the hallmark of religious practice. This new unifying Jewish focus naturally placed the Christians, heretofore a seeming sect of Judaism but now largely Gentile, beyond the designated boundaries of the Jewish religion. Christianity emerged as a religion of its own, distinct from, albeit critically related to, Judaism.[1]

From the time that the distance between Christians and Jews became discernable by those unconnected to these religious groups, a serious issue arose Judaism was a religion tolerated by the Roman Empire. If Christianity was not a sect of Judaism, it would not be tolerated; it would be persecuted by the Romans for its inconsistency with beliefs of the Empire. Christians threatened the social and political life of the Romans by challenging the civic values and pagan ideas that supplied to the Empire communal unity and goodwill of the gods; Christians created new, counter-cultural communities with their own behavioral codes and religious rituals that, among other things, undermined traditional Roman family customs and forbade worship of Roman deities. Indeed, precisely because, avowed monotheists, they refused to worship pagan gods, or any other deity recognizable to the Romans, the Romans viewed Christians as atheists (Lat. *atheos*, "one without a god"). Jesus of Nazareth was not regarded by the Romans as divine but as a troublesome political presence of the past who, inexplicably from their perspective, intruded upon the present in the form of his persistent followers. Persecutions were not always severe in the early Church, and there were times of relative peace. But depending upon the ruler and circumstances in the Empire at a given time, persecutions could involve such significant punishments as the burning of Bibles, the destruction of meeting places, and, famously, the killing of Christians. Among those guilty of the latter were Nero in the first century and Valerian in the third; the systematic and concentrated persecutions in the middle of the third century made martyrs of many still well-known Christians—Pope Sixtus II, Roman deacon Lawrence, and bishop of Carthage Cyprian among them. It often has been observed that the Christian Church was built with the blood of the martyrs. To the consternation of the Romans, the persecutions enlivened rather than extinguished the Christian movement.[2] This situation persisted until 313 A.D. when Constantine, son of the Christian Helena now listed among the Church's saints, issued with his co-emperor Licinius in the East the Edict of Milan tolerating all religions. This edict allowed Christians to worship freely, it returned to the Church property that had been confiscated during the persecutions, and it ended Christian martyrdoms at the hands of the Romans.[3] But the influence of the martyrs was not to be lost. Greatly admired by their fellow Christians during the first three centuries of the Church because of their "grace-ful" refusal to deny faith in Christ and their resulting imaging of Christ in the Passion as they were put to their deaths, the martyrs remained the standard for Christian commitment to the gospel. The Church's initial "official" saints, these holy men and women inspired a host of traditions that became prevalent features of medieval Catholicism.

Well before Constantine's edict of toleration in the early fourth century, then, the martyrs had a special place within Christianity's cult of the dead which only grew in prevalence once the religion gained political validation. What were the features of this cult? [One, martyrs' death anniversaries were celebrated by their communities. Two, martyrs' gravesites were gathering places for the faithful. Three, martyrs' relics were prized by their companions in the faith. Four, the martyrs and later other saints were invoked for their intercessory power. Five, related to their intercessory role, the saints, including martyrs, were by late Antiquity often understood as catalysts for the spiritual development of those devoted to them. And, six, distinct literary traditions developed for memorializing the venerated Christians.] Each of these facets of veneration will receive brief attention here.

Commemoration of Martyr Death Anniversaries

Written shortly after the death at the stake and by stabbing of Polycarp, bishop of Smyrna, in Asia Minor in 155 or 156 A.D., *The Martyrdom of Polycarp* is the earliest-known record of the commemoration of a martyr. It reports that, after his killing, Christians gathered the bishop's bones with reverent care and buried them, then made plans to celebrate annually his martyrdom in memory of all of the martyrs and in preparation of those who would be martyrs. Such annual celebrations of martyrdoms had become popular by the third century, when a feast of the eminent disciples Saints Peter and Paul was placed on the Church's liturgical calendar once it became tradition to honor the early martyrs along with those recently killed. The studies of Josef Jungmann, scholar of the liturgy of the early Church, showed that, in North Africa, the earliest documentation of veneration of martyrs occurred in 180 with a dozen killed together from Scilla (or Scillium, in Numidia), followed by that of Perpetua and Felicitas after their deaths at the beginning of the third century. In Rome, annual commemoration of martyr deaths is first attested in the first half of the third century, when Popes Callistus, Pontianus, and Fabian, along with presbyter and notable ecclesiastical writer Hippolytus, were venerated first, followed by martyred bishops and perhaps others esteemed by fellow Christians. After 250, other Christian martyrs were honored liturgically, including Lawrence and the virgin martyrs Agnes and Cecilia.[4] In the fourth century after Christianity became a tolerated religion, the annual commemoration of martyr deaths became commonplace. The formerly relatively modest monuments at martyrs' gravesites—often small, open chapels constructed on the surface above the underground burial chambers, where services, occasionally even the Sunday liturgy, could be celebrated—became grand basilicas which might attract great crowds on any given saint's feast day. Saints' feast days became abundant; of twenty-four feasts mentioned in an early calendar for Roman churches, the *Depositio Martyrum* of the

Chronograph of 354, all but two—Christmas and *Petri Cathedra*—are martyr feasts.[5]

Once the age of the martyrs came to a close with Constantine, spurring more growth in the official calendar of feast days throughout the fourth century, another breed of "martyrs" came to be venerated—the "confessors," those who publicly proclaimed their faith at risk of martyrdom. While the martyrs were honored and emulated from the earliest days of the persecutions, albeit not at first objects of a distinctive cult, the confessors had a special place in the Church, too. Initially they also were called martyrs, even by such as famous second- and third-century Latin theologians Tertullian and Cyprian. Eventually, however, the name "confessor" came to be used to describe a type of witness's adherence to the faith despite imprisonment and torture that did not result in death. Many of these witnesses were made honorary deacons, and Hippolytus's *Apostolic Tradition*, which provides insight into liturgical practices of the second- and third-century Roman church, suggests that they might properly be regarded as presbyters,[6] the functional equivalent of today's priests. But it was not until the late fourth century, in the case of Martin of Tours, pagan and soldier turned Christian monk, missionary, and bishop, that one of the confessors was placed in the Western church's festal calendar. It was done then with the clear liturgical statement that Martin is a witness in the tradition of the martyrs.[7] He was the first in a line of new "saintly" figures who would be understood to have "martyred" their senses to the world, in "white" rather than "red" martyrdom,[8] a goal which was then to find stark emphasis in the monastic movement that Martin is credited with pioneering in the West. As will be shown in chapter 4, monasticism's ascetical focus drew many who were concerned that life "in the world" after Constantine's edict was no longer a sufficiently rigorous path of Christian discipleship.

Gravesites as Gathering Places

As evidenced by gathering spaces at tombs in the catacombs and in cemeteries above the ground outside of Rome (for it was Roman law that burials occur beyond the city walls[9]), as well as by references in literature of the time, gravesites of martyrs compelled Christians from the early days of the persecutions. Following Jewish tradition of recognition of martyrs, not only date of death but place of burial was important to Christians; feast days of martyrs were to be celebrated at the tomb.[10] Unfortunately, a common practice of holding gravesite vigils became a sometimes problematic custom for Christians. Saint Augustine's *Confessions* recounts Monica's penchant for participating in gravesite activities, taking "cakes and bread and wine" to "the memorial shrines of the saints," until Saint Ambrose, then bishop of Milan, banned the practice.[11] Appropriated by Christians from the pagan ritual of bringing refreshments to the tombs of relatives and friends,[12] these "refrigeria"—meals with the deceased—were occasionally given to excessive, unbecoming behavior, especially in the evenings.[13] Yet Christian adoption of Roman practices was not only that but also adaptation of those practices to Christian belief; the Roman custom of honoring the deceased on their birthday turned into Christians' funeral banquets in honor of the dead (even with empty places saved for the dead[14])—but on their death anniversary, their "rebirth" day. Sometimes a banquet for the poor was offered at these Christian ceremonies, and the Eucharist was celebrated.[15] Due to efforts of bishops, the coincidence of the feasting at the gravesites and the Eucharistic celebrations there eventually became an intentional connection, with the construction of the basilicas containing martyr remains in the altar.[16] Even before then, a mature Christian interpretation of the banquets in the presence of the martyrs was that of the place and the possibility—in the form of the shared meal—of a foretaste of that which might be experienced in the next life as promised in Isaiah 25:6: "On this mountain the Lord of hosts will make for all peoples a feast of fat things, a feast of wine on the lees, of fat things full of marrow, of wine on the lees well refined."[17] It was peace in God that was sought by Christians, "relief from purgatorial pains"[18] for the Christian departed, as Christians of the later Middle Ages would say. Pilgrims from many ages, even early on, expressed this idea in their frequent gravesite graffiti. "May thy soul be refreshed," wrote one pilgrim at the grave of a departed Christian. "Januaria, take thy good refreshment, and make request for us," wrote another concerned not only for peace in God for the departed, but for the departed's intercession for other Christians as well.[19] Belief in the saints' ability to act as intercessors—and, indeed, powerful ones—also was reflected in the gravesite custom of "incubation," staying the entire night in the shrine of a martyr or saint for the purpose of winning his or her protection.[20]

A quotation from the fourth-century Latin poet Prudentius reveals the great pull of the Christian gravesites for the faithful of Antiquity, as well as shows how fervent was the belief in the intercessory power of the saints, as will be examined at more length in subsequent sections. In writing about his visits to the altar at the gravesite of Hippolytus, Prudentius exclaimed that

> I have myself poured forth my supplications there when I have been sick in body and mind, and never have I failed to obtain relief. Numerous are the debts I owe to Hippolytus, for Christ

our God has given him power to grant whatsoever any man may ask of him. Hence, from sunrise even to sunset the people may be seen flocking hither to pay their devotions to the saint; and not the Romans only, rich and poor, men, women, and children, but long trains of people from Albano and all neighbouring cities; and even from Nola, Capua, and other more distant places.[21]

That the crowds of Christians coming to visit the martyr graves eventually could not be contained in the underground chapels was partial impetus for construction in Constantine's day of the martyr churches in the cemeteries above ground.[22] Already before the end of the persecutions, in addition to the construction of aboveground chapels to memorialize martyrs, new, wider, more public entrances had been required in the catacombs in order to accommodate the many pilgrims seeking access to Christian graves, particularly those of the most popular martyrs.[23] While in Rome the gravesites remained relatively fixed in location until invasions of the Lombards in the eighth century when martyr bodies were moved inside the city or given to churches elsewhere to ensure safety of the remains, outside of Rome even dismemberment of the bodies occurred beginning in the middle of the fourth century, in order to supply relics to Christian churches everywhere.[24] As a not insignificant aside, the "translation" of martyr bodies to altars of basilicas, as an episcopal project, had the effect of presenting the bishop as "the visible *patronus* beneath the invisible *patronus*," Peter Brown has pointed out; this rendered originally "private" activities of the cult "public" ones.[25] As will be shown in chapter 4, the saints' perceived role as patrons became especially prominent in the Middle Ages.

Relics as Prizes of Faith

As the age of the martyrs came to a close and Christians began to reflect upon a new method of witness to Christ, heroic virtue and miraculous power became preeminent determinants of sainthood. But belief in the miraculous power of the relics of saints is attested much earlier than the age of Constantine. The impulse that led Christians to gather and honor the bones of beloved Bishop Polycarp after his martyrdom also is observed, for example, in *The Martyrdom of Perpetua*, where one of Perpetua's companions in martyrdom, Saturus, is recalled dipping a soldier's ring in his wound from a leopard bite, producing a relic for the solider presumably to be effective in Saturus's death.[26] As stated in the previous section, in and after the fourth century when the persecutions were but a memory, albeit a vital one in the cult of the martyr-saints, the collection and distribution of the remains of the martyrs and then of other saints became customary—so much so that trafficking became an issue, involving such as the odd and sometimes odious practices of fragmentation, transference, sale, and occasionally theft of bodies. However, with its abundance of martyr-saint bodies, Rome, especially, instituted severe sanctions against disturbance of the remains of the dead.[27]

Why the interest in the bodies of saints? As Lawrence Cunningham has explained, the Christians who would be martyrs were usually exemplary in Christian living before their final sacrifice and were therefore understood as the "locus of spiritual power" even during their lives, much as Jesus and the apostles were seen to have had supernatural powers of healing and of other miracles.[28] Yet it was after their death that the real power of the saints could be manifested, it was thought, for then the saints were in the company of Jesus Christ. "It was at the sanctuaries where their bodies were buried or by the application or veneration of parts of their bodies or objects touched to their bodies (*reliquiae*—relics) that the martyrs and confessors were most potent," wrote Cunningham.[29] In fact, on the popular level, enthusiasm borne by the belief in the presence of the saints in their tombs and relics at times appears to have overshadowed recognition of the more powerful material presence of Christ in the Eucharist, an obvious source of concern to bishops who were anxious to underscore the distinction made clearly already in the third and fourth centuries, to be ratified at ecumenical council in the eighth century, between *latria* (the worship of God) and *dulia* (veneration of saints). However, it is also true, as has been described of Christian gravesite activities, that the sense of the presence of the saints in their material remains was connected with the Eucharist before the basilicas of the saints. The catacombs hold numerous halls and chambers that attest to the worship services held there.[30] And Prudentius gave evidence of the practice when he wrote about the crypt near the city walls wherein "lies the body of S. Hippolytus, near to the altar of God; so that the very table from whence is distributed the bread of life is also the faithful guardian of the martyr's corpse; the same slab preserving his bones for the eternal judgment, and feeding the Romans with holy food. Marvellous is the devotion of the place, and the altar is ever ready for those who will come to pray."[31]

Also in connection with early Christian enthusiasm for relics, a custom apparently developed of being buried with relics as an expression of hope in resurrection along with the saints.[32] Orazio Marucchi, in his now century-old but recently re-issued book, *Christian Epigraphy*, related evidence of the early Christian practice of preserving martyrs' blood "with special care," keeping it close at home or in cemetery.[33] Being buried near a martyr, too, was a desire, one sometimes acted upon at the expense of the walls to the original gravesite.[34] Marucchi's study of Christian epigraphy at Roman gravesites underscores the popularity of this practice and its attendant problems, namely damage to monuments and—as compared to the attention given to the saints' example in life and at the moment of death—a sometimes inordinate attention to the physical location of martyr bodies at rest such that Church authorities had to intervene.[35] The practice is well attested in a sample of inscriptions from a variety of cemeteries: "Serpentius bought himself a tomb from the *fossor* (grave-digger) Quintus near the grave of the martyr S. Cornelius"; "Januarius and Silana bought themselves a tomb to hold two bodies near the grave of S. Felicitas"; "They prepared a sepulchre for their daughter above the acrosolium near the grave of the martyr S. Hippolytus."[36] If one could not be buried near a martyr, the date of one's death could at least be linked to a martyr feast. A particularly elaborate inscription from the catacombs of Syracuse serves as an example: "Euskia, the blameless one, who lived a life of goodness and purity for twenty-five years, died on the feast of our lady Lucia (S. Lucia), for whom no praise is adequate. She was a perfect Christian, well pleasing to her husband, and endued with much grace."[37]

Invocation of the Saints as Intercessors

It is evident from inscriptions found at the catacombs that, in the first centuries of the Church, even before the Edict of Milan, Christian veneration of martyrs already included the practice of invocation for intercession. In the cemetery of Priscilla, one of the oldest sections of the Christian catacombs with tombs dating nearly to the apostolic age,[38] intercessory inscriptions are as early as the third century. A brief sampling can provide an insight into the still early Christian understanding of the power of the relationship of Christians to each other—living or dead—in Christ. "Oh Father of all, thou that hast created Irene, Zoe, and Marcellus, receive them to thyself. To Thee be glory in Christ," one inscription prays from the floor of the Acilii vaults.[39] "Claudius Philotas to his beloved brother Theodorus. May we live in God (Jesus Christ, Son of God the Redeemer),"[40] another asks. Some inscriptions address gravesite visitors and evidence the early established practice of holding liturgical services at cemeteries. Those who visit the tomb of a girl are asked that "when you come to offer common prayer (*precibus totis*) to the Father and the Son, remember the beloved Agape, *sit vestrae mentis Agapes carae meminisse,* that God may take her into His glory."[41] Many other simple pleas to the departed buried in the cemetery of Priscilla show the early grounding of the now common notion of the "communion of saints" in the life of the Church's faithful. "Oh Marinus, be mindful of us twain!" "Pray for thy children!"[42] "To . . . son Philemon who lived happily for two years with his parents. Pray for us, together with the Saints!"[43] And in other Christian cemeteries, too, intercessory prayers were frequent on tomb inscriptions. Some prayed for the departed member of the community even while they asked for the dead's own prayers, as one in the cemetery of Domitilla entreats, "Augendus, live in the Lord, and pray for us!"[44] Such intercessory inscriptions were not concerned with the miraculous, but with the help that all Christians can and do offer to each other and especially with the help that those Christians who are closest to Christ can extend to others on the way to him.

Tomb graffiti became popular with the legalization of Christianity. From the fourth through the eighth centuries, up until the time that the martyr bodies were transferred into the cities, many pilgrims scratched their names and prayers onto the walls of the catacombs.[45] These graffiti pleas reveal that the hope and belief in the intercessory power of the martyrs that was common in the first three centuries of the Church only grew after that.[46] Gravesite visitors' prayer scribblings were expressions of confidence in the martyrs' and later the "canonized" saints' eternal life with God. "Oh Lord, on the intercession of the martyred Saints and of S. Helena, save thy servants John, . . ."[47] "Saint Sixtus, keep Aurelius in your prayers!" "Peter and Paul, pray for Victor!" "Marcellinus and Peter, pray for Gallo, a Christian!" "Hippolytus, keep in mind Peter, a sinner!"[48] But not all such petitionary prayer dealt with the desire for forgiveness and eternal life and peace. A prayer directed to a martyr in the cemetery of Priscilla is striking for its similarity to that which will be seen for particular material causes in the later Middle Ages: ". . . Crescentio, heal my eyes for me!"[49] Cunningham noted that the seemingly endless stream of pilgrims who visited Christian burial places did so with "official" intercessors in mind. The Church guarded the burial sites of its saints and, from the time the persecutions came to an end, it more and more regulated public cults of saints. Martyrs and burial places were listed in the *Martyrologium* and/or the *Kalendarium*, the book of martyrs and the calendar of feast days, respectively.[50]

Early Christians clearly assumed that the distinction between life and death did not constitute a barrier to mutual assistance through prayer. Perpetua's memoir records evidence that veneration of her and her companion martyrs included belief in such power of their intercessory prayer: Perpetua's intercessory prayer for her dead brother Dinocrates was believed to have successfully "relieved [him] of his suffering," as revealed to her in a vision while she awaited in prison her death.[51] In *On the Resurrection of the Body*, written near the turn from the second to the third century, Tertullian taught that intercession of the living might relieve suffering of the dead; in *On Monogamy* he mentioned the Eucharist being offered for the dead.[52]

The Saints as Spiritual Mentors

Brown has called the saint of late Antiquity a "Christ carrier."[53] Noting that, in the Greco-Roman world, human "exemplars" or "classics" functioned as bonding agents from one generation to another, he has shown that the very function of "late antique" pagan, Jewish, and Christian writers was to provide in literature the prototypes or models that would inspire and instruct readers in becoming "classic [timeless] persons."[54] Past ages had viewed one's tutelage with a personally-picked teacher as the normal process for forming oneself into the ideal; for Church Fathers such as Saint Gregory of Nyssa (ca. 335–395), this meant a return to Adam's likeness to God before the Fall. Christianity's unsurpassed emphasis on the union of the divine and the human—in the person of Christ—meant that the Christian exemplar was both revelatory and transformative to an unprecedented degree, since God himself is "the Exemplar behind all exemplars."[55] According to Gregory, wrote Brown, "In Christ, the original beauty of Adam had blazed forth; for that reason the life of the Christian holy man could be treated as a prolonged and deeply circumstantial 'imitation of Christ'"[56] for the purpose of "bring[ing] that elusive touch of the majesty of Adam into the present age."[57] Indeed, throughout time, men like Moses had appeared to reveal the original purity of the image, thought Gregory, calling others to become believers; they connected those who saw in them their exemplars to those who served as these exemplars' own models.[58] In the Christian exemplar, "Christ was thought to dwell at the root of the self" such that "the protection of the saint was certain to bring close to the believer the deeper paradigm of Christ himself."[59] (This notion and the many activities connected with the early cult of the saints can present the saints as spiritual "mentors" for other Christians, a theme that will be explored further late in this study.) As chapter 2 showed in review of biblical material relating to the saint as model, this is consistent with the theology of the New Testament, especially in Paul's epistles, wherein he wrote of Christ being manifested in those who imitate him.

The Saints in Hagiography

The power felt in the martyrs and other saints was that of Christ manifested in them. The deaths of witness and the lives of heroic virtue that resulted from that grace were remembered in narratives about the saints that are today classed under the genre title "hagiography" (Gk. *hagios*, "holy," and *graphein*, "writing"). It could be said that the account of protomartyr Stephen in the New Testament provides a model or basis for the two earliest types of Christian hagiographical documents, consciously so or not; yet scholars note that hagiographical literature, especially as it would develop in Christianity, drew upon Jewish and Hellenistic biographical traditions as featured in the Old Testament and in classical pagan texts, respectively.[60] Aside from the obviously homiletic nature of the report of the dialogue between Stephen and apparently the Sanhedrin (Acts 6:12), the Jewish council in Jerusalem that had judged Jesus (e.g., Mt. 26:59; Mk. 14:55; Jn. 11:47), the account anticipates the later *Acta*, or "Acts"—transcripts of the conversation between the martyr and the Roman magistrate that led to a Christian's death. The *Acta* were read in early Christian liturgies in some locales.[61] The presentation of Stephen's final moments and death (Acts 7:54–60), which he faced in exemplary imitation of Christ, is a concise *Passio*, or "Passion," of which the aforementioned *The Martyrdom of Perpetua* and *The Martyrdom of Polycarp* are famous instances. By the fourth century, the Passions were connected with liturgical commemoration of martyrs, in that they were read in segments (followed by a prayer and/or song) during the vigils held on martyr feast days at the gravesite "crypt-churches" of the martyrs; immediately following Mass was celebrated.[62] Greatly inspiring for the Christian community, Brown has explained that in the reading of the *Passio* the past was pulled into the present; the saints were in the church, their earthly torments and/or holy lives represented so vividly that the power of their heavenly state was palpable.[63] Belief in the power at work in the martyrs, the later saints, and the relics of each led to a development in the literature that in the mind of many is most identified with the term "hagiography," because it became the pervasive and—until recent history—popular means of presenting the stories of the saints. Called *Legendum*, or "Legend," it effectively subsumed the earlier traditions via stories that featured exaggerated accounts of the power of the martyrs and/or saints to endure the pains of persecution heroically and to function as a conduit of God's grace throughout life and in death.[64] The name itself comes from the Latin *legere* which means "to read" or "to recite" which, as noted, Christians did aloud at liturgical services on feast days of saints. Another related type of literature that became prominent as Christianity entered its fifth century, sometimes a component of the *Legendum*, was *Libelli Miraculorum*, "small books" or stories of miracles collected, circulated, and, of course, read in churches on saints' feast days.[65] It is notable that the various forms of *Vitae*—recordings of details of the lives (and/or deaths) of saints—were not apparently even from the beginning simply devotional readings for individual members of the Church but products and cultivators of the cult of the saints and of the liturgy. And they were coincident with a wide array of other vehicles for marking and promoting the impact of the saints on the Church and the world, including recordings of saints' sayings,[66] depictions of the saints in art, the translations of saintly remains, the naming of churches after saints, etc.[67]

Conclusion

It is a matter of some importance that activities of the early Christian cult of the saints may bear resemblance to pre-Christian practices in Judaism. In the deuterocanonical book 2 Maccabees, suggested to have been written in the first century B.C. about events under the Seleucid Empire of a century earlier, two passages are especially intriguing in that they exhibit belief in the power of prayer of those on Earth for the dead as well as in intercession of those in Heaven for those still earthbound.[68] The belief that prayer of the living is efficacious for the dead is reflected in 12:41–46, wherein Judas Maccabeus and his men, during their attacks upon neighboring peoples as retaliation for and resistance against persecution and forced hellenization of Palestinian Jews, discover on the bodies of their own fallen fighters forbidden pagan idols.

> So they all blessed the ways of the Lord, the righteous Judge, who reveals the things that are hidden; and they turned to prayer, beseeching that the sin which had been committed might be wholly blotted out. And the noble Judas exhorted the people to keep themselves free from sin, for they had seen with their own eyes what had happened because of the sin of those who had fallen. He also took up a collection, man by man, to the amount of two thousand drachmas of silver, and sent it to Jerusalem to provide for a sin offering. In doing this he acted very well and honorably, taking account of the resurrection. For if he were not expecting that those who had fallen would rise again, it would have been superfluous and foolish to pray for the dead. But if he was looking to the splendid reward that is laid up for those who fall asleep in godliness, it was a holy and pious thought. Therefore he made atonement for the dead, that they might be delivered from their sin.

The belief in intercession of the dead for the living is reflected in 2 Maccabees 15:11–16, where recounted is Judas's preparation for an attack of Nicanor, a general of Antiochus IV Epiphanes, the Seleucid ruler who incited the Maccabean war by his defilement of the Temple altar with pagan sacrifices in 167 B.C. (The Maccabee family's success in retaking Jerusalem and its subsequent purification, restoration, and rededication of the Temple led to the now annual commemoration, called "Hanukkah," of eight-day dedication events.[69])

> He armed each of them not so much with confidence in shields and spears as with the inspiration of brave words, and he cheered them all by relating a dream, a sort of vision, which was worthy of belief.
>
> What he saw was this: Onias, who had been high priest, a noble and good man, of modest bearing and gentle manner, one who spoke fittingly and had been trained from childhood in all that belongs to excellence, was praying with outstretched hands for the whole body of the Jews. Then likewise a man appeared, distinguished by his gray hair and dignity, and of marvelous majesty and authority. And Onias spoke, saying, 'This is a man who loves the brethren and prays much for the people and the holy city, Jeremiah, the prophet of God.' Jeremiah stretched out his right hand and gave to Judas a golden sword, and as he gave it he addressed him thus: 'Take this holy sword, a gift from God, with which you will strike down your adversaries.'

Intercession generally was a feature of Judaism. As chapter 2 noted, Elijah served as an intercessor. God also listened to Abraham when the father in faith pled on behalf of the few righteous in Sodom—namely Lot and his household—that God not destroy them along with "the wicked" of that city and Gomorrah (Gen. 18:22–25). God listened to Abraham when he prayed for a divine blessing upon Ishmael even as the divine plan of ratifying the covenant through Isaac was revealed (Gen. 17:15–21). He listened to the plea of Moses on behalf of the Hebrews that God not "consume them" (Ex. 32:10) for their creation and worship of the golden calf as Moses attended the Lord atop Mount Sinai and awaited the stone tables (Ex. 32:7–14). He listened to Moses again when he appealed to him not to carry through his plan to "strike them [the people of Israel] with the pestilence and disinherit them" (Num. 14:12) because of their lack of trust in the Lord as they approached Canaan and found it occupied (Num. 14:1–24). And God's punishments were softened when Moses and Aaron prostrated themselves to make atonement for the people in order to obtain God's mercy upon those who rebelled against the brothers' privileged place in God's plan for the Israelites (Num. 16:20–24, 41–50). In the story of Job, God himself initiates the process whereby one human being intercedes for another and he specifies that this should occur through an act of prayer. God "restored the fortunes of Job" only "when he [Job] had prayed for his friends" (Job 42:10).[70] Job is deemed a worthy intercessor after a profession of faith ends his struggle: "I know that thou canst do all things, and that no purpose of thine can be thwarted. . . . Therefore I have uttered what I did not understand, things too wonderful for me, which I did not know" (Job 42:2–3). "I had heard of thee by the hearing of the ear, but now my eye sees thee" (Job 42:5). The power of Job's selfless devotion to his new vision attracts his friends to its source. They offer the sacrifice that God demands of them so that Job will pray for them a prayer that would only be accepted by God from a servant who spoke of him "what is right" (Job 42:8).

The suggestion of God's expressed wish for his righteous to intercede for others is a feature of other Old Testament accounts, too. In the Book of Isaiah, the Lord is said to have been displeased at the injustice that had taken hold among his people, and "He saw that there was no man, and wondered that there was no one to intervene. . ." (Is. 59:16). In the first Book of Samuel, the prophet makes the remarkable statement to the people of Israel upon their request for his prayerful intercession for their sins (1 Sam. 12:19) that "far be it from me that I should sin against the Lord by ceasing to pray for you; and I will instruct you in the good and the right way" (1 Sam. 12:23).[71] Psalm 122:6 encourages pilgrims to Jerusalem to "[p]ray for the peace of Jerusalem!" And in yet other passages God is shown to listen to the pleas of his people, and the supplications of his righteous ones have a special audience.[72] As his discourses at the end of the Book of Job reveal, God is intimately involved in all of his creation, with human beings at the center of his redemptive plan. He blesses his people, and it is his desire to do so; he is under no constraint: "Who has given to me, that I should repay him? Whatever is under the whole heaven is mine," said the Lord to Job (Job 41:11).

So, also, did martyrdom itself find precedent in Judaism. Again in 2 Maccabees (6:7–17), in pericopes difficult to date and, scholars believe, likely inclusive of legendary elements, found are Jews thrown to their deaths or burned for practicing their faith. In 2 Maccabees (6:18–7:42), repeated in 4 Maccabees (5–18), the elderly and influential scribe Eleazar and seven brothers and their mother are tortured and killed on the order of Antiochus IV Epiphanes for their refusal to eat pork and foods sacrificed to idols, which would have constituted idolatry and blasphemy, as well as for their refusal to adopt Greek ways generally.[73] Such martyrdom accounts were designed to inspire, and inspire they did, not only Jews but Christians, who then produced their own accounts of refusal—to compromise their faith in Christ—even in the face of death.[74]

Ancient shrines and sanctuaries attest to the Jewish practice of honoring martyrs, too. There is evidence of postexilic Judaism's veneration of the martyrs Maccabees and Isaiah.[75] Strikingly, early Christians incorporated veneration of Jewish martyrs into their own cultic activity surrounding the saints. "The tombs and relics of the prophets, some of whom were also martyrs, of the martyrs of Judaism (the Maccabees), and of the patriarchs received the same honour as that which the Church paid to the martyrs' bodies and resting-places," reported J.P. Kirsch in his century-old study, *The Doctrine of the Communion of Saints in the Ancient Church*.[76] Here, Kirsch also noted that Old Testament patriarchs and prophets were named along with Christian martyrs in the *Memento* when the Eucharist was celebrated,[77] as well as in early Christian writings about apostles and martyrs.[78] Remarkably, even today it is not unusual to hear Catholics from the East, especially, mention "Saint Abraham" or other Old Testament "saints," many of whom have appeared alongside Christian saints on the walls and ceilings of the more ornate of churches built in the fourth into the twentieth centuries both in the East and in the West. Non- or pre-Christian figures from the New Testament also have been honored, including John the Baptist and the criminal who died on a cross beside Jesus with the promise that he would join Christ in his Kingdom (Lk. 23:39–43).[79]

Evidence of these Jewish practices belies the still occasional claim that the early Christian cult of the saints was pagan in origin. Still, it is no secret, as noted in the review in this chapter, that some activities of the cult of the saints mimicked those of Roman pagans; yet, as also noted, they were not simply adopted, but adapted to Christian belief. In later chapters theological anthropology will be considered (how the human person is constituted with respect to the Creator), and this may offer helpful perspective on religious practices that have commonality among various world religions, past and present, even when the understanding of these practices does not agree among those engaged in them. And so early Christian cultic activity directed to the saints is not simply a continuation and development of Jewish practices, either. The impetus for honoring the saints was the resurrection of Christ. In his triumph over sin and death, his followers perceived a new reality of communion between the living and the dead, a reality *in* Christ that allowed for mutual assistance of members of this communion even across the divide of death. The theology of this communion of saints will be discussed in detail in future chapters. For now, chapter 4 will continue the historical survey begun here, turning to activities of the cult of the saints in the Middle Ages.

Terms for Study

Acta/Acts
Asceticism
Confessor
Council of Jerusalem
Doctor of the Church
Ecclesial
Ecclesiastical
Episcopal
Exile, The
Fall, The
Hellenization
Jamnia

Legendum/Legend
Libelli Miraculorum/Miracle Stories
Monasticism
Orthodox
Passio/Passion
Presbyter
Relic(s)
Revelation
Salvation
Theological Anthropology
Theology
Vitae/Written Lives of Saints

Suggested Readings

Cwiekowski, Frederick J. *The Beginnings of the Church*. Mahwah, New Jersey: Paulist Press, 1988.

In this valuable study of the Church of the New Testament period, Cwiekowski situates the mission of Jesus and the development of the early Church in historical context, providing background for and interpretation of the biblical account.

The Martyrdom of Polycarp. At New Advent [online]. Available from http://www.newadvent.org/fathers/0102.htm. Accessed 1 September 2011.

As is *The Martyrdom of Perpetua*, this famous document is a widely published "Passion" account. Accounts of the trials of martyrs, called "Acts," also are important sources; recommended are the Acts of Justin Martyr, of Cyprian of Carthage, and of the Scillitan martyrs.

Marucchi, Orazio. *Christian Epigraphy: An Elementary Treatise with a Collection of Ancient Christian Inscriptions Mainly of Roman Origin*. Translated by J. Armine Willis. Cambridge: Cambridge University Press, 1912. Reissued by Adamant Media, 2004.

A fascinating record of early Christian epigraphs, this book provides not only rough facsimiles of Christian gravestones along with English translations of epigraphs, but description of Christian cemeteries and symbols used therein, as well as breakdowns of epigraphs according to types, social standing of the departed, and ancient feast days. Inscriptions' reflections of Christian doctrine and sacraments also are studied, and a final section reviews "graffiti" left in the catacombs by early Christian pilgrims.

Four

FROM WITNESSES TO PROTECTORS: THE DEVELOPMENT OF THE CULT OF THE SAINTS IN THE MIDDLE AGES

Reference to the Middle Ages is to a vast length of time in Western European history, from the fifth century to the fifteenth century, beginning with the fall of the Roman Empire in 476 and ending definitively with the Protestant Reformation at the dawn of the sixteenth century. By association, it implies also Eastern Christianity, to the extent that developments in the West and the East impacted each other. It was not until the eleventh century, halfway through the Middle Ages and Christianity itself, that the Christian communion separated into "Orthodox" Christians in the East and "Catholic" Christians in the West, and it was not until the fifteenth century, near the end of the Middle Ages, that attempts at reunion stalled.[1] Catholic and Orthodox Christians, therefore, share some traditions of veneration of saints and list many early saints in common. Yet growth in and evolution of practices of veneration in the West's Middle Ages cemented the place of the saints in the lives of the Catholic faithful in a particular way that in part defined the piety of Western Christians up to the time of the Protestant Reformation and, in some respects, until Vatican II.

Saint Augustine of Hippo (354–430), one of the most famous of Christian saints and of Christian theologians, as well as one of the most famous of Western historical personages generally, stands as a marker for the turn from Antiquity to the Middle Ages. As he neared his death, he interpreted the events leading to the demise of the Roman Empire and, thus, to Antiquity, in his famous work *The City of God*. Rome, already conquered by the Visigoths in 410, was after Augustine's time sacked by the Vandals in 455 and lost its final emperor in 476 when he was deposed by a Germanic warrior named king of Rome.[2] But this was not the end of Christianity in the West. On the contrary, declared the official religion of the Roman Empire only a century before, in 380 under Theodosius I, Christianity became a unifying element in Western culture and politics, influential even in economic and military life, while other institutional structures in the West were weak and in disarray. The medieval years witnessed the Holy Roman Empire, the Crusades, and the founding of universities which taught "Scholasticism," a rigorous method of philosophy and theology which, following in the tradition of Saint Augustine and others, explicitly recognized reason as capable of deepening faith and therefore used formalized rational inquiry to examine the tenets of faith. By the thirteenth century in which lived Saint Thomas Aquinas (1225–1274), the most prominent of the Scholastics and, along with Augustine, considered the greatest of Catholic theologians, traditions of veneration of saints were longstanding. Indeed, many of these traditions, like Scholasticism, were characteristic of the observed life of the Church and, because of the Church's influence, they were prevalent features of medieval life on the whole, as evident in the content, style, and tenor of literature and art of the time. The form in which they existed shows that the medieval world had a palpable sense of the spiritual realm. Angels, demons, spirits all interacted with the Christian faithful in space and time, assisting them or tempting them, as the case may be, in a tumultuous world looking for truth. What it meant to live as a saint and how the medieval faithful venerated saints were impacted by this worldview. This chapter will review activities of the medieval cult of the saints, as well as consider the types of saints that appealed to medieval Christians. Although occasional reference will be made to ways in which "popular" activities of veneration were sanctioned by the Church at this time, it will be the next chapter that will consider liturgical and canonical validation of the saints and their cult(s).

Medieval Veneration of the Saints

Veneration of saints in the Middle Ages was large and colorful, but not discontinuous with that which has been reviewed of the early Church. Necessary to capture the spirit and scope of the medieval cult of the saints, then, is only an explanation of the development of literature of and about saints, of pilgrimages and other devotional activities associated with saints, and of practices of invocation for intercession of saints.

Literature

Writings *of* saints, whether autobiographical, theological, or spiritual, have been popular with Christians throughout history. Augustine's *Confessions* and Thomas's *Summa Theologiae* may be no less impactful on the Church today than they were when written. But writings *about* the saints have been indispensable to preservation of memory of saints and, in a certain way irrespective of customs of culture, to education of other Christians in the way of discipleship. It is between the fourth and the sixth centuries that the formal hagiography mentioned in chapter 3 developed for the transmission of the stories of the lives of the saints.[3] With its emphasis on the miraculous and its love of legend, this style of literature remained popular until recent centuries and, for many, still might be the most recognizably Catholic mode of storytelling about the saints. Scholars note that the model for this classical hagiography was the story of Martin of Tours by Sulpicius Severus, produced near the time of Martin's death at the end of the fourth century but still widely read and imitated well into the Middle Ages.[4] As mentioned in chapter 1, this variety of pious volume has been criticized and even dismissed in recent centuries precisely for its legendary character, so compelling to medieval Christians but failing to engage most modern readers now accustomed to historical-critical studies of figures of the past. As chapter 6 will discuss, it was harshly criticized by Protestant reformers in the sixteenth century and, a century before that, by some who sought to be Catholic reformers. The most fantastic of this type of literature was given to invention of episodes and sometimes of saints themselves, even if unintentionally, due to the medieval religious imagination that emphasized the otherworldly. Along with the legends, especially as they came to be read by bishops at the occasion of the addition of a new saint to a calendar, came a *Translatio*, an account of miracles and other extraordinary events that occurred while the saint's body was exhumed and moved to a shrine.[5] The martyrologies that in the early centuries of the Church were simply lists sometimes had by the Middle Ages accompanying stories. These were read in monasteries as part of the Divine Office, today called the "Liturgy of the Hours," featuring daily prayers at set hours that included psalms, chants, and Scripture readings.[6]

Pilgrimages and Other Devotional Activities

The setting of *The Canterbury Tales* is no anachronistic literary device adopted by Geoffrey Chaucer; the pilgrimage was a standard feature of medieval life. Christians wherever they lived wanted to visit the place of the religion's origin, and so the Holy Land was a popular attraction from the time of the visit of Saint Helena. And Rome, the resting place of so many martyrs for the faith, attracted Christians from far and wide. Therefore, visits to gravesites of martyrs and saints became pilgrimages to distant locations. Yet it was not simply tourism but devotion in the tradition of the ascetics that drew the masses. The journey itself was important, as an event of prayer, a means of purification and/or penance, and an act of veneration of relics disclosing Christ in our midst, even while answers to prayers, including miracles, were sought. This spiritual dimension issued in an official function of the pilgrimage in the life of Church, fostering a major tradition summarized concisely in a single understated sentence of *The Oxford Dictionary of the Christian Church*: "From the 8th cent. the practice of imposing a pilgrimage in the place of a public penance added to the number of pilgrims, so that throughout the Middle Ages they were organized on a grand scale and provided for by special ecclesiastical and civil legislation."[7] Substantial penances would contribute to the popularity of indulgences which will be discussed in later chapters. One of the most frequented of pilgrimages was that to Santiago de Compostela in Spain, where the body of Saint James, apostle of Jesus, is thought to have been rediscovered in the ninth century. A chapel built over the sepulchre containing his remains was expanded to a church which was partially destroyed at the end of the tenth century, but at the end of the eleventh century the Romanesque Cathedral of Santiago was built to welcome the many pilgrims who would make the journey in succeeding centuries. Roads leading to the Cathedral from various directions featured chapels, churches containing relics, hospices and inns, hospitals, monasteries, money changers, and even cobblers, all attending to the physical and spiritual needs of travelers on the sometimes perilous journey of weeks or even months. Before setting out, pilgrims would receive the sacraments of Confession and Holy Communion; then they and their special pilgrimage insignia would be blessed.[8]

The notion of undergoing a journey inspired other types of devotions involving the saints, such as the "Stations of the Cross." Originally, anciently, the "Stations" were the actual locations of the Passion of Christ in the Holy Land, but eventually pictures were produced and located in churches elsewhere, to foster the practice of meditation on Christ's suffering even among those unable to make a long trip. Featured in the pictures and mentioned in the accompanying devotional prayers were, and are, Mary and some of the saints, including the Veronica of legend who is said to have used her veil to wipe Jesus' face while he carried the Cross. Other images and icons, too, including statues, were involved in the devotional life of medieval Christians. Vast and varied religious images were contained in the great basilicas and cathedrals, growing ever more abundant and elaborate, that greeted pilgrims at their destinations. Some appeared in manuscripts, which talented and patient scribes ornamented vividly according to scriptural and theological themes. The Church was the foremost patron of art and music in the Middle Ages, and of later times, commissioning now famous works from illuminated religious texts to the great architectural structures adorned with such as the paintings of Giotto and Duccio that were, and remain, instructive for countless Christians in historical and theological content and in spiritual sensibility. Many of these works depict biblical figures and saints, educating Christians in Jewish and Christian history and inspiring them to live more virtuous lives in imitation of those who faithfully imitated Christ. They also were, and are, viewed sacramentally, in the broad sense of moving the affections and intellect to consciousness of the presence of God in time and place. As chapter 1 already noted, they were honored due to their possibility in and witness to he who made them possible.

Devotional activities connected with saints such as public or private novenas (prayers repeated nine times over a period of days or weeks, as will be described in chapter 7) also grew in number and popularity during the Middle Ages. Often recited before or after Mass, novenas for Advent and for mourning are known of medieval Christians.[9]

Invocation for Intercession

The biblical foundation for invocation and intercession of Christians for one another was reviewed in chapter 2. Chapter 3 showed that Christians of the early Church began invoking the martyrs and then other saints. In chapter 12, the theology of this practice will be studied. For now, then, it must only be affirmed that invocation of saints for their intercession only increased in the Middle Ages, particularly as a result of the saints' popular ascendance to the role of patron, discussed later in this chapter. Saints in the medieval world were petitioned not only for spiritual but for material needs, as attested by long lists of causes with which individual saints are associated as patrons even today. Indeed, as the next chapter will explain, the intercession of a particular Christian, as a result of invocation after his or her death, became the final criterion "proving" the individual's residence in Heaven and, hence, his or her sainthood.

Lives of the Medieval Saints

In the new situation of Christians after Constantine, the saints followed in the steps of the martyrs as eminent Christian disciples, but the focus of attention became their states of life rather than their manners of death (although their attitude in death was often admired as their final demonstration of their love of God throughout life). Saints became known as such because they led heroically virtuous lives. And those who honored the saints developed a profound sense of the power of saintly lives to transform and to protect. The medieval sensibility regarding the saints can be glimpsed through the then most prominent, sometimes overlapping, types of saints: ascetic, monk, cleric, Church Father, pope, scholar, mystic, ruler, conqueror, patron, and miracle worker.

Ascetics

Asceticism is a movement or program of "training" or "exercise" (from the Greek *askesis*, "ascesis") in moral or spiritual development. Involving rigorous self-discipline, including and especially self-denial, it is not confined to Christianity and, in fact, was known by Christians in the forms practiced by Greek philosophers to cultivate virtue. From the beginning of Christianity, though, *ascesis* took on special meaning, in light of the sacrifice of Christ and the call to his disciples to follow him. In the Second Letter to Timothy, purportedly Paul wrote of the obstacles he faced in preaching the message of Christ. In doing so, he used the language of renunciation, of willing endurance of pain and persecution, of spiritual progress through trial and battle: "For I am already on the point of being sacrificed; the time of my departure has come. I have fought the good fight, I have finished the race, I have kept the faith. Henceforth there is laid up for me the crown of righteousness, which the Lord, the righteous judge, will award to me on that Day, and not only to me but also to all who have loved his appearing" (1 Tim. 4:6–8).[10] Imitation of the one whose earthly life ended with death on the Cross would mean disciples would have their own crosses to bear, as Jesus himself is recorded as instructing in the Gospel of Mark: "If any man would come after me, let him deny himself and take up his cross and follow me. For whoever would save his life will lose it; and whoever loses his life for my sake and the gospel's will save it" (Mk. 8:34–35).[11] Paul's First Letter to the Corinthians uses the image of an athlete to describe the mastery of self required in the Christian's cross-bearing that leads to union with Christ: "Every athlete exercises self-control in all things. They do it to receive a perishable wreath, but we an imperishable" (1 Cor. 9:25).

The earliest saints—the martyrs—were the models for asceticism, in that they renounced their very lives for the Kingdom of Heaven of which Jesus spoke. But, as Paul expressed powerfully in his letter for the Colossians, already in this life all Christians are called to "die" to the world: "Set your minds on things that are above, not on things that are on earth. For you have died, and your life is hid with Christ in God. When Christ who is our life appears, then you also will appear with him in glory" (Col. 3:2–4). And so Christians contemporaneous with the martyrs (and some of the martyrs themselves, before their deaths) heard other gospel calls to renunciation, too, for example in Jesus' answer to the affluent young man who asked him what he should do to gain eternal life: ". . . 'If you would be perfect, go, sell what you possess and give to the poor, and you will have treasure in heaven; and come, follow me'" (Mt. 19:21).[12] In addition to renunciation of private property, fasting was undertaken; in the Gospel of Matthew Jesus instructs disciples to fast not like hypocrites but "in secret" (Mt. 6:16–18), and in each of the synoptic gospels Jesus is asked about when his disciples should fast (Mt. 9:14–17; Mk. 2:18–22; Lk. 5:33–39). Paul preached that some were to renounce marriage, living life-long as celibate (1 Cor. 7:29–40); this state came to be viewed as a sign of the Kingdom.[13] Virgins and widows appear to have been supported by the early Christian community, in turn offering intercessory prayer, spiritual guidance, and service to the Church[14]; the early third-century text *Apostolic Tradition*, which deals with Church organization and liturgical rites, attests as tradition already by that date the consecration of virgins and the appointment of widows.[15] Jesus himself had said that ". . . there are eunuchs who have made themselves eunuchs for the sake of the kingdom of heaven. He who is able to receive this, let him receive it" (Mt. 19:12).

As the age of the martyrs came to a close and new styles were sought for the diligent Christian life, religious disciplines such as poverty, fasting, and celibacy were famously adopted by the Desert Fathers—hermits who removed themselves to remote locations, originally the Egyptian and Palestinian deserts, to contemplate, pray, fight demons and extinguish the passions, for closer union with God.[16] "This is virtue: emptying one's mind of the world. As long as the senses are occupied with things, the heart cannot stop imagining them. Passions do not cease nor evil thoughts come to an end without the desert and solitude," wrote Eastern Saint Isaac of Nineveh, late seventh-century bishop who committed himself to a solitary life of prayer, Scripture study, and theological writing.[17] These ascetics, perceived by other Christians to be achieving a state of spiritual perfection in their love of Christ, were magnets for pilgrims and followers.[18] So, too, were the Stylites—those who, like their fifth-century founder, Saint Simeon, lived on pillars where they prayed, provided spiritual advice, and studied and mediated theological controversies.[19] The tradition of "anchorites" and "anchoresses" (Gk. *anachoresis,* "withdrawal") who practiced prayer and mortification in settings of silence also led to the development of solitary lifestyles that by the latter Middle Ages were sometimes close to population centers; some famous ascetics lived—without break—in "cells" attached to parish churches, into which the Eucharist and meals were given to them through windows and from which they read and wrote, made clothing and other items for the poor, and dispensed spiritual direction.[20]

As the Middle Ages progressed, monasticism came to represent the ascetic life. There, for the most part, disciplines of self-deprivation were balanced by those developing Christian communal life. Yet mendicant orders (i.e., orders of beggars) such as the Franciscans practiced and, by example, encouraged even among Christians outside of the monastery a penitential style of life that included sometimes the severe physical mortifications of self-flagellations, strenuous fasts, and the donning of hair shirts and chains. The aim of these abnegating activities was closeness to Christ, particularly by devotion to him in his Passion, a spiritual focus arising from a deep consciousness of his humanity (as well as his divinity).[21]

Religious and Clerics

Monasticism, "religious life," grew out of the ascetic movement after the example of Antony of Egypt. Considered the founder or "father" of monasticism, Saint Antony lived a century from the 250s to the 350s. His story, *Life of Antony*, purportedly written in the fourth century by Saint Athanasius (ca. 296–373), Alexandrian bishop and Church Father, recorded details of his stunning call to live the "eremitic" life—that of a hermit. Hearing the gospel passage in Matthew wherein Jesus instructs the rich young man to live a life of poverty in discipleship of him, Antony understood the words at a moment as from God directly to him. He immediately heeded the call, withdrawing to the desert, only to have many followers seek him out for guidance in their own spiritual lives.[22] In the East, this tradition took two forms beyond that of the strictly eremitic life—life in community (i.e., in large common settings) and life as both communal and individual (i.e., in small-group settings).[23] The former meant not distinct religious orders as arose in the West but different monastic houses in a single communion of monks and nuns; the latter meant two- to six-person "semi-eremitic" groups, such as those living as anchorites, or "lavra," in their separate quarters but overseen by an elder.[24] In the West, organized into different communities observing a "rule" of life (i.e., prescribed patterns of activity), desert-tradition disciples became the foundation of monastic life as that half of the Christian world would come to know it. Monks, their monasteries, and the various religious orders that would develop from the ascetic movement proliferated especially after Saint Benedict of Nursia (ca. 480–547) established his rule in the sixth century. Founding the now-famous monastery at Monte Cassino, Benedict, sometimes referred to as Western monasticism's "father," ordered a community committed to poverty, chastity, obedience (the now standard vows of those in religious life), and stability (a vow unique to the Order of Saint Benedict). This "cenobitic" form of life—that of living in community—became in many ways the ideal state for a Christian in the Middle Ages, a life adopted separately by men and women who sought an intensive form of discipleship issuing in spiritual growth.

As for clerical life, the bishop (Gk. *episcopus*, "overseer"), the primary pastor in any given locality of the Church, was always admired by the flock. As seen in chapter 3, some of the most famous bishops of the early Church were martyrs. Some others, if not that, were Fathers of the Church and its greatest apologists (i.e., those who explained and defended the Christian faith). They also apparently were presbyters (Gk. *presbuteroi,* "elders"), as evidenced by their description in the New Testament where the functions of the two positions are not clearly delineated, perhaps because there was in fact as yet no clear distinction. Many scholars write of the "presbyter-bishops" of the early Church. In the second century, though, as the Church grew geographically, organizationally, and theologically, certain bishops were elevated to a distinct role above other presbyters, the latter's province being a smaller geographical area—a parish—within a local church. Deacons were designated to assist bishops, resulting in a tripartite order of clerical ministry.[25] Not until the fifth century, in part due to the influence of Jewish ministerial traditions, were the presbyters now distinct from the bishops uniformly called "priests," exercising their "sacerdotal" ministry not only because of their connection to their bishops but from their own role ministering to the community. Already by the third century the role of deacons had been subordinated to that of both bishop and priest.[26] Collectively and separately, in the Middle Ages as in Antiquity, these esteemed offices placed their holders in the line of focus of the Christian faithful. While the controversies of the Middle Ages over lay investiture, simony, benefices, and clerical celibacy certainly involved apparently less than sanctified images, a host of pious clerics ascended to sainthood, in the eyes of the faithful in their own time as well as for all time. Some of these individuals were members of religious orders, now referred to as "regular" clergy; others were "secular" clergy, not in "religious life" but employed in the service of a particular diocese.

Church Fathers, Popes, and Scholars

As the early Middle Ages continued to host Christological councils which began under Constantine to fight theological heresies concerning Christ, Church Fathers past and present were appreciated for their contributions during the formative period of the Church to theological understanding of Christian revelation. Their names were invoked at the councils as authorities whose thought could settle disputes about orthodoxy. Many were admired also for their purity of life; some had been martyred. Many became known, then, as saints. So, too, were popes remembered and honored as saints, when martyred or when holiness of life shone through their unique pastoral role in the Church, a role that grew in prominence and power during the Middle Ages. In this period, the Church Fathers became known additionally as "Doctors" of the Church; after the Middle Ages others were given this title, among them selected monks, mystics, and ascetics, as well as scholars who, in addition to having a reputation for sanctity, are recognized for their deep and lasting impact on the Church through their teachings about the faith. The Christological councils settled the definition of Christ, but theological reflection upon him did not end with this; Christians continue to try to deepen their comprehension of that which Christ has revealed. "Fathers" of the Church were so named informally, popes obviously have official status in the Church, and "Doctors" of the Church have received this designation from a pope or from an ecumenical council. All Doctors must be saints.

Mystics

Saints and Doctors of the Church Catherine of Siena (d. 1380), Teresa of Ávila (1515–1582), and John of the Cross (1542–1591), as well as Saints Hildegard von Bingen (1098–1179) and Francis of Assisi (1181–1226) and Blessed Julian of Norwich (d. 1423), among many others, were captivating presences in the Church of the Middle Ages and beyond, despite lack of ecclesiastical validation during most or all of their lives and faced with occasional criticism from those who resented their gifts. In a world in which the invisible and the visible were strongly perceived as coinciding in time and space, mystics were admired for their graced experience of union of soul with God and appreciated for their poetry, spiritual reflections, autobiographies, treatises of mystical theology, artistic images, and music that issued from this union and which, centuries later, are considered Christian classics. They also fascinated with the extraordinary phenomena that attended some of their mystical experiences, such as the stigmata, visions, bilocations, levitations, inedia, hearing of voices, and reading of hearts. But, most importantly (and the reason that those canonized were so), they inspired with their perfected charity borne by their mystical communion with the God who is love (1 Jn. 4:16). This is the test of true Christian mysticism—transformation of the mystic in and for exceptional love of God and neighbor. As Saint and Doctor Bernard of Clairvaux (1190–1153) wrote in his *On Loving God*: "Happy the man who has attained the fourth [and highest] degree of love, he no longer even loves himself except for God."[27] In a letter attached to this famous treatise, as a postscript concerning charity, he wrote:

> I maintain that true and sincere charity proceeds from a pure heart, a good conscience and unfeigned faith [1 Tim. 1:5]. It makes us care for our neighbor's good as much as for our own. For he who cares for his own good alone or more than for

his neighbor's, shows that he does not love that good purely, that he loves it for his own advantage and not for the good itself. Such a man cannot obey the Prophet who says: 'Praise the Lord, for he is good [Ps. 117:1].'[28]

If the early medieval accounts of mystical experiences exhibited language and concepts from Platonism—albeit employed in Christianity as proper to that context—such as Augustine's famous description of the mystical "ascent" shared with his mother at Ostia shortly before her death,[29] as the Middle Ages progressed a mystical piety of devotion to the humanity of Christ developed.[30]

Rulers and Conquerors

With Church and state intertwining at various levels throughout the Middle Ages, rulers, and/or those with political influence over rulers (sometimes popes, clerics, and/or monks), were logically in the mind's eye as well as the physical line of vision of the Christian populace. Saintly characteristics were readily noticed; close admirers documented them in the style of the time, in stories usually more encomium than historical biography. Given that means of consolidation of power was by marriage or by conquest, if not or not also by inheritance, social mores later rejected did not deter even conquerors from being regarded as saints. Saint Louis, King Louis IX of France (d.1270), for example, is criticized today for his participation in the late Crusades, although he was known during his lifetime as a just ruler. Cultural sensibilities influence even the Church, even though it is called to be a sign to the world. Christians, who are to challenge the world where that is needed, are human beings who cannot totally disengage themselves from the assumptions of their times, a fact seen in the past view of saints principally as patrons.

Patrons

In a study of the cult of the saints in Western Christianity, Brown noted that the saints came to be understood as patrons styled after those of the system that dominated socio-economic life in Europe. He showed that in large part it is Augustine who is to be credited with providing the theology for this developing vision of the role of the saints in the lives of those still on their earthly journey. In book ten of the *City of God*, Augustine asserted that those who have proven through their martyrdom that they are servants of God have the ability to draw others closer to God. They can do so in a way angels cannot, because they are servants of

God at the same time that they are our fellows. That we may become their fellow servants, they are available to assist. The move Augustine made was significant, Brown explained:

> Augustine's solution summed up a drift in Christian sensibility: the need for intimacy with a protector with whom one could identify as a fellow human being, relations with whom could be conceived of in terms open to the nuances of known human relations between patron and client, is the hallmark of late-fourth-century Christian piety. It insensibly tended to oust reverence for beings, who, as gods or angels, had owed their position to their role as intermediaries between men and beings other than men in the soaring hierarchy of the late-antique universe.[32]

With regard to saints as patrons, these "invisible companions" were more than intercessors. Following upon ancient tradition, men and women of the fourth and fifth centuries so closely identified with their heavenly patrons that the tendency was toward assimilation of their identity, as explained in chapter 3 following Brown's studies. One's personality was developed by a deepening sense of connection with the personality of the companion or patron; "the patron saint still has the ancient quality almost of an unconscious layer of the self."[33] Understood to be united closely with Christ, the patron saint could provide stability to the one still negotiating his or her way through earthly existence. Brown remarked:

> The later spread of Christian names reflects the need to link the identity of the individual to a saint. A Christian name stood for a new identity associated with a new birth. For the 'rebirth' promised at Christian baptism derived its full meaning from an ancient model of the formation of the personality.[34]

Even today, individual Catholics and other Christians claim as their patron saint one whose name is given at Baptism. Catholics also have a special connection with the saint whose name they choose at Confirmation. But that which is particularly striking about the medieval view of saints as patrons is that those in Heaven were sometimes thought by a poorly-catechized Christian populace to be able to provide not only spiritually but materially for those who invoked them; they were seen to be able to grant favors as earthly patrons granted favors, but on a grander scale. As will be evident by the conclusion of this study, this is a notion theologically untenable and objectionable for its effective displacement of the role of Christ.

As the Middle Ages progressed, individual saints came to be associated with all manners of causes, some now of untraceable origins but others tied to the history of (localities, occupations, events, etc.) or to legends related to particular saintly intercessors or "protectors."

Miracle Workers

As the notion of saints as protectors became prominent, so, too, did their status as miracle workers. Cunningham noted that for a period beginning in the sixth century, the miraculous became the sole criterion for declaring one a confessor and worthy of a cult and that miracles performed after death as an act of intercession were especial indicators of the status as a "saint" of such an exemplary Christian. This had an immediate consequence of deemphasizing the faithful lives of the confessor-saints.[35] Yet it is also the case that the ascetics of the early Church had been thought popularly, too, to possess miraculous powers, and not at the expense of admiration of their lives of holiness. As ascetic practices grew into the movements summarized of the Middle Ages, their aim was first of all sacrifice for imitation of and union with Christ.[36] In short, the holy and the miraculous co-existed in the Middle Ages; the miracles associated with saints were signs of sanctity.[37]

Conclusion

Although special issues involving Mary will be dealt with in chapter 13, a few words must be offered here about the devotion to her that revealed her as preeminent among saints and even angels in the minds and hearts of medieval Christians. Venerated from the early days of Christianity, Mary appeared already in the frescoes of the Roman catacombs.[38] In the Middle Ages she was pictured prominently in churches East and West, as Mother of the Lord, ever-virgin, as Queen of Heaven, as Mediatrix and powerful intercessor. Behind the pictorial images was the developing theological understanding of her role in the work of her Son. As chapter 13 will consider, while in the Gospel of Mark she seems a peripheral figure in the ministry of Jesus, in later-written gospel accounts she is indispensible as the virgin mother of the savior who plays an integral part in his ministry, one to be admired by her Son's followers. The *Protoevangelium of James*, legendary in character, originally called "The Nativity of Mary" and probably written in the second century, provided fuel for Christian fervor surrounding Mary, offering an account of her pious early life up to the nativity of Christ.[39] In early writings of the

Fathers she is the "New Eve" and virgin mother of Jesus.[40] Devotion to her as *Theotokos* (Gk. "God-bearer," or "Mother of God") was permanently validated by the ecumenical Council of Ephesus in the fifth century. Christians found in her an image of and a mother of the Church, a spiritual mother of the faithful[41]; they dedicated churches to her,[42] the one who, through her Son, played a critical role in human redemption. They also identified with her humanity, sanctified beyond others', but suffering as others', in her grief and compassion for her suffering Son.[43] Piety toward Mary led, before the close of the Middle Ages, to a variety of formal Marian prayers and the prayer tradition of the "Angelus"—recitation of the "Hail Mary" three times per day, at morning, midday, and evening.[44] As well, the rosary, utilizing a prayer sequence anticipating that known today, rose in popularity. From this would later spring confraternities wherein Mary devotees committed to sharing spiritual favors and receiving frequently the sacraments of Confession and Eucharist, in addition to praying the rosary regularly.[45] Hymns to Mary were written and widely sung. From the tenth century, in monasteries especially, but also eventually among secular priests and the faithful at large, recited was the Office—or the shortened "Little Office"—of the Blessed Virgin Mary.[46] In sum, Mary was accorded *hyperdulia*—a term used by Saint Thomas Aquinas and other medieval theologians to refer to the exceptional form of veneration given to her alone by virtue of her unique role in "salvation history," to use a contemporary reference.[47]

Popular veneration of Mary and the saints was ratified by liturgical developments and the formal canonization process that emerged in the Middle Ages. To these the next chapter turns.

Terms for Study

Anachoresis	Patron
Angel	Pilgrimage
Apologist	Pope
Cenobiticism	Priest
Council of Ephesus	Religious Order
Deacon	Rosary
Desert Father	Sacrifice
Eremiticism	Salvation History
Evangelical Counsels	*Theotokos*
Invocation	*Translatio*/Translation Miracle
Mysticism	Accounts

Suggested Readings

Saint Athanasius. *Saint Anthony of the Desert.* Translated by Dom J.B. McLaughlin from Migne's Greek text. Rockford, Illinois: Tan Books and Publishers, 1995.

An important Christian text due to its spiritual insights displayed by Antony, as well as its documentation of the beginnings of monasticism, interestingly, the story was instrumental in the conversion of Augustine, according to his *Confessions* (Book VIII, paragraphs 14, 15, and 29).

Saint Benedict of Nursia. *The Rule of Saint Benedict in English.* Edited by Timothy Fry, Imogene Baker, Timothy Horner, Augusta Raabe, and Mark Sheridan. Collegeville, Minnesota: The Liturgical Press, 1982.

This most influential of rules in Western Christianity, the foundation of the Order of Saint Benedict and model for other monastic rules, Saint Benedict's document deals in remarkable detail yet brevity with both spiritual and practical matters of life in a monastic community.

Saint Catherine of Siena. The *Dialogue.* Translated by Suzanne Noffke. New York and Mahwah, New Jersey: Paulist Press, 1980.

Saint John of the Cross. *The Dark Night.* Translated by Kieran Kavanaugh. New York and Mahwah, New Jersey: Paulist Press, 1987. Also *The Dark Night of the Soul.* Translated by Allison Peers. New York: Image Books, 1959.

Blessed Julian of Norwich. *Showings.* Edited and translated by Edmund Colledge and James Walsh. New York and Mahwah, New Jersey: Paulist Press, 1978.

Saint Teresa of Ávila. *The Interior Castle.* Translated by Kieran Kavanaugh and Otilio Rodriquez. New York and Mahwah, New Jersey: Paulist Press, 1979.

These classical selections of mystical texts from Italian Dominican Catherine, Spanish Carmelites Teresa and John, and English anchoress Julian provide glimpses of the experiences referred to as "mysticism," as well as impart spiritual insights gained from interpretation of these experiences. Although John and Teresa lived beyond the customarily assigned ending date for the medieval era, their mystical texts develop the mystical tradition as it existed in the late Middle Ages represented in the works of Catherine and Julian. The three saints are Church Doctors.

Egeria. *The Pilgrimage of Egeria.* Translated with introduction by Patricia Wilson-Kastner. In *A Lost Tradition: Women Writers of the Early Church.* Lanham, Maryland, and London: University Press of America, 1981.

Written in the fourth or the fifth century by a Christian woman of means who journeyed to Jerusalem, Constantinople, and other Christian and Jewish holy sites, Egeria addressed this account of her travels to a group of devout women of which she was a member. Discovered in the nineteenth century in a manuscript of the eleventh century, Egeria's report has been especially prized for her detailed descriptions of Holy Week liturgical services in Jerusalem and for her personal observations about people and history connected to the biblical and religious sites she visited.

Sayings of the Desert Fathers: The Alphabetical Collection, rev. ed. Translated by Benedicta Ward. Kalamazoo, Michigan: Cistercian Publications, 1984.

This extensive collection transmits to present generations the spiritual wisdom given to visitors of the Desert Fathers centuries ago. Other sources of sayings from the desert ascetics, as well as description of the personalities and lives of these admired for their faith, include Laura Swan, *The Forgotten Desert Mothers: Sayings, Lives, and Stories of Early Christian Women* (New York and Mahwah, New Jersey: Paulist Press, 2001). Presenting thematically the reflections of desert dwellers is *The Desert Fathers: Sayings of the Early Christian Monks,* trans. Benedicta Ward (London and New York: Penguin Books, 2003). Providing a translation and explanation of a late fourth-century account of activities of Desert Fathers written by monks who traveled to Egypt to be inspired by the famous holy men is *The Lives of the Desert Fathers: The Historia Monachorum in Aegypto,* introductory chapters by Benedicta Ward, trans. Norman Russell (Kalamazoo, Michigan: Cistercian Publications; London and Oxford: A.R. Mowbray, 1981).

Sulpicius Severus. *Life of Saint Martin.* Translated by Bernard M. Peebles. In *The Fathers of the Church.* Vol. 7. Edited by Joseph Deferrari et al. New York: Fathers of the Church, 1949:101–140.

This text, for centuries serving as model for biographies of saints, provides example of classical hagiography as it imparts the novel story of Martin, sometimes credited as founder of Western monasticism and the first non-martyr to be entered into the Western church's festal calendar.

Five

OFFICIAL AND UNIVERSAL VENERATION OF SAINTS: LITURGY AND CANONIZATION

Expressions of communion with the dead that initially were spontaneous and local became, in the Middle Ages, officially sanctioned in a variety of ways. It is in the "liturgy" (a term derived from the Greek *leitourgia* meaning "work of the public" and as applied to the Church meaning "public worship") that the saints found their essential place in the life of the Church. Indeed, the truth of the fifth-century saying from Prosper of Aquitaine that "the law of worship is the law of belief" (Lat. *lex orandi, lex credendi*), meaning that worship is an indication of correct doctrine,[1] can be seen readily with respect to the cult of the saints, as well as in the history of Christianity as a whole. Along with liturgical validation of veneration of the saints came rules and procedures for determining the proper objects of veneration; this led to the process of "canonization," the addition of names to the list of official saints. This chapter will consider liturgical developments and the canonization process that emerged in the Middle Ages with lasting effect.

Liturgical Veneration of the Saints

Where the saints are concerned, cult and liturgy are intertwined historically and theologically. The earliest forms of liturgical veneration of the saints already have been glimpsed in the review of early Christian cultic activity. But two important liturgical developments occurred after Christianity was legalized. The first was the greater prominence given to the saints in the Mass. The second was the addition of the expression "communion of saints" to the Apostles' Creed, along with a deepening of the understanding of the significance of the reality that this term came to denote for the faithful, living and dead. These events underscore the prevalence of early and medieval veneration of saints, as well as show the Church's vivid consciousness of the power of the saints' perceived proximity to Christ.

Liturgical Development

Scholars of early Church liturgy note that, in the fourth century, Masses
for the commemoration of martyrdom anniversaries at the gravesite
basilicas of the martyrs in the West, unlike in the East, began to
distinguish themselves by their prayers from other Masses. Eventually
the martyrs and saints gained prominent mention not only in liturgies
on feast days of saints but in all Masses. Augustine's Sermon 159 attests
that, already by the early fifth century, the martyrs were honored at
the altar and prayers were offered for the dead there, during the
commemorations.[2] In the West, and particularly in Rome, initially the
Preface at the altar came to reflect the honor paid to the martyrs in view
of the "victory of Christ." The *Muratorian Fragment*, a list of books of
Scripture that survived from the early Church and that was discovered
in the eighteenth century, thanks God that this victory is, in the martyrs,
"repeated which was first won in the Head."[3] It recognizes "these
[who] have confessed that name in which alone salvation is determined
for us" and thanks God, who, "so that we may be enabled to confess
it, . . . teachest our weak faith by their witness and strengthenest it by
their intercession."[4] As the Middle Ages dawned, in the fifth and sixth
centuries, the martyrs were for the first time mentioned not only in the
Roman liturgy's Preface, in the Prayer of Thanksgiving then distinct
from the Canon, but in the Canon itself—the Eucharistic Prayer, the
central prayer of the Mass.[5] There, their specific names were given,
"inserted into the *Communicantes* and the *Nobis quoque*, thus giving
expression to the desire to offer the sacrifice in union not only with the
whole Church on earth but with the Church triumphant in heaven,"
noted Jungmann.[6] V.L. Kennedy, in a thorough study issued in 1938
and revised in 1963, *The Saints of the Canon of the Mass*, explained
that the saints found their way into the first intercession of the Canon,
the commemoration or *Communicantes*, first in Masses for the dead
and then in Masses otherwise. There they joined prayers for the
Church, for bishops, and for the offerers among the living, in a list
referred to as a *Memento*. This tradition led to the development of "a
companion prayer," the *Nobis quoque*, the second intercession in the
Canon, a *Memento* of the dead "with a remembrance of saints to
parallel the structure of the *Memento* of the living with its
Communicantes." Kennedy estimated this feature to be borrowed from
the Eastern tradition, originally including John the Baptist and Stephen
and later including other saints not mentioned in the *Communicantes*.
Eventually, "the *Nobis quoque* becomes an integral part of the Roman
Canon, so much so that it is said in every mass even when the *Memento*
of the dead is omitted."[7]

Also becoming liturgical tradition at the beginning of the Middle Ages was the recital of the Litany of the Saints on the Easter Vigil. Earlier in the Church, the liturgy already included a "Mass of the Catechumens" and "A Mass of the Faithful," known today also as the "Liturgy of the Word" and the "Liturgy of the Eucharist." Those not yet baptized were excused from the Mass before the preparation of the gifts, receiving instruction elsewhere while the baptized participated in the most sacred part of the Mass. The Mass of the Faithful began with an intercessory prayer for the varied needs of the particular community, derived from practice of the synagogues.[8] Eventually, this prayer was moved to the Mass of the Catechumens and therefore was recited by the entire community.[9] By the time of Pope Saint Gregory the Great (540–604), these petitions were issued in the form of a standard litany (invocations spoken by a priest or deacon with responses by the faithful) that included the saints.[10] After Gregory's liturgical reforms, the Litany was preserved in its length only for the Easter Vigil, with shortened litanies remaining for feast days for a time but only the *Kyrie* ("Lord have mercy, Christ have mercy, Lord have mercy") surviving for Masses generally.[11]

As the Middle Ages progressed, the notable liturgical development with regard to the saints was an expanding calendar of feast days. A feast day for a saint customarily was held on his or her death day (especially in the case of a martyr), the day of the translation of a saint's relics, or the day of a church's dedication.[12] Before Constantine, calendars had been local, containing martyrs, and eventually bishops, of importance to particular Christian communities.[13] In the East especially, they also sometimes included Old Testament figures, popular with the many pilgrims who visited the Holy Land. But once Christianity became legal, local calendars began to include saints of importance for the whole Church, as well as saints venerated only locally. Eventually the sanctoral calendar (i.e., a calendar of saints' feasts) of Rome became that of the Western church entire,[14] due largely to Rome's prominence among all of the local churches. Successor to Peter, the "rock" of the Church (Mt. 16:18–19), the bishop of Rome was regarded particularly in the West as having primacy over other bishops. And Rome had been at the center of the persecutions; in these, Peter and Paul had perished, in addition to many others whose bodies so precious to the Church now were interred in Rome.[15] While the Eastern churches tended to retain just the local calendars of the early saints,[16] the Roman calendar increased in both size and scope. By the sixth century, after Martin of Tours, other non-martyrs had been added to the Roman calendar: Stephen; the two Johns regarded as saints; the "Holy Innocents," the children killed by Herod the Great in his quest to prevent the survival of Jesus; and Michael the Archangel.[17] And the Christological councils in the fourth through the eighth centuries resulted not only in new feasts celebrating the mysteries of the life of Christ but, following the definitive pronouncement of the Council of Ephesus that Mary is *Theotokos*, feasts observed first in the East and then in the West celebrating Mary's unique role in Christ's salvific work. Initiating the "liturgical cultus of Mary," these included the Nativity of the Blessed Virgin Mary, the Dormition or the Assumption of Mary, the Annunciation, and the Purification or Presentation of the Lord—the latter two often counted as Christological feasts.[18] (During this period, too, the feast of the Exaltation of the Holy Cross was added to the Roman calendar, in addition to feasts for dedications of churches. The Nativity of the Lord, Christmas, celebrated in the West, and the Epiphany, celebrated in the East and then the West albeit with different meanings, were added in the fourth century.[19]) These and the other feasts that were set, especially the many in and after the great reforming pontificate of Saint Gregory VII (1020–1085), were subordinate to Easter—the first and foremost Christian mystery—and its Sunday observances.[20] Nevertheless, by the later Middle Ages "almost every day of the year was now the feast of a saint, and a yet more closely woven network of feasts of Our Lord and of Our Lady was spread over the entire liturgical year," noted Theodor Klauser in a study of the Western liturgy's history.[21] The move toward papal control over the canonization process that will be discussed later in this chapter was a final factor decreasing the prominence and growth of local Western calendars[22] with the universal assertion of the Roman Sanctorale—the cycle of feast days of saints celebrated liturgically, known as the "Proper of Saints." The Sanctorale is observed in concert with the Temporale—the cycle of the central Christian mysteries celebrated through Christmas, Paschal, and Ordinary liturgical seasons.

Creedal and Theological Development

The term "communion of saints" found its way into the third article of the Apostles' Creed (the paragraph focusing upon the Holy Spirit) by the fifth century.[23] Debate exists about its precise original doctrinal meaning, with some arguing that a notion that existed in the East connected to the communion of saints and meaning "participation in holy things" such as the Eucharist may have found implicit inclusion in the Apostles' Creed there and then influenced the understanding of the term when it was inserted into the Creed in the West.[24] Others argue that, while this notion originated in the East, the term itself arose first in the West,[25] developing out of its reflection upon the means of forgiveness and ultimately salvation which was first represented in the Creed by the expression *communio sacramentorum*.[26] Regardless, by the time that the precise term *sanctorum communio* appeared in the Creed in the West, if not before, evolving understanding of the relationships among the sacraments, forgiveness and salvation, and the community to which these apply rendered the expression "communion of saints" a personal rather than a strictly sacramental statement that referred to the entire community of the faithful through the ages. This community included "patriarchs, prophets, martyrs, and all other righteous men who have lived or are now alive,"[27] as described by one Christian writer at the turn of the fourth to the fifth century. It included those who "deserve to be venerated worthily, forasmuch as they infuse into us, through their contempt of death, the worship of God and the yearning for the life to come,"[28] in the words of a later fifth-century Christian thinker. In the case of either of these personal interpretations, the reference to the communion of saints came to be associated with the ancient custom of praying for the dead and of asking the dead to pray for the living. Concurrently, it can be understood to have retained the sacramental dimension that was reflected by the early Church in the already-mentioned graveyard inscriptions with liturgical references and in statements of Church Fathers such as Tertullian about the solidarity that exists between the living and the dead. As the Middle Ages arrived, in *Confessions* Augustine recalled the death of Monica, praying that "as a result of these confessions of mine may my mother's request receive a richer response through the prayers which many offer and not only those which come from me"[29] and remembering the funeral Mass and its "prayers which we poured out to you when the sacrifice of our redemption was offered for her."[30] In the late sixth century, in a discussion of Purgatory in his *Dialogues*, Gregory I ("the Great") taught that those in Purgatory might be aided in their release by the power of the prayers of the faithful on Earth and in Heaven.[31]

Development of the Process of 'Canonization'

Even after martyrdom was no longer a threat, or indeed a real possibility, when Christians had to amend their definition of that which is required to live the gospel in the new age, the martyrs were still held in high esteem. So much was this the case that a local Council of Carthage in 410 decided that existing altars memorializing martyrs should be eliminated and that no new shrines should be introduced unless they met one of two conditions—they were placed on sites that had an integral connection with a martyr's life and/or death, or they contained relics. Several centuries later the Second Council of Nicaea decided that every church altar should contain the relics of a saint.[32] By then the feasts of martyrs and saints were common and martyrologies and other calendars had begun to reflect the interest of the universal as well as the local church. And yet the path to establishment of new saints remained a local enterprise until the tenth century. Before then, the only formal process that had developed was the submission to the local bishop of the *Vita*—the written biography of a would-be saint that included an account of the individual's virtues, miracles, and death. Even then, the impetus for a declaration of sainthood came from the faithful who sought approval for veneration of one they remembered as holy and experienced as a miracle worker. If the bishop or a regional synod judged the evidence sufficient to prove a reputation for holiness, the body of the one deemed a saint would be translated to an altar and the name would be added to the local calendar on a new feast day assigned for liturgical recognition of the saint.[33] From there, a series of events in the increasingly regulated ecclesiastical process of canonization placed the pope in the position of final judge.

Bishop Ulrich of Augsburg's was the first "authenticated" sainthood case to be validated by a pope, when John XV authorized the translation of Ulrich's remains after meeting with bishops in council at the Lateran in 993 A.D.[34] In 1170 A.D., Pope Alexander III—he who canonized Archbishop of Canterbury Thomas Becket and required penance of Henry II, King of England, for Becket's murder—decreed that the pope's approval was required even for local veneration.[35] In 1234 A.D., Pope Gregory IX published pontifical laws, called *Decretals*, that declared the pope alone to have the authority to canonize. In the fourteenth century, the Avignoise popes (1309–1377)—those who resided in Avignon, France, rather than in Rome during a particularly turbulent political period—expanded canonization procedures as they refined administrative methods of the Church in the overall. It was at this time that a legal trial was firmly established as the means of ensuring the worthiness of those who would be canonized. The prosecutor of the cause represented the petitioners; the "Promoter of the Faith" or "Defender of the Faith"—often described as the "Devil's Advocate"—represented the pope. Weighty testimony was required from dignitaries whose words could be trusted, else the case would not be heard.[36] Yet local communities continued to venerate their own patron saints throughout the Middle Ages, a seemingly contradictory circumstance that finally was resolved by the categorization of those venerated into *sancti* ("saints") and *beati* ("blesseds"). Saints were those venerated universally by validation of the pope; blesseds were those venerated locally by validation of bishops at the behest of local populaces.[37]

Later developments in canonization procedures were expansions beyond the medieval system as the Church responded to needs presented by the times. Following the sixteenth-century Council of Trent which answered the Protestant Reformation, in 1588 Pope Sixtus V created the Sacred Congregation of Rites to prepare canonizations and to authenticate relics.[38] Absolute papal authority over the causes of saints— at the level of beatification as well as at the level of canonization—was established in the first part of the seventeenth century under the papacy of Urban VIII; his production of a one-volume work of his decrees and commentary tightened the methods for examination of causes.[39] From his pontificate on, disallowed was any form of public veneration before papal declaration of one as a blessed. Exceptions were made only in the cases of ancient cults or those that had written evidence of the support of Church Fathers and the approval of earlier popes.[40] Pope Benedict XIV, a canon lawyer, then offered an expansive review and examination of the canonization process in a set of volumes called *De Servorum Dei beatificatione et Beatorum canonizatione* ("On the Beatification of Servants of God and the Canonization of Blesseds") issued between 1734 and 1738. This work was incorporated into the Church's Code of Canon Law in 1917, four years after Pope Saint Pius X split the Congregation of Rites into a division for liturgical issues and a division for canonizations. In 1930 Pope Pius XI added an historical section to the Congregation, to deal with examination of ancient causes. This became part of the Sacred Congregation for the Causes of Saints created by Pope Paul VI in 1969 from the division of the Congregation of Rites that dealt with canonizations; thereafter the Congregation of Rites dealt only with the liturgy.[41] This was the last major step in the evolution of the canonization process until the system was significantly revised in 1983, as will be discussed in chapter 8.[42] Journalist Kenneth Woodward, granted unprecedented access to the Vatican Congregation that today is responsible for causes of saints, described the essence of the formalized canonization procedure until 1983 in his book *Making Saints: How the Catholic Church Determines Who Becomes a Saint, Who Doesn't, and Why:*

> [R]efinements in the saint-making process came chiefly from outside influences. The development of history as critical science, for example, gradually affected how the congregation handled texts, though it had a less perceptible effect, . . , on the writing of *vitae*. More important, the development of scientific medicine greatly reduced the number and kinds of 'divine favors' which could be accepted as miracles. But the determinant 'science' remained canon law and its requirements. The primary evidence remained that of eyewitnesses, and the primary focus was on proving martyrdom or heroic virtue. Even the operative Latin term used by the church, *processus*,

means 'trial.' Thus, if the purpose of papal canonization, as it emerged in the modern era, was to arrive at a theological truth—namely, the candidate is indeed with God in heaven— both the form and, what is more important, the *spirit* of the process were judicial.[43]

What was the process until 1983? It will be reviewed here in brief, and chapter 8 will identity its elements that survive today.[44] The formal process began after a fifty-year waiting period, sometimes waived, during which stirrings that sometimes involved fundraising and distribution of promotional printed materials (such as prayer cards and biographies) occurred at the local level to elicit interest in and private devotion to one with a reputation for holiness. The aim: popular support for the cause of the individual concerned so as to obtain the local bishop's support. With his approval, the official proceedings commenced.

First, in the "Ordinary Process" or "Informative Process," the bishop held local tribunals and/or otherwise gathered evidence for and against the sanctity of the candidate or "servant of God." In addition to testimony of witnesses, also studied were existing writings, published and unpublished (even letters), plus any other known statements of the candidate, to assure that they did not contain heretical or heterodox thought. From 1940, a designation of *nihil obstat* ("nothing hinders") was required of any files concerning the candidate at the Vatican, to eliminate the possibility that negative information known to any other arm of the Vatican might not be known to the Congregation for the Causes of Saints (and, before then, to the Congregation of Rites). If any miracles of intercession were believed to have occurred, preliminary information was collected about their circumstances. When the local examinations yielded the judgment that the candidate was, indeed, holy and orthodox, and that no public cult had formed in devotion to him or her (for this would be ground for halt of a cause, since ecclesiastical approval must be given for such in the form of beatification or canonization[45]), the materials collected at this stage were organized into a dossier that was submitted to the Congregation.

Second, in Rome, the Congregation for the Causes of Saints assigned the cause to a "Postulator" who became the representative for the petitioners who submitted the dossier. Upon the dossier the postulator constructed his case for the heroic sanctity of the individual concerned and then, with the "Advocate," the lawyer assigned for the candidate, answered objections of the Promoter of the Faith or "Devil's Advocate." This was sometimes an exceedingly lengthy dialogue lasting even a generation or more; it was meant to ensure that no mistake could be made in the examination of one who might be canonized. Objections satisfied, the postulator compiled a *Positio*—a volume containing the argument for the candidate, as well as the questions of the promoter of the faith and the replies to them, plus other supporting materials. Reviewed by the Congregation's cardinals, prelates, and other personnel, a judgment was made as to the merits of the cause and, if positive, word was given to the pope to elicit his decree that the cause was formally introduced. The Vatican assumed control of the cause, now an "Apostolic Process."

Third, the Apostolic Process was repetitive of many aspects of the Ordinary Process. The promoter of the faith presented new questions, which received answers through new tribunals at the local level, this time under the supervision of the Vatican. Eventually an *Informatio* was produced, arguing a case either of martyrdom or of heroic virtue. The objections and replies exchanged between the promoter of the faith and the advocate continued through levels of the Congregation up to the pope; the historical section was called into service when necessary, as in cases where witnesses no longer lived to supply details of the candidate's life and/or death. If and when objections were answered satisfactorily, the candidate was given the title of "Venerable."

Fourth, miracles were examined. Once venerable, a candidate awaited only proper identification of his or her body, requiring exhumation, and proven miracles of intercession after his or her death. Exceptions were two: one, if the location of the body was not known or the body inhabiting the supposed grave of the candidate proved not to be his or hers, the cause progressed but private devotions at the gravesite were forbidden, and, two, martyrs were routinely beatified in the belief that their sacrifice would not have been possible without the grace of God. Miracles are considered divine validation of the Congregation's determination that the candidate is a martyr and/or was heroically virtuous—the criteria for sainthood. A group of medical experts was, and is, employed for painstaking evaluations to eliminate the possibility that events thought to be miracles might have occurred naturally.

Fifth, in the case of a positive judgment of two miracles of intercession and determination by the Congregation of the appropriate time to proceed to a public declaration, the venerable was beatified, becoming a "Blessed." As now, thus permitted was local veneration— that of a particular diocese or geographical location or of a particular religious order. A Mass was the occasion for the announcement, but— with the notable exception of Pope John Paul II, who, beginning in 1971 established his own custom with regard to beatifications[46]—the pope did not, and does not, preside at the Mass, for he is the pastor of the universal Church and the blessed is not to be venerated universally.[47] The pontiff's presence was, and is, central in the final step.

Sixth, canonization occurred on the occasion of an additional two proven miracles of intercession. Even in the case of a martyr named a blessed without miracles, two miracles were required after beatification for canonization. At the Mass celebrating the announcement of a blessed turned "Saint," the pope did, and does, preside, symbolic of the fact that sainthood requires veneration throughout the Church. A bull of canonization was issued to this effect; the saint is a worthy model and a proven intercessor. He or she was assigned a feast day on the liturgical calendar of the Church universal.

Conclusion

At the end of the Middle Ages saints had become not simply patrons of particular churches or towns (although they were that), not simply intercessors for those privately devoted to them (although they were more likely to be privately invoked by those invested in their cult than by others), not simply exemplars for those called to live as a martyr now that dying as a martyr was no longer likely (although many of the saints were clergy and religious and therefore had special appeal for those committed to these states of life viewed as types of "martyrdom"). They were models and intercessors for all of the faithful; all of the faithful were to venerate them in the corporate action of the Church, if not in private devotions. Even blesseds now, only locally venerated, were named by officials of the Church rather than by spontaneous devotion of private cults that elicited bishops' addition of their names to local calendars. Still, the impetus for the process leading to sainthood was a groundswell of popular fervor in the inspirational memories of and hoped-for miracles from a person known for sanctity. But those named saints in the late medieval world and after, unlike those in the early Middle Ages, were fewer and carefully vetted. As noted in chapter 4, bishops early after Constantine had grown in prominence for their association with the saints, in their protection of martyr gravesites and in their construction of churches in honor of martyrs and then of other holy deceased. But validation of the pope was increasingly sought, for precisely the gains that were achieved: the greater, more widespread attention given to particular saints because of papal declaration; the more careful scrutiny of candidates, ensuring that those "sainted" were more historical than legendary and that in their history they exhibited holiness and virtue heroically; and the placement of saints in a universal calendar of the Church that would be observed in a liturgical cycle of feast days and Sundays to commemorate first the life of Christ and second his work in the saints.

For all of the benefits of papal canonizations, concerns have been voiced about certain effects of the highly regimented official process, past and/or present. For one, as has been the case since the Middle Ages, the ultimately Vatican control of the images of sanctity put before the faithful has guaranteed their validity as models; at the same time few individuals who are not clergy or religious have been canonized, meaning that the models have not been as instructive as they might be if more of them more closely resembled the majority of the faithful in state of life. Two, the papal process removed those venerated from the close connection enjoyed with local communities that was demonstrated in the early cult of the martyrs and then saints, albeit in many locations this has eliminated problematic cultic practices. Three, the number of individuals canonized dropped substantially after the full development of the process described in this chapter, because of the time demanded by the meticulous investigations. Even though this last effect is not necessarily negative, especially given the perhaps overzealousness with which individuals were "canonized" before Vatican oversight, it did result in the apparent delay or effective denial of canonization of worthy individuals as their popularity waned or when their advocate at the Congregation died while the promoter of the faith generated more and more questions for examination. As chapter 8 will show, the 1983 change in the process meant to address such issues.

While in the West the system of saint "making" became more sophisticated and "scientific" as the Church grew in age, size, and organization, in the East procedural changes did not result in the same complexity. As noted, early on in the East, Old Testament patriarchs and prophets, as well as Christ's apostles and the martyrs, received attention as saints, as in the Western portion of the Church; also priests and those remembered as having lived holy and/or ascetic lives were recognized locally, on the authority of the bishop following upon popular acclaim and often accompanied by miracles of intercession either during life or after death. Bishops ("hierarchs") themselves came sometimes to be universally venerated, when remembered for their unique contributions to the life of the Church in, for example, the important areas of doctrine or care for the poor. As in the Catholic Church, those venerated as saints in the Orthodox Church are understood to have been designated so by God, certified by the individuals' outstanding lives and/or miracles. Faith that is orthodox and a life presenting a worthy example are sometimes validated by formal examinations once a popular reputation has become overwhelming, but in the Orthodox Church emphasis is placed upon signs from God. Along with popular devotion, miracles are key indications of sainthood, except in the case of martyrs whose sacrifice is considered proof in itself of God's "glorification" of an individual. Once the Church "glorifies" the one whom God has "glorified," the prayer that is immediately offered for an individual after death becomes prayer to him or her for intercession in death.[48] Orthodox scholar Timothy Ware has noted rare cases in which public cults have formed for saints who, usually for reasons of political repression, have not been officially declared such; martyrs of the Greek church under the Ottoman Empire and, in more recent history, martyrs of the Russian church under the Soviet Union were honored widely but in secret before official validation was possible. An important aspect of veneration of saints in the Orthodox Church is the saints' depiction in icons, "a point of meeting between the living members of the Church and those who have gone before," Ware has explained.[49]

The review in this chapter of canonization procedures stopped short of the current Catholic system but led beyond the Middle Ages through the years of and following the Protestant Reformation. The liturgical developments presented emerged in the Middle Ages but were retained beyond them to the present day. Alongside these developments in the corporate life of the Church, a host of councils and popes pronounced on the theory and practices of veneration of saints. Many of these pronouncements, some already mentioned, will be reviewed in chapter 7. Chapter 6 must stop to consider the theological points made about the saints by the Catholic Church at the time of the Protestant Reformation.

Terms for Study

Altar
Canon Law
Canon of the Mass
Communicantes
Creed/The Apostles' Creed
Divine Office/Liturgy of the Hours
Icons
Lex orandi, lex credendi
Litany (of the Saints)
Liturgy of the Eucharist/Mass of the Faithful

Liturgy of the Word/Mass of the Catechumens
Nobis quoque
Novena
Postulator
Promoter of the Faith/"Devil's Advocate"
Rite
Sanctorale/Sanctoral Cycle
Temporale/Temporal Cycle

Suggested Readings

Christian Prayer: The Liturgy of the Hours. Translated by the International Commission on English in the Liturgy. New York: Catholic Book Publishing, 1976.

This edition includes selections for morning, daytime, evening, and night prayer, plus the Office of the Readings.

Comby, Jean. *How to Read Church History.* Vol. 1, *From the Beginnings to the Fifteenth Century.* Translated by John Bowden and Margaret Lydamore. New York: Crossroad Publishing, 1995. Original edition, *Pour lire L'Histoire de L'Eglise Tome 1,* Paris: Les Editions du Cerf, 1984.

Comby, Jean. *How to Read Church History.* Vol. 2, *From the Reformation to the Present Day.* Translated by Margaret Lydamore and John Bowden. With additional material by Diarmaid MacCulloch. New York: Crossroad Publishing, 1995. Original edition, *Pour lire l'Histoire de l'Église Tome 2,* Paris: Les Editions du Cerf, 1986.

These volumes provide a concise but colorful telling of the history of the Christian Church through the lens of excerpts from historical texts, as well as maps, charts, and illustrations. Cultural, political, social, economic, and theological factors are considered. Chronological tables ending the volumes are helpful organizational tools for recalling notable events and people.

Cunningham, Lawrence S. *A Brief History of Saints.* Malden, Massachusetts, and Oxford: Blackwell Publishing, 2005.

Scholar of the history and theology of saints and their veneration, Cunningham offers in this work a knowledgeable and entertaining overview of saint-related developments from the beginnings of Christianity to the present.

Eucharistic Prayers I-IV. The Roman Missal's *The Sacramentary.* Excerpts at "Changes in the Parts of the Priest in the Order of Mass in the *Roman Missal, Third Edition,*" United States Conference of Catholic Bishops [online]. Available from http://old.usccb.org/romanmissal/priestsparts.pdf. Accessed 20 August 2011.

The *Communicantes* and the *Nobis quoque*—the Commemoration of the Living and the Commemoration of the Dead—can be studied in their current form in the Canon of the Mass (in the Roman Rite) in the four approved Eucharistic Prayers. As per *The General Instruction of the Roman Missal [Third Edition]: Including Norms for the Distribution and Reception of Holy Communion under Both Kinds in the Dioceses of the United States of America and Universal Norms on the Liturgical Year and the General Roman Calendar* (Washington, D.C.: United States Conference of Catholic Bishops, 2011), each of the Eucharistic Prayers contains eight basic parts: thanksgiving, acclamation, epiclesis, institution narrative and consecration, anamnesis, oblation, intercessions, and concluding doxology (paragraph 79).

"Litany of the Saints," in *The Rites of the Catholic Church: As Revised by Decree of the Second Vatican Ecumenical Council and Published by the Authority of Pope Paul VI,* Vol. 2. Translated into English by the International Commission on English in the Liturgy. New York: Pueblo Publishing, 1980.

Known to most Catholics from the Easter Vigil, this Litany also is recited in private devotions and is used at ordinations to the Catholic priesthood. For accommodation to specific circumstances, *The Rites* allows that cantors may add to the standard prayer "the names of other saints (the titular of the church, the patron saint of the place, and the saints whose relics are to be deposited, if this is to take place) and petitions suitable to the occasion" (pages 292–293).

McGonigle, Thomas D., and James F. Quigley. *A History of the Christian Tradition: From Its Jewish Origins to the Reformation.* New York and Mahwah, New Jersey: Paulist Press, 1988.

McGonigle, Thomas D., and James F. Quigley. *A History of the Christian Tradition: From the Reformation to the Present.* New York and Mahwah, New Jersey: Paulist Press, 1996.

A survey of Christian history and theology, brief but impressive in scope, is offered by these volumes which can provide to a student of the saints the background against which have occurred cultic, liturgical, and conciliar events connected to veneration of saints.

Six

HISTORICAL CRITIQUES OF THE CULT: PROTESTANT AND CATHOLIC REFORMATIONS

As the well-known story goes, Martin Luther, caught in a violent thunder and electrical storm, threw himself on the mercy of Saint Anne's intercession, vowing that he would enter a religious order if he escaped being struck dead by lightening.[1] He was spared and, leaving behind plans for law studies, he became an Augustinian friar. A dozen years later, in 1517, he would post his now-famous *Ninety-Five Theses* on the door of Castle Church at Wittenberg, criticizing many Catholic practices of the time related to the saints, as well as Catholic theology of Church authority and the mechanics of salvation. This simple action set off the chain of events that terminated in the Protestant Reformation, through which traditional practices of veneration of saints—such as invocation for intercession of saints as Luther had practiced that stormy night—ended for many Western Christians. Nevertheless, Luther did not completely dismiss attention to the saints, recommending their edifying stories.

> Next to Holy Scripture there certainly is no more useful book for Christendom than that of the lives of the saints, especially when unadulterated and authentic. For in these stories one is greatly pleased to find how they sincerely believed God's Word, confessed it with their lips, praised it by their living, and honored and confirmed it by their suffering and dying. All this immeasurably comforts and strengthens those weak in the faith and increases the courage and confidence of those already strong far more than the teaching of Scripture alone, without any examples and stories of the saints. Although the Spirit performs His work abundantly within, it nonetheless helps very much to see or to hear the examples of others without. Otherwise a weak heart always thinks: See, you are the only one who so believes and confesses, acts, and suffers. For this reason God Himself in Scripture also describes the life, faith, confession, and suffering of the dear patriarchs and prophets along with their doctrine, and St. Peter, too, comforts

Christians with the examples of all the saints and says: 'Know
that the same afflictions are accomplished in your brethren that
are in the world' (1 Pet. 5:9).[2]

As examples only did the saints function for Luther, for reasons beyond
his original critiques of aberrant activities in the cult of the saints of his
time. His use of the term "saint" usually was to designate the wider sense
of the Christian faithful: "If you believe the words of Christ, you are a
saint as well as St. Peter and all the other saints. . . ."[3] And then it was
accompanied by a reminder of human sinfulness: ". . . Scripture, which
teaches us the origin of sin, testifies that there is nothing good in the
nature of man and that the remnant which might be good is put to bad
use."[4] We are all saints and sinners at once, he stated—saints by "that
absolute righteousness which now, as believers in Christ, we only have
imputed to us through the merit of Christ"[5] and sinners in that "feeble
righteousness of our life here on earth, which, strictly speaking, is filth in
His [God's] eyes."[6]

Luther's theology would have invalidated much if not all Catholic
thought and practice about the saints even if he had had no criticisms of
the abuses in the Catholic Church as it entered its sixteenth century. Just
so, the Catholic Church could not have taught, and could not now teach,
differently than it does about the saints, for to do so would be to
contradict its own theology. The abuses of Luther's time are, of course,
excluded; defended they were not in the Catholic response to the
Protestant Reformation, as they are not now. Today, in fact, that which
was in the past called the "Counter Reformation" is preferentially called
the "Catholic Reformation,"[7] in recognition that the ecumenical Council
of Trent that answered the Protestant Reformation did not do only that
but reformed internally the Catholic Church. Despite the sixteenth
century Church's affirmation of traditional thought on the saints,
Catholic teaching leaves room for emphases and practices connected to
the saints (as to other areas of the life of the Church) to change focus
from age to age and/or from culture to culture. Hence, not every of the
popular practices connected to the saints in Luther's time enjoys
popularity among Catholics today. For example, because it is not binding
to invest in the practice of indulgences, many Catholics reared since
Vatican II have never heard this term. If they have heard it, oftentimes
they have not grasped the concept of it in any context other than
historical, precisely in connection with the Protestant Reformation; they
do not realize that the Church still has indulgences.

There is an internal logic to the theology of each of the three major
branches of Christianity—Orthodox, Protestant, and Catholic. While
core affirmations about the salvific work of Christ are shared among the

branches, there are fundamental differences in how these are understood. As a result, and as Christians must be acutely aware in this age of ecumenism, one cannot expect to be able to pluck specific doctrines from one system and import them into another; they will not necessarily fit. That is the case with most Catholic doctrines regarding the saints, because Catholic teaching about the saints stems from the larger framework of its understanding of the workings of nature and grace, which differ from Luther's. In understanding the significance of the Protestant critiques of the cult of the saints, such theological differences are the important issue for anyone who is not of the mind that the sin of committing an abuse—which individuals in the Catholic Church did do, eliciting Luther's opposition—permanently abolishes moral authority. (To the Catholic mind, this notion would eliminate any authority, for it is to be expected that human beings, individually or formed into institutions, may fail, since by definition fallen human beings are imperfect. And, as the medieval axiom went, *abusus non tollitur abusus*—"abuse of something does not eliminate the possibility of its proper use.") A case in point of the inner integrity of each of the Christian "systems" is the Catholic doctrine of Purgatory. Aside from its place in the tradition in the longstanding practice of praying for the dead, as shown to have precedent in Judaism, the Catholic understanding of the relationship between nature and grace (which will be described in more detail in subsequent chapters) posits that human beings need Christ's "justification" *and* sanctification for union with God and that this is a process that is life-long and involves our activity as well as that of God, although ours as empowered and influenced by God's. Conceivably, sanctification could be incomplete at death due to a deficiency in our love of God and neighbor (more particulars of which will be discussed in chapter 14), and this "requires" an explanation of the whereby of God's mercy in which Catholics believe. Admittedly, however, the presentation of the doctrine of Purgatory in the medieval Church seemed to attest little to God's mercy; in fact the penitential system, exacting in the requirement of recompense for sins, rendered Purgatory a locus of grave concern about the afterlife.[8] So conversely, even apart from Luther's criticism of the doctrine on the ground that he believed it to be unbiblical and invented to the financial benefit of the hierarchy via indulgences, the doctrine confounds Luther's system, which does not hold that sanctification impacts the salvation of the human person (even though it occurs with justification) in the Catholic sense in which we must "cooperate," under the influence of grace, with this work of the Holy Spirit in us perfecting us in love of God and neighbor—"works" of charity. The human person's justification by faith alone saves, via the imputation of the merits of Christ; works of charity borne by love of God and neighbor will occur in one justified but are not required for salvation, taught Luther.[9] This explanation affords another example of the inner logic of each Christian branch. Luther's teaching on the dichotomy between the utter sinfulness of the human person and the "saintliness" of the human person's reality by justifying faith alone can seem unduly dialectical to the Catholic sacramental, or incarnational, sensibility, which could not account for a doctrine of double predestination—that some are necessarily saved and others are necessarily damned. But this doctrine can be coherent and was held in the theology of some Protestant reformers, although it was not taught by Luther. To understand such differences in theology, particularly with regard to saints, this chapter will look to Luther's story and his resulting theology of nature and grace, then at specific critiques of Luther pertaining to the Catholic Church's teachings and practices involving the saints, next at Catholic theology of nature and grace in the context of Luther's time, and then at the Catholic response to Protestant critiques of the cult of the saints. Finally, a few ecumenical notes will be offered in conclusion.

Luther's Protestant Reformation Theology

Already before Luther, calls were increasingly loud for reform of the Catholic Church. The Church, and the larger world surrounding it, had experienced swift and significant changes in the years leading finally to the Reformations, Protestant and then Catholic. Major events converged to produce a sense of unrest and of expectation, alternately of imminent destruction or of reinvention: the Avignon papacy leading to the "Great Western Schism" in the fourteenth century, engendering uncertainty in the faithful; the rise of the Western European nation-states that encouraged a more individualistic view of human community than held by the Catholic Church even as it provided a sense of identity and a center of focus for those who felt disenfranchised by the Great Western Schism; the "Black Death" that in only three or four years in the middle of the fourteenth century killed one-third to one-half of the European population, resulting in a social reconfiguration as infrastructures were rebuilt and as wealth was inherited by the only surviving members of families, in addition to a spiritual revitalization in identification with the suffering of Christ and a religious problem in the filling of clerical roles with whomever could be found (even without always the proper spiritual disposition); the emergence of the merchant class which opened new social and economic doors and dismantled the feudal system that for centuries had been an organizing principle for civic and religious institutions geographically and conceptually; the cultural reawakening of the Renaissance that—with the assistance of the invention of the printing press in the middle of the fifteenth century—reintroduced the artistic and scientific treasures of the ancient world; and the movement called "Humanism" that in its inspiration to people to seek their human potential through education had the result of empowering them to question authority and tradition. Christian Humanists sought to be guided by original Christian sources—Scripture and the writings of the Church Fathers. (In their quest, Scripture was encountered in its earliest extant texts, as opposed to the Latin Vulgate that had been translated by Saint Jerome, a Church Doctor, and his assistant Rufinus, in the late fourth century and the early fifth century). Thereby questions arose and were posed increasingly about Church structure, liturgical rites, and use of the vernacular, since it was apparent from these sources that developments had occurred in each of these areas since Christianity's founding. Conduct of the popes at the time exacerbated dissatisfaction in the Church. On the one hand, they, themselves Renaissance Humanists, are to be credited for contributing greatly to the arts and literature, for commissioning still-admired paintings and statues, for collecting artistic and literary treasures of the past for preservation at the Vatican, and for constructing and renovating buildings such as Saint Peter's Basilica. On the other hand, their worldliness scandalized; opulence, nepotism, and political maneuvering among their ranks was mirrored on lower rungs of the Church hierarchy, where occurred simony, bishops absent from their sees, poorly educated clergy, and abuse of indulgences. Luther, influenced by these events with everyone else, was not the first or the last of those who, with deeply religious concerns, wished to restore the Church to purity. Approximately a century before, John Wycliffe and John Hus had introduced, separately, some of the instincts and theology that Luther would take up.

In spite of the fact that Luther became the catalyst for a rupture in Christian unity that persists until this day, he did not begin to speak out with the intention of separating from Catholicism. He posted the *Theses* as normal procedure for an academic disputation. A doctor of theology at the University of Wittenberg, having earned his master's degree and completing further study at the University of Erfurt, his intention was discussion. But the new interest in language translations resulted in the document's conversion from Latin into his vernacular, German, and the new printing press resulted in wide distribution of this and Luther's writings to come. The content and tone hit a nerve with many, and a movement was born that did not pass. Luther's initial critiques were centered upon the abuses connected to indulgences, occasioned particularly by the preaching of John Tetzel and other Dominicans that contributions to the renovation of Saint Peter's Basilica in Rome would earn a special indulgence irrespective of spiritual disposition; the Archbishop of Mainz who had received the approval of Pope Leo X for the offering of this indulgence did not make it clear that no indulgence forgives sin, as will be explained in chapter 14. But in time Luther's issues with the Catholic Church would move beyond practices to differences in theology. It is these, not the abuses pointed out by Luther that would be condemned by the Catholic Council of Trent, that would become the divisive points between Luther and the Catholic Church. As Luther himself wrote to Erasmus in his refutation of that famous Humanist's *The Free Will*, ". . . [Y]ou have discussed the real thing, i.e., the essential point. You have not wearied me with those irrelevant points about the Papacy, purgatory, indulgences, and such trifles . . ."[10] He was referring to the matter of the presence or absence of human free will, as providing the ability of human effort or "merit" in salvation—which he forcefully denied.

Many pages have been written about the impingement of Luther's background upon his spiritual turmoil eventually solved by the religious insight that becomes the centerpiece of a new branch of Christianity. Much of this is conjecture and therefore will not serve this study, but a general reflection upon his context nevertheless sheds light. By all accounts today Luther was a deeply religious person. As a friar, he sought to be a model one, even though, as would become known in his break from religious life, he eventually found repressive its demands. Availing himself of the spiritual disciplines and penitential rites of his time, still he, like pious others, was plagued by a deep sense of guilt for his sinfulness and by anxiety about his salvation. Scholars today identify one source of this turmoil in the penitential system that, in its part modeled after the spirituality of religious orders with their carefully prescribed way of life and spiritual examination, required even from the laity at large constant and careful evaluation of the smallest of actions to identify sin and to make restitution for it. Another source may have been the Nominalist thought with which Luther for a time was aligned due to early contact with it in his academic career. Its founder, William of Ockham (ca. 1290–1350), taught that God's will rather than God's reason was responsible for creation; universal ideas exist only in the human mind. Unlike the Scholastics who preceded him, he therefore did not believe that human reason could begin to grasp anything about God and then try to act in accord with his plan; God's omnipotence had only to be obeyed though not understood. Nominalists, therefore, believed that human beings have some ability to respond to good; we can try as hard as we can to submit to God's will. And by doing this, we can receive the interim reward of his grace (the final reward being eternal life). At the same time, since we cannot begin to understand God, his actions toward us can seem random. Luther was constantly concerned that he was not doing everything that he should or could and consequently he feared for his salvation. His fear was allayed, however, before his 1517 protest of the *Theses*, when, in reflection upon Paul's words in his Letter to the Romans, he found peace in his discovery of a new understanding of the righteousness attributed to human beings by God. The righteousness of God justifies human beings by faith and not by works; thereby we can be clothed in the righteousness or merits of Christ, but in a way that does not involve any merit of our own. This justifying work of Christ applied to us through faith occurs in us when we hear the word of God in the gospel (i.e., the "good news"). Good works that we might perform—and which the justified necessarily do perform—issue from the grace of God; they do not earn the grace of God. Luther's famous slogans of the Reformation, therefore, became "faith alone" (*sola fide*), "grace alone" (*sola gratia*), "Scripture alone" (*sola scriptura*), and "Christ alone" (*sola Christo*). Sometimes labeled "Augustinian," denoting an anthropological emphasis in the thought of Augustine that often is understood differently by Protestant and Catholic Christians, Luther's anthropology was stark: fallen human beings are radically so, with a nature so corrupted as to be incapable of any good of its own. Catholic theology understands fallen human nature as greatly affected but not destroyed. Underlying assumptions about the state of human nature affect the way in which Christians understand God to work with us to save us in Christ. Although Luther's assertions departed from Catholic theology, he did not intend or believe himself to introduce anything new into Christian faith.

Luther's theology of justification by faith alone was in the end a rejection of Nominalism, clearly. Human beings cannot justify themselves; as fallen, we have not the ability to be just. But, by extension, he condemned theological explanations even preceding Nominalism, in a wholesale rejection of the Catholic theology of the academy which he placed under the banner of Scholasticism—the systematic, abstract variety of theology utilizing a dialectical method of question and response employed in the new universities of the Middle Ages. The Scholastic tradition was indebted to the metaphysics and ethical theory of Aristotle which, in Luther's estimation, resulted in a form of Pelagianism, of which he accused Erasmus, too.[11] Pelagianism is a heretical teaching of Pelagius (ca. 350–425), famously opposed by Augustine, that in their free will human beings have "grace" of God by natural constitution. This is unique to human creaturely reality since other earthly creatures act by necessity; we have all that is needed to avoid sin and choose the good as according to the example of Christ, argued Pelagius, who essentially denied that which Augustine called "original sin"[12] in asserting that the

first sin affected humanity only by presenting a bad example. Contra
Pelagianism, the Christian tradition has asserted that free will is not itself
grace. Were that the case, human beings would be saved by their own
efforts and not by the work of Christ. Luther believed that the prevailing
Catholic theology of the time did not sufficiently emphasize this. The
Nominalist conception suggested that we earn grace by our own efforts;
earlier, Scholastics gave pride of place to grace in the belief that only by
grace with which we cooperate can we be sanctified, or transformed, for
the unity with God that is the eternal reward. But Steven Ozment, in his
study *The Age of Reform, 1250–1550: An Intellectual and Religious
History of Late Medieval and Reformation Europe,* judged that Luther
saw little difference in the Nominalist and Scholastic claims:

> . . . Aristotle's definition of moral virtue was as applicable to the
> movement from a state of grace to eternal life as it was to the
> movement from a state of nature to a state of grace. In both
> instances, whether in an initial or in a penultimate stage of the
> Christian's activity, moral effort remained imperative and
> meritorious. By doing one's best in a state of nature one earned
> grace, according to [Nominalist Gabriel] Biel. By doing one's
> best in a state of grace one earned eternal life, according to all
> scholastics. The same pattern appeared on two different levels
> of the religious life. In the final analysis, earning by moral effort
> salvation as condign merit was only a higher form of earning by
> moral effort saving grace as semimerit. To Luther in 1517, the
> former probably appeared to be only a more cautious
> Pelagianism. For although good works were now done with the
> aid of grace, they still remained necessary for salvation.[13]

Luther objected that human free will is a fiction with respect to spiritual
matters: ". . . [W]ith regard to God, and in all things pertaining to
salvation or damnation, man has no free will, but is a captive, servant and
bond-slave, either to the will of God, or to the will of Satan."[14] And so on
another, related count, too, Scholastic theology was anathema for Luther:
its assertion that human beings have and may exercise free will
presupposes the harmony of faith and reason (and nature and grace) that
was, indeed, articulated more precisely by the Scholastics than by
theologians before them. Theology itself, after the original title of Saint
Anselm of Canterbury's *Proslogium,* was defined at this time as "faith
seeking understanding," attesting to the value of reason in examining and
deepening faith.[15] Luther arrived at the conclusion that reason has
nothing to contribute to faith, a gift: ". . . [S]ince God says so, I shall
believe that it is so; I shall follow the Word and shall let my thoughts and
reason be nothing."[16] The Bible is the only reliable sufficient authority for

Christian life; the law (e.g., the Ten Commandments of the Old Testament) shows us our sinfulness—the state he emphasized above individual sins—and the gospel (present in the New Testament but also present in an anticipatory way in the Old Testament) offers us the gift of Christ's forgiveness and salvation.[17] Our experience of being saved was central in Luther's theology.[18]

Beyond the scope of discussion of veneration of saints are the many events that followed Luther's *Theses* leading to the break with the Roman Church. But a few moments deserve mention. Luther's preaching and writings, met by ready ears and eyes in his native Germany and then beyond, established him as father of "Protestant" reformers, a term coined at the protest of a half dozen German princes when in 1529 the Second Diet of Speyer moved to reinstitute Catholicism in German lands that had adopted Lutheranism after the First Diet of Speyer in 1526 allowed each prince to select the faith to be observed in his own geographical area.[19] An attempt to reestablish the ability to choose faith for each area was made in 1530 when the Protestant princes presented the Augsburg Confession at the Diet of Augsburg. But this declaration of the Lutheran faith written by Luther's friend and fellow reformer Philip Melanchthon was not accepted until 1555, nearly a decade after Luther's death in 1546. Before the term "Protestant" was coined, Luther's criticisms of the Church reached a critical point of divergence in theology in 1519 when, in a debate with John Eck, an academic colleague of Luther, Luther in an unplanned remark validated the statements of Hus, the Church reformer who a century before had been declared a heretic by the Council of Constance for certain challenges to papal and conciliar authority and thereby was sentenced to death at the stake. As a result of Luther's remarks, a papal bull threatening excommunication was issued in 1520 insisting that he publicly retract his statements at odds with Church teaching; this Luther burned and he therefore was excommunicated. His theological writings that became the outline for the coming Protestant Reformation began at this time. Condemned in 1521 by the Diet of Worms, a meeting of German secular rulers representing the Holy Roman Empire, Luther was stolen away by supporters and hidden for nearly a year in Wartburg Castle in order to avoid penalty of death. He returned then to Wittenberg to try to ease disquiet that had arisen as some of his followers implemented reforms aggressively. Those among the peasant class who followed him rose up in opposition to the heavy feudalistic demands of their princes; the Peasants' War resulted, netting the princes' killing of many of the peasants, an action that Luther finally approved when his initial suggestions to foster peace failed. In this same year, 1525, Luther, who had left the Augustinians, married another former member of a religious order, Katherine von Bora. In the final approximate two decades of his life he preached memorable sermons, translated the Bible into German, and wrote catechisms and hymns and theological tracts. Even as he was defining his own theological program, other Protestant reformers were spoking off in other theological directions. And the Catholic Council of Trent, prompted in part by the power of the movement that he helped propel, would commence at just about the time of his death.[20]

Luther's Critiques of the Cult of the Saints

It is not difficult to see how Luther's theological differences from the Church of Rome with which he parted are consonant with his critiques of the cult of the saints. His anthropological view of fallen humanity as depraved and his related understanding that salvation occurs only by justification (through faith alone) necessarily resulted in his rejection of Catholic beliefs that underpin the premises of "sainthood" and thereby veneration of any human person, even if sanctified. Additionally, Luther's conclusions concerning Church authority undermined Catholic belief in tradition in the theological sense, including teaching about the "apostolic tradition." For Luther tradition was not wholly unimportant, but it was merely an historical category, not a theological one carrying truth of revelation from one time to another. And so the long tradition of veneration could be dismissed by him without concern that the integrity of the gospel message was thereby compromised; Scripture alone was sufficient for instruction in Christian discipleship, and practices of veneration of medieval Christians were not all explicitly mandated by Scripture.[21]

Luther's criticisms of the Catholic Church's traditions surrounding the saints can be summarized in five related points. One, he objected to the word "saint" being used, against the dominant practice of Scripture, to set some Christians apart from others in perceived holiness. Believing that all Christians are sinners by nature but holy by the grace of Christ, he did not believe that some were holier than others or possessed more grace than others. He rejected the notion that saints' good works were their merits in any degree. Two, he was critical that many stories of saints had been so tainted by legendary material that their value was reduced for Christian instruction and inspiration, and he rejected the practice of emphasizing the saints' goodness rather than their failings through which other Christians could see the promises of Christ realized in them. Three, he did not believe that the saints or any human persons could serve as intercessors or mediators, as Christ alone is *the* Mediator. From his view of intercession or mediation of saints as an event occuring between Christ and his other faithful, Luther inveighed that we need not and should not seek saints' assistance to attain to Christ. Further, he claimed that the practice of invocation of saints lacked scriptural warrant. Four, he believed that veneration of saints was essentially idolatry. While he regularly marked the Marian feast days with preaching, he was critical of the variety of veneration given to Mary by Catholics, which he judged to rival worship of Christ. Five, scandalized by the prevalence of false relics and with practices of indulgences connected with relics (such as the granting of indulgences for pilgrimages to shrines containing saintly relics), Luther condemned the tradition of preserving and venerating relics.[22]

Catholic Theology: Grace Perfects Nature

It is unnecessary and would be nearly impossible to review the entire spectrum of Catholic theology of nature and grace at the time of Luther. The Nominalist thought that Luther eventually scorned and that was quickly discredited even within the Catholic Church despite its pervasive hold in its own time already has been summarized in brief. Chapter 10 will provide a contemporary explanation of the relationship between nature and grace. All, then, that is needed here is reinforcement of the point that both the Nominalists and the Scholastics before them upheld both divine sovereignty and freedom and human freedom. Nature, although fallen and therefore incapable of attaining to God on its own, still has, through grace, the ability, feeble though it may be, to cooperate with God's work to save us. Grace does not replace or substitute for human nature in order to save us; grace perfects human nature, sanctifying it, transforming it, making individuals holy, issuing in works of charity.

Catholic Response to Protestant Critiques: Trent and Beyond

Luther's critiques will not be answered here from the standpoint of Catholic theology of a specific place or time, but from the standpoint of basic Catholic convictions that hold regardless of their articulation through specific thought systems, such as Scholasticism. Particular statements of the Council of Trent that addressed Luther's critiques, if not always directly, will be reviewed in the next chapter; a Catholic theology of veneration of saints articulated from a contemporary perspective will be ventured in chapters 9 through 12.

To the first objection distilled from Luther's thought, that no person is holier or possesses more grace than another and that the good works of those said to be holiest are not at all their merits, Catholics disagree. As stated, Luther's understanding that nature is completely corrupted is not shared by Catholics, who believe that there remains something with which God can work in fallen human nature. Nature cannot save itself and cannot "earn" grace, but, under the influence of grace, it can cooperate with that very grace. Human free will exists, Catholics believe; the goal is that under the power of grace it will become aligned with the divine free will which wants but will not force precisely that for each of us. God invites us into a relationship of love, so there must exist a measure of autonomy so that we can respond to him in the freedom of love. Despite some very precise theological explanations of this human cooperation with God, it remains mystery at root. Theological certitudes affirmed by Catholics—divine sovereignty and freedom and human freedom—validate for Catholics that which Luther denies, namely that one human person can "possess" more grace or be holier than another and in a way in which human freedom is engaged by grace to cooperate in Christ's salvific work. Canonization of saints certainly suggests that such is apparent to us. But canonization of some does not mean that others not canonized are not also holy or that they are without grace, and the Catholic Church does not pronounce nor even think it proper to speculate about whom among the living might be holier than others, although sometimes in cases of especially exemplary lives there is talk among the faithful of "living saints." Catholicism rejects the idea that one's salvation is guaranteed already during earthly existence;[23] in the sixteenth century it thought Luther to assert otherwise in his doctrine of *certitudo salutis*—"certainty of salvation." (In fact, Luther's certainty was in salvation in Christ, but other Protestant reformers would teach instead, or additionally, an individual's guarantee of salvation by Christ; Catholics took this to be Luther's view.) Such "rash presumption of predestination is to be avoided" stated the Council of Trent. In that Council's Sixth Session, in the "Decree Concerning Justification," the Council fathers wrote: "No one, moreover, so long as he lives this mortal life, ought in regard to the sacred mystery of divine predestination, so far presume as to state with absolute certainty that he is among the number of the predestined, as if it were true that the one justified either cannot sin any more, or, if he does sin, that he ought to promise himself an assured repentance. For except by special revelation, it cannot be known whom God has chosen to Himself."[24] Only after death, in the case of canonization, does the Catholic Church declare one's spiritual state, and it does so then only because it believes it has received signs from God. Never does it declare one to be in Hell, since God does not reveal that to us; this does not mean that no one could be in Hell, just as lack of canonization does not mean that one could not be in Heaven. In the end, those who reach Heaven have a fullness of grace in their participation in the life of God—the outstanding underserved end that God the Trinity offers to us and persuades us to accept. On the way to Heaven there is possibility of degrees of grace, even though we cannot identify what these degrees are in one individual or another, as only God—he who knows us better than we know ourselves—could know this.

As for the second criticism, in Luther's time many or most stories of the saints did contain large quantities of legendary material. Many Catholics today agree, if not many did then, that this decreases the stories' value for Christians. Like Luther, many Catholics today also are interested in multifaceted accounts of the saints that show their weaknesses, too; it can be inspiring to see Christ's triumph in the saints despite defects. (Of course, if their weaknesses were too abundant or deep, they would not be canonized.) Many contemporary biographies of the canonized attempt to bring to light just such challenges in the lives of the saints, placing the saints in their historical, personal, spiritual, and theological contexts. But past biographies survive plentifully, particularly due to the difficulty of the task of rewriting centuries of stories, often without possession of the details of saints' lives that are lost to us behind legend. And the old biographies are still meaningful to some Christians. In fact, it is possible that to future Christians the legendary accounts might be more meaningful than the biographies written today. In our criticism of stories lacking in historical contextualization, ironically we sometimes fail to see that the assumption that historical-critical studies are superior betrays in itself a lack of historical-cultural consciousness. It is entirely plausible that a few hundred years from now Christians may wonder about our near-exclusive focus upon historical details which are seen to function as the sole, or virtually sole, arbiter of truth. They may find a new appreciation for the truth contained in the legendary stories about the saints—that is, the evidence such stories provide of the faithful's perception of Christ's dramatic presence in these holy lives. One could argue that the "mythical" quality of past accounts of the saints provides a kind of religious language about Jesus Christ—not about his own earthly history but about his activity or presence in his saints.[25] The saints are of interest to us because in them we see validated our faith in Christ; the saints' stories, even legendary, attest not just to his presence in their historical life but to his power at work through these lives even now as we remember the saints. There are historical and "meta-historical" dimensions to saintly lives.

Regarding the third objection cited, indeed Catholics agree that Christ alone is *the* Mediator. There is no question of any human person filling such a role. Yet in times past poorly-catechized individual Catholics have wrongly looked to the saints as if they could fill such a role. No saint has the power to dispense any favor or to answer any prayer. As subsequent chapters will underscore, God answers prayers. However, the saints are with Christ and to think of them, to "pray to" them, to think of and pray for any dead, is to think of and pray to God. They do not exist apart from him, and they do exist. Christ is happy for us to recognize his presence in their lives and in our memory of them, and, if he, God the Son, in unity with God the Father and through God the Holy Spirit, wills to answer our prayers through the saints' instrumentality, we rejoice to see that ongoing divine action in our lives. To the Catholic mind, this is consistent with the manner in which God works with us always; he answers our prayers by working through the "stuff" of our concrete human existence. Is it not Christ who reaches out to us in the person who helps us in our time of need? All good comes from God; it reaches us through his sacramental presence in our human experience. No one helps by being "between" us and Christ; in another's help they are *in* Christ. And Christ was not between God and humanity; in the Incarnation he *is* still the ever-existing God the Son even as he *is* also human. Holiness comes from the incarnated, resurrected Christ present to us in the Holy Spirit, one with us but also God. Veneration of saints is Christological, and Christology informs our understanding of humanity in reference to Christ (the subject of theological anthropology) which issues in the Church (the subject of ecclesiology), as will be discussed in later chapters. Notions of saints as patrons have been rightly criticized when they have presented the saints as entities functioning seemingly independently. There is no theological harm, however, in associating saints with particular causes, in our recognition that God has worked through them in particular ways for which we are thankful. As for invoking the saints, already it has been pointed out that praying for the dead and asking for prayers from the dead have Jewish precedent. Additionally it has been pointed out that Catholics do not believe that the divide of death places those on the other side beyond our reach. Particularly in the Eucharist we are with them intentionally, joining them in the proper human posture of praise of God. Again to the Catholic mind, there is no need for Scripture to validate the practice of invoking the saints, since that would be required only if the divide of death did sever our relationship with members of the communion of saints. As chapter 2 showed, the scriptural warrant is there for Christians to pray for each other—and even for non-Christians—always, wherever we or others may be with respect to the journey that each human person must make.

The fourth criticism cited from Luther's contentions about the saints, that veneration of saints is idolatrous, already has been addressed in part. Veneration is not idolatry; the distinction was stated officially at the Second Council of Nicaea at the end of the eighth century, as has been noted. That sometimes in the Church individuals carried away by piety take missteps in veneration or misunderstand that which the Church is directing in veneration does not alter the consistent teaching of the Church that only God is worshipped. To venerate the saints is to enhance that worship, since veneration recognizes and responds to God's work.[26] As regards the veneration given to Mary in particular, Catholics recognize that it sometimes has been exaggerated, indeed seeming to rival attention to Christ, as chapter 13 will discuss. Nevertheless, since she is the *Theotokos*, veneration of Mary is properly exceptional.

The fifth and final objection noted from Luther, his disapproval of veneration of relics, as well as his rejection of the indulgences sometimes attached to such, also is simply a point of disagreement with Catholics. Although relics and indulgences are discussed in other chapters, three matters deserve mention here. First, relic veneration is consistent with the sacramental or incarnational sensibility of Catholics. The bodies of the saints and things associated with their earthly existence provide tangible connection to the evidence of Christ's presence in the world in holy lives; such concrete attention to the immanence as well as the transcendence of God is a hallmark of Catholic theology and spirituality. This registers a key point of departure between Luther's theology and Catholic theology generally: where Luther stresses the absence of God vis-à-vis human nature in order to emphasize the magnificence of God's appearance for salvation (an emphasis that is not completely absent in Catholic theology), in general Catholic theology stresses the presence of God to humanity—even in our fallen state—to extol that same undeserved magnificence of God with us always. Second, it is not only the tradition that recommends relic veneration. Scripture contains a number of instances of relic veneration "impulses" which will be noted in chapter 14, and Scripture presents these impulses as laudable. Third, as regards indulgences, the Catholic response to the Protestant objection was ratification by the Council of Trent of the indulgences system, excluding abuses. Catholics see scriptural validation for indulgences and for the "Treasury" of the Church from which they are supplied (both of which will be discussed in chapter 14) in Matthew 16:19 and 18:18, as well as in 1 John 2:2.

Conclusion

Luther's theology established Protestant thought but it does not exhaust it. The initial Protestant reformer's contemporary, John Calvin, cemented the doctrine of fallen human nature as depraved; his systematic reflection upon this and other theological matters is explicated in his *Institutes of the Christian Religion* that came to be regarded as classical Reformation expository from the Protestants. Yet other Protestant churches differentiated themselves from both Luther and Calvin in doctrinal elements large and small. Notably, the Anglican Church emerged from a different set of circumstances than those of Luther or of Calvin; it was formed as a result of the excommunication of King Henry VIII of England, declared head of the Church of England, because of his divorce of Catherine of Aragon to marry Anne Boleyn. Its theology was not a wholesale reaction against Catholicism; indeed, before his famous marital issue Henry had been praised by the pope for his defense—against Luther—of Catholicism's seven sacraments. Already in the sixteenth century, then, there was diversity in Protestant theology. This diversity has only multiplied in the centuries that have followed, perhaps particularly in the American context where many smaller congregations arise sometimes independently of explicit roots in Protestant Reformation theology or deliberately in alteration of it. This means that "Protestantism" should not be taken to refer to a single denomination but to a collection of denominations not in communion with the Catholic or the Orthodox Churches and having in common certain doctrinal presumptions which, in the case of the larger "mainline" denominations, are clearly explicated and publicly available as is Catholic teaching. Many of the larger denominations belong to the World Council of Churches (WCC) that was founded in the middle of the twentieth century to promote ecumenical dialogue. While the Catholic Church is not a member of the WCC, since Vatican II it has been involved in extensive ecumenical dialogue, including with members of the WCC—notably Lutherans. The diversity in Protestant doctrine means diversity in teachings about Mary and the saints.

As a body of documents, the Catholic Church's exhortations to veneration of the saints, no less than the Church's cautions about potential excesses and abuses, are better appreciated against the backdrop of the critiques of the Protestant Reformation. As the documents from the Council of Trent show, to the Protestant challenge the Catholic Church responded, via its own reform, with condemnation of aberrant activities that had emerged in connection with veneration of saints. But at the same time it did not reverse any of its teachings about the saints; it reaffirmed the theology supporting the cult of the saints, as well as the practices of veneration that had been officially validated over the centuries, giving more careful and emphatic definition to theory and practice related to the saints. The watershed moment in the Church that was the Protestant and Catholic Reformations affected and addressed not only Christian history and theology broadly but veneration of saints specifically, then. In fact, teachings about the saints and veneration of saints go to the very heart of the theological differences that resulted in the split in the Western church in the sixteenth century. This is the case notwithstanding the degree or lack thereof of private veneration of saints by Catholics today or the severity or lack thereof of abuses in the past, for, again, it is on the level of theology that lasting ecclesial differences of any type reside, as this chapter has shown. Other chapters will note progress that has been made in our time in ecumenical discussion of Reformation-age issues. For now, the next chapter will review traditional practices of piety involving the saints that survived or arose after the Reformations. It also will present, in summary form, doctrinal statements pertaining to the saints through the Second Vatican Council. These statements continue to dictate the form of the Church's corporate attention to the saints and the Church's popular private traditions of devotion involving saints.

Terms for Study

Apostolic Tradition

Catholic Reformation

Council of Trent

Ecumenism

Excommunication

Faith

Friar

Grace

Hell

Humanism

Justification

Nature

Nominalism

Pelagianism

Protestant Reformation

Renaissance

Righteousness

Sanctification

Scholasticism

Will (Free)

Suggested Readings

The Canons and Decrees of the Council of Trent. Translated by H.J. Schroeder. Rockford, Illinois: Tan Books and Publishers, 1978.

Grasp of the scope and spirit of the Council of Trent, vehicle of the "Catholic Reformation," can be had fully only through acquaintance with the Council's official documents. This accessible English translation of the statements of the only ecumenical council in a space of three centuries from the Reformations to the First Vatican Council is indispensible for understanding the Catholic Church from the Renaissance to the Modern period, as well as now. The influence of Trent, as well as that of Vatican I, was felt upon Vatican II.

Saint Thomas Aquinas. *Aquinas's Shorter Summa: Saint Thomas Aquinas's Own Concise Version of His 'Summa Theologica.'* Manchester, New Hampshire: Sophia Institute Press, 2002. Reprint of *Light of Faith: The Compendium of Theology,* Sophia Institute Press, 1993. Original edition, *The Compendium of Theology,* B. Herder Book, 1947.

A Summa of the 'Summa': The Essential Philosophical Passages of St. Thomas Aquinas' 'Summa Theologica' Edited and Explained for Beginners. Edited and annotated by Peter Kreeft. San Francisco: Ignatius Press, 1990.

Saint Thomas Aquinas's *Summa Theologiae* is issued in five volumes. Of that masterwork, *Aquinas's Shorter Summa* is a distillation by Saint Thomas himself of his thought on the central Christian and characteristically Catholic themes featured in the *Summa.* The volume provides a sample of Scholastic thinking, although it does not adhere to the dialectical method of the *Summa* and other Scholastic works. *Summa of the 'Summa'* is an anthology of Saint Thomas's *Summa,* focusing upon passages of relevance to contemporary readers. Generous footnotes assist readers in digesting the complex but clarifying thought of the "Angelic Doctor."

Seven

THE CORPORATE LIFE OF THE CHURCH AND POPULAR PIETY: THEOLOGICAL REFLECTION AND TRADITIONAL PRACTICES

As its history shows, veneration of saints developed concurrently along two lines—one, the corporate, and, two, the individual or "popular." The two lines are not parallel lines; they necessarily intersect and merge and are mutually conditioning. The Church officially regulates private, popular veneration of cultic variety, and private veneration of the saints by individuals contributes to the fervor with which the Church universally praises God through veneration of those deemed holy by his grace. This chapter will outline corporate and individual practices of veneration and then summarize major official statements of the Church related to the saints and the honor given to them. Finally, by way of conclusion, it will note both cautions and exhortations in the Church's contemporary statements pertaining to the cult of the saints.

Veneration of Saints in the Corporate Life of the Church

Perhaps the most obvious way in which the "Church Universal" venerates the saints is by its formal canonization of them. And its assignment of "solemnities," "feast days," and "memorials" to canonized individuals and its integration of these days (as the sanctoral cycle) into the liturgical calendar of seasons celebrating the Paschal Mystery (the temporal cycle) ensures the faithful's ongoing consciousness of the saints who live in Christ.[1] The saints are incorporated into the Liturgy of the Hours, as well as into Eucharistic celebrations; occasionally the saints receive special attention in the liturgy. As noted in chapter 5, for example, on the Easter Vigil the Litany of the Saints is recited; this prayer consisting of invocations and petitions asks the saints to "pray for us," making it clear that we relate to them not only as models of holiness but as companions in Christ with all of the faithful. And as companions who are now fully united with Christ, they are worthy and effective intercessors. This is especially the case with Mary, who is recognized in special Masses.[2]

As the liturgical history reviewed in previous chapters indicates, the reality of the communion of saints is expressed most powerfully in the Eucharistic celebration. In this, the entire communion of saints, living and dead, is joined together by participation in Christ's offering of his redemptive sacrifice. "And so, with the Angels and all the Saints we declare your glory, . . ," Eucharistic Prayer II affirms of the union of the Church Militant with the Church Triumphant in the saints' perpetual posture of praise of God.[3] *Lumen Gentium* explains:

> It is especially in the sacred liturgy that our union with the heavenly church is best realized; in the liturgy, the power of the holy Spirit acts on us through sacramental signs; there we celebrate, rejoicing together, the praise of the divine majesty, and all who have been redeemed by the blood of Christ from every tribe and tongue and people and nation (see Apoc. 5:9), gathered together into one church glorify, in one common song of praise, the one and triune God. When, then, we celebrate the eucharistic sacrifice we are most closely united to the worship of the heavenly church; when in one communion we honor and remember the glorious Mary ever virgin, St Joseph, the holy apostles and martyrs and all the saints.[4]

Nowhere else is the doxological character of veneration of the saints so evident. And nowhere else is the Church, in Heaven and on Earth, so united, in its proper doxological posture. Indeed, for Catholics, the Eucharist is the very source of the Christian life realized most perfectly in the saints, whom we imitate, through the grace of Christ.

In addition to liturgical veneration, the Church venerates the saints in other ways seen in previous chapters, such as through production, or encouragement of production, of accounts of the lives of the saints. The Church venerates the saints when it acts as patron or promoter of art and various media depicting them, as well as through reference in homilies and in encyclicals and in catechism classes to saints' grace-filled lives. It venerates them by naming churches and parishes after them and by displaying statues, icons, and/or other images of them in churches, albeit sparsely in comparison with ages before Vatican II "so that the christian people are not disturbed, nor is occasion given for less than appropriate devotion," per Canon Law.[5] It venerates them through special prayers and devotions that are approved for the faithful's use and through protection of pilgrimage sites connected to their lives and deaths. Of these latter the Church sometimes offers indulgences. Some of these activities fall into the category of "sacramentals," along with the blessing of items associated with the saints and events such as "May crownings" of Mary in statue. As Vatican II's Constitution on the Sacred Liturgy, *Sacrosanctum Concilium*, defined them, sacramentals are "sacred signs by which, somewhat after the manner of the sacraments, effects of a spiritual nature, especially, are symbolised and are obtained through the church's intercession. By them, people are made ready to receive the much greater effect of the sacraments, and various occasions in life are rendered holy."[6]

In continuity with the early days of Christianity when the faithful gathered at graves of martyrs to celebrate the Eucharist, the Church also venerates the saints by locating their relics beneath church altars—a requirement of Canon Law for fixed altars—and by protecting and regulating the use of relics wherever they may be, requiring that all relics be authenticated and forbidding their sale.[7] Chapter 14 will address specific issues associated with relics, so little discussed today even among Catholics. The 1983 Code of Canon Law refers to two categories of relics—first, "distinguished relics" (which, according to the next earliest Code, of 1917, were parts of saints' or blesseds' bodies or the parts of martyrs' bodies having suffered the fatal wound), and, second, "others which are held in great veneration by the people" (smaller and/or non-bodily relics).[8] In practice the second category of relics has been further delineated, resulting in three classes of relics: bodies of saints or blesseds, items worn or used by saints or blesseds during their lifetime (including instruments of torture for martyrs), and items coming into contact with bodies of saints or blesseds after their deaths (such as pieces of fabric).[9] The general concern about the potential distraction of an excessive number of images applies to relics, too, in the sense that elicited caution on the part of the bishops of the early Church in cases of intense veneration such as that exhibited around Polycarp's martyrdom mentioned in chapter 3: attention to relics cannot overshadow but must always be referred consciously to Christ in whom ultimately all sacred signs have their source. This reminder leads to reflection upon current popular practices of veneration of saints, some of which correspond directly on the level of private engagement to their approval and promotion by the Church at the corporate level.

Veneration of Saints in 'Popular' Practice

While, in looking at the Catholic Church worldwide, private devotion to the saints is less obvious at the beginning of the twenty-first century than it was in the first twenty centuries of the Church, it is no less fervent where it exists. Practices of the early Church survive and, in continuity with them, new forms of veneration have arisen.

Some common practices of popular devotion are so ingrained in the life of Catholicism that among those engaging in them are even Catholics who do not think of themselves as private venerators of the saints. As mentioned in chapter 4, most Catholics, for example, associate their given name with that of a canonized saint who is thereby considered their patron saint; sometimes the life story of that saint is known by the namesake and shared with others. Certainly Catholics know the story of the saint whose name they chose at Confirmation. Many are attuned to the feast day of "their" saint, if not to the feast day of the saint on which their birthday falls. Still others are aware of the saints considered the patrons of their vocation and avocations. Most will remember fondly the stories of the saints in whose honor their childhood parish, their high school, and their current parish were named. And many a Catholic in difficult circumstances has thought of, if not "prayed to," a patron saint of a particular cause. Saints are honored—venerated—by their appearances on religious medals that are worn or kept, on holy cards often containing prayers associated with the saints pictured, and on key chains and dashboard ornaments and auto visor clips that accompany individuals wherever they go. Catholics keep in their homes books about the lives of saints for reference and for meditative reading, some hang icons or images of saints, and some have small statues of saints inside the home—in the living room, the bedroom, the kitchen—or large statues of saints outside the home—in the garden or on the lawn. Whether or not such images are expressly venerated by their owners and other onlookers, that they are produced and kept at all is indicative of the importance for the Church that Catholics and other Christians sense of the figures represented; they evoke respect if not reverence, turning minds and hearts to God who made possible the holy lives remembered. And it would be a rare Catholic who does not have a rosary, even if it is not often used; it is one of the most popular gifts for celebration of reception of a sacrament of initiation into the Church (i.e., Baptism, First Communion or Eucharist, and Confirmation). Such activities pass on and indeed honor the memory of the lives of saints, and they inspire the faithful to imitate such lives, just as in the early days of Christianity the stories and other intentional reminders of the lives of the martyrs honored them while edifying others.

Yet other activities of contemporary Christians demonstrate a greater individual investment in the cult of the saints. Pilgrimages, while lacking the popularity they attained during the Middle Ages, still attract many to sites of the deaths of saints, to sites of key moments of the lives of saints, and to churches containing relics of saints. Santiago de Compostela continues to draw Christian faithful, as does Saint Peter's Basilica at the Vatican and the many other martyr churches of Rome and elsewhere. Some churches are special spiritual attractions for their art and architecture commemorating the lives of saints. So, too, are Marian apparition sites draws, perhaps especially for those praying and hoping for dramatic intercessory events such as cures at Fatima, Portugal, and Lourdes, France, two famous apparition locations officially recognized by the Church. Also retaining popularity are prayer traditions involving the saints, including novenas and the rosary which, interestingly, developed into their current forms relatively late in the history of the Church. Novenas—prayers, sometimes along with scriptural readings and other meditations, repeated for nine consecutive days (or for nine consecutive weeks or hours) with a special purpose in mind (e.g., a need or occasion for oneself, or a saint's feast day)—gained widespread interest in the seventeenth century.[10] The number nine has its significance for the number of days that Mary plus Jesus' other disciples prayed with each other between the Ascension of Christ and Pentecost.[11] Novenas often are undertaken in private, but they may be public, communal activities, too. The rosary, the Marian devotion of prayers and meditations upon key moments in the life of Jesus Christ and his mother, began to approximate its current form in the fifteenth century.[12] A fourth decade of mysteries of the rosary was added by Pope John Paul II only in 2002. Perhaps especially among Eastern Catholics, icons and other images of saints are deliberately used in private as well as public meditation; the images may be contemplated, kissed, touched, or shown other signs of respect. That many of these activities are or involve sacramentals that have an "official" place in the life of the Church illustrates that liturgy and corporate ecclesial activity generally are intertwined with popular piety; the Church officially guides, promotes, cautions, and sometimes absorbs the pious impulses of the *vox populi*— the "voice of the people."

Many practices of veneration of the saints are variations upon invocation and imitation—the profoundest ways of honoring the saints. As stated at the outset of this study, in chapter 1, and as restated elsewhere, such honor is not worship. And, even though the Church highly recommends such individual devotion as an enhancement to participation in the mandatory corporate veneration of the saints, the Church also has always cautioned about the potential misconceptions and abuses that can creep into popular rituals of the cult of the saints. A summary of the primary Church documents through the time of Vatican II directing both public and private veneration of the saints will provide yet more insight than has already been reviewed into the history of both practice and theory of the cult of the saints, giving the definitive meaning and the proper parameters of veneration of the Church's holiest ones.

Official Church Documents Governing Veneration of Saints

The most important statements of the Church on the subject of the saints are those of ecumenical councils. (As regards Mary particularly, papal documents of dogmatic weight will be reviewed in chapter 13.) Six of the twenty-one councils recognized as ecumenical by the Catholic Church—the Second Council of Nicaea, the Fourth Council of Constantinople, the Council of Constance, the Council of Florence, the Council of Trent, and the Second Vatican Council—provide especially critical points of Catholic doctrine relating to veneration of saints.

Second Council of Nicaea (787)

As prior chapters have recalled, importantly, it was at the second conciliar meeting at Nicaea that a formal distinction between *latria* (worship) and *proskunêsis* (veneration, in contradistinction to the adoration of worship) was introduced to solve the dispute that arose in the East over the veneration of sacred images. This Council staked the value of such veneration on the sacred images' relationship to the original image from which their very possibility of existence is derived.

> For, the more frequently one contemplates these pictorial representations, the more gladly will one be led to remember the original subject whom they represent, the more too will one be drawn to it and inclined to give it [...] a respectful veneration (*proskunêsis, adoratio*), which, however, is not the true adoration (*latria, latreia*) which, according to our faith, is due to God alone. But, as is done for the image of the revered and life-giving cross and the holy Gospels and other sacred objects and monuments, let an oblation of incense and light be made to give honour to those images according to the pious custom of the ancients. For 'the honour given to an image goes to the original model'; and one who venerates an image, venerates in it the person represented by it.[13]

Nicaea II's intent was much bolder than merely to provide a rationale for the veneration of sacred images, however. Against the Iconoclasts, the Council stated clearly that such images not only were permitted in churches, but they were *required* there.

> We define that [...] the representations of the precious and life-giving cross, and the venerable and holy images as well [...], must be kept in the holy church of God [...], in houses and on

the roads, whether they be images of God our Lord and Saviour
Jesus Christ or of our immaculate Lady the Mother of God, or
of the holy angels and of all the saints and just.[14]

Fourth Council of Constantinople (869–870)

Nearly a century later, the subject of sacred images was once again
engaged at a council. In its tenth session in 870, the Fourth General
Council of Constantinople came to the defense of pro-image patriarchs
persecuted by three local councils in the East by decreeing that "the
sacred image of our Lord Jesus Christ, the liberator and Saviour of all
people, must be venerated with the same honour as is given to the book
of holy Gospels."[15] It elaborated, underscoring the importance of
images for those unable to read or to grasp the gospel in words and for
all whose sensitivity to the "principal subject" might be enhanced by
images rendered possible by him.

> For, as through the language of the words contained in this
> book all can reach salvation, so, due to the action which these
> images exercise by their colours, all, wise and simple alike, can
> derive profit from them. For, what speech conveys in words,
> pictures announce and bring out in colours. It is fitting, in
> accordance with sane reason and with the most ancient
> tradition, since the honour is referred to the principal subject,
> that the images derived from it be honoured and venerated, as
> is done for the sacred book of the holy Gospels and for the
> image of the precious cross.[...][16]

Council of Constance (1414–1418)

For half a millennium, no significant official statements were made by the
Church with regard to the veneration of sacred images. This period
corresponds with the increasing papal influence, and finally absolute
authority, over the canonization process. If anything, the embrace of
sacred images, especially those of the saints, was now too enthusiastic;
this was one of the reasons that papal involvement was sought in
canonization decisions. Then a century and a half before the
Reformations, the voices of Wycliffe and Hus, anathematized by the
Council of Constance, anticipated later Protestant objections to excesses
by calling for disposal of the entire cult of the saints, along with other
sacramental acts, rather than only the abuses. Wycliffe was a late
fourteenth-century English theologian and philosopher who had been

publicly critical of Catholic doctrine on such central matters as papal authority and the Eucharist. Hus was a Czech priest whose preaching and theological writings in the early fifteenth century continued the thought of Wycliffe. Recognizing the problems that sometimes attended the cult at the popular level, many borne by superstition and emotionalism, nevertheless Pope Martin V in his 1418 bull *Inter Cunctas* affirmed condemnations by the Council of Constance of the "errors" of Wycliffe and Hus by posing as a test of faith against followers of these early reformers this question: "Does he believe and does he affirm that it is legitimate for the faithful of Christ to venerate relics and images of saints?"[17]

Council of Florence (1438–1445)[18]

The doctrine of Purgatory was one of the topics of discussion at the Council of Florence whose purpose was to reunify the Eastern and Western churches which had split in 1054. *Laetentur Coeli*, a Decree of Union that was accepted by Greek and Latin participants at the 1439 Council meeting but that ultimately failed when the Turks captured Constantinople[19] and the Decree did not receive ratification in Eastern territories, affirmed teaching on Purgatory even where the efficacy of prayers and works of the living for the dead is concerned. It proclaimed: ". . . [S]o that they [the souls in Purgatory] may be released from [purgatorial] punishments . . , the suffrages of the living faithful are of advantage to them, namely, the sacrifices of Masses, prayers, and almsgiving, and other works of piety, which are customarily performed by the faithful for other faithful according to the institutions of the Church."[20] Effectively, elaboration on this teaching was provided following the next ecumenical council, the Fifth Lateran Council (1512-1517), in *Cum Postquam*, a 1518 bull of Pope Leo X issued amidst the indulgences controversy leading to the Protestant Reformation. Indulgences, which may be "transfer[red]," "by means of suffrage," to "the living as well as the dead," are "dispense[d] from the treasury of the merits of Jesus Christ and the saints."[21]

Council of Trent (1545–1563)

In answer to the objections of Protestant reformers, in the twenty-fifth and final session of the Council of Trent, Council members issued comprehensive statements on matters pertaining to the cult of the saints. The section concerning veneration of saints deals largely with the saints as intercessors and is worthy of complete representation here.

The holy council commands all bishops and others who hold the office of teaching and have charge of the *cura animarum*, that in accordance with the usage of the Catholic and Apostolic Church, received from the primitive times of the Christian religion, and with the unanimous teaching of the holy Fathers and the decrees of sacred councils, they above all instruct the faithful diligently in matters relating to intercession and invocation of the saints, the veneration of relics, and the legitimate use of images, teaching them that the saints who reign together with Christ offer up their prayers to God for men, that it is good and beneficial suppliantly to invoke them and to have recourse to their prayers, assistance and support in order to obtain favors from God through His Son, Jesus Christ our Lord, who alone is our redeemer and savior; and that they think impiously who deny that the saints who enjoy eternal happiness in heaven are to be invoked, or who assert that they do not pray for men, or that our invocation of them to pray for each of us individually is idolatry, or that it is opposed to the word of God and inconsistent with the honor of the *one mediator of God and men, Jesus Christ* [cf. 1 Tim. 2:5], or that it is foolish to pray vocally or mentally to those who reign in heaven.[22]

Also notable are Trent's statements on veneration of relics, reflecting, as they do, the ancient belief in the importance of the saintly bodies as communicators of God's grace. "[T]he holy bodies of the holy martyrs and of others living with Christ, which were the living members of Christ and the temple of the Holy Ghost, [cf. 1 Cor. 3:16, 6:19; 2 Cor. 6:16], to be awakened by Him to eternal life and to be glorified, are to be venerated by the faithful," wrote the Council members. More strikingly, these members emphasized that through relics "many benefits are bestowed by God on men."[23] Veneration also is due to images, "not, however, that any divinity or virtue is believed to be in them by reason of which they are to be venerated, or that something is to be asked of them, or that trust is to be placed in images, as was done of old by the Gentiles who placed their hope in idols [Ps. 134:15 ff.]; but because the honor which is shown them is referred to the prototypes which they represent. . . ."[24]

Trent's passage on images underscores the teaching of Nicaea II in its emphasis upon the worship of God, in Christ, that is always either implicit or explicit in the act of veneration of images: "[B]y means of the images . . . , we adore Christ and venerate the saints whose likeness they bear."[25] The likeness to Christ of the images that are the saints themselves is particularly important to a theology of veneration; in it is the relationship of the two traditional emphases in description of the saints—their exemplary character or heroic virtue, and their intercessory, sometimes miraculous power. Both flow from saintly lives of acceptance of grace. As Trent explained, ". . . [G]reat profit is derived from all holy images, not only because the people are thereby reminded of the benefits and gifts bestowed on them by Christ, but also because through the saints the miracles of God and salutary examples are set before the eyes of the faithful, so that they may give God thanks for those things, may fashion their own life and conduct in imitation of the saints and be moved to adore and love God and cultivate piety."[26] Of course, this Council also condemned the abuses that had crept into the cult of the saints. "[I]n the invocation of the saints, the veneration of relics, and the sacred use of images, all superstition shall be removed, all filthy quest for gain eliminated, and all lasciviousness avoided," it demanded. So that not even the possibility of impropriety should easily arise in such matters, bishops were charged with pronouncing on that which would be permitted in their dioceses. They were to have at their disposal the intellectual and spiritual resources of "theologians and other pious men" to make their judgments, and they were to have recourse to synods and the pope.[27]

In addition to these statements from Trent's "Decree on the Invocation, Veneration, and Relics of Saints, and on Sacred Images," this nineteenth ecumenical Council spoke about the saints through related decrees and canons. The doctrine of Purgatory was affirmed, as was the truth of the belief "that the souls there detained are aided by the suffrages of the faithful and chiefly by the acceptable sacrifice of the altar." However, bishops were charged with checking "things that are uncertain or that have the appearance of falsehood" and "things that tend to a certain kind of curiosity or superstition, or that savor of filthy lucre."[28] On the issue of indulgences, Trent defended the ancient practice but mandated that its abuses "be absolutely abolished" so that "the gift of holy indulgences may be dispensed to all the faithful piously, holily, and without corruption."[29] Concerning the sacrifice of the Mass, Trent affirmed that it "is truly propitiatory and has this effect, that if we, contrite and penitent, with sincere heart and upright faith, with fear and reverence, draw nigh to God, *we obtain mercy and find grace in seasonable aid*" [Heb. 4:16].[30] The sacrifice of the Mass benefits the living and the dead: "[A]ccording to the tradition of the Apostles, it is rightly offered not only for the sins, punishments, satisfactions and other necessities of the faithful who are living, but also for those departed in Christ but not yet fully purified."[31] And Trent's statement on "Masses in Honor of the Saints" emphasized the ultimate referent of mention of the saints at the altar: "And though the Church has been accustomed to celebrate at times certain masses in honor and memory of the saints, she does not teach that sacrifice is offered to them but to God alone who crowned them; . . . but, giving thanks to God for their victories, he [the priest] implores their favor that they may vouchsafe to intercede for us in heaven whose memory we celebrate on earth."[32] Finally, the Tridentine Profession of Faith developed by Pope Pius IV at the urging of the Council contains summary passages of historical and doctrinal importance on matters related to the saints:

> I hold unswervingly that there is a *purgatory* and that the souls detained there are helped by the intercession of the faithful; likewise that the *Saints* reigning with Christ are to be venerated and invoked, and that they offer God prayers on our behalf, and that their relics are to be venerated. I firmly assert that images of Christ and of the ever-virgin Mother of God, as well as of other Saints, are to be possessed and retained and that due honour and veneration should be accorded them. I also affirm that the power of *indulgences* was left in the Church by Christ and that their use is very salutary for Christian people.[33]

Second Vatican Council (1962–1965)

It was almost four hundred years after the close of the Council of Trent, to the year, before another significant statement concerning the saints was made by the Catholic Church, and this also occurred at council. The Second Vatican Council framed ecclesial issues concerning the saints, in a comprehensive theology of the communion of saints presented in *Lumen Gentium*. While on the surface the understanding of the expression "communion of saints" appears to be personal in this document, the emphasis on the centrality of the sacred liturgy renders a sacramental connection, too, thereby including both early emphases as the phrase emerged in the Apostles' Creed.

The topic of the cult of the saints is presented in chapters seven and eight of *Lumen Gentium*, where the Council first dealt with "the pilgrim church," which "will receive its perfection only in the glory of heaven, when the time for the renewal of all things will have come (Acts 3:21)."[34] Chapter seven explains the relationship among the disciples who are pilgrims on Earth, those in Purgatory, and those contemplating the Beatific Vision. Since all exist in the same communion of grace "who are of Christ and who have his Spirit," the union between those living and dead is cultivated by "an exchange of spiritual goods."[35] Therefore, "our communion with the saints joins us to Christ," just as our "christian communion among pilgrims brings us closer to Christ."[36] The Constitution provides a brief survey of the history of the veneration of the saints which occurred "from the very earliest days of the christian religion" and which is attested even earlier in Judaism,[37] as has been shown. In the saints, "God shows, vividly, to humanity his presence and his face" through "the lives of those companions of ours in the human condition who are more perfectly transformed into the image of Christ (see 2 Cor. 3:18)."[38] Yet the saints are not only exemplars. Devotion to them which reinforces the unity of the Church also includes our "recourse to their prayers."[39] Through the Lord "and with him and in him they do not cease to intercede with the Father for us, as they proffer the merits which they acquired on earth through the one mediator between God and humanity, Christ Jesus (see 1 Tim. 2:5). . . ."[40] In short, in our veneration of the saints, particularly in the sacred liturgy which unites the earthly and heavenly churches in the Eucharistic sacrifice,[41] we have "example in their way of life, a sharing in their communion, and the help of their intercession."[42]

Obviously key to *Lumen Gentium*'s statements on the communion of saints and its cult of the saints is an understanding of the eschatological nature of the Church; the pilgrim church makes its way toward its heavenly counterpart, drawing inspiration, example, and intercession from the saints united with Christ.[43] In venerating the saints, the Church praises Christ's eschatological victory in the lives of the saints through whom "[h]e speaks to us" and "offers us a sign of his kingdom, to which we are powerfully attracted, so great a cloud of witnesses are we given (see Heb. 12:1) and such an affirmation of the truth of the Gospel."[44] In other words, again, veneration of the saints is doxological.

Chapter eight of *Lumen Gentium* deals specifically with "our lady," Mary, Mother of God, who is venerated first among Christ's saints owing to her unique relationship to him.[45] "Redeemed, in a more exalted fashion, by reason of the merits of her Son and united to him by a close and indissoluble tie,"[46] Mary's special role in God's plan of salvation was fulfilled in her obedience to God's will in the Incarnation,[47] her prominence in and her support of her Son's public life and mission (including her perseverance "in her union with her Son until she stood at the cross"),[48] her prayerful wait along with the apostles for the day of Pentecost, and her assumption into Heaven conforming her even more fully to her Son.[49] Mary's role as "mother to us in the order of grace," by her cooperation "in the work of the Savior in restoring supernatural life to souls,"[50] reveals the power of Christ's mediation between God and human beings.[51] Now with her Son in Heaven, she intercedes for us.[52] Her unique relationship to Christ renders her "a type of the church in the order of faith, charity, and perfect union with Christ,"[53] and members imitate her "as the model of virtues" and "motherly love."[54] The document emphasizes the special cult of Mary which has existed in the Church since the Church's inception, due to the fact that "Mary has by grace been exalted above all angels and humanity to a place after her Son."[55] Accorded exceptional veneration, therefore, she is "a sign of certain hope and comfort to the pilgrim people of God," existing now in her glory in Heaven as "the image and beginning of the church as it is to be perfected in the world to come."[56]

Supporting the extensive treatment of the communion of saints in *Lumen Gentium* is Vatican II's *Sacrosanctum Concilium*, cited earlier in this chapter for its definition of sacramentals. Because this document deals with the liturgy, the connection to the cult of the saints comes in reference to the Sanctorale. Of note in its brief statements is its dual emphasis, as expected, on the companions who are saints and both models of virtue and intercessors: "Raised up to perfection by the manifold grace of God and already in possession of eternal salvation, they sing God's perfect praise in heaven and pray for us." In including the saints on the liturgical calendar, "celebrating the days on which they died, the church proclaims the paschal mystery in the saints who have suffered and have been glorified with Christ." Further, "it proposes them to the faithful as models who draw all people to the Father through Christ, and through their merits it begs for God's favor."[57] This Constitution affirms that "[t]he saints have been traditionally honored in the church, and their authentic relics and images held in veneration." Yet while "the feasts of the saints proclaim the wonderful works of Christ in his servants and offer to the faithful fitting examples for their imitation," the feasts cannot displace the central focus upon Christ through whom saintly lives are possible: "Lest the feasts of the saints take precedence over the feasts which commemorate the actual mysteries of salvation, the celebration of many of them should be consigned to particular churches, nations, or religious families. Only those should be extended to the universal church which commemorate saints of truly universal importance."[58]

Conclusion

Official cautions about abuses and excesses connected with the cult of the saints, as has been shown, have been necessary from the beginning when the early Christians venerated the martyrs and their relics. And cautions were reiterated at and since Vatican II. *Lumen Gentium* urges that Church members, particularly pastors, be vigilant "to remove or correct any abuses, excesses or defects which may have crept in here or there." It underscores that "the authentic cult of the saints does not consist so much in a multiplicity of external acts, but rather in a more intense practice of our love. . . ."[59] In *Lumen Gentium*'s chapter on Mary, there is caution "to refrain as much from all false exaggeration as from too summary an attitude in considering the special dignity of the Mother of God."[60] While it encourages that we "rightly illustrate the offices and privileges of the Blessed Virgin which always refer to Christ, the source of all truth, sanctity, and devotion," it also urges that we "refrain from whatever might by word or deed lead the separated sisters and brothers or any others whatsoever into error about the true doctrine of the church."[61]

In his apostolic exhortation *Evangelii Nuntiandi*, issued a decade after Vatican II's close, Pope Paul VI explained that

> [p]opular religiosity, . . . has its limits. It is often subject to many distortions of religion and even superstitions. It frequently remains at the level of forms of worship not involving a true acceptance by faith. It can even lead to the creation of sects and endanger the true ecclesial community.[62]

Therefore,

> [p]astoral charity must dictate to all those whom the Lord has placed as leaders of the ecclesial communities the proper attitude in regard to this reality, which is at the same time so rich and so vulnerable. Above all one must be sensitive to it, know how to perceive its interior dimensions and undeniable values, be ready to help it to overcome its risks of deviation.[63]

The 1983 Code of Canon Law also guards against abuses. Most emphatically, Canon 1187 mandates, as noted previously in this study, that "[o]nly those servants of God may be venerated by public cult who have been numbered by ecclesiastical authority among the Saints or the Blessed."[64] Canon 885 of the Code of Canons of the Eastern Churches echoes this.[65]

Despite the cautions, exhortations to veneration have remained prominent in the tradition. As mentioned in chapter 1, *Lumen Gentium* boldly states that, excesses aside, the faithful should "be taught that our relationship with the saints in heaven, provided that it is understood in the full light of faith, in no way diminishes the worship of adoration given to God the Father, through Christ, in the Spirit; on the contrary, it greatly enriches it."[66] *Evangelii Nuntiandi* not only validated but encouraged traditional forms of veneration of the saints. "Popular piety," or "religion of the people," is "rich in values" when it is "well oriented, above all by a pedagogy of evangelization." Indeed, it "can be more and more for multitudes of our people a true encounter with God in Jesus Christ."[67] Issued on the heels of a 1974 synod of bishops on evangelization, this document was especially inspired by the comments of bishops in Latin

America who reported on the prevalence of traditional practices of piety in their own time and culture.

> One finds among the people particular expressions of the search for God and for faith, both in the regions where the Church has been established for centuries and where she is in the course of becoming established. These expressions were for a long time regarded as less pure and were sometimes despised, but today they are almost everywhere being rediscovered. During the last Synod the Bishops studied their significance with remarkable pastoral realism and zeal.[68]

Pope John Paul II's 1987 apostolic letter *Duodecimum Saeculum* similarly attested to a new interest in our own times in traditional practices of piety. Twelve centuries after Nicaea II, John Paul II noted the attraction and value of sacred images for many contemporary believers: "Over the past several decades we have observed a resurgence of interest in the theology and spirituality of Oriental icons, a sign of the growing need for a spiritual language of authentically Christian art."[69] The pope reiterated Nicaea II's grounding of the veneration of sacred images in the doctrine of the Incarnation, since "art can represent the form, the effigy of God's human face and lead the one who contemplates it to the ineffable mystery of God made man for our salvation."[70] Notably, John Paul II also mentioned the especial value of veneration of images for our particular time: "The rediscovery of the Christian icon will also help in raising the awareness of the urgency of reacting against the depersonalizing and at times degrading effects of the many images that condition our lives in advertisements and the media, for it is an image that turns towards us the look of Another invisible one and gives us access to the reality of the spiritual and eschatological world."[71]

Also to be noted among contemporary exhortations to veneration is Canon 1186 of the 1983 Code of Canon Law which finds correspondence with Canon 884 in the 1990 Code of Canons of the Eastern Churches:[72] "To foster the sanctification of the people of God, the Church commends to the special and filial veneration of Christ's faithful the Blessed Mary ever-Virgin, the Mother of God, whom Christ constituted the Mother of all. The Church also promotes the true and authentic cult of the other Saints, by whose example Christ's faithful are edified and by whose intercession they are supported."[73]

In the same year in which the most recent Code of Canon Law was issued, Pope John Paul II revised canonization procedures. This is the subject of the next chapter.

Terms for Study

Apparition	Paschal Mystery
Encyclical	Sacramental(s)
Evangelization	Second Council of Nicaea
Feast Day	Shrine
Hyperdulia	Solemnity
Memorial	Vocation

Suggested Readings

Blessed John Paul II, Pope. *Rosarium Virginis Mariae*. At the Vatican [online]. Available from http://www.vatican.va/holy_father/john_paul_ii/apost_letters/documents/hf_jp-ii_apl_20021016_rosarium-virginis-mariae_en.html. Accessed 1 September 2011.

This apostolic letter issued on October 16, 2002, encouraged Catholics to pray the rosary and to learn from Mary how to contemplate Christ. To emphasize the ultimately Christological character of the rosary, the late Pope added to the rosary a fourth decade. The new "mysteries of light," or "luminous mysteries," focus upon key moments of Jesus' public ministry, from his baptism to the Passion, and they complement the longstanding "joyful mysteries," "sorrowful mysteries," and "glorious mysteries."

Lovasik, Lawrence G. *Favorite Novenas to the Saints: Arranged for Private Prayer on the Feasts of the Saints*. [Totowa], New Jersey: Catholic Book Publishing, 2006.

Published collections of novenas abound, often in pamphlet form. This very small book offers twelve novenas, involving twelve different saints in conjunction with their feast days. Each novena contains a meditation upon the life of the particular saint, scriptural passages, a novena prayer or prayers to and with the saint, occasionally including litanies, and a petitionary prayer to God asking that he might answer through the intercession of the saint.

Odell, Catherine M. *Those Who Saw Her: The Apparitions of Mary*, rev ed. Huntington, Indiana: Our Sunday Visitor, 1995.

This book offers the stories of the few Marian apparitions that have been "approved" or "recognized" by the Catholic Church, also providing brief accounts of the seers after their encounters with Mary and of the Church's examination of the events. It also offers brief history and theology of the Church's understanding of and response to the miraculous, including Marian apparitions.

Sacrosanctum Concilium, in *Vatican Council II: The Basic Sixteen Documents; Constitutions Decrees Declarations*, rev. trans.

Edited by Austin Flannery. Northport, New York: Costello Publishing, 1996:117–161.

The Constitution on the Sacred Liturgy, this document discusses the purpose and the place of the liturgy in the Church's life and outlines the focuses of liturgical reform. Of special interest for the study of saints are chapters on sacraments and sacramentals, the Divine Office, the liturgical year, and sacred art and furnishings in churches, as well as an appendix offering the "Declaration of the Second Vatican Ecumenical Council on Revision of the Calendar."

Tylenda, Joseph N. *Saints and Feasts of the Liturgical Year.* Washington, D.C.: Georgetown University Press, 2003.

A handy reference volume suitable for devotional reading, this compact book identifies feast days on the current universal calendar of the Catholic Church's Roman Rite, according to the 2002 Missal. Brief but informative biographies are offered for each of the saints on the calendar, and a glossary at the end provides definitions for terms commonly encountered in saints' *vitae.*

Eight

RECOVERED EMPHASES AND NEW PROCEDURES: VATICAN II AND THE 1983 CONGREGATION FOR THE CAUSES OF SAINTS REFORM

In the 1960s and 1970s, many Catholic churches were emptied of statues, the Stations of the Cross, and other religious images or icons, if these were not only relocated to inconspicuous locations or covered, as with paint. This was done in the spirit of Vatican II's guidelines for church architecture and interior design, as well as in the spirit of the times. In recent years, still under the guidelines of Vatican II but with consciousness of the fittingness of original interior elements of churches' design to their exterior architectural styles, as well as of the appropriateness of maintaining in older churches elements of historical and theological importance, restoration of churches has sometimes included reinsertion of original features. And replacement of statues and removal of overcoats of paint on walls and ceilings have occasionally meant the reemergence of terrestrial and celestial worlds alike, inhabited by biblical figures, angels and saints.

In a curious way, the disappearance of the saints from churches and then their reintroduction there is analogous to a perhaps still-evolving consciousness with regard to the saints—living icons—since Vatican II. Long-held tendencies in veneration of the saints were meant to be checked by the late Council where they were deemed insufficiently grounded in worship of Christ. So it might have been a matter of course that, as chapter 1 noted, despite the fact that Vatican II imbedded veneration of saints in the life of the Church by placing its instruction on the saints in the Dogmatic Constitution on the Church, the saints seemed to recede from public prominence in the Church at large in the years shortly after the Council. Yet the saints never lost their theological importance in Catholic theology, and the pontificate of John Paul II emphasized this by its prolific canonizations, as well as beatifications, particularly after the 1983 reform that in effect sped processes so that a greater number of worthy candidates could be submitted to Catholics for "imitation, veneration and invocation."[1] And Mary and the saints have been a fertile conversation topic in ecumenical dialogue, so indispensable are they to Catholic theology that there can be little understanding about core doctrine among Christian denominations if the saints are not discussed. So to the casual observer traditions surrounding the saints might have seemed to have been hidden in churches as under cover of paint and in the Church as under cover of "history books" (i.e., those written before Vatican II and containing that which some regarded as mere past customs). But within decades of the Council's end the saints were spotted again where the cover of paint obscuring them was removed and the books featuring them were reopened to pages reminding that many beliefs about and practices surrounding the saints are not mere customs but part of the unbroken tradition preserving and communicating revelation. Precisely because of Vatican II's Christological concerns, it is good that the saints are seen prominently. They are mentioned at the altar and are imaged elsewhere in churches because it is Christ who is shown to be triumphant in them, giving hope to all in the communion of grace fashioned by him in the Holy Spirit. The saints' place in the Church, as signs and even as vehicles of Christ's grace, exists in a manner sacramental; their depictions in churches where the faithful gather for liturgy can remind us of this.

In this chapter, to be reviewed are the changes in the system for causes of saints in and since 1983, plus critical features in the existing process that identifies as blesseds and saints those whom God has made such. The Church only declares as saints those whom God has revealed to be so. The system that it follows is designed to ensure that we see accurately God's work. This consists of a thorough historical examination of the life and/or death of a could-be saint to determine if an individual is a martyr or was heroically virtuous, plus an equally rigorous examination of possible miracles to ascertain if God has answered prayers through the instrumentality of an individual, in which case he has shown that individual to be with him in Heaven and therefore a saint. The miracles confirm that which human investigations suggest.

New Process and Norms

Pope John Paul II's 1983 reform of the process of canonization, far-reaching as it was, is explained in only six computer-printed pages that one can run from the Holy See website. His apostolic constitution *Divinus Perfectionis Magister* was issued to establish a streamlined system that would nevertheless be as rigorous as the old procedures in its examination of causes. As was noted in chapter 5, processes could be cumbersome, sometimes stalled for great lengths of time while answers were sought to questions and more questions of the "Devil's Advocate." Additionally, in a shift back toward the custom of early ages when bishops had prominence in the causes of saints, the new system sought to allow greater episcopal involvement, "[i]n light of the doctrine of the Second Vatican Council on collegiality"²—the teaching that all of the bishops, in a communion or "college" with the pope as head, share the duty and authority to pastor the Church (i.e., to shepherd it, or to guide it, spiritually). Anyone familiar with the procedure before 1983 will readily identify the major change—the absence of the prolonged legal process that was the characteristic feature of the former system. Rather than the extended dialectic that ensued between the promoter of the faith and the advocate for the cause, the new system insists upon the same scrutiny by reliance upon the thoroughness and honesty of those charged with examining and judging causes.

The constitution promulgating the newer system describes the procedures to be followed in three phases covering 1) the role of bishops in the initiation of causes, 2) the structure and responsibilities of the Sacred Congregation for the Causes of Saints, and 3) the steps to be followed by the Sacred Congregation for the Causes of Saints in the examination of causes. Another document, *Normae Servandae in inquisitionibus ab Episcopis faciendis in Causis Sanctorum* (for short, *Normae Servandae*),³ provides norms to be followed by bishops in their local inquiries into causes. The two documents together dictate the entire process, which will be outlined in brief here. Updates to the process will follow.

In the first part of *Divinus Perfectionis Magister*, supplemented by the norms for bishops overseeing causes, the new procedures specify that a bishop has the authority and the responsibility to begin gathering information on deceased members of the Church regarded as exemplarily holy, normally these who died in his diocese. At least five years must elapse after death before a cause can be initiated, and no more than thirty can pass without determination by a bishop that no deception on the part of the petitioner was intended with the delay. An exception is permitted in ancient cases, defined as those in which written materials, and not eyewitness accounts, are the only sources available as testimony to martyrdom or to heroically virtuous living. A "Petitioner" for the cause, one who is assigned to see the cause through the various stages, appoints a "Postulator" approved by the bishop. The postulator, who must have expertise in theology, canonical issues, history, and the workings of the Congregation for the Causes of Saints, has the responsibility of investigating the life of the candidate, called a "Servant of God," for signs of sanctity and/or martyrdom. Additionally, he must demonstrate the benefit to the Church of the cause, as the Church does not claim to or intend to canonize every holy person but only those whose lives and/or deaths are particularly edifying. The postulator also manages finances for a cause. A report of the results of these initial examinations must be submitted to the bishop with a formal petition. Included must be a biography or chronological account of actions in life and at death of the servant of God that shows discovered evidence of virtue or martyrdom and a reputation for sanctity and miracles. Additionally, a list of individuals who can testify to the presence or absence of martyrdom or virtue, plus copies of the servant of God's published writings, must be submitted to the bishop. The bishop consults the Conference of Bishops or other bishops in his geographical area to decide whether or not a cause is warranted. The petition is to be publicized in the appropriate dioceses to allow the faithful to submit evidence for or against the cause; in the case of negative information the postulator examines the issue(s) raised to see if there is truly a detriment. If after this the bishop determines that a cause would be viable, he has reviewed by two theological censors the published writings of the servant of God to ascertain whether or not the works are free of anything contrary to faith and morals. If these pass scrutiny, any unpublished writings of the servant of God, including personal documents, plus any relevant historical documents, are examined by historical and archival experts. Then a new report is submitted to the bishop, along with the writings; the report contains a list of the servant of God's documents, statements regarding the documents' authenticity and value, and an assessment of the personality of the servant of God as gathered from the writings. At this point the bishop sends to the Congregation for the Causes of Saints a preliminary report on the servant of God and a statement about the importance of the cause; the Holy See in turn advises whether or not there is any reason known at the Vatican why the cause should not proceed. If not, in the case of recently deceased servants of God, the bishop prepares for tribunals by providing to a "Promoter of Justice" all materials gathered thus far, so that questions can be developed that will reveal the character of the life and death of the servant of God. In ancient causes, rather than the evidence gathered at tribunals, reputation of the servant of God is studied, along with any evidence of a recent cult.

Local witnesses are called to testify before the bishop or his delegate. (The bishop may appoint a delegate for any portion of his oversight of the local process.) Questions are prepared in advance by the promoter of justice or other expert, based upon the contents of the report submitted to the bishop; for the purpose of clarification, though, at a tribunal the bishop may pose questions beyond those prepared. Eyewitnesses are required, including family members, friends and acquaintances, and, in the case of those in religious life, individuals from outside as well as inside the religious order. Other honest witnesses may be called if necessary. Priests, confessors, and spiritual directors may not be called to offer anything revealed in the confessional or in discussions pertaining to matters of conscience; nor may the postulator of the cause concerned serve as a witness. The bishop may call additional witnesses, too, to offer testimony supportive of or detracting from the cause. Witnesses may elect to submit written statements, under oath of authorship and of truth of contents. Notarized transcripts of the trial are confirmed by the witnesses themselves and, in the rare case in which the promoter of justice is not present at testimony, they are given to him for his review and remarks, including any suggestions about additional examinations. All experts involved in the gathering of witness accounts take an oath as to the thoroughness and integrity of the examinations.

As a matter distinct from the examination for martyrdom or heroic virtue of a candidate, witnesses also are called to testify about reports of miracles. Medical doctors who treated patients who experienced a cure by apparent miracle describe in detail the illnesses and the circumstances of healing of these who invoked one whose cause is in process, or they relay their opinion to another competent party who testifies. Written documents may be submitted when experts cannot or will not appear personally to testify, accompanied, as in the case of other witness statements, by an oath of authorship and of truth of the contents of the documents. The bishop authenticates all witness statements with his signature and his seal; all of the witness documents and transcripts also are authenticated by the signature and the seal of a notary or public official. In the case of a reported miracle occurring in a territory other than that in which the cause is initiated, the bishop presiding over the local process instructs the bishop in whose territory the purported miracle occurred to carry out the examinations; the latter retains in the chancery the original acts from his investigations and sends a copy to the bishop calling for the inquiry.

The conclusion of the local examinations begins with several steps to ensure completeness of the materials supporting the cause: the bishop carefully collects all of the proofs; the promoter of justice examines all of the documents and requests additional inquiries, need be; and the postulator may examine the acts and supplement proofs with additional witnesses or written materials. The bishop then inspects places where evidence of a cult might appear, such as at the servant of God's tomb, the residence where he or she lived, and the location of his or her death. He then must prepare a declaration attesting to compliance with the decrees of Pope Urban VIII forbidding a public cult prior to the success of a cause.[4] Next a report is prepared summarizing all activities; this is added to the acts of the local process. A transcript in duplicate is made from the acts and carefully compared to the original to ensure accuracy, a notary initials each page and stamps with his seal, and the closed and sealed original is placed in the chancery archive. The two transcript copies with supporting documents, also closed and sealed, are sent with all of the writings of the servant of God and the reports of the theological censors to the Congregation for the Causes of Saints. The bishop also sends a letter to the "Cardinal Prefect" at the Congregation, validating the veracity of the witnesses and the acts. Separately, the transcript of miracle inquiries along with all supporting documents, including a report on the reputed miracles, is sent to the Congregation.[5]

The second section of *Divinus Perfectionis Magister* describes the variety of positions involved in the work of examining causes, and later voting on them, once bishops' materials have arrived at the Vatican. At the top of the [Congregation,] which in the early stages of causes only guides bishops in the local procedures, is the [cardinal prefect,] as assistant to the pope. [A cardinal prefect heads each congregation of the Roman Curia, the collection of departments overseeing administrative and pastoral matters for the Church at large.] Assisting him is a [secretary] who coordinates between the Congregation and outside parties including the local bishops, participates in conversations about the causes and votes on them along with the cardinal and bishops of the Congregation, and prepares the voting report for the pope. Assisting the secretary is an [undersecretary] who ensures that all rules of law in causes are followed. Assisting the undersecretary are [other officials.] A "Relator General" heads a College of Relators that has the direct duty of studying causes. Individual "Relators" work with "Collaborators" (who are not part of the Congregation); they prepare the *Positio* (the formal document making the case for the cause by outlining the virtues or martyrdom of a candidate), they serve as resident experts at meetings of theologians, and they provide historical contextualization to assist "Consultors"—those employed in the study of causes for their expertise in history and theology. A designated relator writes the *Positio* on miracles and participates in meetings of medical doctors as well as of theologians. The relator general has responsibility for running meetings of consultors. A [Prelate Theologian"] or ["Promoter of the Faith"] (*not* acting as Devil's Advocate) meets with voting theologians, prepares the meeting report, and, as a non-voting expert, attends meetings of the cardinals and bishops. Finally, a board of experts in medicine is employed in the Congregation for the task of investigating events submitted as possible miracles. In addition to studying causes of saints, the Congregation has charge of authenticating and preserving relics.

Specifying the order in which the many individuals involved in the cause of a possible saint execute their tasks, the third section of the apostolic constitution outlines five basic steps. First, the undersecretary checks that all rules of law have been satisfied by the work of the local bishop submitting a cause and he announces his finding at a meeting of the Congregation. Second, in a decision that the law has been followed, a relator and a collaborator are assigned to produce the *Positio* on the virtues or martyrdom of the servant of God. If warranted, the *Positio* is evaluated by consultors with expertise bearing upon the servant of God's context in life; sometimes other scholars, too, are employed at this task. Third, the *Positio*, once it has satisfied all parties involved thus far, is given to theological consultors who vote on the cause's value. They and the prelate theologian raise any issues for further study in the servant of God's life and/or death and, with issues answered satisfactorily, votes of the consultors and the judgment of the prelate theologian are forwarded to the cardinals and bishops of the Congregation for their consideration. Fourth, a relator produces a separate *Positio* on purported miracles. This is forwarded to the medical board that studies thoroughly and rules upon the physical occurrences and then submits its findings. At a meeting of theologians, then a meeting of the cardinals and bishops, reviewed are the medical judgments to determine whether or not an event that the medical board cannot explain by natural processes is in fact a miracle. Fifth, the decisions of the cardinals and bishops are forwarded to the pope for his decision as to whether or not the servant of God is deserving of a public cult.[6]

For the accomplishment of each step, abundant meetings and communications occur both at the local level and at the Congregation. Many minute details are involved in performing each task in the process, including those of logistics. Indeed, the care that is required from beginning to end of a cause still can require many years even in the new system. With the elimination of the legal trials featuring the Devil's Advocate as the major check in the process, it is particularly critical in the current system that every phase be executed with "objectivity and completeness," as Pope Benedict XVI emphasized in a 2007 address to postulators of the Congregation.[7] In that spirit, several elaborations have been given under his pontificate.

Updates to Process

Among documents that have been issued clarifying and/or modifying aspects of the process of beatification and canonization since the death of Pope John Paul II is a 2005 "Communique by the Congregation for the Causes of Saints" establishing several standards: the "pontifical act" of beatification is to be celebrated by a papal representative, usually the prefect of the Congregation for the Causes of Saints, rather than the pope himself;[8] the beatification rite is to occur in the diocese of the servant of God becoming a blessed or in another appropriate location, unless a special case is made officially for the rite of beatification to occur in Rome; and the beatification rite is to occur during the celebration of the Eucharist rather than that of the Word or during the Liturgy of the Hours, "unless special liturgical reasons" intervene to make it appropriate for it to occur at these other moments.[9] These directives were affirmed and received additional attention in new procedures issued for the rite of beatification, with the central aim of distinguishing clearly between beatifications and canonizations and allowing local churches to have a prominent role in the beatification rites of servants of God from their own dioceses.[10]

Recently, too, to guarantee assiduousness in investigations at the diocesan level where causes are initiated, new instruction has been issued to assist bishops in applying the norms established in 1983 for local inquiries. *Sanctorum Mater* reinforces the indispensability of a reputation for sanctity and/or martyrdom before a cause is initiated, then outlines carefully the steps to be followed through the inquiry phase of a process when information is gathered and validated about one who might be a saint and who has the renown of a saint already in the memory of many.[11] In a letter for the Congregation for the Causes of Saints in conjunction with a plenary assembly at which the new instruction was a subject, along with miracles and martyrdom, Pope Benedict XVI emphasized several particular cautionary matters for today: a cause cannot be advanced in the absence of an undeniable reputation for holiness; scientists are to examine events proposed to be miraculous to ascertain whether or not they are extraordinary (i.e., they cannot be explained by natural processes) but it is the role of theology to ascertain, in faith, whether or not an extraordinary event is a miracle; miracles must be physical, not moral, in keeping with the tradition of the Church; and "true martyrdom according to the perennial theological and juridical doctrine of the Church" is present only as a result of "irrefutable proof of readiness for martyrdom, such as the outpouring of blood and of its acceptance by the victim[s]" as a "witnessing to their faithfulness to Christ, to the Gospel and to the Church," as well as "hatred of the faith" on the part of the persecutor who kills, which may be apparent "directly or indirectly but always in a morally certain way."[12]

On this long road to declaration of one as a blessed and then a saint, deserving of special attention are two hinging elements of the process— the *Positio*, the fruit of careful human investigation into the life and death of a servant of God, and the miracle examinations, the results of which are understood as corroboration by God of human conclusions.

Human Investigations, Divine Confirmation

The *Positio*, the record of the examinations of the life and death of a servant of God, is a summary compilation of the proceedings of a cause. It includes the *Vita* that has been standard from the days in which bishops named saints for their own territories, although today the *Vita* relies upon critical methods to bring to light the uniqueness of a candidate as situated in a particular historical and cultural milieu rather than, as was a goal in the past, to show that a candidate is similar to those already named saints. It is unlike earlier hagiographical forms that incorporated legendary elements into stories of saints, differing from these in being the instrument through which an historically accurate and complete portrait of the servant of God emerges. Just as at the stage of local inquiries any negative information must be gathered with the positive, at the *Positio* stage any negative elements of the life of a servant of God must be given an account, even if that should net negative votes on a cause. *Positiones* now show, then, that and how one served as a disciple of Christ in a way unique to one's time and place and expressive of one's genuine personality under the influence of sanctifying grace. If a servant of God is to be judged worthy of beatification and canonization, the life story must communicate clearly and honestly the virtues that the servant of God evidently possessed heroically. These will be from among the classical virtues—theological (faith, hope, and love) and cardinal (prudence, justice, temperance, and fortitude). But they perhaps also will include "associated virtues"[13] such as those appropriate to state of life or to personal circumstances. In the case of a martyr, the account of the death is the focus. Heroic virtue and/or martyrdom "proofs" also may be offered separately, in an *Informatio* that argues for their evidence. Also included in the *Positio* is all of the testimony gathered, at tribunals or elsewhere, along with documentary support. The *Positio* moves through stages in its production, as the relator studies all of the materials submitted to the Congregation and summarizes and assembles them appropriately, as any questions of the prelate theologian—the promoter of the faith—are answered, and as the document is refined for the final votes by the theologian consultants, the cardinals and bishops of the Congregation, and the pope, in that order. An affirmative vote from the pope is followed by his decree of heroic virtues or of martyrdom; henceforth the servant of God is "Venerable." The writing of *Positiones* can require years.[14] In length, they are hundreds of pages, if not thousands.[15] When they issue in a positive final judgment as to the servant of God's sanctity, only miracles of intercession as a result of invocation remain to be required for beatification and canonization of a servant of God.

The evidence of sanctity available to human eyes is exterior—heroic virtue and martyrdom. Only God can see the interior transformation that he effected or the lack thereof. But human eyes can see the miracles that God performs through a servant of God's instrumentality, albeit careful human investigation is required here, too, to ensure that our eyes do not deceive us, so to speak, and that our judgments are as honest and correct as possible. To this end, the medical committee of physicians formed for service to the Congregation for the purpose of examining purported miracles, the *Consulta Medica,* undertakes a rigorous review in a process analogous to that examining sanctity. It determines whether seeming miracles are "inexplicable" or "not scientifically explainable" (and therefore possibly a miracle) or, instead, "natural" (possibly scientifically explainable, that is, explicable or maybe explicable by other than supernatural factors and therefore not able to be considered miracles). Inexplicable events are then judged by theologians to be miraculous or not; if miraculous they must be proven to have occurred as a result of invocation of the particular servant of God in question in order for them to serve as proof that the individual is with God in Heaven.[16] Most miracles today are medical cures, perhaps the most readily identifiable potential instances of dramatic divine activity and certainly the most easily examined according to modern scientific processes, although other types of physical miracles have not been excluded from consideration. A decrease from the number of miracles required for beatification and canonization in the system in place before 1983, today one miracle of intercession from invocation is required for a servant of God to be declared a *beati*, except in the case of martyrdom when this requirement can be waived; a second miracle of intercession from invocation (a first for martyrs)—occurring after beatification[17]—is required for a blessed to be declared a *sancti.*

In spite of the fact that discrete human judgments during a cause in progress could be flawed, at the conclusion of a process, recent Vatican directives have stated that, in the naming of a saint, "[p]ontifical infallibility is involved."[18] As noted in chapter 5, the pope himself presides at the liturgical celebration announcing a canonization and honoring the one canonized, signifying the universal veneration that is binding upon the faithful for the new saint among all of the other saints. The pope presents the newly canonized, among his or her other roles, as a model of discipleship of Christ for imitation by others. One can see how this could satisfy the conditions of papal infallibility as defined at the First Vatican Council (1869–1870): ". . . [T]he Roman Pontiff, when he speaks *ex cathedra*, that is, when carrying out the duty of the pastor and teacher of all Christians in accord with his supreme apostolic authority he explains a doctrine of faith or morals to be held by the universal Church, through the divine assistance promised him in blessed Peter, operates with that infallibility with which the divine Redeemer wished that His church be instructed in defining doctrine on faith and morals; and so such definitions of the Roman Pontiff from himself, but not from the consensus of the Church, are unalterable."[19] These precise conditions, though, have been in visible effect in declarations of sainthood only since canonizations, now distinct from beatifications, have been the province of popes, raising theological questions beyond the scope of this study.

Conclusion

A popular way of conceiving of miracles is as divine interventions. From the standpoint of Catholic theology, this is unintelligible, since Catholicism's sacramental sense is of God as present to creation always, keeping it in existence and enlivening it with his persuasive love. All being has its source and sustenance in he who is being itself. He does not break into history only at select moments. Instead, then, miracles should be understood as profound instances of God's presence, dramatic manifestations of his ongoing work among and through human beings—those in his image and likeness (Gen. 1:26–27) called to and empowered by grace to reflect his loving activity. The means of this salvific work is Christ, and so profound moments of grace in the present must be compared to and consciously connected to the miracles of Jesus during his earthly ministry as recounted in the New Testament. Experientially, even for Christians, unusually dramatic, positive events that are inexplicable from the perspective of science may feel like instances of divinity "breaking into" time and space, but people of faith are able to understand such occurrences in the context of Jesus' revelation of his nearness to us always. Thereby current extraordinary events can be understood as miracles of the resurrected Christ who is with us in the Spirit. Christ ever-present to us is not seen now only in miracles, though.

In the living icons that are the saints, even when they are not being invoked for miracles or otherwise, we also see and respond to Christ. The saints' exemplary lives through the grace of Christ, their companionship with us in Christ through our commonly redeemed humanity, and their nearness to Christ resulting in their willingness to serve perpetually as intercessors, compel us in a way analogous to miracles' draw. They give us evidence of God among us, of Christ not just past but present, persuading us to our finality and the finality of all in the fullness of the Kingdom of

God established in and through the Incarnation—the Word made flesh (Jn. 1:14). "Saints normally bring forth other Saints and closeness to them, or even only to their footsteps, is always salutary: it cleanses and raises the mind and opens the heart to love for God and for the brethren. Holiness sows joy and hope, and responds to the thirst for happiness that people also feel today," said Pope Benedict XVI to the Congregation for the Causes of Saints about the importance of the saints to the Church on Earth.[20] The possibility of the saints' efficacy for others will begin to be analyzed systematically in the next chapter.

Terms for Study

Beatification

Blessed

Cardinal Prefect

Collaborators

Consulta Medica

Consultors

Informatio

Miracles

Papal Infallibility

Petitioner

Positio

Prelate Theologian/Promoter of the Faith

Relators (College of)/Relator General

Roman Curia

Sacred Congregation for the Causes of Saints

Secretary/Undersecretary

Servant of God

Venerable

Suggested Readings

Blessed John Paul II, Pope. *Divinus Perfectionis Magister.* 25 January 1983. At the Vatican [online]. Available from http://www.vatican.va/ holy_father/john_paul_ii/apost_constitutions/documents/hf_jp-ii_apc_25011983_divinus-perfectionis-magister_en.html. Accessed 1 September 2011.

This apostolic constitution issued on January 25, 1983, established new procedures for the causes of saints, dramatically revising the process that had been in place for centuries with occasional modifications.

Congregation for the Causes of Saints. *New Procedures in the Rite of Beatification.* [29 September 2005.] At the Vatican [online]. Available from http://www.vatican.va/roman_curia/congregations/csaints/documents/ rc_con_csaints_doc_20050929_saraiva-martins-beatif_en.html. Accessed 1 September 2011.

This document provides a history of beatification and canonization, including the emergence of the distinction between the two states, and it reviews the history of the rite of beatification. Additionally, as its purpose, it establishes criteria and guidelines for that rite, with a view to clarifying its difference from the rite of canonization in both form and meaning.

Congregation for the Causes of Saints. *Normae Servandae in inquisitionibus ab Episcopis faciendis in Causis Sanctorum* (New Laws for the Causes of Saints: Norms to Be Observed in Inquiries Made by Bishops in the Causes of Saints). 7 February 1983. At the Vatican [online]. Available from http://www.vatican.va/roman_curia/ congregations/csaints/documents/rc_con_csaints_doc_07021983_norme_ en.html. Accessed 1 September 2011.

Issued on February 7, 1983, this document provides norms for the new procedures for causes of saints established by *Divinus Perfectionis Magister* on January 25, 1983.

Woodward, Kenneth. *Making Saints: How the Catholic Church Determines Who Becomes a Saint, Who Doesn't, and Why.* New York: Touchstone, 1996.

Chapters two and three of this book, written after the author and journalist was given unprecedented access to the Congregation for the Causes of Saints, provide "insider" reviews of and commentary on the procedures for examination of causes before and after 1983. Chapter six presents procedural and theological issues involved in the examination of miracles today.

Nine

THE CHRISTOLOGICAL CENTER: CATHOLIC DOCTRINE AND ECUMENICAL CONVERSATION

In the beautiful Trinitarian prayer known as *Saint Patrick's Breastplate* is a powerful Christological stanza:

> Christ be with me,
> Christ within me,
> Christ behind me,
> Christ before me,
> Christ beside me,
> Christ to win me,
> Christ to comfort and restore me,
> Christ beneath me,
> Christ above me,
> Christ in quiet,
> Christ in danger,
> Christ in hearts of all that love me,
> Christ in mouth of friend and stranger.

The prayer in whole, creedal in tone, Celtic in sensibility, thoroughly Catholic in sacramental consciousness of created reality, is a vow of belief in and commitment to God the Trinity. It is deeply reflective upon the three-personed God as operating in his creation, in Christ, through the Holy Spirit, pulling us toward the Father. The Christological content bespeaks our instrumentality in the ongoing work of Christ, following upon Scripture and tradition. This instrumentality is the basis for understanding the saints' roles in the Church. Saints are "made" through the grace of Christ, and his presence in any human being seeks unity not only of that individual with him but of every member of the "Mystical Body" with Christ its Head. To recognize this work of Christ in and through all human beings is to see the communion of saints in its full vitality. Without adopting the objectionable medieval imaginings of the saints in Heaven dispensing favors to those who pay them requisite honor, acknowledgement of Christ at work to save each and all is acknowledgement that those in the communion of saints can be affected by others and can affect others; we can even share spiritual "treasures" in that we can make efficacious offerings for each other. Venerating the canonized saints in the communion of saints is grateful advertence to this reality; it is response to Christ, an acceptance of his grace in consciousness of his love for us and its effect upon all human beings.

This chapter will lay the groundwork for study in subsequent chapters of the roles of the saints. It will do so by considering the concepts of intentionality and of symbol to help explain the making of saints and the veneration of saints, respectively. Intentionality is a philosophical concept that can be appropriated in a specifically theological way. The notion of saints as symbols is ancient, often de-emphasized today, but indispensible for full comprehension of the work of Christ in and through his saints according to the theological tradition of Catholics and some other Christians. This chapter also will look at critical Christological issues, raised in ecumenical conversation, about the ontology of saints and veneration of them. It will conclude with a reflection to be continued in the next three chapters upon the ecclesial function of saints, that is, their roles in the Body of Christ, the Church.

Intentionality and the Making of Saints

"[T]he question of God is implicit in all our questioning," wrote twentieth-century Catholic theologian Bernard Lonergan.[1] The short explanation for this is that, since human beings are made for God, and we are therefore directed to God as our end, all that we will and do, and all that we think, ultimately is in reference to God, whether or not we are conscious of this. How could this be? A look at an interim end within our ultimate end will illustrate. Human beings die; until then we age, inevitably. Human beings are not immutable; we change, progressing and/or regressing. As this occurs, all of our thinking, feeling, and doing condition the person we are becoming in time. Our choices, our attitudes, even about the physical aspects of our existence, influence our future or, rather, our stance toward and in it, such that the way in which we age is in part due to our acceptance of and preparation for it, or lack thereof. We can think of this stance in terms of intentionality. Theologically, the very possibility of our intentionality, as well as exercise of it, was given by God. On the one hand, it exists from God's bringing us into existence as rational creatures related to himself and, on the other hand, from our response to this reality in the form of the posture we adopt toward it. In God's material creation only human beings, intellectual creatures, have the capacity to understand anything about God and to respond. And, given that all interim ends exist within the one end of God who is our destiny (if we will accept him), our stance toward them is always in some way a stance toward God. Theologians relate this fact to our capacity for "self-transcendence." Because our "power to know and love, assent and consent, grasps particular being against the background of being in general; . . . all its particularized knowledge is implicitly based on the unthematic awareness it also has of Being *simpliciter*, . . . of God, . . . of the mystery above us and within us," wrote Rahner with Herbert Vorgrimler. "Consequently the transcendentality of the human spirit is the essential foundation of the person, of responsibility, of religious experience . . . , and of the possibility of God's self-communication in grace and revelation."[2] In the sense in which the term "intentionality" is being used in this and in subsequent chapters, it is the possibility of engagement of that transcendentality.

To return to the example of our aging, if we live without care about the person that we are becoming as time passes, refusing to make choices for the good that will nurture our humanity and lead us closer to eternal life in God, we are closing our part of the ongoing conversation that God has with each of us. This can be emblematic of or affect our stance toward our ultimate end, then. Even the small movements of our attitudes and choices in daily activities are in some part responsive to the ultimate end in which all exists. This means that, on the level of cognition (i.e., our thinking and knowledge), all of our queries, even about temporal matters, are directed beyond their immediate concerns to the ultimate reality, God. And, on the level of volition (i.e., our willing), all of our actions, even some that do not seem particularly significant in their performance, are a response to God. Further, since we are not simply minds, which are finite, limited at that in our case, our affection (its own kind of knowing) fully actualizes our stance toward God. Wrote Lonergan: "[B]eing in love with God is the basic fulfilment of our conscious intentionality."[3] He explained: "Just as unrestricted questioning is our capacity for self-transcendence, so being in love in an unrestricted fashion is the proper fulfilment of that capacity."[4] Love guides and brings to their peak state our intellectual and moral conversions (i.e., those dealing with truth and value),[5] for "[r]eligious conversion is . . . a total being-in-love as the efficacious ground of all self-transcendence, . . ."[6] So

> [t]hat fulfilment is not the product of our knowledge and choice. On the contrary, it dismantles and abolishes the horizon in which our knowing and choosing went on and it sets up a new horizon in which the love of God will transvalue our values and the eyes of that love will transform our knowing.

Though not the product of our knowing and choosing, it is a conscious dynamic state of love, joy, peace, that manifests itself in acts of kindness, goodness, fidelity, gentleness, and self control (Gal. 5, 22).

To say that this dynamic state is conscious is not to say that it is known. For consciousness is just experience, but knowledge is a compound of experience, understanding, and judging. Because the dynamic state is conscious without being known, it is an experience of mystery. Because it is being in love, the mystery is not merely attractive but fascinating; to it one belongs; by it one is possessed. Because it is an unmeasured love, the mystery evokes awe. Of itself, then, inasmuch as it is conscious without being known, the gift of God's love is an experience of the holy, . . .[7]

Rahner's comments about intentionality provide a more technical understanding of the matter of our directedness to God in all of our faculties such that, whether or not we accept God, all of our knowing and willing and loving is response to him, positively or negatively,[8] explicitly or implicitly. He explained in his *Theological Dictionary* co-authored with Vorgrimler that

[i]nsofar as grace is in germ, that is, really and efficaciously, a participation in the life of God and the whole spiritual activity of man is thus already (here and now) directed towards the essentially supernatural beatific vision (possession of God), we can speak of man's cognitive intentionality being elevated by grace ('illuminated', Scripture says) and directed to a supernatural formal object—the infinite reality of God himself; and this intentionality, so directed, forms the non-objective and non-specific 'horizon', in a kind of fundamental existential situation, within which everything of moral and religious (that is, existential) significance is contained and ordered to its last end.[9]

Rahner also recognized, though, the necessity of the exercise of our free will (under the influence of God's grace, as will be discussed in chapter 10) to accept this end. The elevated intentionality gifted by God must have our assent to be fully operative:

The end realized or to be realized in freedom and the predetermined end . . . as the self-realizing end (*finis quo*) has to be set by the free act, creatively, in continual hope. Hence it cannot be simply regarded as the actuation of a potentiality, such as takes place outside the field of freedom. . . . The goal of freedom, even where God himself is the end and absolute future (at least as the *finis quo*), is in the concrete the new goal freely chosen among many possibilities and creatively mapped-out. The past, even as potentiality, is left behind by this incalculable future, in the light of which man understands himself creatively.[10]

The saints lived, and do live, at the highest state of conversion—that of being in love with God and with all in God. But any virtue, including love, is a gift that cannot be demanded of God in any way, even while it is never given without human cooperation or human free will would be undermined. We are not born saints, loving God perfectly from the start. God's love begins the process of our conversion and our return of the love of God (through the influence of the power of his own love) ends the process, but, in between, our intellect and our will condition our love. That is why the saints are instructive and efficacious in our journey; their struggle to allow themselves to be converted through love presents both example and assistance to us. As Lonergan wrote, ". . . [T]he gift of God's love occupies the ground and root of the fourth and highest level of man's intentional consciousness. It takes over the peak of the soul, the *apex animae*."[11] This is the goal for every human person, this unity with God that is observable, as in the case of the saints who are symbolic of Christ who became one with us in his humanity. The saints reveal dramatically his loving presence among us; they are "sacraments," or icons, of this.

Symbol and Veneration of Saints

When we speak of the effect of the canonized saints upon us as we are moved and respond to the grace of Christ shining in and through them, we are recognizing the symbolic capacity of saints. Today there is a tendency in discussion of the saints to emphasize the meaning of the human element of veneration—the deliberate response to God through honor of that associated with him. But without attention to God's presence in those things that are associated with him not simply by inference but by his activity, we fail to recognize and pay true honor to them and we fail to offer fullest worship to God who made them possible. The saints are symbolic in the religious sense—"sacramentally"—in that they are signs and instruments of God's grace, disclosing in a manner efficacious Christ and his work in the world. The resurrected Christ is encountered in every time, especially in human beings radically open to him and thereby sanctified by him. To follow the tradition as articulated by Saint Bonaventure (d. 1274), God the Trinity, revealed to us definitively in the Incarnation, is reflected throughout his creation, at the level of vestige in all creaturely reality, at the level of image in rational creatures (human beings), and at the level of similitude in intellectual creatures conformed to God through his grace (saints, whether canonized or not).[12]

The possibility of human beings functioning symbolically exists in our ability to express ourselves freely and deliberately in reference to our Maker for whom we were created and in whom we realize our true selves. Rahner went so far as to claim that "all beings are by their nature symbolic, because they necessarily 'express' themselves in order to attain their own nature."[13] Even if this is the case, human beings, rational creatures, are symbolic in a unique way because our expression of ourselves properly implies our relationship to God, our end. We are inspired by others because of their capacity to disclose the divine-human relationship in their concrete circumstances of acceptance of God. Human beings, therefore, not only can function as symbols but were created to respond to symbols. And so the saints, who exercised their elevated intentionality for union with God through their willing and loving engagement with his creation and its redemption through the presence of the risen Christ, are potentially revelatory and even salvific for us. In responding to these neighbors as symbols, or sacraments, we respond to God. In venerating the saints, we follow not only the second but also the first of the two great commandments. Rahner claimed that the two—love of God and love of neighbor—are functionally one.[14] The loving action directed to us through the saints is the grace of Christ communicated through mere human symbols of his victory and our hope. So a theology of symbol provides a key to understanding how veneration of those whose lives reflect near-perfection in love can "mediate" grace to us. Our love of the saints is love of Christ because they have reached the fullness of their being in him. The Catholic doctrine of *anamnesis* (Gk. "memorial")—that through the grace of Christ we can recall his sacrifice in a manner that re-presents it in the present—includes this aspect of unity of the Mystical Body with its Head, and it thereby shows how veneration of the saints (i.e., *dulia*) is always a response to the offer of the grace of Christ (i.e., *latria*). More about the saints as symbols will be said in chapter 10. (And Appendix 2 expounds upon this summary of Rahner's theologies of symbol and of *anamnesis*.)

Ecumenical Conversation Concerning Christ and His Saints

That which has been stated thus far should make it evident that a critical value of the saints to the living is derived from the saints' symbolic status and our intentional response to them in that regard. It can be said that the saints are symbolic of and for our relationship with Christ, the "real symbol"—the concrete, definitive sign of God's will and action to save us, which, as the next chapter will show, constitutes a persuasive and empowering invitation of God to us.[15] As this chapter has shown of Catholic thought, because human beings are made in the image of God— and therefore are "naturally" symbolic in a way surpassing other created earthly beings—and because we possess intentionality that has been "elevated" by and in reference to its Giver, intentional investment in our relationship to God realizes increase in the symbolic reality, a reality which thereby becomes intensely revelatory, and "grace-ful," and compelling to others in its communication of human meaning and possibility. The Catholic concern not to violate the tenets of divine or human freedom in any conception of this divine-human dynamic has rendered the word "cooperation" a mainstay in description of the human response to God's initiative—a response that is itself elicited by God's grace. Divine and human freedom is a matter that will be discussed in some detail in the next chapter. For now, though, it will aid to explain briefly why the language of "cooperation," with the concept behind it, legitimizes veneration of saints for some Christians (Catholics, primarily) while its denial invalidates veneration of saints for some other Christians (many or most Protestants). This will be an occasion to introduce important ecumenical conversation on Christological issues that impact understanding of the saints.

The valuable dialogue between Catholics and Lutherans in recent decades, producing such important documents as the *Joint Declaration on the Doctrine of Justification*, has fostered understanding of the extent to which Catholics and Protestants agree on the wherefore of the salvific work of Christ and where the real differences exist, absent the inflamed rhetoric of the sixteenth century and in possession of "new insights" gained by both Churches in the course of their "respective histories."[16] The *Joint Declaration* announced that Lutherans and Catholics agree that "justification is the work of the triune God. . . . Christ himself is our righteousness, in which we share through the Holy Spirit in accord with the will of the Father." Therefore, "[b]y grace alone, in faith in Christ's saving work and not because of any merit on our part, we are accepted by God and receive the Holy Spirit ['who works through Word and Sacrament in the community of believers' to give faith which 'is itself God's gift'[17]], who renews our hearts while equipping and calling us to good works."[18] There is nothing whatsoever that we can do to gain salvation by our own efforts; without the grace of God we cannot even will to be with him.[19] Catholics, then, decidedly do not mean that human beings "cooperate" with God in the sense that we merit his grace and salvation or in the sense that we are equal partners with him in this. The document explains: "When Catholics says that persons 'cooperate' in preparing for and accepting justification by consenting to God's justifying action, they see such personal consent as itself an effect of grace, not as an action arising from innate human abilities."[20] Lutherans reject the notion of cooperation[21] because, unlike Catholics who believe that a personal decision is involved in sin properly speaking,[22] they understand concupiscence—which Catholics see as an inclination to sin that remains after Baptism due to original sin[23]—to be in itself sin. Therefore, even those who have been justified remain sinners (as well as become saints, in the general sense, due to the righteousness of Christ applied to them).[24] Both Lutherans and Catholics recognize "a preservation of grace and a growth in grace"—traditionally known in Catholicism as the process of sanctification. On the one hand, Lutherans "emphasize that righteousness as acceptance by God and sharing in the righteousness of Christ is always complete." On the other hand, "they state that there can be growth in its effects in Christian living." These good works are the result of justification; they are in no way merited by human beings, yet there will be the "reward" of eternal life in their wake "in the sense of the fulfillment of God's promise to the believer."[25] Catholics emphasize the progressive transformation of the human person that requires our cooperation, seeing the true Christian life as a journey of increasing "communion with Christ." The document explains: "When Catholics affirm the 'meritorious' character of good works, they wish to say that, according to the biblical witness, a reward in heaven is promised to these works. Their intention is to emphasize the responsibility of persons for their actions, not to contest the character of those works as gifts, or far less to deny that justification always remains the unmerited gift of grace."[26]

Catholics as other Christians hold to "the primacy of grace."[27] It is through the Incarnation of the Son of God that the Triune God invited humanity into his life. Christ, the second person of the Trinity (or the second *hypostasis*, to use the original Greek description), the Only-Begotten of the Father who is the Unbegotten, took on human reality in approximately 4 B.C., retaining his full divinity but becoming fully human as well. As affirmed in 451 A.D. at the fourth Christological council, the Council of Chalcedon, Jesus Christ is the "Hypostatic Union," the union of two natures, divine and human, "without confusion or change, without division or separation,"[28] in the Son of God who is one in Being with the Father and with the Holy Spirit. His sacrificial death and resurrection for the redemption of fallen humanity established the possibility for us of eternal life, for he, sharing a human nature with us, permanently established humanity's possibility of participation in the life of God. Through the Holy Spirit, Christ remains present to us in time and space, seen especially where love overcomes the evil that is sin, such as in the saints. "The entire existence of the saints is given shape into its very roots and brought to maturity through the grace of Christ. Without this grace the saints have no significance for the church, but by it they become witnesses of the love of God for humanity," in the words of the document *Communio Sanctorum: The Church as the Communion of Saints*, another product of Catholic-Lutheran conversations.[29] The saints are venerated by Catholics in the understanding that such doing attests to this grace of Christ.[30] The saints themselves are "witnesses of Christ in that the Lord meets us in them, for the church is his body: Just as all life currents proceed from Christ into all his members, so all spiritual connections among the members are mediated through him. . . . Christians thus remain forever bound to one another, even beyond the dividing line of death."[31]

The unity of Christians with one another because of all Christians' unity with Christ, involving the sharing of spiritual "favors" which Catholics and some other Christians seek with the canonized saints, shows the intersection of Christology and ecclesiology. Future chapters will show that ecclesiology and theological anthropology are joined by reflection upon Christ's saints in their roles for the Church. And it is not inappropriate that some theologians have of late taken an increasingly pneumatological approach (i.e., one of focus upon the Holy Spirit) to explicate the communion of saints, including the canonized saints within this communion. It is the Holy Spirit, in the Gospel of John the other "Paraclete" or "Counselor"[32] promised by Jesus Christ to provide spiritual direction (Jn. 14:16–17, 26; 15:26; 16:7–15) and in Acts the empowering agent to make Christ's disciples his witnesses throughout the world (Acts 1:8), who was given at Pentecost (Acts 2) and who formed and sustains and nurtures the Church. These connections among theological areas of reflection are inevitable, because the Son who became Incarnate now has his Mystical Body of human disciples who form the Church by the empowerment of the Holy Spirit and who, when they are sanctified, have a similitude to Christ—*the* model for our lives—that demonstrates the graced existence that all are called to live.

All Christians are called to holiness; all Christians are called to be saints. *Lumen Gentium* asserted of "the universal call to holiness"[33]: "[A]ll Christians in whatever state or walk in life are called to the fullness of christian life and to the perfection of charity, . . . In order to reach this perfection the faithful should use the strength dealt out to them by Christ's gift, so that, following in his footsteps and conformed to his image, doing the will of God in everything, they may wholeheartedly devote themselves to the glory of God and to the service of their neighbor."[34] As such, all Christians should become, as in images conjured by *Saint Patrick's Breastplate*, the loving hearts and witnessing friends and strangers in whom Christ is disclosed. And, as does this prayer, all Christians must recognize Christ at work in the world—in self and in others—and respond to this, intentionally, in faith and love, such as through the religious act of veneration of saints.

Conclusion

This chapter has emphasized that both divine activity and human activity are involved in the making of saints and in veneration of them; divine activity is always prior, and human activity is always at the prompting of God and through his grace. All goodness, even in us when we "cooperate" with the loving divine initiative, comes from God. In the past, sometimes the critical focus of veneration was saints' symbolic capacity and instrumentality in the dispensation of grace. Divine activity was sensed preeminently, admittedly sometimes without the proper distinction drawn between God's action and that of the saints, with the effect of the saints seeming themselves almost divine. There was, perhaps, a preoccupation with that which the saints are "doing" for us now that they reside in the "divine" realm. In the present, as stated earlier in this chapter, the meaning of human acts of veneration often is the main focus of reflection upon veneration of saints, as well as upon other aspects of worship of God. Therefore human activity is sensed preeminently, although not without cognizance of God's initiative in creating, sustaining, nurturing, and calling all to the divine-human encounter to which we respond in our religious response of veneration of saints. Properly, we must have this interest in the value of acts of veneration and at the same time acknowledge the efficacy of the saints in our progress toward God. We can do this, without reverting to wrong notions about the saints, by stressing the sacramental reality of all of creation but particularly of the saints. This rightly places the discussion of veneration of saints in the context of the Mystical Body—the Church—of which Christ is the Head.

It is because of our profoundly communal, ecclesial reality in Christ that Mary and the saints are our companions and can serve as models and as intercessors for us. Their loving—which is to say free—intentions and actions have helped us and can help us, and ours can help each other. This sharing of spiritual resources is central to the Catholic sensibility. Yet the two great commandments are linked not only in Catholic thought and practice but in Scripture.[35] The First Letter of John tells us that a love of God that does not involve love of neighbor is a lie (1 Jn. 4:20–21). Rahner wrote in affirmation of the scriptural message: "There is no love for God that is not, in itself, already a love for neighbor; and love for God only comes to its own identity through its fulfillment in a love for neighbor." He explained: "Only one who loves his or her neighbor can know who God actually is. And only one who ultimately loves God . . . can manage unconditionally to abandon himself or herself to another person, and not make that person the means of his or her own self-assertion."[36] Pope Benedict XVI's first encyclical, *Deus Caritas Est*, addressed exactly this matter in discussion of the necessary centrality of the Eucharist in the life of Catholics as the source of the *agape* love that elicits and informs charitable activities of individual Christians and of the ecclesial Body wholly.[37] As neighbors, the saints, then, must be loved if God is to be loved. The Catholic sacramental sense that affirms that God is mediated through the things of this world recognizes love of another made in the image and likeness of God as the basic act of response to divine love. And respond we must, if God is to be worshipped in his earthly creation. As Leontius of Neapolis said in the seventh century, a century before the Second Council of Nicaea which would codify the relationship between religious or holy images and God,

> Through heaven and earth and sea, through wood and stone, through relics and church buildings and the Cross, through angels and humans, through all creation visible and invisible, I offer veneration and honor to the Creator and the Master and Maker of all things, and to Him alone. For creation does not venerate the Maker directly and by itself, but it is through me that the heavens declare the glory of God, through me the moon worships God, through me the waters and showers of rain, the dew and all creation, venerate God and give him glory.[38]

To emphasize, our veneration of Mary and the saints is related to our worship of God; truly it is a form of worship of God. For, as chapter 7 showed Nicaea II to have said, "'the honour given to an image goes to the original model';[39] and one who venerates an image, venerates in it the person represented by it."[40] The saintly models—living images or icons—who are also intercessors, are not empty symbols; nor are they divine. They are free subjects whose radical submission to Christ allows his grace to be manifest dramatically in them before us. In them we see Christ. Veneration of Christ's saints is a profound religious, indeed intentional, act in reference to the promise of our "share" in the eschatological victory that he has won. *Lumen Gentium* stated: "No creature could ever be counted along with the Incarnate Word and Redeemer; but just as the priesthood of Christ is shared in various ways both by his ministers and the faithful, and as the one goodness of God is radiated in different ways among his creatures, so also the unique mediation of the Redeemer does not exclude but rather gives rise to a manifold cooperation which is but a sharing in one source."[41] The cooperation in the work of Christ of the canonized and of those who venerate them will be the focus of study in the next three chapters, where the roles of the saints will be examined, each in turn.

Terms for Study

Anamnesis	Intentionality
Christology	Mystical Body of Christ
Council of Chalcedon	Pneumatology
Creation	Redemption
Ecclesiology	Symbol
Holiness	Trinity, The
Hypostatic Union	Virtue

Suggested Readings

Bilateral Working Group of the German National Bishops' Conference and the Church Leadership of the United Evangelical Lutheran Church of Germany. *Communio Sanctorum: The Church as the Communion of Saints*. Translated by Mark W. Jeske, Michael Root, and Daniel R. Smith. Collegeville, Minnesota: Liturgical Press, 2004. Original edition, *Communio Sanctorum: Die Kirche als Gemeinschaft der Heiligen*, Paderborn: Bonifatius, 2000.

The back cover of this volume explains: "*Communio Sanctorum* is the product of the official German Catholic-Lutheran Dialogue and the first major Lutheran-Catholic ecumenical statement since the groundbreaking Joint Declaration on the Doctrine of Justification in 1999. It focuses on the ecclesiastical issues that the Joint Declaration identified as the remaining obstacles to Lutheran-Catholic communion. The metaphor of the church as the communion of saints serves as a framework for addressing ecumenical issues such as sacraments, ministry, the role of the church in salvation, and the papacy." The fruit of a "Bilateral Working Group" formed in 1987, this volume summarizing dialogue drew upon, among other sources, not only the *Joint Declaration on the Doctrine of Justification* from the Lutheran World Federation and the Roman Catholic Church, but *Church and Justification* from the International Roman Catholic-Lutheran Joint Commission and *The Condemnations of the Reformation Era: Do They Still Divide?* resulting from Protestant-Catholic Dialogue in Germany.

The Lutheran World Federation and the Roman Catholic Church. *Joint Declaration on the Doctrine of Justification.* Grand Rapids, Michigan, and Cambridge, U.K.: William B. Eerdmans Publishing, 2000. Original edition, *Gemeinsame Erklärung zur Rechtfertigungslehre,* Frankfurt am Main: Verlag Otto Lembeck; Paderborn: Bonifatius-Verlag, 1999.

Lutheran-Roman Catholic dialogue produced this important ecumenical declaration in the last days of the twentieth century. The document is found easily in a number of sources, some online. This volume also includes the *Official Common Statement* of ecumenical intent and its *Annex* of clarifications of key theological points.

The One Mediator, the Saints, and Mary: Lutherans and Catholics in Dialogue VIII. Edited by H. George Anderson, J. Francis Stafford, and Joseph A. Burgess. Minneapolis, Minnesota: Augsburg Fortress, 1992.

This eighth volume resulting from Lutheran and Roman Catholic dialogue in the United States of America in the latter half of the last century offers a biblical, historical, and theological overview of issues of Catholic and Lutheran doctrine regarding "saints," along with essays from noted theologians on specific issues that have been divisive since the Protestant Reformation. This 1980s conversation was explanatory and investigative in nature, seeking to facilitate understanding and to identify points of agreement and lack thereof.

Ten

THE SAINTS AS COMPANIONS:
A CONTEMPORARY UNDERSTANDING

Of the roles of the saints, that of companion is perhaps the most easily misperceived in our time, even though it might appear to be the most accessible to understanding. In fact, exaggerations and abuses of the past connected to the saints as intercessors and models occasionally might be traced to faulty notions of the relationship of the saints to others on the most basic level of companion. It is easy to see, for example, how the saints' intercessory role could be mistaken as that of powerful entities who can dispense even miraculous material favors at their own will, if they are affirmed to be in Heaven but imagined to be active there and on Earth in the way of living patrons who move the world by their influential connections. In that case the saints, in the celestial realm, would be believed to have extraordinary supernatural force of their own that is formidable against the most difficult of situations faced by those on Earth. It is also easy to see how reaction against this idea could lead to the equally mistaken notion that the saints are nothing more than exemplars, no more inspiring or instructive than an idealized character in a novel or a film. In that case, our consciousness is emptied of the presence of Christ in the lives of the saints who, now nearest to him, can be transformative of our own lives by his grace operative through all who accept him. Even Catholics vigilant about their faith can fall prey to aberrant ideas and practices as they rightly invest in the Church's veneration of saints but might unsuspectingly err in their manner of veneration due to lack of knowledge of the full teaching on the saints.

Contemporarily-popular beliefs in the larger culture that can supplant correct thinking about the saints as companions often stem from theologically unorthodox notions about the relationship between the living and the dead. These can issue in practices such as engagement in séances, use of mediums, and even trust in earthly advisors with supposedly special supernatural connections who assist dead in "crossing over"—popular fodder for current television programs. Ironically, such can be compelling even to Christians who have no interest in the cult of the saints or who vehemently oppose it because of its belief in the relevance of the saints to us despite that they are dead, although the ideas behind such activities are far beyond any Catholic notions of communion—and communication—with the dead. Indeed, from the vantage point of Catholic teaching on the saints they are grossly deviant—speculative, superstitious, and baseless in Scripture and tradition. This certainly is not to say, however, that the saints cannot "speak" to us of the path of our own discipleship as we travel through the trials and failures, and joys and successes, of the earthly life that they already have negotiated. Superstition and idolatry must be barred absolutely, but correct use of religious imagination in veneration of saints can be of great use, making one more fully conscious of God's work in one's life through the community of grace that the saints disclose profoundly. The concern of the next few chapters is theology rather than spiritual exercise, however—matters related yet distinct.

The long tradition of the Church affirms that the saints are companions, models, and intercessors each and all. Of these roles, that of companion is the possibility of that of model and of intercessor.[1] Therefore, right theological understanding of the saints as companions can ensure right theological understanding of the saints in their other roles, as well as facilitate a deeper comprehension of the human condition shared by saints and sinners alike. *Lumen Gentium* provides the lead to consideration of Catholic teaching on this most fundamental role not only for saints but for every human person "destined" for God.

Lumen Gentium on Saints as Companions

In the words of *Lumen Gentium*, the saints are our companions because "[e]xactly as Christian communion among pilgrims brings us closer to Christ, so our communion with the saints joins us to Christ, from whom as from its fountain and head flow all grace and life of the people of God itself."[2] Not only instruction on the saints' function as companions, but the whole tradition of Catholic theological anthropology is contained in this short but dense statement. The rest of this chapter will in effect dissect it. *Lumen Gentium* itself does not do so; as a summary document of Church doctrine, it assumes the tradition and provides shape for its ongoing theological reflection.

In what way are the saints companions, if not as otherworldly friends intimately and virtually materially involved in our daily lives in the world of space and time? The starting point for answering this is in the relationship between God and human persons that was discussed in terms of our intentionality in the last chapter. To explain the divine-human relationship more fully in this chapter, it will serve to begin with the basic observation that, in the Christian understanding, God in his sovereignty and freedom created us and redeems us. To know this is to know the essence of human existence.

The first paragraph of the current *Catechism of the Catholic Church*'s Prologue instructs: "God, infinitely perfect and blessed in himself, in a plan of sheer goodness freely created man to make him share in his own blessed life. For this reason, at every time and in every place, God draws close to man. He calls man to seek him, to know him, to love him with all his strength."[3] Of course the reference to "man" is to "woman," too. We are each and all to be a reflection of God's love. God did not have to create us; he did not have to save those whom he created when we failed to live up to our vocation; he did not have to offer us a supernatural destiny. These are borne by his love, which enables us to respond in love and to be saved by love. God who has revealed himself as Love (1 Jn. 4:8) is under no external constraint; he is free. Our true freedom is realized only from acceptance of, alignment with, that freedom within which we exist. In the words of 1 Jn. 4:19, "We love, because he first loved us." The old *Baltimore Catechism,* used in religious instruction before Vatican II, imprinted this teaching in Catholic minds via the question-and-response method. Its sixth question in the first of thirty-seven lessons asked about the reason for the creation of human beings: "Why did God make you?" The answer: "God made me to know Him, to love Him, and to serve Him in this world, and to be happy with Him forever in the next."[4] Ever operative in Catholic theology, irrespective of Catechism versions, the belief that God made us for himself has a corollary: we will never be happy without him, for this would be not to realize our purpose—our true selves. As Saint Augustine famously prayed to God in his *Confessions,* "You stir man to take pleasure in praising you, because you have made us for yourself, and our heart is restless until it rests in you."[5] But how do we reach our destination in God whom we hope to contemplate for eternity after departing this life for fuller participation in his? How do we attain to this, the "Beatific Vision"—the vision of God as he is in himself? It is only by grace that this can occur, all Christians agree. As was shown in the chapter 6 review of Protestant and Catholic thought at the time of the Reformations, as well as in the chapter 9 review of ecumenical conversation, the disagreement among Christians has been about the way in which grace operates vis-à-vis human nature, not about the fact that it does do so to save us.

The matter of the divine-human relationship, brought to fruition in God's sovereign, free initiative to persuade us in our freedom to return his love, was the subject of a major discussion in Catholic theology a couple of decades before Vatican II, as theologians of the *Nouvelle Théologie* offered various new articulations of the seeming paradox of human beings' situation of existence in the order of "nature" with a destiny (in the sense of God's intention but not predetermination) in the supernatural order, which we experience in and by grace.[6] Rahner entered the conversation and, to many minds, offered an explanation of the relationship between nature and grace that, while not the only possible one, was satisfactory. Reviewing this will shed light on the Catholic understanding of the human person, who, in every case, even if the goal is not evidently or actually realized, is called to be a saint even in the special sense of profound holiness. To understand the saint as companion, then, is simply to understand correctly the saint as human, albeit in a fulfilled state of love of God and ultimately in union with him and thereby with other human persons. The saints are our companions as other Christians are our companions, in a communion—the communion of saints—fashioned by the grace of Christ. This communion is possible and is that which it is—a group of individuals whose "destiny" depends in part upon their relationship to each other—because those within it share with all human beings the same nature and the same existential situation (that is, the same situation of existence and our experience of it). Members of the communion are on a common journey, then, of nature being led by grace, that must be made by each as related to all, in God.

Saintly Companions in Catholic Theology

Rahner began his explanation of the relationship between nature and grace[7] by noting that human beings exist in a supernatural modality; we are merely human, but made for, directed to, surrounded and permeated by, the supernatural—which is to say God, or his grace. "Grace" is a theological term whose definition can be multivalent. This is undoubtedly the case because it refers to that which is not human but of God. And God, as Rahner underscored, is the "Absolute Mystery"[8]—not in the sense of a puzzle that will be solved when we put all of the pieces together, but in the theological sense of that which is beyond our human capacity to understand completely. Even in the Beatific Vision, human beings will ever love and contemplate God, coming to deeper and deeper understanding of him, but never exhaust this process. There will always be something more to learn about God; otherwise he would not be God, the Infinite. The Absolute Mystery has no limits or boundaries, whereas we, finite, do. In Rahner's theology, grace is defined as "divine self-communication." Clearly it is not a "thing," therefore, but God's gift of God's very self— Father, Son, and Holy Spirit, the Triune God. Receiving the gift of the "self-communication of God," in Christ, by the power of the Holy Spirit, is receiving the Giver himself (although not in such a way that we become divine).[9] All human beings live with a yearning for this, under influence of an offer of it and in hope of its fulfillment in eternal life in God.

To explain more precisely, as created by God, human beings have, naturally, an "obediential potency"[10] or openness to God and his grace that might have remained only that. But God chose, in his sovereignty and freedom, to orient it to grace (although it is not grace itself). This rendered the originally mere openness now a desire for the Beatific Vision, eternal life with God, which is attainable through grace. Human beings' natural end proper to "pure nature" was subsumed by a supernatural end not due to our nature but forever a constituent part of our concrete human reality via a supernatural gift of God. Rahner called a "supernatural existential" this sublation of our obediential potency in the assignment of a new end. The supernatural existential gave us the capacity to accept grace, *as grace*—a gift. It established our freedom to respond to God, since he is the Giver of the supernatural end which is himself.[11] Now capacitation to accept grace anticipates an offer of grace, and in some of Rahner's later writings he referred to the supernatural existential as this offer. He did so without erasing the distinction between the offer of grace and the God-given ability to accept grace, but he did make the point that the offer of grace—before any response of the human person—is itself a kind of grace, in that the offer persuades its own reception: "God's self-communication as offer is also the necessary condition which makes its acceptance possible," he wrote in his *Foundations of Christian Faith: An Introduction to the Idea of Christianity*.[12] It, like the gifted capacity to receive grace, in freedom, is a perpetual element of our existence as human. Yet, again, it is not "natural," as we are, but "supernatural."[13]

The distinct moments of offer of grace and capacitation to accept grace are analogous, both to each other and with respect to God's activity. It is important to remember in reviewing such highly technical explanations as Rahner's that human categories of action are being used to describe God's ongoing salvific will for us. This is, of course, our manner of understanding revelation and ensuring that we remain faithful to it, since we do not have the mind of God. Rahner's concept of the supernatural existential affirms the proclamation of Scripture and tradition that our experience as human does not find its fulfillment in earthly, material reality (although this is not unimportant, our body being a dimension of our human existence that therefore is to be saved as part of the whole human person). Human fulfillment is found in union with God, who never ceases to try to persuade us to accept freely his offer. He will, however, allow us to refuse it; this is accomplished by "moral guilt"[14] which is incurred by exercise of our freedom against God—rejection of his grace—during the course of our earthly life. A positive response to God's offer results in a progressive conversion—sanctification of the human person—whereas a negative response does not.[15] Depending upon an individual's "existentiell decision,"[16] then, the supernatural existential can exist in us either "in the mode of 'yes'" ("deliberate and obedient acceptance") or "in the mode of 'no'" ("protest" or "rejection").[17] This decision is revisable during a lifetime, but, at death, a person's "fundamental option" toward his or her existential situation—of being human, finite, with all of the imperfection and guilt that that which is mere "nature" entails but also, in the case of a positive fundamental option, of being conscious of and accepting of the undeserved supernatural end that we are enabled to receive—is finalized and effective in the complete transformation of the human person.[18]

The supernatural existential exists in the self-bestowal of God in the Christ event (the incarnation, ministry, passion, and resurrection of Christ) through the presence and power of the Holy Spirit who was present to creation from its beginning.[19] So the effects of Christ's work are not bound by time although the work itself occurs in time. Christ "constitutes the climax of God's self-communication to the world, . . . *both* the absolute promise of God to spiritual creatures as a whole *and* the acceptance of this self-communication by the saviour." In him, a divine subject with a fully divine nature and a fully human nature, "there is an absolutely irrevocable self-communication on both sides [the divine and the human], and only then is it present in the world in a historical and communicable way."[20] In language that many Catholic theologians might use, in Christ "objective salvation" has been accomplished; all that God "must" do for our salvation (without this being understood as any conditions placed upon God) has been done and is being done. Yet "subjective salvation," our acceptance of salvation in Christ, must yet occur in each individual.[21]

To relate this explanation of our human reality in God to the discussion in the previous chapter, since the concrete reality of human beings that includes "the transcendental character of the ordination to the end" in God functions as a moral "ought" in our lives,[22] and we thereby live the supernatural existential either in the mode of acceptance or of rejection, we necessarily exercise our intentionality for greater union with God, or not. Our "intentional" response to God is itself influenced by "grace" in the very form of the offer of his self-communication manifested in our elevated intentionality.[23] To restate this, because the kind of self-bestowal of God upon human beings that is the "antecedent offer"[24] of God's self-communication exists regardless of an individual's fundamental option, human beings experience God as that which Rahner referred to as the transcendental horizon of our existence—that which is not limited by space and time. As the last chapter explained, we have an awareness of that which is—Being, God. This awareness occurs in a state of "elevation" in which the immediacy of God's presence is not associated with any object in the world, as well as reflexively and deliberately in association with particular objects in the world.[25] God's self-communication to human beings occurs in the temporal order, thus the unthematic, "original transcendental experience of God in grace"[26] is necessarily mediated through worldly categories, which is to say those of history, those involving materiality. And so we are conscious of God's presence in the things of this world, most especially in other people, since human beings are made in the image and likeness of God and have the capacity to recognize God's offer of himself and to respond to this, thereby conforming more nearly to him and disclosing him more clearly than can other creatures. This is easy to grasp through reflection upon how we come to understand the love of God— through the love of our parents, our children, and other family members, through our friends, our co-workers, and sometimes even caring and generous strangers. Experience of God, then, is mediated emphatically through love of neighbor, our "original relationship with God" which is enabled and elicited by God's grace,[27] although we also experience God, for example, through the beauty of his creation and through knowledge about his creation gained by use of our divinely-gifted intellect.

"[T]he unique and the highest act of love of neighbour," wrote Rahner, is "the love of Jesus Christ,"[28] the preeminent, unsurpassable categorial mediator of God's personal communication (i.e., *the* symbol or sacrament of God in history). Yet since *the* Mediator is known in the neighbors who have life through him and who are lenses to him especially in cases of a positive existentiell orientation[29] (which is to say a positive fundamental option for God), when we deliberately love neighbors in consciousness that they reflect and mediate God's love, we engage in a religious act of free human response to God.[30] Again as the last chapter noted, veneration of the saints is such a religious act; saints are honored for their association with God, for the fact that they disclose God in holy lives that would not be possible without his grace. Therefore, *dulia* of the saints and *latria* of God are united,[31] such that Rahner wrote of "the veneration of the saints as adoration of God"[32] (without, of course, confusing the saints with God, since, again, only God is worshipped). The neighbor who is a saint has not "simply an implicit unity" with Christ that could still be lost by adoption of a negative response to God's offer of self-communication, but one "explicit and definitively complete"[33] because it is a radically affirmative response to God, in grace, that has been ratified in death. Rahner concluded: "This means that it ['love of the saints'] has one advantage over love of neighbour in the ordinary sense: the theological and christological character of love of neighbour here comes clearly to the fore."[34] And yet we can participate in this kind of love only if we have learned to love the neighbor "who confronts us in the body here and now."[35] Therefore, love of the saints as the neighbor is mediated love of God,[36] but love of other neighbors is this love's possibility and also puts us in "an immediate relationship with God in Jesus"[37] in which we realize our "full creaturely reality."[38] Remarked Rahner: "To put it in biblical terms, only he who has encountered the Christ whom he does not yet recognise in his brother and sister can then go on to encounter him in manifest and explicit form, at latest in the judgment."[39] The saints themselves are, of course, those who have done this.

In summary, human beings respond to God, in praise, via truly religious acts, whenever they honor and love those who disclose him. Those who disclose God in his encounter with us most fully are those who themselves have loved God greatly through love of the neighbor, for these transformed individuals are symbolic of Christ in the Catholic sense of participating in that which they signify, as chapter 9 explained; they are especial "mediators" of the Mediator[40] who seeks to transform all through loving relationships issuing from and leading to him. It is in the unabating interpretation of the saints as, again, "sacraments," "icons"— symbols—revealing and re-presenting Christ, and in the unwanning practice of the Church of responding ritually to this symbolic reality, that the saints' roles as companions, models, and intercessors should be understood.[41] The belief that in the saints we see and respond to Christ himself is reflected in the Church's tradition already in the New Testament, in passages reviewed in chapter 2 such as the presentation of Stephen's ministry, trial, and martyrdom (Acts 6–7) as imitative of Christ's and Paul's entreaties to fellow Christians to imitate him as he imitated Christ (1 Cor. 4:15–16, 11:1) who is "manifested in our bodies" (2 Cor. 4:10–11). Saints are symbolic of Christ because they lived the supernatural existential in the mode of acceptance to an extraordinary degree, thereby functioning as especial lenses, in time and place, through which we see Christ who revealed our proper end.

Rahner's complex explanation of the divine-human relationship— wherein God, sovereign and free, lovingly creates and then remains present to us in and through his creation, offering for and to our freedom his very self for our unity with him (a unity that is gift as end and means)—shows that our experience of grace is inherently communal. For Christians, the communal reality is expressly ecclesial. And in the Church the saints have an important function. Following Saint Paul, Rahner observed that especially in "the great saints in whose creative example quite new possibilities of Christian life can be seen,"[42] there is a visible unity of charisms given to individuals for their sanctification and for the building up of the Church.[43] He claimed that this is of the essential "charismatic element" of the Church.[44] Saint Paul recognized many charisms—such as prophesy, preaching, teaching, and healing (1 Cor. 12)—as beneficial to the Body of Christ (of which the saints are a permanent part). But it can be asserted that it is the charism of love that "makes" a saint. The other charisms, if not accompanied by love, do not fulfill the two great commandments (Mt. 22:35–40; Mk. 12:28–34; Lk. 10:25–28) which constitute the essential Christian life that in its fullness leads to martyrdom and/or to heroic virtue. The greatest charism of love (1 Cor. 13), the "more excellent way" (1 Cor. 12:31) that is offered to all, creates, strengthens, and transforms the Church. In the saints it does so by forming them into steadfast companions, models, and intercessors—roles that exist in each member of the Church (and of humanity) in potentiality but that are present and perfected in the saints to our benefit. In the saints we are shown dramatically the relationship, in the grace of Christ, in love, between the individual and the community. Since these sanctified individuals are symbolic of the presence of Christ, prisms of his love, our recognition of their roles—through our acts of veneration—can be acts of love. The roles of the saints are inextricably related and equally significant in the life of the Church because they result from the concurrence of individual and ecclesial graces to which we are drawn to respond and that is efficacious for all. But, as was claimed at the outset of this chapter and as has now been explained, the role of companion is foundational for the roles of model and intercessor, because it is derived directly from human beings' given shared nature and existential situation, whereas the other roles result from a willing positive acceptance of this reality.[45]

Special Issues in Saintly Companionship

Despite the warnings at the beginning of this chapter about ways in which Christians should not understand the saints as companions, those who know even a little about the history of the saints will remember that during their lifetime some saints had visions of or heard voices of those dead and in Heaven. Joan of Arc (1412–1431), for example, heard the voices of Saints Catherine, Margaret, and Michael, among others, informing her of her calling by God to save France from England's occupation. Bernadette Soubirous (d. 1879) saw Mary as the "Immaculate Conception" at Lourdes, France, in one of the reported Marian apparitions that chapter 7 noted has been accepted as authentic by the Catholic Church. Such events are rarely recorded, though; even more rarely are they validated by the Church. Even when they are, Catholics are not bound to believe in them, although Catholics who do not give them credence are not to be scornful of those who do or to make a public spectacle of their own position. Falling into the category of private revelations, the truth of such events is in part suggested by the degree to which they build community and transform individuals. Private revelations never add anything to the revelation of Christ, whom Christians recognize as the full, definitive revelation of God—his Word. These revelations may, however, aid some individuals in seeing something in the revelation of Christ that they had not previously noticed or fully grasped, pulling them into a deeper understanding of Christ's revelation.[46] Private revelations and other miraculous events that are studied but not approved by the Church are deemed either "not contrary to the faith" (a benign judgment) or "not worthy of belief" (a direction to Catholics to cease any attention to them). These designations were developed by Pope Benedict XIV in the eighteenth century in his *On the Beatification of Servants of God and the Canonization of Saints* mentioned in chapter 5. The Church is on the side of caution in such affairs. It does not encourage expectation that one might receive such unusually dramatic encounters; at the same time one must be open to any way that God chooses to manifest his presence.

Another controversial matter among Christians that attends the doctrine of the companionship of the saints among all human beings is, as mentioned in chapter 6, the doctrine of Purgatory validated at the Council of Trent. Using language and concepts of contemporary Catholic theology introduced in recent chapters, this doctrine can be explained as simple attestation that, in death if not in earthly life, a positive existentiell orientation will mean complete transformation of the human person. Purgatory offers no possibility of a reversal of one's earthly disposition toward God; a negative response to God's offer of self-communication will not net transformation after death, as it does not net transformation during life, and therefore it can never end in the Beatific Vision. Judgment occurs at the moment of death as a finalization of one's fundamental option. The fundamental option should not be viewed as a scorecard of individual right and wrong thoughts and actions during life (although it is reflected in and is confirmed or revised by our thoughts and actions) but as an overall, pervasive attitude for or against God and the human situation that exists only in relationship to him. So why might it be that one who has said "yes" to God during life is not fully sanctified at death? As will be discussed in chapter 14 in the context of the subject of indulgences, there could be unrepented venial sins or repented mortal sins at the end of one's earthly existence; a choice for God does not mean that one will never err, but it does mean that one will accept willingly, and even desire, the process of "punishment" or purification, in addition to forgiveness, that must be endured to put one back in right relationship with God and others. If this does not occur in life, it must occur in death. Although literature and art, especially of the medieval period, have offered elaborate descriptions of Purgatory, such conceptions need not be entertained by Catholics today. That which Dante (Alighieri) envisioned and described in his *Divine Comedy* may in reality be only a moment at death that incurs no such torment—or not. Current Catholic instruction on this and other matters of the afterlife will serve as final reflection for this chapter.

Conclusion

What eternal life will mean for us, concretely, is as much the object of faith as ever, although perhaps less the subject of speculation given contemporary admission of our inability to grasp that which has not been revealed to us or can be only marginally comprehended by our finite, limited minds. We are not bidden to accept every past, sometimes fanciful conception of life after death, such as the popular elaborations of medieval Catholics. Equally, Christians are right to reject elaborations of our own time, some of which have arisen, surprisingly, from secular sources, as mentioned early in this chapter. As the Sacred Congregation for the Doctrine of the Faith submitted in its 1979 document, *The Reality of Life After Death*,

> Neither Scripture nor theology provides sufficient light for a proper picture of life after death. Christians must firmly hold the two following essential points: on the one hand they must believe in the fundamental continuity, thanks to the power of the Holy Spirit, between our present life in Christ and the future life (charity is the law of the Kingdom of God and our charity on earth will be the measure of our sharing God's glory in heaven); on the other hand they must be clearly aware of the radical break between the present life and the future one, due to the fact that the economy of faith will be replaced by the economy of fullness of life: we shall be with Christ and 'we shall see God' (cf. 1 John 3:2), and it is in these promises and marvelous mysteries that our hope essentially consists. Our imagination may be incapable of reaching these heights, but our heart does so instinctively and completely.[47]

The Congregation cautioned that "[w]hen dealing with man's situation after death, one must especially beware of arbitrary imaginative representations: excess of this kind is a major cause of the difficulties that Christian faith often encounters."[48] It stressed the privilege of Scripture in this matter: "Respect must however be given to the images employed in the Scriptures. Their profound meaning must be discerned, while avoiding the risk of overattenuating them, since this often empties of substance the realities designated by the images."[49] So in recognizing the propriety of a level of apophaticism in regard to the details of the promise of eternal life, at the same time the Congregation insisted upon the minimum affirmations that must be made by believers who call themselves Christian. It outlined key points that are held by the Catholic Church in accordance with Scripture and tradition. The Church professes the resurrection of the dead, which is a resurrection of "the whole person."[50] It believes "that a spiritual element survives and subsists after death, an element endowed with consciousness and will, so that the 'human self' subsists." It validates the legitimacy of the term "soul" to describe this spiritual element, despite its occasional ambiguity in the Bible.[51] It insists that its prayers, funeral rites, and religious acts offered for the dead be upheld in "every way of thinking or speaking."[52] Following Scripture, the Church awaits "'the glorious manifestation of our Lord, Jesus Christ' (*Dei Verbum*, I, 4), believing it to be distinct and deferred with respect to the situation of people immediately after death."[53] It upholds the meaning of the doctrine of the assumption of Mary as "the fact that the bodily glorification of the Virgin is an anticipation of the glorification that is the destiny of all the other elect."[54] And it affirms that the possibilities for life after death are not predetermined.

> In fidelity to the New Testament and Tradition, the Church believes in the happiness of the just who will one day be with Christ. She believes that there will be eternal punishment for the sinner, who will be deprived of the sight of God, and that this punishment will have a repercussion on the whole being of the sinner. She believes in the possibility of a purification for the elect before they see God, a purification altogether different from the punishment of the damned. This is what the Church means when speaking of Hell and Purgatory.[55]

With this guidance in the conceptualization of the afterlife that is now enjoyed by those in the heavenly church, chapters 11 and 12 will consider the saints' roles of model and of intercessor, played in death as in life.

Terms for Study

Beatific Vision	Mediator, The, vs. mediators
Catechism	Passion, The
Charism	Religious Imagination
"Fundamental Option"	Resurrection, The
Human Nature	Soul
Living Icons	"Supernatural Existential"

Suggested Readings

Catechism of the Catholic Church: With Modifications from the 'Editio Typica.' Translated by the United States Catholic Conference. New York: Doubleday, 1997. Original edition, [*Catechismus Ecclesiae Catholicae*], Cittá del Vaticano: Libreria Editrice Vaticana, 1994.

The student of Catholic saints would benefit from reviewing, at the least, paragraphs of the *Catechism* dealing directly with doctrine on the saints, veneration of saints and images, and intercessory prayer: 686, 688, 828, 946–959, 1717, 2012–2015, 2028–2030, 2129, 2131–2132, 2156, 2634–2636, 2647, 2673–2679, 2682–2684, and 2692.

A World of Grace: An Introduction to the Themes and Foundations of Karl Rahner's Theology. Edited by Leo J. O'Donovan. Washington, D.C.: Georgetown University Press, 1995.

In twelve essays of different theologians on topics including theological anthropology, grace, Christology, ecclesiology, Christian morality, and more, this volume provides a broad treatment of Karl Rahner's influential thought.

Eleven

THE SAINTS AS MODELS:
A CONTEMPORARY UNDERSTANDING

"When reading the accounts of the patriotic deeds of French heroines, especially the *Venerable* JOAN OF ARC, I had a great desire to imitate them; and it seemed I felt within me the same burning zeal with which they were animated, the same heavenly inspiration," wrote Thérèse of Lisieux, now a canonized saint and Church Doctor, in her autobiography published after her death under the title *Story of a Soul*.[1] Theologically, the inspiration is known as grace that moved Thérèse and those whose lives she admired. As has been theme in previous chapters, grace can be powerfully evident in the lives of those who have radically accepted God. Indeed, in this sense we see Christ in the saints; the wonder of saintly lives is that they are possible through divine power manifest in them with their graced positive response to God in Christ. Grace works with nature to perfect it, as has been said of the Catholic understanding, and perfection draws others by the persuasion of grace. This follows from the basic principle articulated at the Second Council of Nicaea and ratified at other councils reviewed in previous chapters: religious images, including living icons, can mediate the grace of Christ, pulling our emotions and consciousness to God who is their ultimate source and encouraging our veneration of them to enhance our worship of God.

Centuries before the controversy over iconoclasm, in an exploration of proper scriptural interpretation, Saint Augustine wrote that "whatever else appeals to the mind as being lovable should be directed into that channel into which the whole current of love flows. Whoever, therefore, justly loves his neighbor should so act toward him that he also loves God with his whole heart, with his whole soul, and with his whole mind. Thus, loving his neighbor as himself, he refers the love of both to that love of God which suffers no stream to be led away from it by which it might be diminished."[2] Augustine argued that we are to use rather than enjoy all that "is to be loved for the sake of something else"; only the "eternal and immutable" is to be enjoyed,[3] that is, "the Father, the Son, and the Holy Spirit, a single Trinity."[4] It would be an "abuse"[5] not to acknowledge that human beings are not ends in ourselves but, made in the image and likeness of God (Gen. 1:26–27), reflective of and directed

153

to God who is our source and goal.[6] This is another vantage point from which to consider the neighbors who are saints because they have made their commitment to God completely, who by their canonization have been established as explicit religious symbols, who elicit our love of them because they are especially disclosive of the love for us of God who made and has sanctified them. When we love the saints for our love of God, we can see the way to loving other human beings, and ourselves, for God. For, as explained in the last chapter, the roles of the saints that can assist in pulling us to God our destiny exist in potentiality in all human beings. Through grace, any and all of us might become living icons, companions who are models and intercessors for others.

To the benefit of the living is veneration of the saints. Canonizations occur for those in the pilgrim church. Now at rest in God, a definitive state that cannot be lost since death is the living out of one's "fundamental option" made in the earthly life ended and not to be revised, the designation of "saint" does not profit those in the heavenly church. Saints already enjoy the Beatific Vision, the final goal of human beings in which all other good things that come to us are summed up. Using our religious imagination, we can surmise that, in their completed transformation, the saints, seeing God as he is, want that which he wants—the salvation of all—and that they are or would be pleased to be canonized if that will inspire earthly members of the communion of saints. But we can equally assume that they would be as happy to see someone else canonized if another would be more inspiring to those still on the journey to God. Since the Catholic Church does not claim or aim to canonize all who may be in Heaven, and Catholics hope that there are more in Heaven than have been canonized, the concern must be to canonize only those who are truly saints and who will edify earthly pilgrims. This is a critical point in understanding veneration of saints. The saints are honored for their relationship with Christ, but our impetus for honoring them arises from a sense of the importance, in Christ, of their "sainted" status for other human beings. Veneration of saints occurs in the Church's acknowledgement and celebration of the orientation to God of all human beings and God's redemptive, sanctifying work to bring this to fruition in us as in the saints. This will be explored in this chapter, which considers the saints in their role of model.

Lumen Gentium on Saints as Models

"[T]he outstanding practice of the christian virtues and the wonderful graces of God" have "recommended to the pious devotion and imitation of the faithful" those "closely united with us in Christ," *Lumen Gentium* confirms of the ancient tradition of the Church. Among these are "the apostles and Christ's martyrs," "the Blessed Mary Virgin and the holy angels," and those who elected "to imitate more closely the virginity and poverty of Christ."[7] In this document, then, the saints are defined not only in relation to God in Christ, but in relation to their fellow human beings, including and particularly those in the pilgrim church—the "wayfarers" on Earth.[8] Our companions in the community of the living and dead faithful, they compel us with their exceptional holiness manifested during their lifetime and being lived out in their "afterlife." The symbolic or sacramental "power" of the saints as models attracting us to God in disparate historical contexts—theirs past and ours present—is conveyed clearly in *Lumen Gentium*, as [summarized in chapter 7: "In the lives of those companions of ours in the human condition who are more perfectly transformed into the image of Christ (see 2 Cor 3:18) God shows, vividly, to humanity his presence and his face. He speaks to us in them and offers us a sign of his kingdom, to which we are powerfully attracted, so great a cloud of witnesses are we given (see Heb. 12:1) and such an affirmation of the truth of the Gospel."[9]]

God created history; his manner of redeeming us was to enter history, to become human in the person of the Son, while remaining divine. He redeemed us from within, through love, and, hence, as described of Christ in the second century by Church Father Saint Irenaeus, bishop of Lyons, "not by violence . . . , for that is the proper way for a God who persuades and does not compel . . . [H]e pours out the Spirit of the Father to unite God and humanity and bring them into communion, bringing God down to human beings through the Spirit and, conversely, bringing humanity up to God by his own incarnation."[10] Products of grace working upon nature, the saints can serve as conduits of God's activity in history just as any human persons open to the grace of God can mediate, in Christ, his ongoing presence to and persuasive influence upon us. A commonplace example suffices to give the simplest of evidence both of God's redemptive presence in creation and the sacramental status of "God-willing" human beings who in effect present invitations to us to accept the communion that God offers: one's difficult day can be converted from an experience of alienation to an experience of inclusion when an attentive person notices that something is wrong and gives a knowing, encouraging smile and/or makes a caring inquiry. Theologically, it can only be that that person chose to offer charitable gestures because he or she was open to the grace of Christ and in that openness he or she noticed that which Christ always notices—one's need for help. Christ reaches us through others' acceptance of his grace, as well as through other aspects of his creation. When we recognize Christ in the actions of others, we affirm his work in them and we are inspired to allow him to work similarly through us.

We tell the stories of the saints precisely to remember and to be thankful for their holiness through Christ that inspires us, as was stated in the concluding words offered in chapter 1 of the early hagiographical document *The Martyrdom of Perpetua*. We are not drawn to that which has been accomplished in saintly figures by nature but, as explained in previous chapters, by grace that transforms nature with our cooperation. It is possible to imagine a situation in which human persons could be models for each other on the level of nature alone—that which theologians refer to as "pure nature," which as shown for the Catholic theology of Rahner is a theoretical state in which human beings were created with an openness for God but not with the call to an end in him. Yet since in reality the human being, and the human community, is not directed to a merely natural end but to a supernatural one (in God), focus only upon the "natural" example that human persons might be for others would be a failure to recognize God's offer of self-communication, to use Rahner's language. As lenses through which we see Christ in different contexts, Rahner regarded the saints as *"creative* models of the holiness which happens to be right for, and is the task of, their particular age."[11]

The "witnesses" who are the saints encompass a host of life states, historical and geographical contexts, and personalities and cultures. One can look at the array of saints of the Church and find "proof" of Christ's redemptive presence in all times and places, through the diversity of that which he has created. Again as Rahner wrote, the saints "create a new style; they prove that a certain form of life and activity is a really genuine possibility; they show experimentally that one can be a Christian even in 'this' way; they make such a type of person believable as a Christian type."[12] He explained that this is the unique function of the saints, who are of "the very essence of the Church" and "of vital importance for her constitution," for the Church "must represent in a historically tangible manner the victory of God's grace"[13] in order for Christ's work to be completed in the fullness of the Kingdom that he preached. Christ's saints "'. . . give example to other Christians and so promote the increase of his Mystical Body'."[14] For "the Church has a genuine history, a unique history of salvation and hence also of holiness. Even though the 'essence' of Christian holiness remains always the same, it does not simply always 'happen' in the 'same way' in each Saint." Hence, Rahner wrote of "a history of holiness, i.e. the always unique, unrepeatable history of the appropriation of God's grace and of the partaking of God's holiness. . . ."[15]

In the words of *Lumen Gentium,* the saints are models because through these "who have faithfully followed Christ we are inspired anew to seek the city which is to come (see Heb 13:14 and 11:10)" and "to arrive at perfect union with Christ, which is holiness."[16] Now that the saints are with Christ, the memory of their historical existence—their holy earthly lives—is not their only value to us, though, as must be remembered if we are not to diminish them. *Lumen Gentium* states: "It is not only by reason of their example that we cherish the memory of those in heaven; we seek, rather, that by the practice of fraternal and sororal charity the union of the whole church in the Spirit may be strengthened (see Eph 4:1–6)."[17] As has been stated, their other roles of companion and intercessor are intrinsically, inseparably related to that of model. While it may be the case that in a given time and place, one or another of the saintly roles is more the focus of the faithful's attention because it appeals especially to a particular people, in fact the three roles are always operative, for the reason that the ongoing relationship between God and human beings establishes their possibility in every human person and effects their realization in the saints. This will be further underscored later in this chapter.

Saintly Models in Catholic Theology

The biblical material in chapter 2 proclaimed Christ as *the* model, but it also attested to the exemplars that are Christ's disciples in imitation of him and through his grace. Transformation can come of imitation of Christ. When the saints are understood in their function in the Catholic sense of symbol or sacrament, whereby they become transparent to Christ in that we see him vividly in them due to their radical openness to him through which he works, eliminated are theologically incorrect ideas and habits cited in chapter 10 such as viewing the saints as dead companions to be contacted by mediums, thinking of the saints only as inspirational ideals and thereby ignoring the mediated grace of Christ present in them, and disregarding the saints as special intercessors despite their sanctified image and likeness of God. The Catholic Church is making an ontological statement in veneration of saints: Christ truly is present to each and every one of us, regardless of time and space. We are directed to him as our goal, welcomed into a communion of acceptance of this supernatural reality. The saints are models because they are exemplary, sanctified, true and lasting companions in that communion. Modeling the Christian life in various contexts, they orient our thoughts and deeds to Christ who is their source and ours, rendering us more pliable to God's work in our lives. It is significant that supposed saints who lack verifiable historical reality, including some who in the history of the Church have drawn fervent pious attention, were expunged from the liturgical calendar after Vatican II. For invented characters, even though they may be inspiring and mediate grace to us (in that they can move us intellectually and emotionally), cannot demonstrate the actual presence of God to history (except in the sense that authors created them, possibly as a result of their own experiences of or as graced individuals). In contrast, in the lives of the saints Christ's presence in the Holy Spirit is tangible, demonstrating that holy lives are possible by grace and that graced lives promote the progress of the Church and the world toward the Eschaton.

The communal mechanism of the saints' lives—which, even when not emphasized everywhere in the Church never ceases to be apparent in the liturgy, in the Eucharistic celebration when the earthly Church adopts the proper posture of human beings that is full praise of God, joining with those in Heaven who are in this posture perpetually—is the point of canonization. The divine-human relationship, which entails relationship among human persons, issues in the ecclesial reality that recognizes the concrete connection between the living and the dead in the communion of saints. The distinctive "churchly" dimension of saintly lives cannot be described but Christologically (i.e., in terms of the work of Christ), even though it is the work of the Holy Spirit that forms and sustains the Church, because the saints are those in whom human possibility has been brought to fruition in nearness to Christ, the Mediator between God and humanity, and with whom our communion with Christ is fully actualized. Honoring these lives of imitation of Christ is recognition of grace perfecting human beings through the instrumentality of others, and this builds up the Church—again, the very function of canonized saints. The grace evident in the saints is efficacious for all who recognize it; this is an essential element of the sacramental dimension of the Church itself, whose members are to realize in the world the love of Christ.

Special Issues in Saintly Modeling

There was a time when the saints were among the first to come to mind when Catholics sought models for their lives. Today there is often the claim that the contemporary person is not inclined to seek models. Yet there would seem to be no shortage of interest in and emulation of the famous, fueled by media images and the conditioning of mass culture. And the laudable tendency to try to follow in the footsteps of admirable family members and friends still is present. Certainly it is good to follow examples wherever they are good, but do the models with us in the present fulfill the same role as those who have completed their lives— those whose stories have their end? True it is that at times there are people among us who are viewed as living saints, but, even in these cases, after death, in the Catholic Church, examinations into their lives and confirmations of miracles take place to ensure that our veneration is validly placed. Additionally, there is undeniable fittingness to veneration of the dead rather than the living: this safeguards the humility of the living. And the saints are unique in that they are not examples for one area of life to which we happen to be attuned by personal interests or relationships; they are examples for a purity of life in the overall that should be the goal of all. Many religious traditions hold up those who exemplify noble ways to live. In the Christian tradition, those held up have tended to represent certain patterns of life. In this chapter some of the most prominent of these will be reviewed, with attention given to specifically contemporary concerns. After this survey, considered will be demographic matters of the day that suggest new categories of saints or that may eventually influence the number of saints in the usual categories.

Saintly Types

When one biographer of Saint Thérèse of Lisieux, Ida Friederike Görres, wrote of the period of Thérèse's life in which she first found herself captivated by the saints, she noted that the young girl who would become a Carmelite nun at the age of fifteen was like other pious Catholics of her milieu in viewing the saints as "types" or "abstractions," "the embodiment of innumerable features of historical saints" whom others were to imitate in order to become yet other instances of a certain "standard of perfection."[18] This is in contrast to the way of understanding saints today—as unique instances of the grace of Christ operating in and through particular individuals with distinct personalities in specific periods and cultures. The goal is not for any other to become another Saint Thérèse but for each individual to become a special icon of Christ's grace triumphant. The canon of saints hints of a picture in progress depicting Christ's work throughout history. The saints show what a life of Christ looks like in a specific historical moment and state of life and such. Given this uniqueness of each saint, and in consciousness of the fact that a given saint could be regarded under the rubric of more than one of even the traditional "types," in a sense there are as many classifications of saints as there are saints and therefore labeling might seem counter-productive. And yet the human mind organizes to apprehend and to comprehend, so even today we tend to categorize saints. But they are a rich diversity of personages within any category, and we know that any given saint, whether old or new, might be viewed in multiple ways.

The earliest chapters of this study showed that the earliest saints were the martyrs and the confessors of the young, persecuted Church. Chapter 4 outlined types of saints prominent in the Middle Ages: ascetics, including virgins and widows; members of monastic communities and clerics; Church Fathers, popes, and scholars; mystics; rulers and conquerors; patrons; and miracle workers. Because so many saints are from the long past, these categories remain standard for viewing saints today, although some of the saints within these categories could also be viewed as other now common types such as missionaries, founders of charitable institutions, and healers. So here the classical categories will be presented once more, with conceptual modifications to accommodate current circumstances and attitudes.

Martyrs

Christian martyrs and confessors still are made. In recent centuries, persecutions have resulted in Christian martyrs in China,[19] Korea,[20] Uganda,[21] Vietnam,[22] Mexico,[23] and elsewhere. Those imprisoned and tortured for the faith today are analogous to the confessors and martyrs of the early Church, although in contemporary cases there is sometimes ambiguity that did not exist in pre-Constantine instances. Then, as *Acta* show, those who suffered atrocities and sometimes by these means died were targeted specifically for their adherence to Christian faith despite threat of punishment that might be fatal. Contemporary martyrdoms are not always as clearly defined. Not only contempt for the faith but political, social, and even economic motives might impel the torturers and murderers, even while religious motives lead the persecuted to the stances that make them targets. Figures of South America in recent centuries provide examples. Archbishop of San Salvador Oscar Romero was assassinated in 1980 while celebrating the Eucharist, after his repeated criticism of a corrupt government responsible for gross violations of human rights of the poor.[24] Four missionaries also were deliberately killed in 1980 in El Salvador: Maryknoll sisters Maura Clarke and Ita Ford, Ursuline sister Dorothy Kazel, and Jean Donovan.[25] When the Church has canonized individuals in similar circumstances, it has had to determine that the essential measure of a Christian martyr is present—that one died for faith in Christ. As noted in chapter 8 to have been reiterated recently by the current pope of the ancient definition of Christian martyrdom, a killer's hate for that faith (if only "indirect") also must be a factor. Finding this, sometimes new kinds of Christian martyrs have been asserted. In his book reviewing the history and method of canonizations in the Catholic Church, Woodward noted that, at the canonization Mass for Maximilian Kolbe (1894–1941), Fransiscan missionary and founder of the "Militia of Mary Immaculate" promoting devotion to Mary,[26] Pope John Paul II declared the new saint a "martyr."[27] Fr. Kolbe volunteered to

take the place, in Auschwitz, of a married man with children, when the
Gestapo chose ten prisoners to kill as retaliation for the escape of one. He
was tortured before being fatally injected with carbolic acid.[28] As
Woodward assessed this move, ". . . [S]ome saint-makers insist, John Paul
II sanctioned the concept of the martyr for charity as a new category of
saint—and with it the possibility of bestowing the title of martyr on a
wider range of candidates."[29] Saint Maximilian had died for a Christian
virtue. So, too, Woodward noted, had Maria Goretti (1890–1902), the
now popular saint who died by multiple stabbings while fighting off a
neighbor's rape attempt when she was only eleven years of age.[30] She was
to be venerated as "martyr of chastity," declared Pope Pius XII at her
beatification.[31] Despite any novelty of such canonizations with respect to
the sorts of martyrdom they present, the notion of true Christian
martyrdom by defense to death of "any human good in so far as it is
referred to God" appears in Saint Thomas's nearly eight-hundred-year-
old *Summa Theologiae*, and he attributed it to Saint Jerome's even eight
centuries earlier commentary and "a gloss." Wrote Thomas: ". . . [A]ll
virtuous deeds, inasmuch as they are referred to God, are professions of
the faith whereby we come to know that God requires these works of us,
and rewards us for them: and in this way they can be the cause of
martyrdom."[32]

Ascetics

While in extreme forms ascetics are rare today, from a Catholic
perspective shared by some other Christians, ascetic practices are an
essential component of imitation of Christ who sacrificed his very life.
From a broad perspective on asceticism, therefore, it is not too bold to
say that from the ascetic tradition has sprung every saint. Some
Christians feel called to observe ascetic practices more rigorously than
others, though. Members of religious orders generally live the more
traditional ascetic call; among these especially observant of it are those
belonging to "cloistered orders"—communities of men and women,
separately, who commit to living life within monastery and convent
walls, shut off from the larger world in lives of prayer and reflection.
The severe physical mortifications of past centuries are discouraged; in
fact, the psychological framework of our culture tends to view such
extreme activities as questionable in terms of their authentic religious
value. And, particularly since Vatican II, there has been encouragement
to the faithful to concentrate on doing the positive rather than or in
addition to the negative (i.e., contributing something versus sacrificing
something) in living the Christian calling. Still, there are subtle ways in

which many Christians practice asceticism without naming it as such. Christians discipline themselves to observe the liturgical life of the Church and to engage in private prayer and reflection. They fast during prescribed times of the liturgical year and perhaps at other times, too, as well as "offer up" time, attention, services, and money for the good of others. They commit to living by a moral code that precludes activities that can be accepted as normal by the larger culture, refusing to participate knowingly in activities that subjugate others solely for personal benefit and observing traditional ascetic calls such as chastity (i.e., using sexuality in accordance with state of life). They accept in faith suffering that befalls them, sometimes consciously offering it for the alleviation of the suffering of others. Others more deliberately involved in ascetic practices engage in private devotions—novenas, Eucharistic adoration, Liturgy of the Hours, etc.

Monastics and Clerics

Monasticism, representative of the principle ascetic tradition, is one of the distinctive characteristics of Catholicism, although it exists in other Christian traditions, too, namely among the Orthodox and the Anglican/Episcopalian unions. Since Vatican II, numbers in monasteries have dwindled, but founders of religious orders have been some of the most frequently canonized in this time period, bringing new attention, and with this sometimes novices, to little-known orders. Traditionally monastics and clerics have comprised the greatest numbers of the canonized, inspiring the faithful with their lives of sacrifice. For increase in vocations to religious orders, as well as increase in vocations to the priesthood, the Church frequently prays. Without clerics, the central liturgical element of Catholicism could not be as it is, a fact that poses the principal difficulty of the current "priest shortage." This prominence of the priest, along with the worldly favors that he as well as those in religious orders give up, brings him quickly to the mind of the faithful when they consider lives of sanctity. As chapter 8 showed, such visibility is important in the identification of possible saints; a popular reputation for holiness is impetus for the opening of a cause.

Church Fathers, Popes, and Scholars

According to custom, the age of Church Fathers is considered to have ended in the eighth century, and the list of nearly fifty Eastern or Greek Fathers (i.e., those whose writings were in Greek) and nearly forty Western or Latin Fathers (i.e., those whose writings were in Latin), although informal, has been "set" since approximately that time. Most of the Fathers are considered saints, not only by Catholics but also by the Orthodox, although they were added to the canon of saints before there was an official process for canonization. Their reputation for holiness, along with their admirable defense of the faith, recommended them. The list of popes, however, obviously is extended with time. So, too, though, has the list of popes canonized grown with time's passage. Interestingly, by popular acclaim and custom, almost every individual who served as pope was canonized until the tenth century when the first canonization *by* a pope occurred. Since then only a dozen popes have been declared saints, including only one of late history—Pius X (1835–1914). However, other recent popes—Pius IX (1792–1878) and John XXIII (1881–1963)—were beatified by Pope John Paul II, in 2000.[33] And the cause of John Paul II (1920–2005) himself was underway shortly after his death, the customary five-year waiting period waived by Pope Benedict XVI;[34] only an intercessory miracle is required for this blessed to become a saint. Other popes have garnered the popular interest that could lead to beatification and/or canonization. Fifty years after the death of Pope Pius XII (1876–1958), there is still strong sentiment in memory of his faith, at the same time that controversy reigns due to disagreements about the meaning of his low public profile on behalf of the Vatican during the Holocaust.[35] Not only the number of popes but the number of people in total being canonized decreased dramatically once a formal process was put in place. Remedying this was, as previously discussed, one of the primary reasons for the 1983 modification of the process. Since then, popes of late history still in ready memory would be, as is in fact the case, the most likely among the popes to be promoted, without diminishment of the observed holiness of life of earlier popes, some who served the Church during tumultuous times or in a rapidly-changing and challenging world.

As for scholars, since the Scholastics few have been declared saints. Accounting for this might be the special problems of examining their large volume of writings and the higher risk that such thinkers will, in their exploratory work, be viewed as heterodox at least for a time. Suggested by Woodward is also a lack of emotional pull that the life of a scholar has for the rest of the faithful.[36] Among those who have been canonized are Edith Stein (1891-1942), the philosopher and Carmelite known as Teresa Benedicta of the Cross, killed among the six million Jews murdered by Hitler's Third Reich, she in the gas chambers of Auschwitz, targeted because she was a Jewish convert to Catholicism and the Nazis aimed to punish Catholics in retaliation for a letter of Roman Catholic bishops in Holland protesting treatment of the Jews.

Saint Edith studied with the notable philosopher Edmund Husserl. Her own philosophical writings, influenced by the work of Saint Thomas Aquinas, came to be widely published. Interestingly, she translated personal writings of John Henry Cardinal Newman,[37] another scholar, recently beatified by Pope Benedict XVI.[38] A relatively new phenomenon, particularly where philosophy, theology, and related disciplines are concerned, unlike in the age of Scholasticism and for centuries afterwards, many scholars today are lay persons, who are not represented as prominently as clerics and monastics in the canon of saints.

Mystics

Most of the great mystics of the Church are medieval, the time of "the growth and flowering of mysticism," to borrow description from two titles of works by Bernard McGinn, a contemporary scholar authoring a five-volume study of the history of Christian mysticism.[39] Although many of these figures are among the most famous of Christian saints, it is the rare Padre Pio (1887–1968)—the Capuchin friar known for his sense of the supernatural in his ministry of counseling the faithful who sought him out from many corners of the world—who enters the process today with a "classical" mystical reputation. In part this may be because of the emphasis now on cultivation of the sense of sacramentality that results in a "mysticism of everyday life" or a "mysticism of ordinary life," in the words and theology of Rahner,[40] that can and should be had by all. We can become more and more consciously attentive to the universal human, concrete reality of being offered the self-communication of God, regardless of whether or not we are given by grace the soul's unusual heightened experience of God described by the great mystics. From a Catholic point of view, mysticism in this special sense could not be divorced from experience of the supernatural dimension of human life generally; thinking otherwise we would be, rather than Christian, as Gnostics,[41] believing that some have a secret source of knowledge of God, or, as Pantheists,[42] believing that the world is identified with God. These are heresies. Mysticism of any form or degree is a gift to individuals—and it can as well be a gift to the Church, as apparent in the cases of saints who are mystics, for, as explained in chapter 4, the true test of authenticity of mystical experience is growth in charity, which, as explained in chapter 10, builds up the ecclesial community. No one can manufacture or demand of God a mystical event. While ascetical activity can help prepare any individual for mystical consciousness, in Christianity, unlike in some other religions, mystical experience is understood to come only from divine benevolence, as life in God at all is divine gift.

Rulers, Patrons, and Miracle Workers

The categories of rulers and conquerors, patrons, and miracle workers, understood in the way of the past, are not today principal paradigms for viewing saints canonized in the present or for considering those of the past, with a few exceptions. "Rulers" in the Church such as bishops (who are always clerics but also "overseers"), more appropriately designated also as "servants," form a large group of saints. As for saints as patrons, while it is true that there are patron saints for virtually any cause that could be imagined, the multiplicity of social systems that exists today—most far different from those of the Roman Empire and of medieval Europe in which Western Christianity developed—has helped us to see clearly how these earlier systems' influence produced the wrong popular perception of the patron role of saints (i.e., of saints as independent entities capable of fulfilling our needs on their own). This means that saints are not now viewed essentially as miracle workers, either, nor should they be so viewed. Miracles are in the Catholic Church deemed a requirement for divine confirmation of human judgments that particular lives were saintly, as noted in chapter 8, but regarding saints as dispensers of miracles is dangerous theologically, usurping in our consciousness that which is only the province of God. As will be underscored in the next chapter, only God works miracles, even if through saints. Only God answers prayers. Nevertheless, it is appropriate not to be wholly dismissive of the impulse of earlier Christians that led to their occasionally dominant view of saints as patrons and miracle workers since, again, the power of God is present to history, at work in all who accept him, productive even of miracles where he so chooses. If this activity of God is recognized especially in the cases of saints, this is fitting. But favoring exclusively these categories for viewing and honoring the saints is disallowed for problems past.

Saintly Demographics

Focus upon types or categories of saints leads to consideration of demographics. Although God, not the Church, produces saints, certainly in our current consciousness of the influence of history and culture upon our impressions, it is not impossible to think that, in our recognition of saints, in the Church's history the Catholic faithful have exhibited certain tendencies, even if unconsciously. Noted today, for example, is the preponderance of male saints; comparatively few saints and blesseds are women (although some of these are among the most widely known), and many of these are from the early Church. Among saints of the Middle Ages who remain popular today are individuals who left a life of privilege to embrace poverty, if not also the other evangelical counsels, to pursue spiritual perfection and/or to serve those less fortunate. Saint Francis of Assisi is famous of these, rejecting the affluent life of his parents, successful cloth merchants, to serve the growing urban population of his town— especially the poor and marginalized, including lepers. Compelling then and in more modern times are those who used their power and influence to further the aims, often missionary, of the Church. Saint Katharine Drexel (1858–1955), from a wealthy family of Philadelphia, donated her fortune and her life to the Sisters of the Blessed Sacrament for Indians and Colored People, an order that she founded to educate and otherwise serve these populations through the establishment of schools.[43] Geographically, most saints emerge from traditionally Catholic, developed, and older, countries.

Since the initial impetus for a cause still comes from the local community, such trends of past and present are no wonder. Although they undoubtedly have multiple causes, God's will not excluded, from the standpoint of human perception one principal one may be visibility, as mentioned earlier in this chapter with regard to clerics whose role puts more men than women in the large public pastoral position that, for good reason when performed well, keeps them in mind even long after their death. Geographical areas with long Catholic histories have ready-made contexts for interpreting the lives of those remembered fondly as those of exceptional holiness, and the faithful in these locations are more likely to engage in the private activities of veneration that issue in a cause. And certainly these usually developed parts of the world, schooled in saint-making and saint-venerating, are more likely to have in place the machinery, as it were, to advance a would-be saint to and through the process—which is not the case in much of the "Third World." From contexts where there have been few Catholic saints in the past, though, new styles of saints may emerge consistent with the Church's vision of Christian discipleship and evangelization. The work of Blessed Mother Teresa (1910–1997) in India represents a type of Christian outreach to all, regardless of creed, unlike missionary endeavors of the past that explicitly sought conversions to Christianity. In North America, Blessed Kateri Tekakwitha (1656–1680), a Native American convert to Catholic Christianity who retained her cultural heritage, represents the Church's consciousness that the revelation of Christ comes to us in time and place, received by us through culture and even personality. If the process of Catholic Worker Movement founder Dorothy Day (1897–1980) results in canonization, she will represent the Church's social justice initiative that has become a prevalent focus in the past century. This focus also will be represented by any who might be found to have been saints in South America, especially in the 1970s and 1980s when liberation theology was young, standing for the common people against corrupt social and governmental systems. In Asia, aside from martyrs for the faith, in time memory of holy lives led during, say, the underground church of China may produce candidates for sainthood. The growing African church, whose reach is far in its supply of clerics to areas of the world affected by the priest shortage, may also offer an assortment of new types of saints from the diverse social, political, economic, and religious contexts of its large continent.

Clerics and religious will continue to be canonized, but, in this age of the laity, we might expect in the future to find more married saints and single "non-vowed" saints than in the past, as lay Catholics become more attuned to signs of sanctity among their own ranks. The largest segment of the Catholic population marries, yet relatively few saints have been married; those who were receive much attention, partly for their novelty. Usually imbedded in a family of saints or related to historically-significant individuals (a not improbable reason for their prominent notice by the faithful which resulted in canonization), saints who were married are some of the most famous: Peter, first of the apostles of Jesus; Monica, mother of Augustine; Elizabeth and Zachariah, parents of John the Baptist; Anna and Joachim, parents of Mary; and, of course, Mary and Joseph, parents of Jesus; among others. Some individuals declared saints have been married but their spouses died or divorced them before the better portion of their lives for which they became canonized. These include, recently, Elizabeth Ann Seton (1774–1821), mother of five who founded the parochial school system in the United States, and, anciently, Helena (d. 330), mother of Constantine. Among current married candidates for sainthood are the parents of Thérèse of Lisieux, Louis (1823–1894) and Zélie Martin (1831–1877), who were beatified in 2008.[44] Saintly married lives serve as models of "mutual love" that "becomes an image of the absolute and unfailing love with which God loves man [and woman],"[45] teaches the *Catechism*. Married individuals who are heads of families also can become exemplary in the call to live out Christian families' status as "a *domestic church*," an "ecclesial communion"[46] of "faith, hope, and charity,"[47] wherein "its members learn to care and take responsibility for the young, the old, the sick, the handicapped, and the poor."[48] Single Catholics, also fewer in canonized number than clerics or members of religious orders, are more represented among the canonized than the married. In an age in which the population of single, never-married Catholics appears to be growing at least in developed countries, and in which divorced and widowed Catholics raise the not-married population to almost half of the adult church in such as the United States,[49] models of the single, non-vowed life[50] are instructive for many faithful. While Jesus can provide *the* model for the single life in particular even as he provides *the* model for all Christian lives in general, and while Jesus' single disciples of the first century provide exemplary imitations of the life of Christ, it nevertheless is helpful to see saintly models—in this state of life as well as in the others— from each age. Of all of the Christian vocations, the Church has had the least direction for the non-vowed single one, summed up in one paragraph in the *Catechism of the Catholic Church*: "Some forgo marriage in order to care for their parents or brothers and sisters, to give themselves more completely to a profession, or to serve other honorable ends. They can contribute greatly to the good of the human family."[51] Saints Paul and Mary Magdelene are among the canonized who continue to inspire with their images of discipleship in the single state.

Whatever past or present categorizations of saints are employed, the criteria for sainthood under the Church's formalized process will remain exceptional sanctity, as evident in martyrdom or in heroic virtue (or in both). Yet the favored models, particularly of those canonized for heroic virtue, may change from time to time. The "types" of saints popular in the past reveal that the extraordinary path of discipleship has inspired the faithful. That may be the case for many faithful in the present, too, but today there also is perhaps especial interest in "saints of the ordinary," to use a variation on the phrasing often employed by Pope John Paul II in remarking upon the "universal call to holiness" recognized by Vatican II, as mentioned in chapter 9. These are saints whose states and patterns of life are those of the ordinary faithful, yet their living of these states and patterns is done exceptionally—in a manner revealing the operative self-communication of God, grace, moving them into nearer proximity to Christ and to closer resemblance of him. Thereby the Church and the world are advanced in progress toward the Kingdom of God in its fullness.

Conclusion

Those engaged in the earthly journey to final rest in God "seek from the saints 'example in their way of life, a sharing in their communion, and the help of their intercession,'"[52] as has been noted to be stated in chapter seven of *Lumen Gentium*. The roles for the pilgrim church of "the brothers and sisters who sleep in the peace of Christ"[53] are at the service of the Eschaton. Permeating human lives at least as offer, and in a particular way evident in the saints, grace is persuading nature, pulling all toward the moment in which, again in the words of *Lumen Gentium,* "the universe itself, which is closely related to humanity and which through it attains its destiny, will be perfectly established in

Christ (see Eph 1:10; Col 1:20; 2 Pet 3:10–13)."[54] Each of the roles of
the saints exists and has significance in its place in "the renewal of all
things . . . (Acts 3:21)" by which the Church "will receive its perfection
only in the glory of heaven."[55] So the roles spring from the same source
(of Christ's grace working upon human nature), exist in reference to the
same goal (of the fullness of the Kingdom), and are the fruit of the same
reality (of grace perfecting human nature which thereby becomes sign
of and inspiration for others to accept Christ's redemptive activity). The
honor given to the saints, then, is a product of our consciousness, first,
of the redeemed creation gifted by Christ which the saints "prove,"
and, second, of the special function of those sanctified in God's
persuasive presence to us. The holy lives possible only through the grace
of Christ perfecting or sanctifying nature reveal God's love which asks
for and empowers our like response of love as demonstrated by the
saints: "Being more closely united to Christ, those who dwell in heaven
consolidate the holiness of the whole church, add to the nobility of the
worship that the church offers to God here on earth, and in many ways
help in a greater building up of the church (see 1 Cor 12:12–27)."[56]

To venerate canonized saints is to participate deliberately in the
communion of saints, searching for the fullness of loving companionship
of others in Christ, including those finally and fully joined to Christ. The
saintly companions are models because they lived and continue to exist
in Christ, who is our goal. And they are effective intercessors because,
with Christ, they now participate as fully as we might in the life of God,
but they remain one with us in nature. Imitation of and invocation of
them are acts of love of Christ and his saints, acts of hope in our
redemption by Christ, and acts of faith in Christ's salvific intercessory
work in all of the faithful, particularly in the saints. Upon the saints'
intercessory role the next chapter will reflect.

Terms for Study

Abbot   Spirituality
Gnosticism   Vow, Religious
Novice

Suggested Readings

Saint Augustine of Hippo. *Confessions*. Translated by Henry Chadwick.
Oxford and New York: Oxford University Press, 1991.

Saint Teresa of Ávila. *The Book of Her Life.* In *The Collected Works of St. Teresa of Avila.* Vol. 1. 2ⁿᵈ rev. ed. Translated by Kieran Kavanaugh and Otilio Rodriguez. Washington, D.C.: ICS Publications, 1987.

Saint Thérèse of Lisieux. *Story of a Soul: The Autobiography of Saint Thérèse of Lisieux.* 3ʳᵈ ed. Translated by John Clarke. Washington, D.C.: ICS Publications, 1996.

Perhaps the three most famous autobiographies in Christianity, these classics represent the lives and thoughts of saints in three distinct periods of Christian history.

An eminent work of theological and historical significance for Christian spirituality and doctrine, *Confessions* has been popular for sixteen hundred years. A masterful account of a life of graced transformation, the first nine books are Augustine's autobiography to the time of his religious conversion; the final four chapters are the saint, bishop, and Church Doctor's theological and philosophical reflections upon key Christian themes of the divine-human relationship. In addition to the many now famous moments of Augustine's spiritual pilgrimage, of special interest are his recollections of his interactions with other influential saints of his time—Monica, his mother, and Ambrose, bishop of Milan and now also a Doctor of the Church.

Carmelite nun, mystic, and reformer of her religious order, Teresa was the first woman to be given the title "Doctor" of the Church, in 1970. She wrote several works that have become spiritual classics; among them is her autobiography.

Thérèse's autobiography gained instant popularity following its release shortly after her death by tuberculosis at twenty-four years of age in 1897. For its exceptional instructional value in the life of faith, its content earned her the title of "Doctor" of the Church in 1997.

Görres, Ida Friederike. *The Hidden Face: A Study of St. Thérèse of Lisieux.* Translated by Richard and Clara Winston. San Francisco: Ignatius Press, 2003. Original edition, *Das Senfkorn von Lisieux,* 8ᵗʰ rev. ed., *Idas Verborgene Antlitz Eine Studie über Therese von Lisieux,* Freiburg im Breisgau: Verlag Herder, 1959.

This contemporary biography of the "Little Flower" studies the saint in her religious, historical, cultural, and even psychological context, following the basic chronological outline of Thérèse's autobiography while providing interpretive background for it.

Thomas of Celano. *Saint Francis of Assisi: First and Second Life of St. Francis with Selections from The Treatise on the Miracles of Blessed Francis.* Translated by Placid Hermann. Chicago, Illinois: Franciscan Herald Press, 1988. Reprint, Qunicy, Illinois: Franciscan Press, 2000.

The earliest biography of Saint Francis, the first part of this text was completed within a few years of Francis's death in 1226; the other parts followed in the next couple of decades. Thomas of Celano was a member of the Order of Friars Minor during and after the life of Francis. His account has been a primary source for innumerable studies of the founder of the Franciscans.

Thomas à Kempis. *The Imitation of Christ*. Translated by Richard Challoner. Rockford, Illinois: Tan Books and Publishers, 1989.

This edition contains, as supplements to the famous text of spiritual instruction, "practical reflections" and prayers at the end of chapters.

Twelve

THE SAINTS AS INTERCESSORS:
A CONTEMPORARY UNDERSTANDING

Belief in intercession of the saints is grounded in faith in the enduring salvific work of Christ, whose mission was to establish the Kingdom of God by literally dying to this world yet remaining its source of salvation. The place of human beings in this can be expressed in the theology of symbol that has been presented, a theology that is an antidote to spiritualistic practices or to individualist notions of saints as companions who are entitatively powerful, because it eliminates ideas of saints as placed between other human beings and God. As previous chapters have explained, even as dead, the saints remain our companions in nature and existential reality, albeit for them these facts have come to graced fruition; saints are transparent to the creative and redemptive power of God because they have reached the end of the human journey and now rest in Christ. We remain in communion with them because of Christ, and it is to our benefit that we recognize this and consciously, deliberately react to it. Saints' nearness to Christ during their earthly existence makes them efficacious models for us, and in their death they are now also perpetual intercessors.

A "guarantee" of the saints' intercession in the afterlife to a degree not possible for even the holiest of people during earthly life is a result of the saints' final acceptance, in death, of God's offer of self-communication. Whereas requests for prayers of individuals in the pilgrim church may or may not be heard (depending upon how carefully others are listening and how caringly they respond), prayers "to" saints will be heard (although no more so than prayers addressing God directly), since the saints are united most closely with Christ. There are no areas of Heaven over which saints have purview themselves; intercession of the saints "works" because of Christ. But how does it work? While we will not attain full comprehension of this matter in this life, we can ponder it as an act of contemplation of the greatness of God's work. This chapter intends to do just this, beginning with words of *Lumen Gentium* on the reality of the communion of saints that exists only in Christ, *the* Intercessor.

Lumen Gentium on Saints as Intercessors

As noted in chapter 7, *Lumen Gentium* reminds that from Christianity's beginning those in the communion of saints from the pilgrim church have prayed for the dead, and the Church "has always venerated" the martyrs, Mary, and the angels, and "has asked piously for the help of their intercession."[1] The communion, in Christ, of those venerated and all others in the heavenly and earthly churches, recommends invocation.

> It is most fitting, therefore, that we love those friends and coheirs of Jesus Christ who are also our sisters and brothers and outstanding benefactors, and that we give due thanks to God for them, 'humbly invoking them, and having recourse to their prayers, their aid and help in obtaining from God through his Son, Jesus Christ, Our Lord, our only Redeemer and Savior, the benefits we need.' Every authentic witness of love, indeed, offered by us to those who are in heaven tends towards and terminates in Christ, 'the crown of all the saints,' and through him in God who is wonderful in his saints and is glorified in them.[2]

This passage contains the answer to the question of why we should invoke the saints if the saints have no power to answer prayers themselves and since prayer to God alone is not only possible but essential to the Christian life. The "merit" of invocation of saints is that it joins us intentionally and profoundly to all of those in permanent communion with Christ, in our common faith in the efficacy of Christ's redemptive work, in our hope for our transformation through Christ's redemption, and in our love of Christ in the neighbor. In our request that our prayers be joined with those of the saints, we can have confidence in saints' ready prayerful assistance and, if God so wills, in their participation in his fulfillment of our needs. Yet it must be remembered always that, as intercessors, the saints are but conformed to Christ[3] and thereby simply "cooperate" in his work as the Intercessor (Heb. 7:25). Their nearness to him simply establishes in them an especially effective instrumental capacity in his work, whereas earthly intercessors may inconsistently have the openness to Christ that allows any human person to serve as a conduit of God's response to our prayers.

> Once received into their heavenly home and being present to the Lord (see 2 Cor 5:8), through him and with him and in him they do not cease to intercede with the Father for us, as they proffer the merits which they acquired on earth through the one

mediator between God and humanity, Christ Jesus (see 1 Tim 2:5), serving God in all things and completing in their flesh what is lacking in Christ's sufferings for the sake of his body, which is the church (see Col 1:24).[4]

Invocation of the saints is truly directed to worship of God, since the saints' symbolic, iconic, sacramental function in God's gift of his grace, where he so chooses, makes them transparent to the risen Christ. As Rahner insisted, the saints intercede not as "intermediaries"[5] but as neighbors who have been transformed by God's grace. This is why, in religious acts of veneration, opening ourselves to the neighbors who are saints, human beings engage in the "*basic* act of love of God *and* of neighbour."[6] In invocation of saints, a form of veneration, we assume, trustingly, with our neighbors in the heavenly church, the humble, worshipful posture that is due to God and that is held permanently by intellectual creatures in their fulfilled state.[7] We testify to faith in God's promise that human beings do not cease to exist or become irrelevant in death; in our death God welcomes into his very life the very selves that we are, in a purified, loving state.

Saintly Intercessors in Catholic Theology

From the biblical texts concerning petitionary and intercessory prayer that were reviewed in chapter 2, three main points should be taken. The first point is that Scripture clearly instructs us to engage in petitionary prayer. Petitionary prayer is efficacious when engaged in in faith, and faith is evident in the degree of confidence in and persistence of prayerful requests, as well as in requests' alignment with the revealed will of God. Petitions will be so aligned when elicited by the Holy Spirit, who guides us in prayer. The second point is that Jesus not only taught but engaged himself in petitionary prayer that exhibited the very conditions just named. And his petitionary prayer expressed his desire for union among his disciples as he and the Father are united (Jn. 17), as well as his desire for his indwelling with the Father in the community of believers so that this community would serve as a beacon to the world of unbelievers (Jn. 17:20–21). For this purpose, he gave the "glory" to his believers that the Father gave to him (Jn. 17:22). The responsibility for each other of the members of the community of disciples enlivened by the power of the Spirit is expressed in Jesus' commands to "love one another" (Jn. 13:34, 15:17) and "to wash one another's feet" as "your Lord and Teacher . . . washed your feet" (Jn. 13:14). It is expressed pointedly in such as the Letter of James urging intercessory prayer: "[C]onfess your sins to one another, and pray for one another, . . The prayer of a righteous man has great power in its effects" (Jas. 5:16). The third point is that, from the beginning of Christianity, there was an impulse toward prayer for both the living and the dead. This communal impulse was intimately linked with the early Christians' hope for the Eschaton, a reality, in Christ, that Christians grasped as impinging upon life in the earthly present even as it fulfilled its promise for the departed faithful, affecting human existence on both sides of the grave.

These points arise, obviously, from faith. Faith sometimes raises questions; we are creatures endowed with the faculty of reason, as noted in chapter 4 and beyond, so use of reason can clarify and deepen faith. Questions arising from the biblical injunction to petition God are about the integrity of divine and human freedom in petitionary prayer and about the sovereignty of God (i.e., his absolute power and perfection). Traditional Christian belief is in God's immutability, or impassibility. God is perfect, simple or indivisible; he does not change. So if our prayer, in faith, will cast a mountain into the sea if we ask it (Mk. 11:23–24; Mt. 21:21–22), does this not threaten divine sovereignty and freedom? Or, if this prayer is efficacious because God willed that we ask that the mountain be cast into the sea, does this not threaten human freedom? Why should request be made to God if the Father "knows what you need before you ask him" (Mt. 6:8) and wills to fulfill those needs? And why should prayer of one person be efficacious for another? Contemporary theologians and philosophers have given much ink to exploration of this paradoxical reality of petitionary prayer and the form of it that is intercessory prayer. Their musings help us to understand why and how it works. But we must begin by exploring the basic premise of freedom in the divine-human relationship.

Divine Sovereignty and Freedom, Human Freedom

In the classical view of time and the eternity of God, Saint Severinus Boethius (ca. 480–524) held that God exists outside of time, seeing all "in His eternal present."[8] God therefore knows all in "one ever present glance,"[9] not as a temporal sequence of events as in human perception of reality. Nevertheless, this places no conditions upon human freedom, since, although God knows all, none of that which he knows constitutes future for him. Boethius wrote: "[T]he same future event is necessary with respect to God's knowledge of it but absolutely free and unrestrained when it is examined in its own nature. . . [F]ree acts, when referred to the divine intuition, become necessary in the conditional sense because God's knowledge provides that condition; on the other hand, viewed by themselves, they do not lose the perfect freedom of their nature."[10] God in his simplicity is sovereign, free, immutable, omniscient, but these realities do not encumber human freedom. Further, in our human freedom, we can legitimately pray to God and trust that he will respond, for, since God's vision "runs in unison with the future nature of our acts," meaning that it encompasses our future as well as our past and present, he is ever "dispensing rewards to the good, punishments to the evil."[11]

Contemporarily, views of time and eternity are debated. Some philosophers argue that, even without creation, God's existence and vision cannot properly be said to be the simple "glance" Boethius or his followers claim, since "[a] state of affairs must last for a period of time; . . . [so] God cannot be omnipotent or omniscient just at an instant," in the words of Richard Swinburne.[12] On this ground, Swinburne has deemed the argument for divine eternity to be incoherent. He found properly scriptural and in keeping with the early tradition of the Church prior to its appropriation of neo-Platonic thought[13] the notion of God as "everlasting" rather than eternal, and he argued that it can avoid thought of God as "time's prisoner" if God's subjection to time is by his own choice.[14] God has willingly instituted "a succession of qualitatively distinct mental acts" into his life, resulting in creation, which means that he willingly has incorporated a temporal order within himself.[15] Without creation, God could have perpetually engaged in "his one act of self-awareness" of indeterminable length, had he so chosen.[16] Swinburne's belief is that a doctrine of God as everlasting provides that which a classical Christian theist most wants to safeguard (God's sovereignty), without falling into that which he identified as the problem with a view of God as eternal—the difficulty of explaining how "if God has an existence outside (our) time, he can have any relation to the events of time which would be in any way analogous to 'causing' or 'observing' them."[17] He claimed that change in God is a logically necessary belief if God's omniscience is to be upheld: "[I]f God was to be omniscient at any time, he would need to know what was happening at that time; and so, as the world changed, he would need to change with it."[18]

There are those even within the "timeless" tradition who hold that "the divine 'moment' has duration and thus is a period."[19] But they part ways with those espousing the "everlasting" view in rejection of the stipulation that "if God causes the beginning or continuing existence of the world, and perhaps interferes in its operation from time to time, his acting must be prior to the effects that his action causes. . . , [and] his awareness of events in the world must be later than those events."[20] God's omniscience and immutability are incompatible only if God is considered a *temporal* being—which he is not, they argue.[21] Adherents to Boethius's view of divine eternity can recognize that we speak analogically of God's "eternity" in contradistinction to our temporal existence. To say that God is outside of time, that God is eternal, that his is an atemporal existence, is to say that he is a "perfect being" with "an indivisibly persistent present actuality."[22] Philosophers Eleonore Stump and Norman Kretzmann have explained that, in divine "eternality," [23] "the eternal present persists, encompasses time, and is unbounded. In those respects it resembles temporal duration enough to make it helpful to speak of eternity as extended, . . . On the other hand, because it lacks succession, it fails to resemble spatial and temporal extensions in being divisible." Therefore, it should not be thought "on the basis of the characteristics it does share with temporal duration that it must also be like it in all other respects. . . ."[24] They followed William Alston in suggesting a conceptual aid in the notion of the "specious present"[25]—a brief span of time within which a series of moments are experienced as the "now."[26] God's specious present might be understood as the eternal present which includes all time, such that God is at the same "place" in relationship to each and every temporal reality. This would explain both God's omniscience and omnipresence, and it offers a means of resolving the apparent dilemma involved in upholding a version of the classical doctrine of God's immutability while affirming God's personal interaction with us in petitionary and intercessory prayer. [27] Even though eternality and temporality are different modes of existence, there is no gulf between God and human beings precluding communication since, "from an eternal viewpoint, every present time is present, co-occurrent with the infinite whole of the eternal present."[28] This means that God "cannot *fore* know anything," but he knows of all temporal events, "as they are present" to him "in the whole of eternity."[29] Equally, the fact of God's presence to all of temporal reality does not necessarily bind him by the conditions of the temporal sphere.

In the same vein, but from a theological vantage point, Rahner suggested that past and present speculations alike about God have been conditioned by the tendency to think of him in spatio-temporal terms and misunderstand the fundamental Christian affirmations about his eternity and its relationship to his created world.[30] God is said to be eternal because he is present to creation but transcends it.[31] Time, which is of the temporal world, is both created by God's loving gift of himself (which issues in an "other") and the condition that makes possible his free gift of himself to that which is other than and completely dependent upon him—namely, human beings.[32] The "once and for all now" of God is a fullness of time achieved through God's self-bestowal upon the world.[33] Even in his most profound involvement with creation—the Incarnation— wherein he takes on a "personal history of his own in time, and 'in the

world' itself," God's immutability remains intact "in himself."[34] To say
that God exists outside of time is to recognize that all exists in him who
is unconditioned (i.e., who is infinite, unbound by anything or anyone).
To say that the world has time is to recognize that it had a beginning. The
Church's doctrine on creation and time is, in Rahner's words, "a saving
statement ('evangelium') addressed to men and . . . an appeal to their free
decision ('law') to accept 'irrevocably' the definitive salvation in a
definitive exercise of freedom."[35] For, unlike other earthly creatures,
human beings have a spiritual and free existence which points beyond the
finite. This reality is the possibility of eternal life. Rahner maintained
that, in the experience of human beings who have Christian hope in
eternal life, "[e]ternity is not a further projection of history into another
dimension of time, but the sheer reality of the history itself as
accomplished and complete."[36] So for human beings, eternity is not
simply a prolongation of this life, nor is it a disjunctive reality coming
after this life. "In reality, it is *in* time, as its own mature fruit, that
'eternity' comes about. . . : it [eternity] eliminates time by being released
from the time that was for a while so that the definitive could come about
in freedom," wrote Rahner.[37] We "become immortal in our life"[38] through
moral decision wherein the human person "constitutes himself as having
a valid end."[39] He explained: "In this decision the subject is immediately
presented, in his being and his act, as something incommensurable with
passing time," as someone who transcends time, grasped by the
"immediate presence of the eternal."[40] This common human experience
of transcendence is validated for us as real in God's word of revelation,
which provides the meaning of human existence. In Scripture God is
revealed as "Absolute Mystery" with whom the dead now live in fullness,
wholly transformed, body and soul.[41] Rahner offered this depiction:

> Eternal life is not the 'other side' so far as our personal history
> is concerned, but rather the radical interiority, now liberated
> and brought to full self-realization, of that personal history of
> freedom of ours which we are living through even now and
> which, once it has been fully brought to birth in death, can no
> longer be lost. The only further development which it can still
> achieve then is to lose itself in a loving immediacy to the
> ultimate Mystery of existence called God, and thereby discover
> its own fullness.[42]

The distinction between life and death, therefore, is derived from the fact
that life after death "is something radically withdrawn from the former
temporal dimension and the former spatially conceived time, and a state
of final and definitive completion and immediacy to God which is
absolutely disparate from space and time."[43] But continuity is maintained

by God's "universal, infralapsarian salvific will" for all of humankind which is manifested from human inception as an offer of divine self-communication to each and all.[44] By God's graciousness, the possibility of a "salvific relationship of freedom to God"[45] is a part of the very structure of the human being, making it possible for us to receive actual grace in free acceptance,[46] as explained in chapter 10. Within our concrete reality as oriented to God, petitionary prayer, including the intercessory variety, may play a special role in preserving both divine and human freedom.

Petitionary and Intercessory Prayer in Divine and Human Freedom through the Sovereignty of God

Affirming Christian belief in a perfect and loving, eternal God, Stump ventured a theory about the point of petitionary prayer. In a 1979 article, "Petitionary Prayer," she asked, "Why should prayers be included in God's plan as causes of certain effects? And what sense is there in the notion that a perfect and unchangeable God, who disposes and plans everything, fulfills men's prayers asking him to do one thing or another?"[47] She proposed that petitionary prayer checks the relationship between God and human beings, providing a critical function precisely because God extends himself so fully to us as Father and as friend, etc. In relationships of inequality, there is always a danger that the superior's even loving condescension toward the other will either dominate or spoil—dominate if the inferior party is "so overcome by the advantages or superiority of his 'friend' that he becomes simply a shadowy reflection of the other's personality" and spoil if inferior parties become "tyrannical, willful, indolent, self-indulgent, and the like" due to "the power at their disposal in virtue of their connections." God's requirement of petitionary prayer before he answers some of our needs and desires allows "omniscient, omnipotent, perfectly good" God to extend himself in friendship to "a fallible, finite, imperfect person"[48] without oppression or overindulgence. In this case, we are given the freedom to request God's help or not, and, when we do so and receive it, we are in a position to recognize his goodness and to give the proper thanks to him.

Stump's theory extends beyond petitionary prayer for oneself to intercessory prayer for others. She proposed that our prayers for others also help maintain the necessary distance in God's relationship with human beings, since it may be that God will not "intervene" in the lives of those for whom we pray or will not do so in certain ways without our invitation. In relationships among human beings, the assistance of those who are in a position to help is sometimes sought for a friend when it is clear that he or she needs help but will not seek it himself or herself. Sometimes the friend will not accept the assistance, but a potential helper may at least offer and perhaps make it as easy as possible for the friend to accept. Stump looked to *Confessions* to provide an example of how intercessory prayer might have worked in Augustine's famous case: "[A]s Augustine tells it . . . , God responded to Monica's fervent and continued prayers for Augustine's salvation by arranging the circumstances of Augustine's life in such a way that finally Augustine himself freely asked God for salvation."[49] Might Augustine's story have turned out differently without Monica's prayers? Stump postulated that "God would have saved Augustine without Monica's prayers but not in the same amount of time or not by the same process or not with the same effect. Augustine, for instance, might have been converted to Christianity but not in such a way as to become one of its most powerful authorities for centuries."[50] Implicit in Stump's argument is the belief that intercessory prayer also helps the one who prays, making him or her happier or favorably influencing his or her relationship with God in recognition of his love and care.[51]

Where the saints are concerned, in Rahner's explanation of petitionary and intercessory prayer, since human beings, living and dead, exist in the same modality of existence from their creation,[52] there is not an insurmountable, unknowable divide between life and death that would prevent the efficacy of intercessory prayer. Yet the living have not fully realized the possibilities of their "graced" existence. The dead who are hidden with Christ have done so and, eternally of the communion of sons and daughters of God, joined finally to Christ, they now intercede along with him on behalf of those still on the journey. Their fullness in eternity, in the ultimate mystery, is our "true future" which "comes to meet us."[53] We cannot plan or conjure or control this future, but can only respond positively to God's invitation to us to it,[54] which was established in the Hypostatic Union.[55] Our acceptance of our lives unconditionally is our first step into this future[56] that embraces not only individuals but the totality of the world, "determining where its consummation is to be achieved,"[57] or when the Kingdom of Heaven of which Jesus spoke will come into its fullness. Human beings participate in bringing about the Kingdom by accepting "in knowledge and freedom" the consummation of the "finite reality of the world" in God.[58] One way in which this acceptance is expressed is in religious acts such as veneration that recognize that God's promises have been fulfilled in the lives of those who have completed their earthly pilgrimage. God's promises to us mean, as Rahner effectively concurred with Stump, that petitionary prayer in general is "absolutely certain to be heard"[59] yet leaves God to answer it in the way that he wills.

> That such prayer combines a great measure of 'self-will' (for
> one presents to Him one's *own* desires) with a supreme degree

of submissiveness (for one *prays* to Him whom one cannot compel, persuade or charm but only beg), that here there is a mingling and an incomprehensible fusion of the greatest boldness with the deepest humility, of life with death, this makes the prayer of petition in one respect not the lowest but the highest, the most divinely human form of prayer. Why else is the Lord's Prayer not a hymn but a sevenfold petition?[60]

Following the Gospel of Matthew's chapter 6, verses 25 through 33 on faith, Rahner's starting point for reflection upon petitionary prayer was the recognition that God tends to our needs prior to any explicit petitions from us.[61] In these verses of the Sermon on the Mount, Jesus tells his disciples:

> Therefore I tell you, do not be anxious about your life, what you shall eat or what you shall drink, nor about your body, what you shall put on. Is not life more than food, and the body more than clothing? Look at the birds of the air: they neither sow nor reap nor gather into barns, and yet your heavenly Father feeds them. Are you not of more value than they? And which of you by being anxious can add one cubit to his span of life? And why are you anxious about clothing? Consider the lilies of the field, how they grow; they neither toil nor spin; yet I tell you, even Solomon in all his glory was not arrayed like one of these. But if God so clothes the grass of the field, which today is alive and tomorrow is thrown into the oven, will he not much more clothe you, O men of little faith? Therefore do not be anxious, saying, 'What shall we eat?' or 'What shall we drink?' or "What shall we wear?' For the Gentiles seek all these things; and your heavenly Father knows that you need them all. But seek first his kingdom and his righteousness, and all these things shall be yours as well.[62]

Yet as scriptural passages reviewed in chapter 2 showed, Christ also taught us to petition God. As with all prayer, petitionary prayer is efficacious (even if we do not receive from it that for which we explicitly ask) because it is elicited by the grace of God. Ultimately, stated Rahner, "whatever it seeks apart from God it wants only if this is consistent—by the disposition of God which has been unconditionally accepted—with the fundamental desire for God."[63] In petitionary prayer human beings unreservedly place ourselves at God's mercy, understanding our true relationship of dependence upon him, recognizing that "the exigencies of concrete earthly existence are in God's hands."[64] There is nothing in Rahner's theology of petitionary prayer that would necessarily overrule

Stump's suggestion that petitionary prayer guarantees that God's initiative does not cancel the free will with which he has gifted us. However, as a theology rather than a philosophy of prayer, and as a theology that has a profound sense of the structure of the human being as oriented to God as source and destination, Rahner's explanation gives great weight to the human consciousness of desire for God that is intrinsic to petitionary prayer. This is the fundamental merit of all prayer—that it responds, under the influence of grace, to God's own summons, with a will to union with him.[65] The very definition of prayer is to come into the presence of God at his call, and the saints are always in God's presence praising him; hence, they are always praying. For what do they pray? Rahner claimed that petitionary prayer for others is inevitable if it will be truly Christian.

> If the one Holy Spirit is to move us all, and there is one body because we have been baptized by this Spirit into one body (I Co 12:13) and if we must therefore—because we are members of the one body of Christ—with one mind bear each other's anxieties, then everyone ought to pray for everyone else. Apostolic prayer is a Christian duty.[66]

According to Rahner, invocation of the saints bespeaks a deep sense of the love of God which Catholic Christians believe enlivens each of us in life and in the afterlife in a way that has meaning for others and that assists all in the communion of saints in attaining the fullness of personal spiritual existence. It is "the courage of that love" that trusts that "every life lived in faith and love is of permanent value and significance for all, and that the redeemed man in the state of blessedness receives and lives this significance of his life."[67] Invocation of a particular saint is in fact invocation of all the saints, "an act by which we take refuge in faith in the all-enfolding community of all the redeemed." In Christ, all are united in love, and, since "each is responsible for all," the saints who are joined with Christ will not fail to intercede. In the lovely words that conclude Rahner's article "Why and How Can We Venerate the Saints?,"

> They are our brothers [and sisters] who have already attained their perfection, and they entreat the God of the living to let that light shine upon us too which is the manifestation of his own love and the blessed eternity of his own life.[68]

The saints' prayers for us do not yield only answers to the specific petitions for which we invoke them. Applying the thought reviewed in this chapter on the value of petitionary prayer as aligning us with the will of God in both divine and human freedom, we must believe that the kind of petition that is intercessory prayer favorably influences both the relationship between God and those for whom prayer is offered and between God and those who pray. (And certainly it must be beneficial for the relationship between those praying and those for whom prayer is offered, too.) Intercessory prayer draws all human parties involved more deeply into the Christian life and into the very life of God which embraces all. So, yes, because the saints are fully transformed by grace in the completion of their history, their perpetual posture of worship of God is at the same time a perpetual openness to being conduits of God's blessings upon us, which means we might receive blessings through their instrumentality if we invoke them. But that is not all. If the saints are perpetual intercessors because of their unceasing love of God and neighbor, then our invocation of them, as well as our deliberate religious attention to them as companions and models, realizes a change *in us*. We attain, through grace, a deeper commitment to the Mystery that is God who is our end, whether or not we receive the specific "favor" requested of God by invoking them. The critical result of our invocation of saints is our adoption of the receptiveness to God's will that was the characteristic attitude of the saints' earthly lives. As the foregoing chapters have made clear, the Catholic understanding is that, when this humble attitude is made definitive in each of our deaths, as in the deaths of the saints, it will come to fruition in an eternity of participation in the life of God wherein we will forever love God and neighbor. In this we see once again the intrinsic links among the roles of the saints, the reason for which these holy ones are canonized. Still joined in nature and faith with their earthly brothers and sisters (as companions to us), they edify us with their commitment to Christ (as models for us), which persuades us to invoke them (as intercessors for us) as we answer God's call to live more and more in consciousness of our life and destiny in him.

In summary of and brief excursus upon this chapter's conclusions about petitionary and intercessory prayer, God always responds to our prayers, albeit perhaps not always in the way we expect or wish. We exist always within God's offer of self-communication, and petitionary prayer is a response to that persuasive reality. Positive orientations toward God should produce prayers that seek his will even while other specific results may be requested by the petitioner. We may not know for what we should pray; an innate tendency toward selfishness, as well as an inability to see the whole, can bar this knowledge. We may pray that that which we think we need will indeed be God's will. Sometimes the specific requests made in prayers are not fulfilled, but whatever God does as a result of our prayer is toward fulfillment of his plan from within the context of the circumstances in which he reaches to us. God's constant offer of grace does not restrict our freedom, but empowers it. And because our freedom and indeed our personal realization grow in tandem with our alignment with his will, there is no adversarial relationship between divine and human aims, no restriction of freedom on the side either of God or of humanity. God is sovereign even as he is responsive to the free actions of human beings which he has persuaded and which he has empowered from the outset; he himself, who created history, has ordained that its completion will be realized through human beings. The way of eschatological completion involves, then, our graced response to God in love, which always occurs in the context of community. So petitionary prayer must be offered for others—that is to say, it must include intercessory prayer—if it is to be genuinely Christian. Prayer promotes our loving, salvific relationship with God, as members of the communion of saints which exists in Christ. The saints are always with Christ. We are with Christ when we intentionally recognize him and respond to him in his saints, as well as in other human beings. Invocation of the saints is intentional recognition of our place in the communion of saints which transcends time and space; in intercession Christ is shown dramatically as present and triumphant in the communion of the Church and in the community of humanity.

Special Issues in Saintly Intercession

On the subject of the saints as intercessors, matters of peculiar interest and/or concern today include a not uncommon deemphasis of this role, questions about the saints' consciousness of our specific prayers, and issues with the traditional language for invocation. Deserving of attention, each of these topics will receive brief guiding remarks here.

Deemphasis today of the saintly role of intercessor is an understandable temptation in order to avoid the medieval tendency to focus principally or wholly upon the miraculous that might come through a saintly patron, but, from the standpoint of Catholic theology, it can lead to a disregard of Christ himself. As *Lumen Gentium* was quoted earlier in this chapter, "Every authentic witness of love, indeed, offered by us to those who are in heaven tends towards and terminates in Christ, 'the crown of all the saints,' and through him in God. . . ."[69] Since all human persons can serve as intercessors (of Christ *the* Intercessor for us with God the Father), ignoring the saints' given and enhanced capacity in this regard ignores the reality of the grace of Christ present in the communion of saints and profoundly so in those perfected by it. The ontological and organic communion of the faithful that exists in Christ is duly recognized in invocation of those who are believed to be with him and in him. This is the case whether invocation of saints occurs on the corporate or the private level; these dimensions merge in the Church's canonizations which take place only with official validation of intercessory miracles resulting from private invocation and showing that an individual is in Heaven.

With regard to the saints' consciousness of our invocation of them, a usual assumption when we say that our prayers can be answered through the instrumentality of saints is that they hear our prayers. After all, we can only know particular saints as intercessors when we or others receive results from God after invoking them. But it is logical to wonder whether or not the saints must hear our prayers for this to occur. This chapter's contentions necessarily lead to the conclusion that, if the saints hear our prayers when they are invoked, they hear them in and through Christ. Theologically, it is permissible to think that saints do hear the individual prayers of Christians. But, for those uncomfortable with any degree of speculation about the afterlife, it is perhaps not necessary to think so in order to uphold the tradition of intercession by invocation of saints. Saints could be understood to intercede in the sense that, in their fixation upon Christ, they are so completely aligned with the will of God who loves all, who is forever ready to assist us in our need even before we ask, that they are already always praying for us in their love for us, in their love for God, and in their openness to his activity in and through themselves. If this conception seems to lack a desired specificity in our invocation of saints, especially given that the saints in Heaven "see" God but do not have the mind of God and therefore cannot "divine" our particular needs, we might be helped by recalling that they, as did Christ, have traveled the earthly journey. Our needs and prayers are not likely to offer anything novel for them; there is a sense in which they, simply from their human experience, know the types of things for which we will cry to Heaven and could anticipate them in their own prayers—if these prayers need to be thought to be anything but the basic expression of the desire for God's will to be done, which is the perfect content of prayer, as demonstrated by the "Our Father," "The Lord's Prayer," given to us by Jesus.

Finally, concerning the language of invocation, although ancient custom of the Church validates use of the expression "praying 'to'" the saints, the expression "praying 'with'" the saints must be as valid, it is perhaps less easily given to theological confusion, and it might be helpful in ecumenical dialogue. Communicating more clearly than the traditional language the relationship among Christ, the saints, and the petitioners united in the Body of Christ with its Head, it also has the merit of conveying the important fact that the saints are engaged in unending worship—and thereby prayer—in which we consciously join them when we invoke them. In Christianity, worship always has the communal dimension. In invoking the saints, praying "with" them, we are readied for our ongoing conversion, in the company of and with the assistance of others, in Christ and led by the Spirit. To put this in the systematic language that has been used throughout the last few chapters, invocation and other religious acts of veneration of saints uniquely express a fully reflective and deliberate intentionality directed to God as the end of each and every member of humanity who, under the influence of grace, will accept him.

Conclusion

Among the saints, Mary, *Theotokos*, is preeminent. In the tradition of the Church, she has always stood with but "apart" from other saints—both in the particular sense of those canonized and in the general sense of all of those in the communion of saints—as the human being most united with Christ, her Son. Where invocation of saints is concerned, it is she to whom Christians have appealed first. Because of Mary's unique role, veneration of her—either for its presence or its absence—has been the focus of especial attention in ecumenical conversation. Catholics and Orthodox have paid her great honor; Protestants traditionally have been concerned that such effusiveness endangers the worship due to God alone that all Christians hold cannot be compromised, for, indeed, this would deny the very meaning of Christ and his work. Analogous to "high" and "low" Christologies, or Christologies "from above" and "from below"—so named for their emphasis or for their starting place in reflection, Christ's divinity or his humanity—are "high" and "low" Mariologies that result from the manner of observing Mary's role in the mission of her Son. As Nicholas Ayo has observed, a Mariology from above "emphasizes the privileges of Mary and her closeness to God," usually with comparisons to but also with contrasts to Christ on matters related to his divinity (such as sinlessness and reign in Heaven); a Mariology from below "emphasizes the humanity of Mary and her closeness to the human Jesus and to the disciples of Christ," usually with comparisons to but also with contrasts to Christ on matters related to his humanity (such as solidarity with humanity which is redeemed through him).[70] In this time of Catholic reassessment of Marian piety and of ecumenical conversation among Catholics, Protestants, and Orthodox, Mariologies of both varieties are apparent, even at extremes, as will be considered in the coming chapter.

Terms for Study

Immutability/Impassibility (of
God)
Intercessory Prayer
Perfection/Simplicity (of God)

Petitionary Prayer
Platonism
Sovereignty (of God)
Temporality

Suggested Readings

Holy Cards.
  Prayers invoking saints often are spontaneous, but formal prayers
requesting the intercession of saints that can be found in various types of
prayer books also are preserved accessibly on the back of traditional holy
cards that can be found in most Catholic religious goods stores.

Thirteen

MARIOLOGICAL DEVOTION: CATHOLIC DOCTRINE AND ECUMENICAL CONVERSATION

The first passage offered in a collection of quotations about Mary from Pope Benedict XVI speaks of her special place in the communion of saints, because of the unique disclosure through her of God's presence to us in Christ. God is praised in veneration of Mary and of all of the saints.

> We do not praise God sufficiently by keeping silent about His Saints, especially Mary, "the Holy One" who became His dwelling place on earth. The simple and multiform light of God appears to us exactly in its variety and richness only in the countenance of the Saints, who are the true mirrors of His light.
>
> And it is precisely by looking at Mary's face that we can see more clearly than in any other way the beauty, goodness, and mercy of God. In her face we can truly perceive the divine light.[1]

Discussions about the saints find their genesis and terminus in the subject of Christ, but they find their delimitation—the boundaries of anything that might be attributed to human persons as objects of Christ's salvific work—in the subject of Mary. As the first (in the Annunciation) explicitly to accept Christ as the Messiah, she is *Theotokos*, "Mother of God," the first disciple and, thereby, even before disciples recognized themselves as members of a religious movement that would be distinct from Judaism, the first member of the Church.[2] Traditionally she has been honored under a host of titles, including "Blessed Virgin," "New Eve," "Mary Immaculate," "Our Lady," "Queen of Heaven," "Handmaid of the Lord" (Lk. 1:38), and, as Vatican II affirmed, "Advocate," "Helper," "Benefactress," and "Mediatrix."[3] Some of these have been deemphasized by Catholics since Vatican II; Vatican II's *Lumen Gentium* itself cautioned that the titles it cited affirming Mary as an intercessor are to be "understood in such a way that it [invocation of her] neither takes away anything from, nor adds anything to, the dignity and efficacy of Christ the one Mediator."[4] Some Marian titles were deemphasized or even rejected in the Protestant

Reformation. Indeed, Marian piety, so prevalent among Catholics and Orthodox, has, in its Catholic form, been a lightening rod in the Western divisions of Protestant and Catholic Christians. Yet, although it was sometimes exaggerated among Catholics in the past, today the apparent disparity is striking between the encouragement of recent popes to private Marian veneration and the seemingly marginal place of Mary in Catholic devotional life. Still, the importance of Mary to the Church has never escaped the attention of Catholics and many other Christians, even though traditional practices may not always hold sway. And although Marian piety has been virtually non-existent among Protestants after Luther, who himself honored Mary as a model of humility,[5] today there is new interest in and discussion of her importance for all Christians by those who feel neglectful of her following the mutual antagonism of Protestants and Catholics for years after the Reformations. In the West, Marian devotion, if not Mary herself, came to be seen as a symbol of Catholicism. But, as the new millennium dawned, something was happening as regards interest in Mary; ecumenical dialogue about her has been fruitful.

Especially in studying Mary, it becomes apparent that, in the roles of the saints, distinct areas of theology intersect. Theological anthropology and ecclesiology are joined because, as chapter 10 showed, the grace given to sanctify the saints also builds up the Church as a result of the saints' function within the Church. Christology is eminently involved, particularly where it is concerned with the ongoing salvific work of Christ evident in holy lives. And, because Christ's unending presence to us occurs in the Holy Spirit, pneumatology also is concerned. The saints, then, are not neutral figures in theology; attention to them or lack thereof impacts theological reflection in multiple ways, as history has shown. In the case of Mary, although devotion to her has sometimes driven Christological reflection (including in moments in history where piety seemed, wrongly, to posit her as the key for us to attain relationship with her Son), at other times, such as now, reflection upon Christ rightly has driven brands of devotion to her. This is no more evident than in her prominent reinstatement, even by Christians who have not venerated her, to in a place of importance in the Church in and since the latter half of the twentieth century, in consciousness of her unique and indispensable role in the mission of her Son. Attention to Mary's role is always conditioned by culture and tied to doctrinal emphases of the times, as is the case with all theological reflection and practices. But, irrespective of these influences, her perceived status and the particular variety of veneration due to her must stem in any age from primary reflection upon her Son's person and work, as was the justification for the Council of Ephesus's claim that she is *Theotokos*.

To survey the entire history of Marian veneration and its doctrinal connections is more than can be done in one chapter of a book devoted to the veneration of saints generally, especially in the Catholic context in which Mariology's scope is vast. So it must suffice here to focus upon the general outlines of traditional devotion and official doctrine, then to review briefly the shape of recent Marian studies, then to explain the Catholic Marian dogmas, and finally to note points of convergence and divergence in ecumenical dialogue about Mary.

History of Marian Devotion and Doctrine

As biblical scholars Raymond E. Brown, Karl P. Donfried, Joseph A. Fitzmyer, and John Reumann concluded in their study of the late 1970s, *Mary in the New Testament: A Collaborative Assessment by Protestant and Roman Catholic Scholars,* differing views of Mary among Christian traditions today owe to the weight given to some New Testament passages over others, as well as to post-New Testament writings that "were increasingly positive in portraying Mary as a disciple par excellence and as the virgin."[6] Christians reared against the background of traditions of unabashed Marian piety sometimes are not conscious of the relatively scant attention, critical as it is, given to Mary in the New Testament.

Scripture's information about Mary is, of course, confined to her movements around the life of Jesus. Scholars note that, depending upon the biblical book, her presentation is either negative (Gospel of Mark) or nameless (Gospel of John and Letter of Paul to the Galatians), to positive (Gospels of Matthew and Luke and the Acts of the Apostles) and even laudatory (Gospel of Luke, by some judgments).[7] In the New Testament writings as a group, she is mentioned in ways and in scenes well-known to Christians: as Jesus' mother; in the context of genealogy; in the angel Gabriel's Annunciation; in the Nativity and, leading up to it, in the departure of the family to enroll in the census required by Caesar Augustus; in the presentation of Jesus in the Temple; in the flight into Egypt due to Herod's murderous plan directed against male children; in the family's trip to Jerusalem at Passover and the subsequent discovery of Jesus in the Temple when he is missing from the party returning to Nazareth; and in reports of attempts of those who encountered Jesus to understand who he is in terms of his relatives. (See Mt. 1:16, 18–25; 2:1–12, 13–23; 13:53–58; Mk. 6:1–6; Lk. 1:21–38; 2:1–7, 8–20, 22–35, 41–52.) Of scenes that have been particularly important for understanding Mary's role vis-à-vis her Son, in the Gospel of Luke, in her visit with Elizabeth (Lk. 1:39–56), Mary's hymn of praise known as the

"Magnificat" is featured (Lk. 1:46–55).[8] In a recollection repeated in each of the synoptic gospels, Jesus refers to his mother and other kin in making the point that discipleship (i.e., doing the will of God) rather than biology is determinative of the true defining relationship with him (Mk. 3:31–35; Mt. 12:46–50; Lk. 8:19–21). In the same vein, in the Gospel of Luke, Jesus, in response to a woman who blesses his mother, calls blessed "those who hear the word of God and keep it" (Lk. 11:27–28). Aside from material from the synoptic writers, in the Gospel of John, Mary is featured prominently in the story of the wedding at Cana (Jn. 2:1–11) where she attests to her Son's power, and she is mentioned as one of the party that subsequently journeyed to Capernaum (Jn. 2:12). Also in this gospel, she appears at the foot of the Cross with, notably, the beloved disciple (Jn. 19:25–27). In the Acts of the Apostles, Mary is mentioned as one gathered with the apostles and other disciples in the upper room of Jerusalem (Acts 1:12–14). Paul refers to Jesus' birth by a woman, "to redeem those who were under the law, so that we might receive adoption as sons" (Gal. 4:4–5).[9]

Much that is "known" by Christians of the life of Mary is derived from extra-biblical sources, chiefly the probable second-century *Protoevangelium of James*. Intentionally convergent with the biblical account of Mary in many scenes, the *Protoevangelium* also provides additional details. It tells of Mary's parents, Joachim and Anna, long childless until an angel appears to each foretelling God's coming gift of the conception of Mary. In thanks to God, upon the birth of their daughter, they keep her isolated in her bedroom until the age of three, so that she will be preserved from contact with anything "unclean." Then, to keep their vow to the Lord that she will be placed in his service, she is taken by them to reside at the Temple until the age of twelve. At that time, the priests, with the guidance and sign of an angel, arrange a marriage for her to an elderly widower, Joseph, who immediately leaves for extensive work on a building project. Mary is visited by an angel who announces to her that she will conceive one she is to name "Jesus," who is "the Son of the Most High." She visits Elizabeth, also with child, remaining for several months before returning to her own home. She is then sixteen years of age. Upon his return, Joseph discovers Mary's condition and, distressed, ponders his proper course, until an angel appears to him to assure of Mary's faithfulness to him and to announce to him the identity of the child she has conceived. Judgments of the Temple priests then ensue, once they discover Mary's condition after the absence of Joseph. But the pair is deemed innocent after undergoing successfully a trial by water ordeal (See Num. 5:11–31). On the way to Bethlehem to enroll in the census of Augustus, they retreat into a cave when Mary goes into labor. After the birth, a midwife exits the cave to tell Salome, a passerby and also a midwife, of the miraculous birth from a virgin. Salome, in doubt of this, assesses for herself Mary's physical condition; for her unbelief, her hand is said to drop off and burn as by fire. At her repentant prayer, an angel instructs her to hold the infant Jesus, and her hand is cured upon doing so. The magi, following the bright star, then bring their gifts to the child. Shortly thereafter, Mary and Elizabeth hide their newborn sons from Herod's killing sweep of all Jewish children under two years of age. Herod has Zachariah murdered for his refusal to reveal the location of his son, John the Baptist.[10]

Supplementing Scripture's picture of Mary is also the early medieval apocryphal *Transitus Mariae*. As with the *Protoevangelium of James*, Christians who may be influenced by it are scarcely aware of it, so seamlessly has it melded into the composite portrait of Mary with which they are familiar. From the *Transitus Mariae*, extant in several different but related texts, Christians learned details of the death of Mary, witnessed by the apostles, at least one of whom is carried by clouds to her death bed. Through the eyes of these apostles, medieval Christians received vivid description of Mary's funeral and entombment, and they were shown her bodily "translation" into Heaven by angels in clouds who arrived at the promise and prompting of the Lord.[11]

The very existence of the *Protoevangelium* and the *Transitus Mariae*, along with Mary's prominent place in other apocryphal texts, shows the special interest that Christians had in Mary already in the early centuries of the Church, an interest that has endured to the present day. Kennedy noted, as evidence of the early attention given to her, her wide depiction in the catacombs and her frequent appearance in the writings of the Fathers[12] where she was often presented according to the "New Eve" typology that was not always wholly positive but often did stress Mary's laudable obedience to God in contrast to Eve's disobedience.[13] The ferocity of the reaction to the denial of her status as *Theotokos* (by Nestorius's faulty Christology anathematized in the third Christological council) shows how fervent was devotion to her by the fifth century. Kennedy observed that it was after the Council of Ephesus's formal dogmatic definition of her as the Mother of God that "her cult began to flourish independently of that of her divine Son."[14] Shortly thereafter the Liberian Basilica at Rome was dedicated to her. Possibly at this point, too, her name appeared in the Roman Canon.[15] In the seventh century, the four great feasts of Mary came to be celebrated in Rome by way of the East,[16] and from there Marian devotional activities reviewed in the conclusion of chapter 4 grew in number and prominence in the course of the Middle Ages. Sally Cunneen's recent research showed that the declaration of Mary as *Theotokos* gave even greater prominence to other roles that by the fifth century were seen of Mary: as "ever-virgin" she became model for the ascetic life and for purity generally; as symbol of the Church she was both set apart from other Christians and allied with them in Christ; as "all-holy" (Gk. *panagia*)—in Eastern Christianity especially—she was symbolic of spiritual as well as physical purity, human lens to the Son who is the image of the Father. Essentially a Christological statement, Mary's role as *Theotokos* was asserted to show the unity of the Son with the Father and the unity of divinity and humanity in the Son. Thereby, it effectively combated heretical notions going back to Arianism—the denial of Christ's full divinity, a position condemned at the Council of Nicaea in 325. But Cunneen and others have made the observation that in its assertion of the divinity of the person of the Son (with two natures—divine and human—in the Incarnation), it had the effect of seeming to separate conceptually the Son from immediate contact with us; it became Mary who seemed closest to us, as Jesus sat at the right hand of the Father in Heaven.[17] Throughout the Middle Ages, resultant tendencies of heightened Marian piety could be witnessed in different times and places,[18] right up to the moment of the Protestant Reformation, after which an extensive Marian piety survived among Catholics until Vatican II. But it is also the case, as mentioned in chapter 4, that, in the late Middle Ages, Mary and her Son received, together with Joseph, as the Holy Family, special attention for their humanity; many Christians came to identify with and become intensely connected with their suffering.[19] From humble Jewish mother of Jesus of Nazareth to powerful heavenly advocate, evolution in the understanding of Mary was not wholly devoid of popular if unconscious associations with pre-Christian feminine symbols of the divine and in part modeled upon the social structure of the Roman Empire with its hierarchical system of patronage, Cunneen and others have noted.

Providing an accurate sense of the place of Mary in the Roman Catholic Church today, especially with regard to the Church's liturgical life, is the Church's calendar. It contains three solemnities of Mary, two feasts universally and one additional feast in the United States, and eight memorials. The solemnities, the most important of Marian celebrations, concern three of the four dogmas promulgated about Mary: the Immaculate Conception (December 8); Mary, Mother of God, *Theotokos* (January 1); and the Assumption (August 15). (The fourth dogma, that of Mary's perpetual virginity, is assumed in the background of all Marian celebrations.) The universal feasts are the Visitation (May 31), which commemorates Mary's visit with Elizabeth at the time of their expectation of the births of Jesus and Saint John the Baptist, and the Birth of Mary (September 8), which evolved from the dedication to Mary's nativity of a church thought to have been built on the site of Mary's parents' home. In the United States, the feast of Our Lady of Guadalupe

(December 12) remembers and celebrates the apparition of Mary to Juan Diego in 1531 near Mexico City. Five memorials are "obligatory." That of the Immaculate Heart of Mary (August 22, but celebrated on the Saturday after the second Sunday from Pentecost) has its origins in a seventeenth-century devotion resulting in a special Mass. Pius XII consecrated the world to the Immaculate Heart of Mary and instituted the feast in the 1940s after the events of Fatima in the early twentieth century. The Queenship of Mary (August 22) became a universal feast on the centenary of the dogmatic proclamation of the Immaculate Conception, although it is connected with the dogma of the Assumption. Our Lady of Sorrows (September 15) recognizes and joins in Mary's suffering at the Cross of Christ; it is dated to a seventeenth-century observation of the Order of Servants of Mary that was added to the universal calendar of the Church in the early nineteenth century. Our Lady of the Rosary (October 7) has been celebrated universally since the beginning of the eighteenth century, although its origins stretch back to the late sixteenth century. The Presentation of Mary (November 21) was inspired by the reportage in the *Protoevangelium* of Mary's entrance into the Temple at the age of three to live, dedicated to God, as per her parents' vow, in the company of holy women. In the East, this feast was celebrated from the sixth century. Extended to the papal territory of Avignon in the late fourteenth century, it was instituted as a universal feast in 1585. The remaining three memorials are optional. Our Lady of Lourdes (February 11), celebrating Mary's appearance to Saint Bernadette in 1858, was established in 1907. Our Lady of Mount Carmel (July 16) was added to the universal calendar in 1726; it originally was established by the Carmelite Order upon its relocation in the West due to its expulsion from the Holy Land. The Dedication of the Basilica of Saint Mary Major (August 5) became a universal Church celebration in 1568, but its origins include the dedication of the church more than one thousand years earlier to commemorate the fifth-century proclamation of Mary as *Theotokos*.[20] One additional feast, the Presentation of the Lord (February 2), and one additional solemnity, the Annunciation (March 25), sometimes have been counted among Marian celebrations.

The solemnities of Mary are, as the teachings that gave rise to them, interrelated. The dogma of Mary as *Theotokos*—a status gifted her by God, on his initiative—points to the Annunciation wherein Mary freely agreed to this role requiring her virginity (hence the title "Ever-Virgin"). And it is because of the role as Mother of God that Mary would play that she was conceived immaculately and that she would be assumed into Heaven. Other Marian celebrations point to specific aspects of Mary's experience and to her role in the work of her Son, as well as to her place in the life of believers in her Son. God chose to enter human history in the radical way of the Incarnation, and he chose to do this contingent upon the free response of a mere human being—Mary. The solemnities, feasts, and memorials of Mary, the vehicle of the Incarnation, celebrate the depth of God's love for human beings. We remember through them not only the power of Mary's faith in her fiat, but the power of God's love in persuading her positive "graceful" response to his plan for human salvation. Of human persons, Mary is the perfect example of discipleship because she allowed God to transform her. She discloses strikingly Christ's triumph over sin. In her we see powerfully the drama of divine-human interaction, of grace and nature, as it results in that for which we all hope—which Catholics understand as sanctification of the human person. It is in the manner of expressing this that different Mariological emphases arise.

Recent Marian Reflection

Since Vatican II, important papal documents have been issued to guide Marian devotion.[21] For example, Pope Paul VI's 1974 apostolic exhortation *Marialis Cultus* encouraged new Mariological reflection that would present Mary in a way faithful to Scripture and doctrine while meaningful to contemporary women and men where past presentations of her are not.[22] Mary is a model of discipleship for all, in any age, for her immediate and complete acceptance of God's will and her "charity and a spirit of service."[23] She is our "sister" who "fully shared our lot" and deserves our devotion, for "Mary's glory . . . ennobles the whole of mankind [and womankind]."[24] Pope John Paul II's 1987 encyclical *Redemptoris Mater* presented Mary as a guide on the Church's journey through the ages.[25] She is "already the eschatological fulfillment of the Church" and her "pilgrimage of faith" serves as "a constant point of reference for the Church, for individuals and for communities, for peoples and nations and, in a sense, for all humanity."[26] In our time characterized by science and technology and rapid change, Mary is "maternally present and sharing in the many complicated problems which today beset the lives of individuals, families and nations; . . . helping the Christian people in the constant struggle between good and evil, to ensure that it 'does not fall,' or, if it has fallen, that it 'rises again.'"[27]

As Catholics among other Christians look anew at Mary, the scriptural passages referring to her have been and are being mined for every insight that they contain into the person and life of the mother of Jesus of Nazareth, whom Christians confess as the Christ. Attentive to history and culture, the result has been the publication of a number of studies that attempt a "reconstruction" of Mary's life based upon that which can be known about her time, place, culture, social role, etc. Such studies use methods of biblical scholarship, anthropology, archeological interpretation, and—especially in feminist and liberation scholarship—considerations of human experience. In contrast, there are those who wish to reassert Marian devotion in a more traditional form that often fixates more upon her current heavenly existence than upon her past earthly one or that views her earthly life through the lens of her current eschatological existence. The former, usually "low Mariologies," have of late come from Protestant thinkers who retain, in fear of idolatry or superstition, sometimes understandable misgivings about Catholic pietistic tendencies with regard to Mary, as well as from Catholic feminist and liberation thinkers who wish to rethink Mary's value to her fellow human beings, especially to women and those at the fringes of society. Mariam of Nazareth, they note, is one of us, albeit from her historical and cultural location of a first-century Palestinian Jew under the domination of the Roman Empire. In her marginalization, poverty, oppression, and lack of education, those who also are powerless can find special identification with her and perhaps even be empowered by her simple faith. Advocates of this view of Mary sometimes juxtapose their presentations against those of the past that have so elevated Mary—and sometimes precisely as a woman—that women, especially, have found her example unattainable and untenable. They argue that Mary's concrete experience has been ignored in favor of her place in the faith life of Christians and that she has been used as a symbol constructed by men of the ideal of women—which, according to custom, is to be submissive.[28] "High Mariologies" have come especially from Catholic Christians concerned that traditional Protestant inattention to Mary's unique role vis-à-vis Christ and thereby to her importance to her companion Christians, along with Catholic "reduction" in Marian devotion since Vatican II that has devalued traditional Marian roles affirmed by the Catholic Church, fails to focus fully upon the salvation (or at least the salvific experience) of women in particular. They assert that proper honor due to Christ is absent with inattention to Mary. Some bemoan the loss of the "feminine face of God"[29] provided to them by Mary who is not divine but who, in her free reception of grace—her fiat—showed in her sanctified image and likeness of God, in a truly exemplary and feminine way, something about God. They miss the emphasis upon her special intercessory role among the saints, in Christ.[30] Each of these positions offers important considerations. But, in exaggerated forms in which the concerns of the other position are completely disregarded, they can undermine key aspects of Marian doctrine of most Christians. Low Mariologies must guard against presenting Mary as just like the rest of us in her role (which she is not) rather than only in her humanity (which she is); high Mariologies must beware of presenting Mary as a "divine" representative (which she is not) rather than a mere human being (which she is) chosen by God, in his freedom and in hers, to be *Theotokos*. When they err at the extremes, they ignore something about Christ (i.e., his personal identity and work) that is the basis upon which all Mariologies must be judged, as well as the basis upon which veneration of all saints is judged. Unchecked low Mariologies run the risk of ignoring the real change in humanity's situation demonstrated concretely in Mary who freely cooperated with God's free and sovereign action in the Incarnation. Unchecked high Mariologies can lose the sense of the graciousness of the gift of our redemption by focusing on the objective fact of Mary's role vis-à-vis Christ but not emphasizing that it did not have to be so (since Mary is the first of the redeemed because God so chose this, not by any deservedness on her own or on the part of humanity) and not highlighting the real circumstances of her life that show her to be one of us.

In these positions it is perhaps not inappropriate to draw an analogy with the oft-noted relationship between the "Jesus of history" and the "Christ of faith."[31] Indeed, some scholars have compared the quest for the "Jesus of history" with that for the "Mary of history."[32] There is a "Mary of history" and a "Mary of faith," although, in the latter case, unlike with Christ, our faith in regard to Mary is not faith *in* her but faith in her role, *in Christ*. These are not exclusive positions; we are concerned with the Mary of history because of our faith in Christ and her role in it, and we must be concerned with the Mary of faith in a way that is grounded in her history, and his, if we are to appreciate fully her significance for us as the first of Christ's redeemed. Emphasis upon the Mary of history nets that which Edward Schillebeeckx termed "church or church-theological mariology" in which "Mary is our sister, an eminent and model member of the church's community of faith." Emphasis upon the Mary of faith nets a "christological mariology" in which Mary is placed "alongside Jesus to such a degree that she – the mother of Jesus, who as Christ is head of his redeemed church – is herself also called 'mother of the church.'"[33] Any proper Mariology must be both ecclesiological and Christological, shedding light upon our humanity as the object of the redemptive work of Christ (the concern of theological anthropology) through the Holy Spirit (the subject of pneumatology). Consciousness of this can prevent exaggerated influences in either direction. "Ecclesiological Mariology" cannot ground its assertion of Mary's exceptional exemplarity without consideration of her unique relationship to Christ, a consideration that certainly is evident in *Lumen Gentium*. And "Christological Mariology" finds its balance in remembering that Mary's unique relationship to Christ is important for us precisely because she is one with us in her humanity and in membership in the Church. If the intrinsically-related roles of the saints have, as has been argued, the impact of building up the Church in that the sanctification of individuals, as possible in Christ, renders companions worthy as models and as intercessors for others, then Mary's case demonstrates emphatically the necessary connections of these theological areas. "Proof" of this is the fact that it was important for the life of the Catholic Church that certain essentially Christological doctrines about Mary be promulgated as dogmas—infallible teachings either by popes (as according to the teaching of Vatican I as outlined in chapter 8) or by ecumenical councils.

Catholic Marian Dogmas

As has been noted, among Catholic doctrines about Mary are four dogmas: *Theotokos* (Mother of God), promulgated at the Council of Ephesus in 431; *Aei Parthenos* (Ever-Virgin), promulgated at a Lateran Synod in 649; the Immaculate Conception, defined by Pope Pius IX's papal bull *Ineffabilis Deus* in 1854;[34] and the Assumption, formally defined in 1950 by Pope Pius XII's apostolic constitution *Munificentissimus Deus.*[35] Although it often is observed that the first three of these dogmas are preeminently Christological statements upon which their Mariological statements rest, it can be argued that all four of the dogmas are inherently Christological statements, attesting to that which has occurred in Mary through the merits of her Son for the benefit of all of humankind.[36] The dogma that Mary is the Mother of God attests to the reality that he to whom she gave birth was God the Son. The title honors Mary because of her unique status vis-à-vis God who condescends (in the good sense of this term) to enter human history to redeem us, if we will accept redemption as did Mary. Mary is the Mother of God according to the "order of grace," *Lumen Gentium* asserts, as noted in chapter 7.[37] God's initiative in the Incarnation asked for her free but grace-enabled positive response to his plan, as it asks for our grace-enabled positive response to his "self-offer." In the words of *Lumen Gentium,* "All the Blessed Virgin's salutary influence on men and women originates not in any inner necessity but in the disposition of God. It flows forth from the superabundance of the merits of Christ, rests on his mediation, depends entirely on it and draws all its power from it. It does not hinder in any way the immediate union of the faithful with Christ but on the contrary fosters it."[38] The term "Ever-Virgin," affirming that Jesus had no biological brothers or sisters, attests to the complete submersion of Mary in her personal mission to support the mission of Christ for humanity universally. This submersion is possible through the grace of Christ, whom she bears. This dogma, then, as that of Mary as *Theotokos,* affirms Christ's divinity (as well as his humanity), as it recognizes the miraculous nature of his birth. Even though, in the history of the Church, Mary's virginity has been a symbol of purity sometimes conspicuously validating the life of celibacy, today an enlarged sense of purity allows us to see her state as emblematic of any human person's proper focus upon God and therefore instructive in discipleship for all states of life.[39] The most-recently promulgated dogmas, of the Immaculate Conception and of the Assumption, attest to the need of all for Christ's salvation and to the actual gift of salvation for all who accept it. That Mary is said to be the Immaculate Conception means that Christ prevented the stain of original sin from applying to Mary at all; that Mary experienced the assumption means that the promise of the resurrection has been realized in a human person, the first member of the Church. These late dogmas deserve special attention.

The dogma of the Immaculate Conception, in its assertion that Mary was conceived "completely free from all taint of original sin," means that she did not lose sanctifying grace, as have all other human beings, and therefore she would not have had "concupiscence," an excessive desire retained even after Baptism that is disordered (by original sin) toward that which does not lead to God (i.e., things of temporality, of the senses). Baptism eliminates the stain of original sin, but it does not eliminate this tendency. Her lack of concupiscence, however, does not mean that, ontologically, she was prevented from being tempted. It does mean that, in her confirmed choice for God, made under the influence of grace, she existed in an existential situation in which she would not turn from God (i.e., she would not give into temptation). To explain, because in her reality permeated by grace she chose God "habitually," she was "fixed" in her comportment toward God in a fulfilled state of a free decision executed. Human beings are creatures of habit, in that human free action leads to habit. Because all human beings—while of the "natural" order—are embraced by the supernatural order in God's offer of self-communication and his capacitation of us to accept this offer which directs us to him as our end and enables us to reach him, good habit can be elevated, by grace, to virtue. (Bad habit can become vice.) Mary was perfected in virtue—the fulfilled mode of being for any and every human person—such that she did not have to wrestle with choice between good and evil, between God and that which is not, not of, or does not lead to, God. She lived in an harmonious state in which her will was joined to God's and she simply did the good. Her freedom was not eliminated; she lived out her freedom in her fullness of personhood deliberately accepted as properly oriented to God. To borrow an analogy that early theologian

Origen (ca. 185–254) employed in a Christological context, "iron which is kept always in a fire" and therefore "takes in fire by all its pores and passages. . . . is entirely made into fire." In such case "nothing is seen in it save fire." Origen asked: "Can we possibly assert that this, which by its nature is plainly a quantity of iron, can at some point take on the quality of being cold when it has been located in a fire and is burning away incessantly?"[40] No, it must be answered. So Mary's love for God, never extinguished or even wavering, did not cool and "permit" of actions counter to God's will, even though he did not curtail the freedom of her will. Despite her immaculate conception, theologians hold that Mary retained the effects of sin—suffering, both emotionally and physically. Key among biblical passages supporting this dogma are the promise of Genesis that triumph will be realized over the serpent (Gen. 3:14) by "the woman" and "her seed" (Gen. 3:15) and the Lukan passages in which the angel greets Mary as "favored one" (Lk. 1:28) and in which Elizabeth greets Mary as "blessed among women"(Lk. 1:42).[41]

An intriguing feature of the document promulgating the dogma of the Assumption is silence on the matter of whether or not Mary died before this event. *Munificentissimus Deus* simply states that "the Immaculate Mother of God, the ever Virgin Mary, having completed the course of her earthly life, was assumed body and soul into heavenly glory."[42] The overwhelming tradition of the Church has been that Mary did die; theologically, it is difficult to explain why Mary would be preserved from this human "end" that even her divine Son experienced, as human. Nevertheless, even though there might seem to be the danger of elevating Mary to the level of Christ in a denial of her death, the document itself leaves open the possibility of Mariologies that have this belief in view of the unique honor properly given to Mary at the prompting of God. Vatican II allowed for conversations about such controverted Mariological matters in its chapter on Mary in the Dogmatic Constitution on the Church: "It [the Council] does not, . . , intend to give a complete doctrine of Mary, nor does it wish to decide those questions which the work of theologians has not yet fully clarified."[43] Among such questions, some theologians would put the language of the two recently-declared dogmas themselves. Originating in the early and medieval Church and influenced by spiritualities prominent at the time of their promulgation, the dogmas' language is not readily accessible to the faithful today.[44] In view of linguistic issues and in the context of ecumenical discussion, the Dombes Group, composed of Roman Catholic and Reformed scholars in France, observed, first, that the formal definition of the Immaculate Conception says only that "from the 'first moment' Mary was preserved from sin," leaving room for interpretation,[45] and, second, that the language of Vatican II in regard to this dogma is more congenial to the Eastern tradition, recalling "that it was customary for the Fathers to refer to the Mother of God as all holy and free from every stain of sin, as though fashioned by the Holy Spirit and formed as a new creature. . . ."[46] As for the definition of the Assumption, this ecumenical group noted the importance of being mindful of the facts of this dogma's stated relationship to the other Marian dogmas and its grounding in Mary's unique relationship with her resurrected Son.[47]

As evident from this brief summary, all of the Catholic Marian dogmas are observant of the sanctifying grace present in Mary who is said, in an early and popular translation of Luke 1:28, to be "full of grace." In Mary, the persuasive love of God met with the graced loving response of the human being for progressive sanctification of human nature. Yet she remains human. Nicaea II's teaching on the distinction yet relationship between worship and veneration holds; Mary is never worshipped. Indeed, the very power of the dogmas is their acknowledgement that that which has occurred in and for her—and through her for all other human beings—is not due to humanity but comes from the unsurpassable love of God though Christ. Catholic Marian doctrines can only be understood correctly and in their true profundity within this context of reflection upon the divine-human drama empowered by the Incarnation of which Mary is the vehicle. Central to all of the Marian dogmas is recognition of this interaction in freedom, an interaction initiated and sustained by God who is sovereign, in which humanity participates by divine gift.

Ecumenical Dialogue

At their formal definition, the dogmas of the Immaculate Conception and the Assumption purportedly surprised other Christians and, ostensibly, made ecumenical conversation more difficult. The dogmas are roundly observed to have been promulgated in times of intense Marian devotion, amidst a flurry of reported and some notably approved Marian apparitions. Yet they followed growing consensus about their unmistakable truth in the form of conciliar and papal statements over a period of centuries. Earlier supporting statements included those of the Council of Trent, which deliberately mentioned in its "Decree Concerning Original Sin" that Mary was excluded from its teaching about original sin pertaining to human beings[48] and which stated in its "Decree Concerning Justification"[49] that Mary was sinless through "a special privilege from God." The papal bull formally defining the Assumption, in particular, was issued in the wake of the world's witness of extraordinary carnage, in "severe calamities," such as World War II, and at a time of turn "away from truth and virtue."[50] The statement about the completed redemption of Mary was to give hope to all and to inspire greater attention to our eschatological goal realized in communion with others, in Christ. Despite the unwelcomeness of the announcements outside of Catholicism, ecumenical dialogue has advanced. On the subject of Mary and the saints, some Lutheran and Catholic theologians have proposed that Catholics be sensitive to the Lutheran concern that veneration of Mary and the saints not threaten the conviction that Christ is *the* Mediator and therefore not require Lutherans to hold the Marian dogmas or to invoke the saints. And these conversation partners have proposed that Lutherans be sensitive to the consistent Catholic tradition of veneration of Mary and the saints and, based upon this tradition's articulation in Vatican II documents, not charge that practices of veneration are counter to the gospel or that they foster idolatry. The intent of these suggestions, which have not been ratified by official statements of the Catholic Church, was to allow further dialogue with a goal of growing unity between Catholics and Lutherans in the future.[51]

It perhaps helps all Christians to remember that the traditions of the Immaculate Conception and the Assumption—and the occasional controversy surrounding them—are not recent; their dogmatic promulgation validated overwhelming and even ancient Catholic affirmation in popular piety, in liturgical celebration, and in theological reflection. Additionally and more importantly in promoting understanding, seen from the Catholic view of the relationship between nature and grace, they are consistent with this and, strong statements, can make the Catholic teaching on nature and grace so clear that some existing intra-religious agreement is made apparent with regard to Mary. That said, for Orthodox Christians, the dogma of the Immaculate Conception poses difficulty on the level of meaning because of their understanding of sin that differs from that which they identify of the West (both Catholic and Protestant) as juridical. And many Protestant Christians reject the teaching for the same reason that it was opposed by several of the great Catholic theologians of the Middle Ages (such as Anselm of Canterbury, Bernard of Clairvaux, Bonaventure, and Thomas Aquinas), in the extended discussion ending with Pope Pius IX's bull of dogmatic definition. Improperly understood, it seems to promote Mary beyond her companions in faith *in nature*; it seems to make her more than human. How could she be saved by Christ if she was never touched by the stain of sin? Properly understood, though, it underscores precisely the Catholic emphasis already noted of divine and human freedom. Mary was conceived immaculately (without the stain of original sin) *because of the divine prerogative. Lumen Gentium* explained: "Because of this gift of sublime grace she far surpasses all creatures, both in heaven and on earth. But, being of the race of Adam, she is at the same time also united to all those who are to be saved; . . ."[52] As the late thirteenth-century theologian Duns Scotus taught, as is anyone who is saved, Mary was saved by Christ, but in a unique way in view of the special role that she would play in the economy of redemption: Mary was preserved from having the stain of original sin even for a moment. This condition was given to her out of God's freedom, before any exercise of her own freedom; it therefore rests entirely upon the gratuitousness of God, entirely upon the merits of Christ. The dogma of the Immaculate Conception is, accordingly, a testament to the triumph of Christ over sin. At the same time, it is a testament to the human possibilities for true freedom under the influence of grace. Mary did not give into temptation, but "ever increased her original gift, . . , by divinely given power she utterly destroyed the force and dominion of the evil one."[53]

While belief in Mary's assumption does not demand a doctrine of her Immaculate Conception, the dogma of the Assumption logically—theologically—follows from belief in Mary's immaculate condition. As *Munificentissimus Deus* states, Mary, "by an entirely unique privilege, completely overcame sin by her Immaculate Conception, and as a result she was not subject to the law of remaining in the corruption of the grave, and she did not have to wait until the end of time for the redemption of her body."[54] Because of her radical conformity to her Son, a condition to which she gave her free assent and to which she was predestined[55] (in the Catholic sense of the supernatural end God offers us and persuades us by grace to accept), Mary Immaculate enjoys now the fullness of the eschatological reality for which we all hope. In Mary, Catholics see emphatically the triumph of Christ. In Mary, Catholics see that true freedom is exercised in trusting commitment, for as God, in freedom, in love, committed to humanity by entering history through the preordained vehicle of Mary, so Mary committed herself, in a continuous loving and free response, to this salvific plan. In Mary, Catholics see the sanctification or holiness to which all, as disciples of Christ, are called—a state resting upon the sovereignty and initiative of God which empowers free acceptance of his love. God's love is revealed profoundly in Mary. In the words of *Lumen Gentium*,

> . . . [W]hile in the most Blessed Virgin the church has already reached that perfection whereby she exists without spot or wrinkle (see Eph 5:27), the faithful still strive to conquer sin and grow in holiness. And so they turn their eyes to Mary who shines out to the whole community of the elect as the model of

virtues. Devoutly meditating on her and contemplating her in the light of the Word made man, the church reverently penetrates more deeply into the great mystery of the Incarnation and becomes more and more like its spouse. . . . [W]hen she is subject of preaching and honor she prompts the faithful to come to her Son, to his sacrifice and to the love of the Father.[56]

Although only the Catholic Church has promulgated any Marian doctrines as dogma, and, as stated, the doctrine of the Immaculate Conception is unique to Catholics, there is some agreement among Christians on three Marian teachings. Most of those who identify themselves as Christians hold at least to the first four Christological councils, the third of which affirmed that Mary is *Theotokos*. This includes all Catholic and Orthodox Christians and many Protestant Christians. The teaching that Mary was virginal throughout her life, before and after the birth of Christ, is held by the Orthodox and by some Protestants, as well as by Catholics. The doctrine of Mary's Assumption is also held by Orthodox Christians, although with no official definition, and it is not rejected by all Protestants. In fact, it was in the Eastern Christian empire that a feast of or anticipating that of the Assumption, called the *Dormitio* (Mary's "falling asleep"), was first celebrated widely. The Eastern emperor made it official for his territory entire in 602. Jungmann reported that already more than a century before this the feast had been celebrated by Christians prizing a church built between Jerusalem and Bethlehem, on a road at Gethsemane, where Mary was thought to have been buried.[57] By the eighth century, the feast celebrating her assumption on the day of that church's dedication—August 15—was widespread, observed even in Rome,[58] its popularity bolstered by the *Transitus Mariae*.

In *Lumen Gentium*, Vatican II expressed pleasure at the unity of Christians of all traditions where Mary is honored as "the Mother of Our Lord and Saviour."[59] Among these, it noted particularly "the eastern Christians, who with devout mind and fervent impulse reverence the Mother of God, ever virgin."[60] The history of Marian devotion dating to early Christianity is one that the Orthodox and Catholics consciously validate in current liturgical and devotional practices recognizing Mary as exemplar of faith for all Christians, as intercessor for all in the communion of saints, and as companion to all on the journey to full union with Christ. Orthodox regard for the *Theotokos* as "Ever-Virgin" and "All-Holy" and "immaculate" has been unrelenting.[61] In *Marialis Cultus*, Pope Paul VI reiterated the ecumenical unity residing in reflection upon and devotion to Mary, citing not only Catholic and Orthodox but Anglican convergences and the latter's contribution to scriptural study of

Mary, in which Reform churches also have participated.[62] This ecumenical dimension of attention to Mary is mentioned, too, in Pope John Paul II's *Redemptoris Mater.*[63]

Conclusion

As Catholics are given to notice in belief that discipleship of Christ is always a communal reality, in Orthodox churches, an "iconostasis," a screen featuring icons of the saints, is positioned between the community at worship and the priest presiding over the liturgy, signifying that the communion of saints is in the company of Christ. We are a people of God; it is a communion of saints that is saved by Christ, of which Mary is the preeminent member because of her unique historical and theological connection to Jesus' person and work. From the Catholic standpoint, as has been stressed in this chapter, key is the emphasis upon Mary's freedom in her positive response to God. Following the ancient tradition of the Church, *Lumen Gentium* asserted:

> Committing herself whole-heartedly to God's saving will and impeded by no sin, she devoted herself totally, as a handmaid of the Lord, to the person and work of her Son, under and with him, serving the mystery of redemption, by the grace of Almighty God. Rightly, therefore, the holy Fathers see Mary not merely as a passive instrument in the hands of God, but as freely cooperating in the work of human salvation through faith and obedience.[65]

Mary does as all human beings might; she serves as a "co-creator" in that, through her acceptance of the grace of Christ, his saving work is manifest in her and is efficacious for others who behold it. She is a locus of God's saving activity, through Christ, for other human beings. For this she "deserves" veneration or, to put it perhaps more correctly, for this other believers "deserve" to venerate her. As twentieth-century Catholic theologian Hans Urs Von Balthasar wrote in a book co-authored with Joseph Cardinal Ratzinger, *Mary: The Church at the Source,*

> The veneration of Mary is the surest and shortest way to get close to Christ in a concrete way. In meditating on her life in all its phases we learn what it means to live for and with Christ—in the everyday, in an unsentimental matter-of-factness that nonetheless enjoys perfect inner intimacy. Contemplating Mary's existence, we also submit to the darkness that is imposed on our faith, yet we learn how we must always be ready when Jesus suddenly asks something of us.[66]

Our consciousness of our closeness to Christ in veneration of Mary should not and does not ignore the Holy Spirit. Recently theologians have noted a dearth of late explicit attention given to the connection between Mary and the Holy Spirit, a connection attested in Scripture and highlighted by the Fathers, and some are pursuing this line of reflection. Mary is the first member of the Church, but the Holy Spirit is responsible for the Church's formation and sustenance. With that thought, the next chapter turns to expressly ecclesial and ecclesiastical matters related to the communion of saints, as validated by Catholic theology particularly.

Terms for Study

Aei Parthenos/Ever-Virgin	Habitude
Annunciation, The	Immaculate Conception, The
Assumption, The	Mariology, "High"/"From
Concupiscence	Above," "Low"/"From Below"
Devotion(s)	*Panagia*/All-Holy
Dogma	Piety
Fiat	Virginal Conception, The

Suggested Readings

Blancy, Alain, Maurice Jourjon, and the Dombes Group. *Mary in the Plan of God and in the Communion of Saints.* Translated by Matthew J. O'Connell. New York and Mahwah, New Jersey: Paulist Press, 2002. Original edition, *Marie dans le dessein de Dieu et la communion des saints*, [Paris]: Bayard Éditions, 1999.

The result of meetings in France, annually since 1997, including Catholic and Lutheran or Reformed theologians and open also to Anglican and Orthodox theologians, this ecumenical work employs a method of comparison and contrast of Catholic and Protestant convictions about Mary in the context of biblical assertions and historical developments associated with Christian attitudes toward Mary. As the back cover of the volume summarizes, the Dombes Group "has taken a fresh look at Mary in Christian faith and concluded that she has been more the victim than the cause of discord." All discussion participants accepted "the virginal conception and motherhood of Mary," despite other areas of disagreement.

Braaten, Carl E., and Robert W. Jenson, eds. *Mary: Mother of God.* Grand Rapids, Michigan: William B. Eerdmans Publishing, 2004.

This ecumenically-oriented collection of essays about Mary by theologians from each of the three major branches of Christianity provides a variety of views of and reflections upon Mary's status and role in the Church.

Coyle, Kathleen. *Mary in the Christian Tradition: From a Contemporary Perspective*, rev. North American edition. Mystic, Connecticut: Twenty-Third Publications, 1996.

In this brief presentation, traditional and alternative contemporary images of Mary are reviewed. A feminist and liberation perspective on Mary, the book also concisely relates history of Marian theology and devotion.

Cunneen, Sally. *In Search of Mary: The Woman and the Symbol*. New York: Ballantine Books, 1996.

A thorough study of the history of Marian devotion, as well as of contemporary directions in Marian spirituality and theology, this work of a Catholic author is ecumenical in nature. Beginning with the New Testament, Cunneen's survey includes Marian theology and art, the cultures in which these have arisen and developed, and even the psychological aspects of various Marian presentations.

Gambero, Luigi. *Mary and the Fathers of the Church: The Blessed Virgin Mary in Patristic Thought*. Translated by Thomas Buffer. San Francisco: Ignatius Press, 1999. Original edition, *Maria nel pensiero dei padri della Chiesa*, Milan: Edizione Paoline, 1991.

Gambero, Luigi. *Mary in the Middle Ages: The Blessed Virgin Mary in the Thought of Medieval Latin Theologians*. Translated by Thomas Buffer. San Francisco: Ignatius Press, 2005. Original edition, *Maria nel pensiero dei teologi latini medievali*, Milan: Edizione Paoline, 2000.

These two volumes offer an extensive study of thought about Mary in the history of the Church. Gambero organized his works according to a rough chronology of events and thinkers, featuring characterizations of key figures and their thought, summaries of their Marian theologies, and quotations from their works.

Gaventa, Beverly Roberts. *Mary: Glimpses of the Mother of Jesus*. Minneapolis: Fortress Press, 1999.

A contribution to ecumenical conversation from a Protestant perspective, this volume offers an analysis of biblical material about Mary, as well as considers early post-New Testament development in Marian thought as evident in the notable second-century *Protoevangelium of James*.

Johnson, Elizabeth A. *Truly Our Sister: A Theology of Mary in the Communion of Saints*. New York: Continuum International Publishing, 2004.

A Catholic participant in ecumenical conversations in recent decades, as well as a leading feminist theologian, in this volume—a companion to her *Friends of God and Prophets: A Feminist Theological Reading of the Communion of Saints*—Johnson worked from the biblical material concerning Mary, as well as from findings of anthropology and archeology and the concrete experience of women, to construct a portrait of Miriam of Nazareth that places her in her historical-cultural context. Offsetting past piety that presented Mary in a manner rendering her unapproachable and/or irrelevant to women and men of our day, Johnson used her portrait to mine the Bible for an understanding of Mary with which contemporary Christians can identify and in which they can find inspiration.

Little Office of the Blessed Virgin Mary. Edited by John E. Rotelle. New Jersey: Catholic Book Publishing, 1988.

The current version of the popular devotional tradition of the Middle Ages, it is derived from sections of the Liturgy of the Hours that are specifically relevant to Mary.

Mary in the Church: A Selection of Teaching Documents. Washington, D.C.: United States Conference of Catholic Bishops, 2003.

This volume includes four recent Marian documents of the Catholic Church: *Behold Your Mother: Woman of Faith*, 1973 pastoral letter of the National Conference of Catholic Bishops; *Marialis Cultus: For the Right Ordering and Development of Devotion to the Blessed Virgin Mary*, 1974 apostolic exhortation of Pope Paul VI; *Redemptoris Mater: On the Blessed Virgin Mary in the Life of the Pilgrim Church*, 1987 encyclical letter of Pope John Paul II; and *Rosarium Virginis Mariae: On the Most Holy Rosary*, 2002 apostolic letter of Pope John Paul II.

Mary's Place in Christian Dialogue. Edited by Alberic Stacpoole. Wilton, Connecticut: Morehouse-Barlow, 1982.

While several decades old, the essays in this volume remain helpful statements of positions and issues that are subjects of discussion among Christians engaged in Mariological reflection today, particularly those with a goal of ecumenical understanding about Mary. One of several books associated with the Ecumenical Society of the Blessed Virgin Mary and featuring contributions from scholars of many Christian denominations, the essays are grouped into eight discussion areas: ecumenical, scriptural, theological, doctrinal, the Protestant tradition, other Christian and non-Christian traditions, historical, and devotional.

Blessed Pius IX, Pope. *Ineffabilis Deus.* At Papal Encyclicals Online [online]. Available from http://www.papalencyclicals.net/Pius09/p9ineff.htm. Accessed 1 September 2011.

This apostolic constitution was issued on December 8, 1854, as a papal bull promulgating the dogma of the Immaculate Conception which is celebrated liturgically on December 8.

Pius XII, Pope. *Munificentissimus Deus.* At Papal Encyclicals Online [online]. Available from http://www.papalencyclicals.net/Pius12/P12MUNIF.HTM. Accessed 1 September 2011.

This apostolic constitution was issued on November 1, 1950, as a papal bull promulgating the dogma of the Assumption which is celebrated liturgically on August 15.

The Protoevangelium of James. At New Advent [online]. Available from http://www.newadvent.org/fathers/0847.htm. Accessed 1 September 2011. Revised and edited by Kevin Knight, cf. *Ante-Nicene Fathers.* Vol. 8. Edited by Alexander Roberts, James Donaldson, and A. Cleveland Coxe. Translated by Alexander Walker. Buffalo, New York: Christian Literature Publishing, 1886.

Apocryphal Works on the Assumption of Mary (*Transitus Mariae*). At *New Advent: Church Fathers* [online]. Available from http://www.newadvent.org/fathers/0832.htm. Accessed 1 September 2011. Revised and edited by Kevin Knight, cf. *Ante-Nicene Fathers.* Vol. 8. Edited by Alexander Roberts, James Donaldson, and A. Cleveland Coxe. Translated by Alexander Walker. Buffalo, New York: Christian Literature Publishing, 1886.

"Classics" of the pious tradition of devotion to Mary, these texts purport to offer historical details of the beginning and end of Mary's life and have been judged to be influential in the scope and quality of veneration of her.

Tavard, George H. *The Thousand Faces of the Virgin Mary.* Collegeville, Minnesota: Liturgical Press, 1996.

This expansive ecumenical study of Mary is from the late internationally-active Catholic ecumenist of the Augustinians of the Assumption who was a Vatican II peritus contributing to the Decree on Ecumenism. Images of Mary are studied from and through a variety of Christian confessional vantage points and "media" (including doctrine, poetry, visions, popular piety, etc.), as well as in relation to the idea of the feminine vis-à-vis God in Asian religions.

Fourteen

CONCERNS:
THE MYSTERIOUS, THE MIRACULOUS,
AND MISCELLANEOUS

Pilgrims visiting the Basilica of Saint John Lateran in Rome can walk
across the street to ascend, on their knees, one at a time, twenty-eight steps
to the *Sancta Sanctorum* ("the Holy of the Holies," as it has been known
since the ninth century), the famous chapel of the popes in the many years
in which they resided in the Lateran palaces. There housed are a multitude
of prized relics including, famously, a probable fifth- or sixth-century icon
depicting Jesus Christ called the *acheropite* image ("an image not painted
by human hand"). The staircase itself, popularly known as the *Scala
Sancti* (the "Holy Stairway"), is purported to be that which Jesus climbed
on the day he faced Pontius Pilate to receive his death sentence.[1] Formal
prayers, available in print at the site, are recited at each stage of the
approximate thirty-minute journey. (The rate of progress to the chapel
varies depending upon the speed of recitation of the prayers and one's
physical ability.)[2] Unevenly worn by the knees of countless faithful, the
wood-encased marble steps are unforgiving. At busy times, discomfort
experienced is increased by the need to recalculate path and readjust position to accommodate others making the trip. Of course the difficulty is
very little compared to the sufferings of Christ, but that is the point. Those
who climb the stairs engage in ascetical activity, willingly accepting pain
in their desire to be united with Christ who suffered for us, in atonement
for sins forgiven by Christ's suffering, and in some meager way responding to the call of Christ to any follower to "deny himself and take up his
cross and follow me" (Mt. 16:24), "complet[ing] what is lacking in
Christ's afflictions for the sake of his body, that is, the church, . ."(Col.
1:24). The prayers recall the torments of Christ, but also his love and forgiveness, during distinct moments of the Passion. And they ask for Christ's
mercy for our entrance into "paradise."[3] In these prayers pilgrims join their
thoughts, emotions, and bodies to a religious act directed to God through
his sacramental presence in relics. In their progress up the stairs, pilgrims
also are conscious of their unity, in the grace of God, with others who are
making this journey and who have made it over the centuries, as well
as with the saints whose relics are near, and with all who rest in Christ

with these saints. They gain a palpable sense of their inclusion in the communion of saints. Additionally, they might gain an indulgence, if other required conditions are fulfilled.

In spite of the fact that some traditional practices that touch upon veneration of the saints are not as prevalent now as they were in the past, those involving devotions, relics, and indulgences remain current among the Church's repository of spiritual aids. Each of these has been mentioned in previous chapters, but, because today they are unfamiliar to many Christians, and no less because they can both captivate and confuse even contemporary faithful who know about them, supplementary explanation is due.

Devotions

There was a time when it would not have been unusual to see a Catholic pray the rosary during Mass—before Vatican II when the form of the Mass itself could seem a private affair of the priest and as a result individuals were spiritually fed by receding into their own devotional activities. Vatican II rightly sought to curtail such private devotions during the Eucharistic celebration which should be the undivided focus of our attention; the Mass now visibly and experientially involves the entire community gathered. Sometimes, depending upon the manner in which the liturgical reforms of Vatican II have been implemented, however, the liturgy can seem to emphasize the horizontal dimension of the Body of Christ—the relationship among human beings because of Christ. The Church evolves in permissible ways in keeping with revelation, since it is an institution containing human beings who change and grow in time, in knowledge, and in culture. The vertical dimension of the Body of Christ—our relationship with Christ, the divine Son become human—has been the emphasis at some points in the past. Those who seek that focus now, along with the other, can turn to devotional practices.

Devotions are not, and will not ever be, equally appealing to all believers, even to Catholic Christians whose history includes, amply, such spiritual practices. But applying the concept of intentionality to such practices can aid in understanding them. As in the case of ascent of the Holy Stairway, all devotions are willing engagements of the faithful in exercises that promote unity—and religious experience of that unity— with God and with other human beings. This is possible because of our elevation to a supernatural realm that does not dissolve nor devalue our historical reality or experience but that pulls us to transcend it by embracing and completing it in consciousness of a destiny beyond it in God's grace. Yet, since God created us as individuals, with unique personalities, where private spirituality is concerned, we should not expect that all of us will respond in the same manner to him and to the reality that he has gifted us. To consider psychological factors of our personalities, more introverted persons (i.e., those who are revitalized by private time) are bound to find especially meaningful quiet religious activities such as devotions that provide necessary time for reflection. More extroverted persons (i.e., those who are revitalized by public interaction) are bound be more attracted to communal, and possibly lively, religious activities. Without recognizing this, we can become unduly critical, on the supposed grounds of theology, of others' spirituality issuing from personality traits that are morally neutral. There are public and private dimensions of Christian life, in that all are called to public worship and in fact nothing occurs outside the context of our status as "people of God," yet private prayer and reflection guide each of us in the individual choices we must make to ratify our commitment to Christ and his Mystical Body of which we are a part. This explains at least in part why some Christians more than others, in possession of knowledge about the history and the theology of veneration of saints, will be interested in private activities of the cult of the saints, in addition to willingly participating in the Church's corporate veneration of the canonized.

Relics

As chapter 6 noted, Scripture would seem to contain evidence of impulses toward relic veneration on the part of those who had faith in Christ and his power manifested even in things he wore and used, as well as his power manifested in those who were closely associated with him and in things that came into contact with them. For example, in the synoptic gospels, there appears the story of the hemorrhaging woman who touches Jesus' garment and is healed of her twelve-year affliction by the power released from Jesus thereby. Although biblical scholars understand her touch of the "fringe of his garment," a prayer shawl by some accounts (Mt. 9:20–22; Lk. 8:43–48), to be an act of homage, in the earliest account of this incident (Mk. 5:25–34), no mention is made of a prayer shawl but only of the woman's touch of Jesus' "garment(s)." Daniel J. Harrington has written that "[her] action is based on the belief that contact with Jesus the powerful person could heal her."[4] Such sought physical contact with Jesus as a person of spiritual power, or with his garment(s), also is reflected in the synoptic gospels where others ill are brought to him to touch him (Lk. 6:19) or "the fringe of his garment" (Mt. 14:35–36; Mk. 6:56) and thereby are healed.[5] In the Acts of the Apostles, stories of healings by physical touch of or presence of the apostles—such as that of the restoration at the Temple of the lame man's ability to walk at Peter's invocation of Jesus' name (3:1–9), of the raising of Tabitha of Joppa at the bedside prayer of Peter (9:36–43), and of the healing of the official Publius's father through Paul's prayer and laying on of hands (28:7–8), followed by other healings through Paul in that vicinity of Malta (28:9–10)—are supplemented by those that explain cures by reference to physical items associated with the apostles whose hands are known to heal.[6] In Acts 5:12–16, sick are placed in the streets so that "as Peter came by at least his shadow might fall on some of them" (5:15). In Acts 19:11–12, as cited in chapter 2, it is recounted that, because of Paul's reputation for miracles, "handkerchiefs or aprons were carried away from his body to the sick, and diseases left them and the evil spirits came out of them." Richard J. Dillon has classed these incidents with that of the earlier-mentioned sick touching Jesus' garment "hem" in Mark 6:56: the power that cures the ailing here "is a function of faith in the living *Kyrios*."[7] It is not out of the question to see in these a connection with a later form of relic veneration, whereby prayers to God in the presence of the remains of his martyrs and saints made his curing presence more palpable.

In Fyodor Dostoevsky's *The Brothers Karamazov*, in a scene at once touching for its portrait of faith in signs of the sacred in the profane, disturbing for its characterization of human propensity for pettiness borne by jealousy, and comical in its presentation of human reaction to the unexpected, members of an Orthodox monastic community in Russia and guests and residents of the town in which the monastery is located gather to pay their final respects to a revered monk-priest and to experience or to witness the enhanced power to heal that he will have in death. Believed during his lifetime to have been a saint, many also wait with happy anticipation the "odor of sanctity," a sweet smell expected to be emitted from his corpse, a phenomenon that has been reported in the case of some saints and one that this community views as proof of sainthood. Instead, as hours pass, the unmistakable stench of decay pervades the room in which his body is laid, until, finally, feigned oblivion to the smell is no longer possible. Mourners are left to speculate about the secret sinful life that he must have led to elicit this sign from God; one attempts to explain that decay does not necessarily disprove sainthood.[8] In the Western church, bodily decay has not been thought to indicate lack of sanctity nor has lack of decay traditionally been thought to prove saintly status, but reports of sweet odors emanating from the dead believed or confirmed to be saints, as well as sightings of incorruptible bodies, post-death blood and/or oil flow from bodies, and bodily movements of the dead such as change of position, have always inspired the faithful. So, too, have miracles—including those of intercession—that have been reported to have occurred in connection with saintly bodies, whether or not the bodies exhibit other exceptional phenomena. "Incorruptibles"—saints or blesseds whose remains, in whole or in part, were revealed upon exhumation not to have decayed despite the fact that no steps were taken to ensure such preservation—are on display in shrines throughout the world but especially in Italy.[9]

Veneration of relics seems in our day to fascinate in a way that both compels and repels those with scant understanding of the tradition, especially where customs mentioned in previous chapters involving preservation, distribution, and display of first-class relics—bodies or parts of bodies of the saints—are concerned. An historical-cultural consciousness can aid. In past ages, before there existed photographs and realistic portraits by which loved ones could be remembered, and when people lived much closer to death in that they had shorter lives, died in homes rather than in hospitals, and themselves prepared for burial the bodies of relatives and friends (rather than sending them to a funeral home), the idea of keeping bones or blood of the dead developed from affection and, in the case of the saints, also belief in miraculous powers. There was no disrespect in practices that seem odd to us today; quite the contrary, these practices were signs of deep regard (although in cases of disagreements about the final resting place of a saint, selfishness could reign, too). Relic veneration is one manifestation of Christian belief in the resurrection of Christ and its promise that our resurrection will be the salvation of the whole human person—soul and body.

Indulgences

Indulgences have a long history, growing out of concern already in the early Church about the sins that individuals commit after Baptism. Baptism, as the *Catechism of the Catholic Church* reminds, "is the first and chief sacrament of forgiveness of sins because it unites us with Christ, who died for our sins and rose for our justification, . . ."[10] This sacrament, by which "*all sins* are forgiven, original sin and all personal sins, as well as all punishment for sin,"[11] also "gives us the Holy Spirit."[12] Baptism does not erase concupiscence,[13] however, so it is not surprising that baptized individuals sin after receiving this initial sacrament of initiation into the Church. The Church has understood that it has the authority, given by Christ (Jn. 20:22–23), to extend Christ's forgiveness to these post-baptismal sins and to impose a penance that allows the penitent to continue the process of conversion, a constant call of Christ to each and all.[14] The sin is forgiven by God, through the Church, in the sacrament of Confession (also known as Penance and as Reconciliation), then, but punishment is due. This punishment is *not* "vengeance inflicted by God" but the residue of sin that must be eliminated in order for the individual to undergo the "complete purification" necessary for complete unity with God.[15] "Eternal punishment" is that of Hell—eternal separation from God due to "mortal sin" (i.e., grave sin that "destroys charity"[16]) that is not repented and therefore not forgiven. For sin forgiven, whether mortal or "venial" (i.e., sin that "weakens charity"[17]), there is always due "temporal punishment" to be satisfied either in this world or in the next.[18] The *Catechism* instructs that "the Christian must strive to accept this temporal punishment of sin as a grace."[19] Indulgences come into play here. In early ages of the Church, penances imposed after sacramental confession could be extensive, not to mention public, and therefore sometimes difficult to fulfill. The custom arose of offering substitute activities for these, with the understanding that the infinite merits of Christ's sacrifice, "with his own precious blood" (cf. 1 Pet. 1:18f),[20] as well as the contributions of the saints acting in the grace of Christ, would supply any deficiency in the penitent's actions. In the sixteenth century such substitute activities included almsgiving to the Church, as well as more traditional activities such as prayers. Chapter 6 discussed Luther's negative reaction to this practice, leading to the Protestant Reformation, prompted by improper preaching about donations to the Church that suggested to believers that indulgences could be purchased.

The definition of an indulgence is given by Canon 992 of the 1983 Code of Canon Law: "An indulgence is the remission in the sight of God of the temporal punishment due for sins, the guilt of which has already been forgiven." The Canon explains: "A member of Christ's faithful who is properly disposed and who fulfils certain specific conditions, may gain an indulgence by the help of the Church which, as the minister of redemption, authoritatively dispenses and applies the treasury of the merits of Christ and the Saints."[21] There are five basic elements to consider in this definition. First, indulgences do not forgive sin. Sin must be forgiven through the normal channels prescribed by the Church, chiefly in Baptism and in the sacrament of Confession, as has been explained. Second, any individual who pursues an indulgence must do so with the appropriate spiritual disposition of one seeking ongoing conversion and unity with God. Third, precise conditions, approved by the Church, must be met for an indulgence to be granted.[22] Such conditions, including the norms for indulgences generally as well as the particular types of activities for which indulgences can be granted, are set out by the Church today in the Apostolic Penitentiary's *Enchiridion Indulgentiarum: Normae et Concessiones*, translated and published in North America by the United States Conference of Catholic Bishops.[23]

The four main types of activities involve invocations, charitable work or almsgiving for the needy, fasts and abstinence, and public witness to faith in Christ.[24] Indulgence grants are also given for recitation of ecclesiastically-approved prayers, litanies, and offices, for reverential visits to "sacred places," plus for "acts of piety, or use of a devotional object," as well as for Eucharistic adoration, recitation of the rosary, participation in the Way of the Cross, reading or listening to sacred Scripture, etc.[25] In each case, precise directions are to be followed in the performance of these acts of Christian faith, hope, and love. An indulgence may be either partial or plenary, "according as it partially or wholly frees a person from the temporal punishment due for sins."[26] In order to receive a plenary indulgence, the specified activities must be carried out with the proper disposition, the individual completing these works must within a few days receive the sacrament of Confession, receive the Eucharist, and pray for the intentions of the pope, and this individual must be free even of venial sin. Absent any of these factors in their fullness, a plenary indulgence is reduced to a partial indulgence.[27] Fourth, the Church has the authority to grant indulgences,[28] just as it was given the authority by Christ to forgive sins. As recounted in the Gospel of Matthew, this authority was given by Christ to Saint Peter the Apostle, whom Catholics consider the first pope: "I will give you the keys of the kingdom of heaven, and whatever you bind on earth shall be bound in heaven, and whatever you loose on earth shall be loosed in heaven" (Mt. 16:19). The authority was extended by Christ to the other apostles, too, as he counseled them in the way to live toward the Kingdom of Heaven (Mt. 18:18). Biblical scholars note that Saint Paul used this power already in the earliest days of Christianity, as recorded in his Second Letter to the Corinthians: ". . . What I have forgiven, if I have forgiven anything, has been for your sake in the presence of Christ, . . ." (2 Cor. 2:10). Fifth, the Church dispenses indulgences from the "Treasury of Merits" of Christ and his saints. As attested in the First Letter of John, Jesus Christ "is the expiation for our sins, and not for ours only but also for the sins of the whole world" (1 Jn. 2:2). Indulgences may be applied to the one who gains them or to those dead and in Purgatory.[29]

The Treasury, also called the "Treasury of the Church," is "spiritual goods of the communion of saints,"[30] which *Indulgentiarum Doctrina*, an apostolic constitution issued shortly after Vatican II to modify the Church's indulgences criteria, states is "the infinite and inexhaustible value the expiation and the merits of Christ Our Lord have before God, offered as they were so that all of mankind could be set free from sin and attain communion with the Father." Pointing to the ancient tradition of Christians offering good works for each other's salvation,[31] the document describes the content of the Treasury:

It is Christ the Redeemer Himself in whom the satisfactions and merits of His redemption exist and find their force. This treasury also includes the truly immense, unfathomable and ever pristine value before God of the prayers and good works of the Blessed Virgin Mary and all the saints, who following in the footsteps of Christ the Lord and by His grace have sanctified their lives and fulfilled the mission entrusted to them by the Father. Thus while attaining their own salvation, they have also cooperated in the salvation of their brothers [and sisters] in the unity of the Mystical Body.[32]

The Treasury is not to be considered "the sum total of material goods accumulated in the course of the centuries."[33] As members of Christ's Mystical Body, each "part" of the Body should function as intended—in imitation of Christ's love, enabled by his grace. When this occurs, the Body grows stronger, as emphasized by Pope Pius XI in his 1928 encyclical *Miserentissimus Redemptor*. He also wrote:

> . . . Christ's expiatory suffering is renewed and in a way continued and completed in his mystical Body, which is the Church. For, to use St. Augustine's words . . . : 'Christ suffered all that he should have suffered; there is now nothing lacking in the measure of his sufferings. His sufferings as Head, then, were completed; yet, for Christ in his body sufferings still remained.' . . . Christ who is still suffering in his mystical Body should want to have us as his companions in the work of expiation. This is required of us also by our close union with him, since we are 'the Body of Christ and individually members of it' [1 Cor. 12:27], and all the members ought to suffer with the Head anything that the Head suffers [cf. 1 Cor. 12:26].[34]

As members of the Body of Christ accept the sacrificial love of Christ, Christ's presence in the world is made more powerful and evident; there is thereby increase in the Treasury. By joining our intentionality to that of the saints who have ratified their commitment to God in life through death, we affirm their choice and follow their path in the pull of their example of charity and of their perpetual intercession—their constant prayer—on behalf of their companions on Earth and in Purgatory. Rahner remarked:

> [T]he 'Treasury of the Church' is nothing else than the salvific will of God, which aims at bringing all men [and women] to perfect charity. And such charity includes reparation and the elimination of the 'punishments for sin', since this salvific will exists as centered on the redemption wrought by Christ and the

holiness of the whole Church which depends on this redemption but is also present through it. And this holiness implies a dynamism which tends to the perfect charity which eliminates all the consequences of sin in every member of this Church.[35]

Perfect charity can be accomplished only in relationship with others. Our salvation depends, in part, upon the *acceptance* of the grace of Christ who, in the words of Pope Pius XII's encyclical *Mystici Corporis* following the prologue of the Gospel of John, is "so full of grace and truth . . . that of his inexhaustible fullness we all receive" (cf. Jn. 1:14–16).[36]

Conclusion

In the conclusion to Jesuit writer James Martin's popular 2006 book, *My Life with the Saints*, he cautioned that we should not look to the saints only as models and as intercessors, only as dispensers of favors, but treat them as true friends.[37] If we can do this, despite that most of us are only fortunate to know the saints through the memory of the Church and its individual members who venerate them and not in the flesh, so to speak, it is perhaps partly by way of our knowledge of the saints garnered through the experience we share with them of being human. In his encyclical *Novo Millennio Ineunte,* Pope John Paul II wrote of the "'lived theology' of the saints,"[38] the experience that many of them have had analogous to that of Jesus Christ himself on the Cross when he felt both his intimacy with the Father and pain that elicited his "final cry of abandonment." "The simultaneous presence of these two seemingly irreconcilable aspects is rooted in the fathomless depths of the hypostatic union," wrote the Pope.[39] Indeed, the possibility of this disjunction was the assumption of humanity—which is other than God—by God the Son. In our humanity, that same pain can exist. Because of the Triune God's invitation to us to salvation (an invitation that directs us to a supernatural realm), however, we know and experience the possibilities of fulfillment and joy in final participation in God. Since the saints no less and perhaps more than the rest of us can experience this dual reality, they know our pain and joy, as does Christ in whom they continue to exist, and we know theirs—because we share the humanity that Christ assumed and "graced." To look at them in their different contexts is to see how this dichotomy played out in their lives. These true companions, friends, model the way to negotiate our path in the Holy Spirit; in their lives and deaths we see their grace-filled "ending" analogous to Christ's when he handed over his spirit to the Father. And they intercede—continually praying for us—with Christ who is our perpetual Intercessor with the

Father. This is why we venerate the saints, testifying to the grace of Christ we see in them and the evidence this gives of the coming fulfillment that Christ promised to all of humanity. To "use" the saints as models and as intercessors is not objectionable as long as we see that they are increased, that they reach their true selves, in Christ, as do all human beings, as related to each other, in "a single mystical person," in the language of a beautiful passage in *Indulgentiarum Doctrina* following upon the tradition of the communion of saints as the Mystical Body of Christ.[40] God has created and has redeemed us in such a way that we are all united in his eschatological Kingdom; we are all making the journey there together. Martin's point, then, reminds us that, in veneration of the saints, our eschatological sensibility cannot be lost (or else we will "use" the saints and others in the wrong way). The saints assist us as we can and do and will assist others. And that recognition leads us to the realization that veneration of saints should drive us into deeper love of those we know in this life. That which we see in the saints that compels us is Christ, and we know Christ also in our neighbor now. We must be able to love in *this* world *and* in the next to function fully in the Mystical Body. The character of true love is that it is unconditional; it transcends time, as God himself who is present in time but who is not bound by time *is* Love. To become a saint is to participate in God through love, which is sacrificial. The final chapter will reflect upon this transcendent dimension of love seen in the saints.

Terms for Study

Baptism	Punishment, Eternal and Temporal
Confession/Penance/Reconciliation	Sin, Mortal and Venial
Incorruptibles	Treasury of the Church/Treasury
Indulgence(s)	of Merits

Suggested Readings

Cruz, Joan Carroll. *The Incorruptibles: A Study of the Incorruption of the Bodies of Various Catholic Saints and Beati.* Rockford, Illinois: Tan Books and Publishers, 1977.

The product of extensive research into the particulars of incorruptible bodies of more than one hundred Catholic saints, the author's introduction provides precise description of the phenomenon and a short explanation of the history of the Church's reaction to it. The chapters that follow offer specific information about each "Incorruptible" featured: a brief biography; the circumstances of the burial, exhumation(s), and translation to shrine; details about the current condition of the body; and reports of miracles associated with the saint, his or her bodily relic, and/or the translation of the relic.

Dostoevsky, Fyodor. *The Brothers Karamazov.* Translated by Andrew H. MacAndrew. New York: Bantam Books, 1981.

First published in 1880, a year before Dostoevsky's death, this novel which is considered a literary masterpiece explores the "great questions" about the meaning of human life and the existence of God. Characters could be viewed as studies of conversion or lack thereof.

Manual of Indulgences: Norms and Grants. Approved by the Apostolic Penitentiary. Washington, D.C.: United States Conference of Catholic Bishops, 2006. Original edition, *Enchiridion Indulgentiarum: Normae et Concessiones,* 4th ed., Città del Vaticana: Liberia Editrice Vaticana, 1999.

This handbook provides current rules governing indulgences, explains the basic types of indulgences, and lists specific prayers and works for which indulgences are granted. Based upon an edition approved in 1999 by Pope John Paul II, it was prepared in accordance with the 1967 apostolic constitution *Indulgentiarum Doctrina,* which established new norms for indulgences, as well as in correspondence to the 1983 Code of Canon Law and updated editions of the Scriptures, liturgical texts, ritual texts, and documents of the Apostolic See. *Indulgentiarum Doctrina* is included as one of the appendices in the volume.

Fifteen

VENERATION OF SAINTS: MEANING AND VALUE OF THE TRADITION

In the late Anglican theologian and novelist C.S. Lewis's *Mere Christianity*, one of his many famous books inspirational to now several generations of Christians, he composed an image of us from the vantage point of God.

> . . . If you could see humanity spread out in time, as God sees it, it would not look like a lot of separate things dotted about. It would look like one single growing thing—rather like a very complicated tree. Every individual would appear connected with every other. And not only that. Individuals are not really separate from God any more than from one another. Every man, woman, and child all over the world is feeling and breathing at this moment only because God, so to speak, is 'keeping him going.'[1]

He continued this reflection by drawing the Christological ramification of this reality.

> Consequently, when Christ becomes man it is . . . as if something which is always affecting the whole human mass begins, at one point, to affect that whole human mass in a new way. From that point the effect spreads through all mankind. It makes a difference to people who lived before Christ as well as to people who lived after him. It makes a difference to people who have never heard of Him. . . .[2]

The Christological content of Lewis's image can be rendered more vividly by adding Christ's saints to it. Lewis himself noted that individuals must appropriate the salvation that Christ has gifted us, that "of passing over from the temporary biological life into a timeless 'spiritual' life."[3] When that acceptance of human beings of our new reality occurs, the "difference" that Christ has made for all becomes powerfully evident in various portions of the "tree." This is an ontological reality. As this fifteen-chapter study has explained, our creation and our salvation exist by God's initiative, to which we can only respond—under the influence of his empowering grace—and to which we must respond. The saints have done so; their response can be efficacious for us, inspiring us by engaging our intentionality on every level (mind, heart, and will) by the power of the sanctifying grace seen in them and thereby moving us to assume their same posture toward God and, through him, toward the neighbor. As religious images themselves, icons that are symbols or sacraments, they are instances of the redemptive work of the Incarnate God, their graced lives making this more powerfully apparent in the world in a way that advances the eschatological goal of all of humanity. From this view, it is not difficult to see that the actions of these companions of ours in humanity, connected with us in our family tree (to use both Lewis's analogy and the Catholic sense of the familial communion of Christians), affect others in the saints' own time of history and after it. But, further, there is also a highly qualified way in which the saints can affect people before their own historical time, too—because they have achieved the "timeless 'spiritual' life" that is really the completion of their historical life. (We are "spirits in the world," to borrow the title of one of Rahner's works.⁴) The saints as individuals emerge only in particular historical moments (which look not so particular from the vantage point of God), but the fact of saintly lives transcends time divisions because it is a sign and instrument of the Incarnation's universal accomplishment. How else could we conceive of Jesus Christ's redemptive effect upon all, if, looking backwards into history, we could not see any righteous, or holy, persons? Chapter 2 showed that the New Testament recognized a host of righteous persons from the Old Testament and chapter 3 showed that the Church has venerated such figures, not to mention angels. And Church Fathers—Saint Justin Martyr, for example—explicitly theorized about Christ's work in those who lived before the Incarnation. According to Justin, the "seeds" of the Logos (from the Greek *logos* meaning "word"), who became the Incarnate Christ, were scattered throughout creation, at creation, because creation came to be through the agency of the Logos of God who would become flesh (Jn. 1:14). Made in the image and likeness of God, human beings, as rational creatures, have always had the ability to recognize and to respond to this reality; we have a "seed-like participation" in the Logos. Whenever and wherever human beings have acted toward goodness, human beings have perceived and accepted the Logos, even if unconsciously—as would have been the case before the Incarnation occurred in approximately 4 B.C. when the Logos was revealed in fullness. Today the Catholic Church extends such reflections to explain the grace that Christians see operative in other world religions, in people who do not confess Christ explicitly but who, in an implicit way consistent with their understanding of that which they believe to be revelation, in fact accept the goodness that comes from the Father through the Son in the Holy Spirit—the Triune God.[5]

The intertwinement of human lives across historical time periods (not in the sense of a backward causality, which is science fiction, but in the sense of the permanent relevance of each and every human being) means that, in Christ, as has been stated in previous chapters but which must be underscored here, human beings do not cease to be important to others for their completion of their earthly lives. Again, we are all ever companions to each other in our humanity and consciously and profoundly so in the transforming grace of Christ which forms us into an ecclesial community—the Mystical Body. How, in particular, are the companions who are saints important to us in this reality? To recapitulate, this study has shown, through review of official statements of the Catholic Church validating Scripture and tradition, and as exhibited in the lived faith life of Catholics and many other Christians, that they are important as models and as intercessors—models for what they, in their holy earthly lives, show us about living in history through Christ, and intercessors for their deliberate care during their earthly existence and now in their heavenly reality for the neighbor in Christ. Because human beings are directed to a supernatural end, hopefully to be joined together finally with Christ and with all others in Christ, the canonized saints (and any others in Heaven) continue to have—and even more fully—an impact upon others as a result of their intentional commitment to Christ. We cannot reduce the saints only to the status of models, then—and especially not to "empty" ones (i.e., those that have no symbolic reality). Nor can we understand their intercessory role rightly without seeing that God may use them as instruments of his gift of grace to us precisely because they are exemplary images—symbols, sacraments—transparent to Christ who revealed to us the depths of God's love. In *The Martyrdom of Polycarp* this transparency of the loving saints to Christ—a transparency that communicates grace to us—is described in recount of Polycarp's sacrificial death in imitation of Christ.

> . . . It was almost as though all the preceding events had been leading up to another Divine manifestation of the Martyrdom which we read of in the Gospel; for Polycarp, just like the Lord, had patiently awaited the hour of his betrayal—in token that we too, taking our pattern from him, might think of others before ourselves. This is surely the sign of a true and steadfast love, when a man is not bent on saving himself alone, but his brethren as well.[6]

In *The Martyrdom of Perpetua*, too, is the claim of Christ's presence in those who accept and imitate his sacrificial love. As Felicitas suffered in delivery of her child shortly before the day of her martyrdom, her jailors mocked her, claiming that her pain in childbirth would be little compared to that of her devouring by wild beasts. She replied: "Now it is I who suffer, but then another shall be in me to bear the pain for me, since I am now suffering for him."[7]

The efficacy of the saints—both through their historical life and through their heavenly life—in every other human person's goal of becoming a saint was mentioned by Pope Benedict XVI in his first encyclical: "The lives of the saints are not limited to their earthly biographies but also include their being and working in God after death. In the saints one thing becomes clear: those who draw near to God do not withdraw from men [and women], but rather become truly close to them."[8] In this encyclical, the Pope wrote of the necessity for Christians to focus not only upon current history (as in our given work for social justice), but upon the invisible that maintains and nurtures history toward its completion. Early Christians had a strong consciousness of our partially-realized eschatological existence, as was evident even in their cultic activities honoring the saints. So, too, have saints in every age had this sensibility. Lewis's image, enhanced by the addition of the saints, helps us to see how and why this is so. Christ's work—or the effect of Christ entering human history—not only spreads exponentially throughout the tree but bears the fruit of saints on the tree. This is the way in which Christ's presence is made known to us outside of his thirty-three years of earthly existence: Christ now works though us, in history. The saints, made such by his presence, make his presence known dramatically. And they become the signs and "graceful" causes of other saints. We meet Christ again and again in those who mediate him by their love. As Cardinal José Saraiva Martins of the Congregation for the Causes of Saints offered in a reflection on the beatifications and canonizations of Pope John Paul II, "The world is changing, yet the saints, while changing with the changing world, always represent the same living face of Christ."[9] We cannot totally dispense with the paradigm of saints as patrons, then, for in the love of Christ mirrored in them, they do help us.

To avoid objectionable notions associated with the particular view of saints as patrons in the Middle Ages and to offer a more contemporary concept for understanding the help that, in their disclosure of Christ, the saints give to us as companions, models, and intercessors, we might consider them "mentors." Past notions of the saints as patrons entertained a sort of descending theology of the saints that did not always stress that they are no more than we are in nature: they are in Heaven, thought medieval Christians, and, as in the case of but even more so than with earthly patrons, they could shower us with favors. A sort of ascending theology of the saints is employed today when saints are thought of almost solely as companions, or friends, for in that case we understand ourselves as helped by them chiefly simply because they are in the communion of saints with us as we progress toward finality in God. This alternative notion has a flaw as significant as that of the old patronage view. The saints are like us in our humanity but not in their realized fulfillment of that humanity; they are not just as other members of the communion of saints who are negotiating their way to God. They have completed the journey that we are making and, in the fullness of their existence in God, they know something (in the Beatific Vision) that we, strictly speaking, do not yet know. They model—via their paths in earthly life—the mode of our completion. And they intercede—always praying for us. A concept of the saints as mentors incorporates both the descending and the ascending view of the saints' value to us *as* saints. In his providence (his plan or purpose for and his care for his creation), God has used and might use the saints to inspire us and to draw us to him; he has answered and might even again answer our prayers through them. They can assist us, then, yet not in competition with Christ or independent of him, but as those among human beings permanently near him. When we imitate the saints or invoke them, it is as kindred spirits to experienced companions in the way of Christ who is *the* Way (Jn. 14:6). As earlier chapters recalled of earlier Christians, there was a time when the saints were viewed as so personally close to living Christians that they were influential in earthly pilgrims' personality development. Without devolving into spiritualistic practices, recognizing the saints' lessons for us, and adverting to these by allowing ourselves to engage wholeheartedly in acts of veneration, could allow us to be helped by the saints at least in the sense of our coming to mirror their intentionality, thereby pulling us into closer union with Christ and neighbor, which is the maturation of human personhood.

Christianity is bold in its testimony to the descending and ascending movements in the divine-human dynamic that is dramatized in the saints. It is a radical claim the religion makes that God entered space and time so that it could participate in him, that the Kingdom of God has thereby begun in history even amidst the suffering and sin in the world which it will overcome, that we see Christ who suffered for us in the poor and the marginalized and in all who are in pain, as well as in the saints (who are sufferers for Christ as well as joyous in Christ). In the saints' imitation of Christ and through the grace of Christ at work in them, we see how Christ responds to suffering; in the saints we see Christ himself working to alleviate suffering of others. We also see human beings, in grace, cooperating in this. A secular view is of a natural human spirit overcoming evil and suffering in the world; in Christianity it is the Holy

Spirit working in us who elicits this work. There is a giftedness to saintly lives (and to all human lives) that is God reaching us in history in a way that enables us to fulfill history and thereby ourselves. The Church itself is not only historical, and, so, as God beckons, it reaches for its fulfillment at the end of ages. Within the Church, we acknowledge and embrace the reality of God forever offering to us our end and means— himself—through, among other ways, our veneration of saints who exist in Christ. To repeat the words of *Lumen Gentium* on this veneration, "Every authentic witness of love, indeed, offered by us to those who are in heaven tends towards and terminates in Christ, 'the crown of all the saints,' and through him in God who is wonderful in his saints and is glorified in them."[10]

Conclusion

It is at times today remarked that some Catholics have lost their belief in or their sense of the meaning and power of the Eucharist—that it is the real presence of Christ. Theologically, from a Catholic standpoint, this belief, and the actual reception of the sacrament of the Eucharist in this belief, should inform every other aspect of our faith, as it empowers every aspect of our life in Christ. Belief in Christ as truly present in the Eucharist leads to the deepest comprehension of what it means for humanity to be joined with God in Christ, in such a way that we are not dissolved into God but participate in his life, remaining wholly the unique selves as related to others that he created us to be, in the communion of saints that encompasses all of history and lives even beyond it. But, finite and fallible, sometimes we are led to greater understanding of truth by grasps of insights at truth's periphery. Concerted reflection upon the saints and veneration of them has the potential to lead Catholics to a profounder understanding of the Eucharist. The doctrine of the communion of saints, which in the Catholic view includes veneration of its holiest members, necessarily drives us to the heart of the Eucharistic mystery, to contemplation of the very purpose of the Incarnation and its atoning sacrifice of the Son of God—the loving unity of all in God. As has been pointed out in the course of this study, in the sacrifice of Christ re-presented in the Mass, through the power of the Holy Spirit, we join the saints in Heaven in thanksgiving to and in praise of God. This should be our constant activity, as it is the saints'. That this was at least becoming the saints' constant activity during their lifetimes, as they were being progressively transformed, is demonstrated in our preserved memories of their lives and in our consciousness of the significance for us of those lives in the saints' afterlife. This is the compelling power of the saints for us, even when we, not yet fully sanctified, are mystified by their self-sacrificial actions imitative of Christ's—even unto willingly-anticipated martyrdoms. To be edified and inspired by the saints, seeing clearly that they are always with Christ, understanding ourselves to be gathered up with them in the central moment of the divine liturgy—the Eucharistic celebration—through the sacrifice of Christ which established our eschatological existence permeated by the action upon us of the Holy Spirit drawing us through the Son to the Father, is to recognize and to welcome the mystery of the saints' sanctified reality which is our hoped-for future, too: "In this the love of God was made manifest among us, that God sent his only Son into the world, so that we might live through him" (1 Jn. 4:9).

Terms for Study

Logos/Word   Providence

Suggested Readings

Butler, Alban. *Butler's Lives of the Saints* Edited, revised, and supplemented by Herbert J. Thurston and Donald Attwater. Allen, Texas: Christian Classics, 1996.

Long considered the standard reference for traditional basic biographical information on the saints, this four-volume work has abbreviated cousins, such as *Butler's Lives of the Saints*, concise, modernized edition, edited by Barnard Bangley (Brewster, Massachusetts: Paraclete Press, 2005). Other sources also offer brief biographies of selected saints: *Our Sunday Visitor's Encyclopedia of Saints* by Matthew Bunson, Margaret Bunson, and Stephen Bunson (Huntington, Indiana: Our Sunday Visitor Publishing, 2003); the "Saints & Angels" section of Catholic Online [online], available from http://www.catholic.org/saints/ (accessed 1 September 2011); the "Saints' Lives" section of Internet Medieval Sourcebook of the Online Reference Book for Medieval Studies [online], available from http://www.fordham.edu/Halsall/sbook.3.asp (accessed 1 September 2011); the New Catholic Encyclopedia at New Advent [online], available from http://www.newadvent.org/cathen/ (accessed 1 September 2011); Bert Ghezzi's *Voices of the Saints: A Year of Readings* (New York: Doubleday, 2000); James Martin's *My Life with the Saints* (Chicago, Illinois: Loyola Press, 2006); and Richard P. McBrien's *Lives of the Saints: From Mary and St. Francis of Assisi to John XXIII and Mother Teresa* (New York: HarperCollins Publishers,

2001). The Martin and McBrien books include figures who have not been canonized by the Catholic Church. An extensive collection of information on the saints is the *Acta Sanctorum* of Bollandist Jesuits in Brussels, a work of more than sixty volumes begun in the seventeenth century and still in progress. The Bollandist enterprise is a rewriting of the lives of the saints, with an historical-critical consciousness, relying on sources available from the times of the saints and organized by feast dates.

APPENDIX 1:
KEY CHURCH DOCUMENTS PERTAINING TO DOCTRINE ABOUT THE SAINTS AND TO VENERATION OF SAINTS (IN CHRONOLOGICAL ORDER)

Definition on Sacred Images, Session 7, The Second Council of Nicaea (787).

Canon 3, Session 10 (870), The Fourth Council of Constantinople (869–870).

Pope Martin V, Bull *Inter Cunctas* (1418), The Council of Constance (1414–1418).

Pope Eugenius IV, Bull *Laetentur Coeli* (6 July 1439), "Decree for the Greeks," The Council of Florence (1438–1445).

Pope Leo X, Bull *Cum Postquam* (9 November 1518), The Fifth Lateran Council (1512–1517).

Decree Concerning the Sacrifice of the Mass (17 September 1562), Session 22, Chapter 2 on "The Sacrifice of the Mass is Propitiatory Both for the Living and the Dead" and Chapter 3 on "Masses in Honor of the Saints", The Council of Trent (1545–1563).

Decree on the Invocation, Veneration, and Relics of Saints, and on Sacred Images (3 December 1563), Session 25, The Council of Trent (1545–1563).

Decree Concerning Purgatory (3 December 1563), Session 25, The Council of Trent (1545–1563).

Decree Concerning Indulgences (4 December 1563), The Council of Trent (1545–1563).

Tridentine Profession of Faith (1564), The Council of Trent (1545–1563).

Constitution on the Sacred Liturgy *Sacrosanctum Concilium* (4 December 1963), Chapter 5 on "The Liturgical Year," paragraphs 104 and 111, The Second Vatican Council (1962–1965).

Dogmatic Constitution on the Church *Lumen Gentium* (21 November 1964), Chapter 7 on "The Pilgrim Church" and Chapter 8 on "Our Lady," The Second Vatican Council (1962–1965).

Pope Paul VI, Apostolic Constitution *Indulgentiarum Doctrina* (1 January 1967).

Pope Paul VI, Apostolic Exhortation *Evangelii Nuntiandi*, paragraph 1259 (8 December 1975).

Canons 1186, 1187, 1190, and 1237 paragraph 2, *Code of Canon Law* (1983).

Pope John Paul II, Apostolic Letter *Duodecimum Saeculum* (4 December 1987), paragraph 11.

Canons 884, 885, 888, and 1242, *Code of Canons of the Eastern Churches* (1990).

APPENDIX 2:
ABSTRACTS OF KARL RAHNER'S THEOLOGIES OF SYMBOL AND ANAMNESIS

Theology of Symbol

"[A]ll beings are by their nature symbolic, because they necessarily 'express' themselves in order to attain their own nature," wrote Rahner.[1] For both divine and human realities, there is a basic multiplicity, a "plural unity" which Christians perceive in the Trinity (which is the basis for asserting that being itself is plural) and which as clearly may be detected in finite beings, since "[e]ach finite being as such bears the stigma of the finite by the very fact that it is not absolutely 'simple.'"[2] In all cases, the "one," in disclosing itself, finds itself in the plural result even as it maintains itself in the origin and the origin preserves the unity of the plurality.[3]

> Being *as* such, and hence *as* one (*ens* as *unum*), for the fulfilment of its being and its unity, emerges into a plurality— of which the supreme mode is the Trinity. The distinct moments deriving from the 'one' which make for the perfection of its unity stem essentially, i.e. by their origin in and from another, from this most primary unity: they have therefore a more primary and basic 'agreement' with it than anything produced by efficient causality.[4]

That which is objectified, which is derivative of the origin, is the "expression" of the origin even as it "agrees" with the origin, in the sense that the resulting plurality allows the original being to fulfill *itself*. "The self-constitutive act whereby a being constitutes itself as a plurality which leads to its fulfilment or rather (in certain circumstances) which is a reality given with the perfection of the being, is . . . the condition of possibility of possession of self in knowledge and love," wrote Rahner.[5]

God's self-expression in its "perfect plurality" effected the Christ event. Since in the highest degrees or instances of the symbolic, "one reality renders another present,"[6] Rahner asserted, "the incarnate word is the absolute symbol of God in the world," the preeminent, unsurpassable sign of God's offer of grace to us culminating in the Cross and Christ's resurrection.[7]

> [T]he cross (together with the resurrection of Jesus) has a primary sacramental causality for the salvation of all men, in so far as it mediates salvation to man by means of salvific grace which is universally operative in the world. It is the sign of this grace and of its victorious and irreversible activity in the world. The effectiveness of the cross is based on the fact that it is the primary sacramental sign of grace.[8]

Stated in more personal terms, because God the Father's universal salvific will for us is truly expressed in the Son, the Word Made Flesh, and, because the unity of the Son with the Father is maintained even in the differentiation, the Father's will is truly present in Christ. Therefore, Christ, through the Paschal Mystery, is the sacrament of our salvation, both resulting from God's offer of grace and becoming the very means of grace. Rahner wrote:

> He is not merely the presence and revelation of what God is in himself. He is also the expressive presence of what—or rather, who—God wished to be, in free grace, to the world, in such a way that this divine attitude, once so expressed, can never be reversed, but is and remains final and unsurpassable.[9]

In looking from an evolutionary standpoint at God's plan executed in history, Rahner asserted that the Father's salvific will "shared" by the Son is expressed also in the Spirit who pursued the goal of its full historical manifestation in Christ. Christ is the constitutive cause of salvation *always* because the Holy Spirit sought him from the beginning.[10] Revelatory and efficacious, the Spirit of Christ guides us in our transcendence toward our goal; in the categorial realm Christ is met in relationship with the neighbor, a central matter of Rahner's doctrine of *anamnesis*.

Theology of Anamnesis

Anamnesis, generally speaking, is the recollection of past events. For Christians, the primary religious event of recollection is Christ's life, death, and resurrection. Since the saints are a permanent part of the Body of Christ, they play an important role in this. The principle of *anamnesis* functions in Rahner's theology on a couple of levels, correlative to his descriptions of 1) human beings' original act of knowledge and freedom bearing upon the actual reality itself—God—and 2) human beings' deliberate objectification of this act in a concept.

    On the first level, the original doctrine itself as Plato's referred to the soul's ability to recollect things known from another existence;[11] Rahner compared it to Augustine's doctrine of *memoria* to explain the necessity and reality of the "*a priori* principle of expectation" in human beings that allows them in their transcendence to grasp that which is met in history.[12] Since we are constituted such that God is our fulfillment, *memoria* responds to that which discloses him. On a most basic level, that which is met in history is the neighbor; the categorial object of the neighbor can mediate God's personal communication, which is revelatory. "It is the environment of *personal relationships* . . . that provides the word in and through which man discovers himself and realizes himself, and . . . comes forth from himself," wrote Rahner.[13] Personal relationships can be said to be the pinnacle of historical experience which reveals to human beings their transcendental nature ever reaching for something in but beyond this world, which theologians have named "grace" and Rahner called the "self-communication of God." *Memoria* ultimately anticipates and hopes for "the absolute bringer of salvation,"[14] God, the Absolute Mystery upon whom human beings come to recognize that in their finite contingency they are utterly dependent. It seeks Christ, who brings our salvation by manifesting his gift of self and making this manifestation an "irreversible event."[15]

On the second level, one that more particularly focuses upon human beings' deliberate cooperation in the realization of God's manifestation in history and their resultant growth in spirit and freedom, human beings find "immediate contact" with the Incarnation in the sacraments where this "past" salvific event is recollected in a way that makes it present even as it simultaneously anticipates the future.[16] Here, past, present, and future could be said to dissolve into the eternity of God. *Anamnesis* is accomplished in the sacraments—most particularly in the Eucharist— because these contain the necessary characteristics of such an event: "it must be accomplished in a personal act and anticipate its ceremonial representation in *anamnesis*; it must affect the celebrants and be of significance for salvation, or more specifically, it must commemorate in advance their future salvation."[17] Because the Church "represents humanity," authority for anamnestic events is given fundamentally to it rather than to individuals.[18]

The two facets of Rahner's appropriation of the concept of *anamnesis* also can be delineated in terms of intentionality. Rahner wrote of a cognitive intentionality "elevated by grace," "in germ," by virtue of its direction toward "a supernatural formal object." But this original transcendental experience is "non-objective" and "non-specific."[19] Within this is another experience—one of deliberate, objectified human response. This latter experience is explicit, thematic, a religious act,[20] as one consciously reflects upon and commits to "the infinite reality of God himself"[21] through an object. Since this occurs *within* the fundamental

existential reality of life in God, such religious acts are properly
anamnestic, which is to say sacramental or symbolic, in a manner given
only to human beings since "man is a being permanently established
within the universe and the unity of history means that those deeds which
he has accomplished in time retain their validity and remain likewise
historically established."[22] The possibility of any event of *anamnesis* is
given by God's "real symbol," Christ.

God's real symbol and the purposeful *anamnesis* of its culminating
event—Christ's sacrifice—intersect in the Eucharist. And at the moment
in the Mass when Christ becomes present to us "substantially,"
intercession is made for the living and the dead in the Canon both before
and after the consecration, thereby uniting the entire Church—Militant,
Suffering, and Triumphant. Forgiveness is asked as the names of the
martyrs and other saints are mentioned because of their proximity to and
suffering for and with Christ. Sacrifices of others close to God—righteous
Old Testament figures Abel (Gen. 4:2–4), Abraham (Gen. 22), and
Melchizedek (Gen. 14:18–20)—are viewed as types of the sacrifice of the
Mass.

Notes

Preface

1 Karl Rahner and Johann Baptist Metz, *The Courage to Pray*, trans. Sarah O'Brien Twohig (London: Burns & Oates and Search Press, 1980), 36, original edition, *Ermutigung zum Gebet*, Freiburg im Breisgau: Verlag Herder, 1977. The context of these comments is the authors' expressed concern to address "the Church's problems with regard to the veneration of saints." Their words, on 35, are yet stronger: "Modern Christians who feel that praying to the saints has 'no meaning' for them must ask themselves whether they are not too conditioned by their own times or spiritually too narrow-minded and mean to describe themselves as true Christians." Even so, the authors insisted that no one should feel obligated to private veneration simply "by a sense of traditionalism."

One: Veneration of Saints: Past and Present

1 "St. Blaise," *Catholic Encyclopedia*, ed. Kevin Knight, at New Advent [online], available from http://www.newadvent.org/cathen/02592a.htm (accessed 7 March 2009), cf. J.P. Kirsch, "St. Blaise," in *The Catholic Encyclopedia* (New York: Robert Appleton, 1907).

2 "St. Nicholas of Myra," *Catholic Encyclopedia*, ed. Kevin Knight, at New Advent [online], available from http://www.newadvent.org/cathen/11063b.htm (accessed 7 March 2009), cf., M. Ott, "St. Nicholas of Myra," in *The Catholic Encyclopedia* (New York: Robert Appleton, 1911).

3 Thomas Merton, *The Seven Storey Mountain* (New York: Harcourt, Brace and Company, 1948), 280.

4 Ibid., 411.

5 Richard Mazziotta, "When the Saints Went Marching Out," *Commonweal* 119, no. 18 (October 23, 1992):14. Michael Whalen, in "Saints and Their Feasts: An Ecumenical Exploration," *Worship* 63, no. 3 (May 1989):194–209, offered a brief summary of the changes made to the liturgical calendar with respect to the feast days of saints. Relying on a number of interrelated Church documents which effected the changes in light of Vatican II reforms, he focused particularly on the "Commentary on the General Norms for the Liturgical Year and the Calendar," summarizing on 205–206 its five basic principles guiding sanctoral cycle revisions: "First, the number of *devotional feasts* was lessened. . . . Second, the *history* of the lives of the saints found in the 1960 calendar was scrutinized. Those with dubious historical backgrounds were (for the most part) removed from the calendar. Third, only saints of *important significance* for the universal

church remained in the general calendar. Fourth, the question of the days on which the sanctoral celebrations were *observed* was examined. . . . Finally, the calendar was made as *inclusive* as possible so that saints from every race and period of time were represented."

6   Mary A. Unkelbach, in "Intercession, the Communion of Saints and Supernaturalistic Metaphysics," *Journal of Religion and Psychical Research* 6, no. 4 (October 1983):260–261, connected intercessory and mystical theologies, suggesting that both have declined in the interest of the Christian populace because attention has been diverted to social justice concerns especially prominent in our time, because a contemporary emphasis on the human Christ has "produced anthropological, sociological and political Christologies" which have "all but stripped [the Kingdom] of its ethereal and supernatural component," and because realizing Utopia has been the objective of contemporary theological reflection.

7   Caroline Walker Bynum, "Material Continuity, Personal Survival, and the Resurrection of the Body: A Scholastic Discussion in its Medieval and Modern Contexts," *History of Religions* 30, no. 1 (August 1990):51–85. Bynam made the point, however, that while the contemporary philosopher is embarrassed or mystified by medieval preoccupations, he or she in a uniquely modern way also has arrived at a focus upon material continuity as a necessary element in preservation of the self.

8   David Matthew Matzko, in "Postmodernism, Saints and Scoundrels," *Modern Theology* 9, no. 1 (January 1993):19–20, gave voice to a prevalent postmodern reaction to the saints on the level of ethics: the saints are a "scandal" in their excessive emotion, simple-mindedness, and faith-centered action, while devotion to them is an affront to universalistic and democratic notions which reject the inherent claim of "inequalities among persons in a hierarchy of goodness." According to Matzko, "autonomy, freedom, and choice" are undermined by sainthood's creation of "possibilities for community, apprenticeship, and veneration." Interestingly, Matzko, on 20, claimed that "among many Catholics, devotion to the saints has continued to be a vital practice which shapes their common life." The breadth of the recent work by Catholic scholars on the meaning of saints which he mentioned on 33, nt. 5, is in and of itself an indication that interest in the saints is not extinct, even though the work of theologians on the matter of the saints today is conducted in the manner of a reappropriation of this aspect of the tradition rather than as a wholesale retrieval of its earlier forms of piety.

9   Gordon S. Wakefield, in "Intercession," in *Mary's Place in Christian Dialogue: Occasional Papers of the Ecumenical Society of the Blessed Virgin Mary 1970–1980*, ed. Alberic Stacpoole (Middlegreen, Slough: St. Paul Publications, 1982):263–270, remarked that many fail to see that intercessory prayer answers precisely the need for individuals not to feel overwhelmed and alone in travails, since in the act of this type of prayer we are given to understand that all cooperate in the anamnesis which is the promise that all shall be well as members of the community help each other in Christ.

10   Marina Herrera, in "Popular Devotions and Liturgical Education," *Liturgy* 5, no. 1 (Summer 1985):33–34, made a distinction between "popular piety" and "clerical piety," asserting that North America lacks the former except in the case of popular devotions which arrived with ethnic settlers and have been preserved in those communities. In the United States "[t]here are no national places of pilgrimage that attract both the curious and the faithful in the same way that the shrines at Fatima, Guadalupe, Knock or Lourdes do." In contrast, public celebrations of feast days and important religious sites, as well as private devotions, hold much importance for many in Latin America.

11   Karl Rahner, "Why and How Can We Venerate the Saints?," *Theological Investigations*, vol. 8, trans. David Bourke (New York: Seabury Press, 1977), 7, original edition, *Schriften zur Theologie*, VII, part II, Einsiedeln: Verlagsanstalt Benziger, [1966]. Published the year after the close of Vatican II, the article's effective contemporaneity with the Council suggests that the Rahner's observations predated the Council. Rahner's frame of reference for his article was Europe, but there is no reason to think that the experience of Catholics was too different on other continents, particularly in countries at "advanced" levels of development.

12   *Lumen Gentium*, in *Vatican Council II: The Basic Sixteen Documents; Constitutions Decrees Declarations*, rev. trans., ed. Austin Flannery (Northport, New York: Costello Publishing, 1996), 48–51. Citations are to paragraph numbers. "The Pilgrim Church" is the name of chapter 7 of this Constitution.

13   Ibid., 50.

14   Elizabeth A. Johnson, in "May We Invoke the Saints?," *Theology Today* 44, no. 1 (April 1987):49–51. Johnson has suggested a reevaluation of the ancestor cult according to and conditioned by the doctrine of the communion of saints.

15   *Lumen Gentium*, 49–51.

16   Rahner, "Why and How Can We Venerate the Saints?," 6. The phrase "the liturgy of perfect glory" is taken from *Lumen Gentium*, 51.

17   Some of these points were made in my article "A Reinterpretation of Invocation and Intercession of the Saints," *Theological Studies* 66, no. 2 (June 2005):381–400, and/or in my dissertation, *The Unity of Dulia and Latria: Karl Rahner's Philosophy and Theology as a Resource for a Theology of Intercession* (Ph.D. diss., Marquette University, 2003). Occasional other sections of this book also may resemble portions of this article and/or my dissertation, even replicating passages in some cases.

18   Rahner and Metz, in *The Courage to Pray*, 83–84, wrote: "Our main problem with regard to the practice of praying to the saints is not so much, or at any rate not exclusively, of a theological nature. . . . Our real difficulty lies in our general lack of human solidarity with the dead. For this solidarity is a necessary prerequisite if we are to venerate the saints honestly and genuinely, not merely according to some official cult established by the Church. Our relationship to the dead should not be misinterpreted in parapsychological or spiritualistic terms, . . . Nor should

it be seen as a phenomenon about which we register nothing but its presence or absence. Our religious duty demands that we do not simply hide behind a supposed failure in our relationship to the dead. It is a duty we can cultivate if we choose, for we have been granted the freedom to discover our reality or to fail to do so, and the same applies to our relationship to the dead."

19   See Victor Paul Furnish, "Saints," *The HarperCollins Bible Dictionary*, ed. Paul J. Achtemeier (New York: HarperCollins Publishers, 1996), 958, who called attention to Paul and the writer of Acts' frequent application of the term to particular churches (e.g., Acts 9:13, 9:32; Rom. 15:25, 26, 31; 1 Cor. 1:2). Furnish also noted that two Hebrew terms rendered in English by the term "saint" refer either to "covenant faithfulness . . . (e.g., Pss. 31:23; 148:14)" or to those "set apart and dedicated to the service of God (e.g., Dan. 7:27)." He remarked: "In both cases, the faithful of Israel are in view, and their 'sainthood' consists in the relationship they bear to the God who has destined them for righteousness and salvation (Pss. 16:3; 132:9, 16)."

20   Unless the source of a Greek or Latin translation is cited by way of footnote pertaining either to the translation itself or to a passage, quoted or otherwise, of which the translation is a part, translations are common and can be found in standard academic references. Particular English equivalents have been chosen for their relevance to the subject at hand.

21   Catherine Murphy, "Cult," *The HarperCollins Encyclopedia of Catholicism*, ed. Richard E. McBrien (New York: HarperCollins Publishers, 1995):385.

22   Canon 1187, *Code of Canon Law Annotated*, ed. E. Caparros, M. Thériault, and J. Thorn (Montréal: Wilson & Lafleur Limitée, 1993): "Only those servants of God may be venerated by public cult who have been numbered by ecclesiastical authority among the Saints or the Blessed." See also canon 834, para. 2: "This worship [the sacred liturgy] takes place when it is offered in the name of the Church, by persons lawfully deputed and through actions approved by ecclesiastical authority."

23   *Dei Verbum*, in *Vatican Council II: The Basic Sixteen Documents; Constitutions Decrees Declarations*, rev. trans., ed. Austin Flannery (Northport, New York: Costello Publishing, 1996), 8. Citations are to paragraph numbers.

24   Ibid.

25   Ibid.

26   *The Martyrdom of Perpetua*, in *In Her Words: Women's Writings in the History of Christian Thought*, ed. Amy Oden (Nashville, Tennessee: Abingdon Press, 1994), 37, para. 21.

27   *Lumen Gentium*, 51.

28   Ibid., 50, cf. 2 Th. 1:10.

Two: The Saints in the Bible: Companions, Models, Intercessors

1   All biblical citations are from the Revised Standard Version, *The New Oxford Annotated Bible with the Apocrypha*, ed. Herbert G. May and

Bruce M. Metzger (New York: Oxford University Press, 1977). For a similar statement to that of Jn. 21:25, see Jn. 20:30–31.

2   *Lumen Gentium*, 51.

3   This form of address is used frequently elsewhere in the epistles, as well, especially throughout Romans, 1 Corinthians, 2 Corinthians, Galatians, Philippians, 1 Thessalonians, 2 Thessalonians, and James.

4   Cf. Col. 4:7, 11; Philem. 1, 2, 24; 1 Jn. 1:1–3; etc.

5   Cf. 1 Cor. 16:20; 1 Th. 5:26; 1 Pet. 5:14.

6   Cited instances are but a sampling; such familial relationships in Christ are referenced throughout the epistles.

7   Cf. Gal. 3:26, 4:6–7; Heb. 12:5–8. This book occasionally supplies bracketed statements for the explicit inclusion of women where implicit inclusion is assumed but where women are most likely to feel their own exclusion by language—usually in cases of biblical statements and of official Church documents. To avoid clumsiness in presenting other historical and theological documents produced before inclusive language became customary, such clarifications are not added to all quotations in this work.

8   The immediate context of Paul's comment was reference to the contribution of the churches at Macedonia and Achaia to a collection for the poor of the church in Jerusalem. It was requested by the church at Jerusalem at the time of an early council there at which it was decided that Gentiles need not become circumcised (i.e., become Jewish) to be members of the Christian community (Gal. 2:1–10). For extended reference to the collection, see also Rom. 15:25–29; 1 Cor. 16:1–4; 2 Cor. 8–9.

9   Cf. Col. 2:1–3; 1 Pet. 1:22, 3:8, 4:8–11. On encouragement of one another in faith and in the life of faith, also see 1 Th. 5:11; Heb. 10:24–25, 12:14–15; Jas. 5:19.

10 Cf. 1 Cor. 10:24; Eph. 4:32; Phil. 2:4; Heb. 13:1–3.

11 Cf. Acts 4:32–37.

12 Cf. Jn. 15:12–17. The commandments of love are a significant focus of attention in the Letters of John. "He who loves his brother abides in the light, and in it there is no cause for stumbling" (1 Jn. 2:10, of pericope 1 Jn. 2:7–11). Christians are "to love one another" (1 Jn. 4:11) because God "first loved us" (1 Jn. 4:19). "God is love" (1 Jn. 4:8, 16). The necessity of loving the neighbor also is stated in Mt. 19:19.

13 Cf. Mt. 22:37–40; Mk. 12:28–34; also Dt. 6:4–5; Lev. 19:18.

14 The opening and closing benedictions of the epistles frequently are explicit in their association of Christian fellowship with the gift of grace. But explicitly Trinitarian references are rare in the New Testament, since first-century Christians were only beginning to reflect theologically upon the relationship of Jesus Christ, Son of God, to the Father—YHWH of the Old Testament—and to the Spirit. The doctrine of God as Trinity will be officially promulgated in 381 at the First Council of Constantinople.

15 See 1 Cor. 3:10–11 for another metaphor about use of gifts of grace: "According to the grace of God given to me, like a skilled master builder I laid a foundation, and another man is building upon it. Let each man take care how he builds upon it. For no other foundation can any one lay than that which is laid, which is Jesus Christ."

16 For additional discussion of the Body of Christ and/or the spiritual gifts afforded its members, see 1 Cor. 12; Eph. 3:1–6, 4:1–6, 5:21–32; Col. 2:9–15, 3:15.

17 For a Christian explanation of love, see 1 Cor. 13.

18 Cf. Gal. 5:14; Jas. 2:8–9.

19 Cf. Mt. 10:24; Lk. 6:40. The injunction to serve appears throughout the New Testament. For a sampling of texts enjoining believers to serve God and/or neighbor, see Mt. 4:10, 6:24; Mk. 9:35; Lk. 4:8, 16:13, 17:7–10; Jn. 12:26; Rom. 12:11; Gal. 5:13; Eph. 6:5–9; and 1 Pet. 2:16, 4:10. Influential upon some of these passages may have been Is. 52:13–53:12, the fourth and final "servant song" featuring a servant whose suffering is redemptive for others. The writers of the epistles frequently proclaim themselves and other faithful Christians to be servants of "Jesus Christ" (Rom. 1:1; 2 Pet. 1:1; Jude 1:1), of "Christ Jesus" (Phil. 1:1; Col. 4:12), of "God" (2 Cor. 6:4; Tit. 1:1; Jas. 1:1), "in the Lord" (Col. 4:7), etc.

20 The Lukan passage is placed in the context of the Last Supper.

21 The content of verses 43–44 appears also in Mk. 9:35: ". . . 'If any one would be first, he must be last of all and servant of all.'"

22 Cf. Mk. 8:34; Lk. 9:23, 14:27. Following the commandments of Christ is obligatory for his disciples; see Lk. 17:7–10. Suffering should be expected when one is in the service of Christ: "Remember the word that I said to you, 'A servant is not greater than his master.' If they persecuted me, they will persecute you; . . ."

23 Given the Church's understanding of and contemporary emphasis upon the duty of Christians to participate in and even initiate the transformation of unjust social structures, it should be noted that the original recipients of the First Letter of Peter were early Christians whose faith was tested constantly by the opposition of the surrounding pagan world and occasionally by that world's outright persecution. On the theme of servanthood, the encouragement to this, in love, occurs throughout the New Testament, including but not limited to epistle passages in Rom. 12–15; 1 Cor. 13; 2 Cor. 6–9; Eph. 5:21–6:9; Col. 3:12–4:5; 1 Th. 4:9–12, 5:12–15; Heb. 13:1–21; Jas. 2; 1Pet. 4:11; 1 Jn.; 2 Jn.; and 3 Jn.

24 William J. Dalton, "The First Epistle of Peter," in *The New Jerome Biblical Commentary*, ed. Raymond E. Brown, Joseph A. Fitzmyer, and Roland E. Murphy (Englewood Cliffs, N.J.: Prentice Hall, 1990), 903–904. Dalton noted that 1 Pet. 2:21b–25 is believed to be "part of a primitive Christian hymn based on Isa 53:4–12" (cf. Goppelt, *Der erste Petrusbrief* 204–7). Against other contemporary opinions positing a later date for this letter, Dalton argued that it likely was written "just before Peter's death, which took place probably in AD 65 in the persecution of Nero (Eusebius, *HE* 2.25.5)."

25 Ibid., 908. Dalton identified 1 Peter 5:1–5 as an "addition to the [domestic] code" presented in 1 Peter 2:13–3:7 and 1 Tim. 3:13, 5:4–19.

26 These leaders are "keeping watch over your souls, as men who will have to give account" (Heb. 13:17).

27 For biblical descriptions of the Parousia, see 1 Th. 4:13–18 and Mt. 24.

28   On the faith of Abraham as an example to Christians, see also Gal. 3:8–9.

29   References to the conduct of Paul and his companions as edification for the faithful appear elsewhere in the New Testament epistles, as well. With regard to the Thessalonian community, see 1 Th. 1:5, 2:1–12.

30   It is important to note that such New Testament statements as appear in 1 Th. 2:15–16 (that the Jews ". . . killed both the Lord Jesus and the prophets, and drove us out, and displease God and oppose all men by hindering us from speaking to the Gentiles that they may be saved—so as always to fill up the measure of their sins. . . .") disclose the tension between Jews and Christians in the first century. The notation for this passage in *The New Oxford Annotated Bible*, 1434, explains: "The severe language reflects the strenuous struggle between Paul and the Jews (Acts 14.2, 5, 19; 17.5, 13; 21.21; 25.2, 7)." Raymond F. Collins, in "The First Letter to the Thessalonians," *The New Jerome Biblical Commentary*, ed. Raymond E. Brown, Joseph A. Fitzmyer, and Roland E. Murphy (Englewood Cliffs, N.J.: Prentice Hall, 1990), 776, reported that some scholars view verses 13–16 as an interpolation: "This is the only place in Paul's writings where the death of Jesus is attributed to the Jews (cf. 1 Cor 2:8)." Christians must remember that Jesus was Jewish, as were all of his earliest followers. First-century Christian communities included "converts" both Jewish and Gentile.

31   Many contemporary biblical scholars believe that the "pastoral epistles"— 1 and 2 Timothy and Titus—were not authored by Paul himself but by one following in his tradition. For a summary of this discussion, see the comments of Robert A. Wild on "Authorship" in "The Pastoral Letters," in *The New Jerome Biblical Commentary*, ed. Raymond E. Brown, Joseph A. Fitzmyer, and Roland E. Murphy (Englewood Cliffs, N.J.: Prentice Hall, 1990), 892. Only seven of the thirteen epistles attributed to Paul are of his undisputed authorship: Romans, 1 Corinthians, 2 Corinthians, Galatians, Philippians, 1 Thessalonians, and Philemon. It was not unusual in the ancient world for a writer to assign another's name to a work in order to continue a tradition of thought, to associate the work with a particular tradition, and/or to elevate the work's authority. Sometimes, too, the one whose name appears on a work employed a "secretary" to communicate his ideas. Regarding Paul's self-designation in Rom. 11:13, see also Rom. 15:15–16 and 1 Tim. 2:7.

32   As validation of this interpretation, I offer replication of nt. 47 on page 397 of my article "A Reinterpretation of Invocation and Intercession of the Saints": "Jerome Murphy-O'Connor explained that 'Christ is the ideal of humanity toward which all believers strive, but since they cannot see him,' Paul's comportment must mirror "the life of Jesus" (2 Cor. 4:10). This is the only authentic hermeneutic. The theme appears with reference to every community that knew Paul personally (1 Cor. 4:16; Gal. 4:12; Phil. 3:17; 4:9; 1 Thess. 1:6; 2:14)' (Jerome Murphy-O'Connor, in *The New Jerome Biblical Commentary*, ed. Raymond E. Brown, Joseph A. Fitzmyer, and Roland E. Murphy [Englewood Cliffs, N.J.: Prentice Hall, 1990] 808)."

33   For the story behind this statement, see 1 Kg. 17–18.

34   Cf. Mt. 6:9–14; Mk. 11:25–26.

35   Cf. Lk. 11:9–13.
36   Cf. Mt. 21:22.
37   See D. Edmond Hiebert, "The Significance of Christian Intercession," *Bibliotheca Sacra* 149, no. 593 (January–March 1992):18–19, for a helpful exegesis of this parable: "God could send forth needed workers without the prayers of Christians, but it is His loving purpose to relate His redemptive workings to believers' intercessory work."
38   Cf. Mt. 22:39, 42, 44; Mk. 14:35–36. For reference to this scene at Gesthemane, see also Heb. 5:7.
39   Cf. Mt. 26:41; Mk. 14:38. For other exhortations of Jesus to petitionary prayer, see Mk. 13:18; Mt. 24:20; Lk. 21:36.
40   The gospels abound with other accounts of healings by Jesus following petitions for such: demons are cast from the possessed into a herd of swine (Mt. 8:28–34; Mk. 5:1–20; Lk. 8:26–39); a hemorrhaging woman is healed (Mt. 9:20–22; Mk. 5:25–34; Lk. 8:42b–48); blind men receive sight (Mt. 9:27–31, 29–34; Mk. 8:22–26, 10:46–52; Lk. 18:35–43); a dumb demoniac is exorcised and speaks (Mt. 9:32–34, 12:22–24; Lk. 11:14–15); a deaf and speech-impaired man is healed (Mk. 7:31–37); the son of the widow at Nain is raised (Lk. 7:11–17); ten lepers are cleansed of their disease (Lk. 17:11–19); and a variety of other unspecified sick and possessed people are healed (Mt. 12:15–16, 14:35–36, 15:29–31; Mk. 1:32–34, 3:7–12, 6:53–56; Lk. 4:40–41, 6:17–19).
41   See Mt. 27:3–5 for an alternate account of the death of Judas.
42   Cf. Jn. 16:25–27, 14:13–14, 15:16, further emphasizing the power in prayer of belief in Jesus' name.
43   The theme of Jesus as "the mediator of a new covenant" is repeated in Heb. 12:24. Compare the Heb. 9:15 reference to Christ who redeems those called from their transgressions to the Is. 53:12 reference to the suffering servant— Israel, who becomes the source of blessings for others—who "poured out his soul to death, and was numbered with the transgressors; yet he bore the sin of many, and made intercession for the transgressors."
44   Robert J. Karris, "The Gospel According to Luke," *The New Jerome Biblical Commentary*, ed. Raymond E. Brown, Joseph A. Fitzmyer, and Roland E. Murphy (Englewood Cliffs, N.J.: Prentice Hall, 1990), 717.
45   The RSV commentators' nt. on 17:20–26 offers: "Jesus' prayer for the Church universal is that it may be indwelt by the Father and the Son and express their unity in *love*, thus fulfilling its mission of leading *the world* to believe."
46   John's mention of the gift of "life" in 1 Jn. 5:16 is a reference to "eternal life," as specified in verse 13. This explains his further comments in verses 16–17 to the effect that we are not bidden to pray for those in a state of mortal sin. Discussion of John's noncommittal attitude toward such prayer is beyond the scope of this project, but it can at least be said that his underlying assumption might be that those who are in a state of mortal sin may have exercised their "fundamental option" (to borrow a term of contemporary theology, especially that of Karl Rahner) for evil and therefore may have closed themselves off from the salvation for which we might hope and pray for them.

47   This passage is from the Sermon on the Mount in Mt. 5–7. Cf. Lk. 6:28. The exhortation to prayer for one's enemies would seem to be implicit in Paul's words to the Romans in Rom. 12:14: "Bless those who persecute you; bless and do not curse them." Jesus punctuates the parable of the unforgiving servant in Mt. 18:35 with the statement that "[s]o also my heavenly Father will do to every one of you, if you do not forgive your brother from your heart."

48   See Acts 14:23.

49   See, for examples of such prayer of Paul and of other epistle writers, Col. 1:3, 1:9; Rom. 1:9; Phil. 1:3–4; 1 Th. 1:2, 3:9–10; 2 Tim. 1:3; and Philem. 4–6. In Col. 4:12, Paul assured the community of one of his fellow missionary's faithful prayers on its behalf.

50   See Acts 27:21–24 for the first story mentioned; for the second story, see Acts 12:12–17. The story in 2 Cor. 12 of Paul's ascendancy to the "third heaven," Satan's subsequent harassment, and Paul's recourse to God, also suggests answered prayer.

51   Cf. Acts 2:43.

52   This story as it appears in Mt. 8:14–15 does not recount others requesting Jesus' aid to Peter's mother.

53   See Geoffrey Wainwright, "Wesley and the Communion of Saints," *One in Christ* 27, no. 4 (1991):341, for an account of Wesley's admission of this story's applicability to the practice of invocation of the saints despite his lack of enthusiasm for this tradition. Said Wesley about Lk. 16:24: "It cannot be denied but here is one precedent in Scripture of praying to departed saints: but who is it that prays, and with what success? Will any, who considers this, be fond of copying after him?," cf. *Explanatory Notes upon the New Testament*, ad loc.; cf. Sermon 115, 'Dives and Lazarus', in *Works* (Bicentennial Edition), vol. 4 (ed. Outler, 1987), 14. In nt. 19, Wainwright reported that "[i]n a letter to Mary Bishop of 9 May 1773 (*Letters*, ed. Telford, vol. VI. P. 26), Wesley, speaking of the 'saints . . . in paradise', declares it 'not improbable their fellowship with us is far more sensible than ours with them . . . They no doubt clearly discern all our words and actions, if not all our thoughts too.'" Wainwright remarked that "[i]f that be the case, then surely, as 'all one body united under one Head' (*ibid.*), we may hope (in a move that Wesley does not here make) that they will *in fact* pray for us, whatever the propriety of our invoking them."

54   A remarkable passage at 1 Cor. 15:29 is taken by some commentators, including May and Metzger of *The New Oxford Annotated Bible with the Apocrypha*, to attest to a practice of being baptized in the name of unbaptized dead "in order that the latter might share in the final resurrection": "Otherwise, what do people mean by being baptized on behalf of the dead? If the dead are not raised at all, why are people baptized on their behalf?" However, others do not concur with this interpretation of Paul's words. See Jerome Murphy-O'Connor, "The First Letter to the Corinthians," in *The New Jerome Biblical Commentary*, ed. Raymond E. Brown, Joseph A. Fitzmyer, and Roland E. Murphy (Englewood Cliffs, N.J.: Prentice Hall, 1990), on 813, for discussion of this matter.

Three: The Cult of the Martyrs: The Saints in the Early Church

1   See Frederick J. Cwiekowski, *The Beginnings of the Church* (Mahwah, New Jersey: Paulist Press, 1988), especially pages 82–83, 93–95, and 132–149, for a concise but deft treatment of the martyrdom of Stephen, the Christian distancing from Judaism in the middle of the first century (as at the "Council" of Jerusalem), and the Jewish-Roman conflict leading to the fall of Jerusalem in war and the succeeding reconstitution of Judaism at Jamnia. On Cwiekowski's interpretation of the events of Jamnia this brief summary is especially indebted.

2   For recent studies of the circumstances of Christian martyrdoms, including a phenomenon of "voluntary" or "radical" martyrdom, see G.E.M. De Ste. Croix, *Christian Persecution, Martyrdom, and* Orthodoxy, ed. Michael Whitby and Joseph Streeter (Oxford and New York: Oxford University Press, 2006), and Paul Middleton, in *Radical Martyrdom and Cosmic Conflict in Early Christianity*, vol. 307, *Library of New Testament Studies*, ed. Mark Goodacre (New York and London: T & T Clark, 2006). For short but expansive review of the meaning of Christian martyrdom, see Robin Darling Young, *In Procession Before the World: Martyrdom as Public Liturgy in Early Christianity*, Père Marquette Lecture in Theology (Milwaukee, Wisconsin: Marquette University Press, 2001).

3   A concise but detailed account of the persecutions appears in the article "Persecutions, Early Christians," in *The Oxford Dictionary of the Christian Church*, 3rd. ed., ed. F.L. Cross and E.A. Livingstone (Oxford and New York: Oxford University Press, 1997):1257–1259.

4   Josef A. Jungmann, *The Early Liturgy: To the Time of Gregory the Great*, trans. Francis A. Brunner (Notre Dame, Indiana: University of Notre Dame Press, 1959), 177. Cf. Kirsch, *Scuola catt.*, 55 (1927), 161–174. The feast honoring Peter and Paul has retained its original date on the calendar—June 29—since its inception. In the East, the feast day originally was assigned to December 28, according to Michael Walsh, ed. *Butler's Lives of the Saints*, concise ed., rev. and updated (New York: HarperCollins Publishers, 1991), 198.

5   Jungmann, *The Early Liturgy*, 178–179.

6   Ibid., 176, cf. Dix, *The Apostolic Tradition*, 18 f. Hippolytus wrote: "[I]f a confessor has been in chains in prison for the Name, hands are not laid on him for the deaconate or the presbyter's office. For he has the office of the presbyterate by his confession." Mk. 13:11–12 is sometimes cited as an exhortation to be a confessor.

7   Ibid., 181. Jungmann explained: "The antiphon for the *Magnificat* at Vespers sounds like an apology: . . . O sanctissima anima, quam etsi gladius persecutoris non abstulit, palmam martyrii non amisit! In short, a saint had, in some sense, to be a martyr!"

8   Daniel R. Grigassy, "Saints, Devotion to," *The HarperCollins Encyclopedia of Catholicism*, ed. Richard E. McBrien (New York: HarperCollins Publishers, 1995):1157.

9   V.L. Kennedy, *The Saints of the Canon of the Mass*, 2ⁿᵈ ed., rev. (Rome: Città del Vaticano, 1963), 83.

10 Theodor Klauser, *A Short History of the Western Liturgy: An Account and Some Reflections*, 2ⁿᵈ ed., trans. John Halliburton (Oxford and New York: Oxford University Press, 1979), 87, original edition, *Kleine abendländische Liturgiegeschichte*, 5ᵗʰ ed., [Bonn], Germany: Peter Hanstein Verlag, 1965.

11 Saint Augustine of Hippo, *Confessions*, trans. Henry Chadwick (Oxford: Oxford University Press, 1992), VI. ii. 2. Citations are to book, chapter, and paragraph numbers. Nt. 3 reports that Ambrose mentioned his ban in *On Elias* 62. Chadwick noted here that Augustine, also, "vainly tried to stop the inebriation at martyrs' shrines in Africa, where (as one letter records) drink was a major social problem."

12 Kennedy, *The Saints of the Canon of the Mass*, 106.

13 Jungmann, *The Early Liturgy*, 140–141, 179, and 183–184. Jungmann noted, on 179, that, at the Council of Elvira in Spain in approximately 305, women were forbidden at the cemetery vigils. Cf. C. 35; Mansi 2, 11. On 141, he reported that a problem of the *refrigeria* was their occasional devolution into "excessive drinking parties." James Stevenson, in *The Catacombs: Life and Death in Early Christianity* (Nashville, Tennessee: Thomas Nelson, 1985), 164, original edition, *The Catacombs: Rediscovered Monuments of Early Christianity*, London: Thames and Hudson, 1978, noted that Augustine referred to this custom, sometimes deteriorating and becoming orgies, as "very like the superstitious practices of the heathen."

14 Jungmann, *The Early Liturgy*, 140–141 and 183, DACL 14, 2:2179–90.

15 Kennedy, *The Saints of the Canon of the Mass*, 85, cf. H. Delehaye, *Les origins du culte de martyrs* (Bruxelles, 1933), 24–49, and E. Freistedt, *Altchristliche Totengedäcknistage und ihre Beziehung zum Jenseitsglauben und Totenkultus der Antike = Liturgiegeschichtliche Quellen und Forschungen*, Heft 24 (Münster i. W., 1928).

16 Jungmann, in *The Early Liturgy*, 183, recalled that the *refrigerium* were even held in some of the martyr basilicas, until bishops successfully squelched the practice.

17 As the commentators' nt. for this passage in the RSV indicates, this "cultic feast (1 Sam. 9:13)" became part of the Messianic expectation, of course. This is reflected in references by Jesus to the faithful who will "in the kingdom of heaven" sit at table with the patriarchs (Mt. 8:11) and who now remember him by drinking of the "blood of the covenant" which he would share again in his "Father's kingdom" (Mt. 26:26–29, and similarly Lk. 22:18; Mk. 14:22–25), as well as in the Parable of the Great Banquet in the Gospels of Luke (14:15–24) and Matthew (22:1–14) and the angel's words in the Book of Revelation about those "invited to the marriage supper of the Lamb" (19:9).

18 Orazio Marucchi, *Christian Epigraphy: An Elementary Treatise with a Collection of Ancient Christian Inscriptions Mainly of Roman Origin*, trans. J. Armine Willis (Cambridge: University Press, 1912), 146.

19 Stevenson, *The Catacombs*, 163–165.

20   Kenneth L. Woodward, *Making Saints: How the Catholic Church Determines Who Becomes a Saint, Who Doesn't, and Why* (New York: Simon and Schuster, 1996), 59.

21   J. Spencer Northcote, *The Roman Catacombs: Or, Some Account of the Burial-Places of the Early Christians in Rome* (Philadelphia: Peter F. Cunningham, 1859), 62.

22   Ibid., 63–65. Among accommodations for the growing crowds, Northcote mentioned the creation of "luminaria"—aperatures to open air for better circulation.

23   Ibid., 62–63.

24   Kennedy, *The Saints of the Canon of the Mass*, 86.

25   Peter Brown, *The Cult of the Saints: Its Rise and Function in Latin Christianity* (Chicago: University of Chicago Press, 1981), 39. Brown, in chapter 2, 23–49, showed that this occurred with the Western church's accumulation of wealth through endowments, beyond need even for charitable activities there; the bishops directed funds and attention to the veneration of saints. Cf. A.H.M. Jones, *The Later Roman Empire* (Oxford: Blackwell, 1964), 2:894–910; W. Zeisel, Jr., "An Economic Survey of the Early Byzantine Church" (Ph.D. diss., Rutgers University, 1975); R.M. Grant, *Early Christianity and Society* (New York: Harper and Row, 1977); R. Staats, "Deposita pietatis—Die Alte Kirche und ihr Geld," *Zeitschrift fürTheologie und Kirche* 76 (1979):1–29; Ramsay MacMullen, *Roman Social Relations* (New Haven: Yale University Press, 1974):101–2.

26   "The Martyrdom of Perpetua," 36. Jungmann, *The Early Liturgy*, on 185, recalled that "we find the martyr Saturus dipping the ring of the soldier Pudens in his own blood and handing it back to him as a *pignus* and a *memoria sanguinis*, because he had been very good to the Christians."

27   Jungmann, *The Early Liturgy*, 184–187. Jungmann explained that although initially bishops attempted to discourage or eliminate these practices, Rome found itself finally succumbing to some of them after the fifth century when the Lombard invasions prevented Christians from visiting the graves of the martyrs. The dismembering of some of the bodies occurred as they were transferred into the safer, city churches.

28   Lawrence S. Cunningham, *The Meaning of Saints* (San Francisco: Harper & Row, 1980), 13–15.

29   Ibid., 14. Cunningham, on 13, cited the sensibility of the early Christians that allowed them to grasp at face value the story of the hemorrhaging woman in Lk. 8:43–48 being healed by the power of Jesus emitted through her touch of "the fringe of his garment" (Lk. 8:44). Others have noted that this pericope may give even earlier attestation to an impulse toward relics.

30   Northcote, *The Roman Catacombs*, 59.

31   Ibid., 61–62.

32   Cunningham, *The Meaning of* Saints, 15.

33   Marucchi, *Christian Epigraphy*, 321. According to Marucchi, this is another "fact confirmed by Prudentius, who says that they kept it in their houses, *domi ut reservent posteris*." Also, located at Mastar in Numidia, a cemetary inscription reads: "On June 11th was deposited here the blood of the holy

martyrs who suffered under Florus the president in the city of Milevis in the days of the incense-burning . . ." Marucchi explained the significance of the reference to the "incense-burning": "There is also a record of the days of 'thurification' under Diocletian, when attempts were made to force the Christians to burn incense before idols."

34 Jungmann, *The Early Liturgy*, 182–183, cf. DACL 10:2455 ff.

35 Marucchi, *Christian Epigraphy*, 180–181. Marucchi recounted a case in which Sabinus, archdeacon of the Roman church, chose a gravesite in the porch of the church at St. Lorenzo rather than near the martyr in order to make the point, as summarized by Marucchi, "that the best way to get into touch with the martyrs is to imitate their virtues."

36 Ibid., 174–175.

37 Ibid., 169.

38 Ibid., 55.

39 Ibid., 93. Some scholars contend that intercessory inscriptions were not likely to have appeared before the third century in any Christian cemetery.

40 Ibid., 96.

41 Ibid., 138. Marucchi noted that "[t]his important inscription is not later than the beginning of the third century."

42 Ibid., 154.

43 Ibid., 155.

44 Ibid., 154.

45 Ibid., 439, 448.

46 Cunningham, *The Meaning of Saints*, 37.

47 Marucchi, *Christian Epigraphy*, 444.

48 Cunningham, *The Meaning of Saints*, 37, cf. Marucchi, 439–448. Translations of and this grouping of prayers are accepted from Cunningham. Marucchi, in *Christian Epigraphy*, 164, remarked that in the ancient cemetery of Priscilla, to which traditions connected Peter, this apostle's intercession is invoked on a tomb for the purpose of gaining eternal life for one buried there. On 81, he reported that the appearance of the name "Peter" in burial inscriptions was exclusively Christian, used in honor of the apostle, and attests to "a special cult commemorating the first preaching of S. Peter in Rome."

49 Jungmann, *The Early Liturgy*, 182, cf. DACL 10:2450 (Marucchi).

50 Cunningham, *The Meaning of Saints*, 37.

51 "The Martyrdom of Perpetua," 30–31. Perpetua's recorded conversation with another brother, on 28, in which he asks her to request a vision foretelling her eventual fate, reveals that she had a reputation for being granted her requests of God. In fact, this entire circle of martyrs evidently shared a reputation as successful petitioners, both for their own and for others' behalf. Perpetua's commentator notes, on 35, that each of the martyrs was granted the method of death for which he or she had petitioned God.

52 Mary A. Donovan, "Communion of Saints," *The HarperCollins Encyclopedia of Catholicism*, ed. Richard E. McBrien (New York: HarperCollins Publishers, 1995):339, cf. Tertullian, *On the Resurrection of the Body*, 43, and *On Monogamy*, 10.

53   Peter Brown, "The Saint as Exemplar in Late Antiquity," in *Saints and Virtues*, ed. John Stratton Hawley (Berkeley and Los Angeles: University of California Press, 1987), 8–9.

54   Ibid., 5.

55   Ibid., 5–6.

56   Ibid., 6.

57   Ibid., 7.

58   Ibid., 12.

59   Ibid., 13. The assignment of a Christian name "meant to take at baptism a guide and companion, who could act almost as an ideogram for one's own soul," Brown explained. He contended that "as long as we look at the saints as only distant 'good examples' (as moderns tend to do) or merely as effective 'patrons' (as Late Romans frequently tended to do), we will not touch on a layer of the formation of the Christian sensibility that is, in my opinion, as yet insufficiently explored. . . . Christian believers' map of their own selves, and its capacity for relationships with invisible guides and invisible enemies. Yet few periods in the ancient world devoted such serious and consequential attention to the manner by which the frail essence of the concrete identity could be seen as supported and given consistency through being flanked by hierarchies of protectors thought of as close in their interactions with the believers' souls as if the protectors were aspects of the believers' own selves" (12–13). Death marked "the final meeting of masters and their pupil, . . . and also the moment when, in the meeting of Christ and man, the glory of the human self could be glimpsed in its awesome fullness" (14).

60   See, for example, Lawrence Cunningham, *A Brief History of Saints* (Malden, Massachusetts, and Oxford: Blackwell Publishing, 2005), 21, cf. Patricia Cox, *Biography in Late Antiquity: A Quest for the Holy Man* (Berkeley, California: University of California Press, 1983).

61   Kennedy, in *The Saints of the Canon of the Mass*, 94, reported that Acts were read in North African services. For his documentation, see his nt. 57 offering "Council of Hippo 393, Canon 40; Hefele-Leclercq, *Histoire des Conciles* II, 1 (Paris, 1908), p. 89: Mansi, *Concilia* III, 924."

62   Jungmann, *The Early Liturgy*, 179.

63   Brown, *The Cult of the Saints*, 80–85. According to Brown, the *Passio* was a "*psycodrame*," intensifying the sense of identification between the saint and his or her still earthbound admirer, pulling the latter through the saint's sufferings and final relief and reward.

64   Cunningham, *A Brief History of Saints*, 15–16, 32–34.

65   Cunningham, *The Meaning of Saints*, 16. Cunningham mentioned Augustine's prominent role in the new practice of collecting miracle stories "after the translation of the remains of Saint Stephen the Protomartyr from the Holy Land to North Africa in the year 415. Book XXII of Augustine's *De Civitate Dei* has a long list of miracles and prodigies that had occurred around Saint Augustine's diocese in his own time."

66   Cunningham, in *A Brief History of Saints*, 36, recognized the *Conferences* (records of conversations with desert ascetics in which their pious interior

lives were the focus) and the *Institutes* (descriptions of lives of monks) of Saint John Cassian, a contemporary of Saint Augustine of Hippo.

67 Cunningham, in *The Meaning of Saints*, on 159, encouraged view of hagiography "in that broad sense that encompasses popular art, legends, writings, memories, and such."

68 May and Metzger, *The New Oxford Annotated Bible with the Apocrypha*, 263 of *The Apocrypha*. The introduction to the book supplied by the editors explains that 2 Maccabees is an "abridgment" of a "five volume history, now lost, written by a certain Jason of Cyrene" who "seems not to have been a Pharisee; he may reflect the ideas of Jews at Antioch or possibly Alexandria." Aside from 2 Maccabees, some have cited Baruch 3:4 of the Apocrypha as evidence of Jewish belief in intercession across the divide of death.

69 See 1 Macc.4:42–60 and 2 Macc. 10:1–9 for explanations of the origin of Hanukkah.

70 In Gen. 18:27, echoed in verse 31, Abraham states that it is his own initiative that impels the intercessory process on behalf of the righteous in Sodom. In verses 30 and 32, his initiative is underscored. In Ex. 32:11–14, appealing to the covenant, Moses successfully intercedes with God for his people.

71 The efficacy of Samuel's prayer will be contingent upon the faithfulness of the people. See 1 Sam. 12:24–25. Similarly, Is. 1:15 expresses faithfulness to God as a condition of his reception of prayers.

72 Other Old Testament intercessory texts include Ex. 5:22–23, 2 Sam. 12:16–17, 1 Kg. 17:20–21, 2 Kg. 4:32–33, Ezra 6:9–10, Jer. 29:7, Ezek., 9:8, Ezek. 11:13, and Am. 7:1–6.

73 Regarding the challenge of dating these martyrdom accounts, see G.W. Bowersock, *Martyrdom and Rome*, The Wiles Lectures (Cambridge, New York, and Melbourne, Australia: Cambridge University Press, 1995), 10–13, who argued that the material in 2 Maccabees may have been added as late as 70 A.D. and that the 4 Maccabees material may be dated as only slightly earlier. Cf. Chr. Habicht, 2. *Makkabäerbuch, Jüdische Schriften aus hellenistisch-römischer Zeit*, vol. 1 (Gütersloh, 1976). On the legendary content of these accounts, see Lacey Baldwin Smith, *Fools, Martyrs, Traitors: The Story of Martyrdom in the Western World* (Evanston, Illinois: Northwestern University Press, 1997), chapter 3, especially 51, who followed other scholars' dating of the 2 Maccabees material as the early first century B.C. with editing toward the middle of that century and the 4 Maccabees material approximately forty years after Jesus' birth (50). Cf. *II Maccabees*, trans. and ed. Jonathan A. Goldstein, *The Anchor Bible*, vol. 41A (New York, 1983), 71–83; also *The Third and Fourth Books of Maccabees*, ed. and trans. Moses Hadas (New York, 1953), 95–99; also *The Second Book of Maccabees*, ed. Solomon Zeitlin (New York, 1954), 27–29; also John Downing, "Jesus and Martyrdom," *Journal of Theological Studies*, new series vol. 14 (1963), 280. Middleton, in *Radical Martyrdom and Cosmic Conflict in Early Christianity*, chapter 4, especially 106–115, reviewed some of the contested views in dating the Maccabees martyrdom accounts.

74 Bowersock, *Martyrdom and Rome*, on 12 and 13, argued that Christians developed a "new concept" of martyrdom as "death at the hands of hostile secular authority." See also 14–21 for this argument.

75 Cunningham, *The Meaning of Saints*, 28.

76 J.P. Kirsch, *The Doctrine of the Communion of Saints in the Ancient Church: A Study in the History of Dogma*, trans. John R. McKee (St. Louis, Missouri: B. Herder; London, Edinburgh, Glasgow: Sands & Company, 1911), 233, cf. Hieronymus, *epist.* cviii. *ad Eustochium*, 13, (Migne, P.L. XXII. 889).

77 Ibid., 232, cf. Cyrillus Hieros., *Catech. myst.* v. 9 (ed. Rupp. II. 386–387). On 216, Kirsch offered Cyrillus's own words of identification of these of the Church's departed members—"first the patriarchs, prophets, apostles, martyrs, that God would at their prayers and intercessions receive our supplication."

78 Ibid., 233, cf. Hilarius, *Tract.* in *Ps.* CXLVI. 9 (Migne, P.L. XI. 873).

79 The website for the archdiocese of Dublin, Ireland, and related links share the story of the Church of the Immaculate Conception of Merchant's Quay parish which still is popularly known as "Adam and Eve's Church," after the name of the tavern at which Catholics secretly worshipped during Reformation repression. See http://ireland.archiseek.com/buildings_ireland/dublin/southcity/quays/merchants/adam_and_eves.html (accessed 3 November 2008).

Four: From Witnesses to Protectors: The Development of the Cult of the Saints in the Middle Ages

1 After centuries of tensions cultural, historical, sociological, and theological, in 1054, the patriarch of Constantinople, Michael Cerularius, and Pope Leo IX anathematized each other (actions nullified by both Patriarch and Pope in 1965) over the use of Greek versus Latin and the Western church's addition of the *filioque* (the words "and the Son" after the statement that the Holy Spirit proceeds from the Father) to the Nicene-Constantinopolitan Creed, creating a rupture in Church unity that elicited attempts at reconciliation for the next four hundred years. The sack of Constantinople by the Crusaders in the early thirteenth century greatly imperiled these attempts; although the Council of Lyon in 1274 and the Council of Florence in 1439 sought to end the division, a Decree of Union was rejected by the Orthodox, officially by a Synod of Constantinople in 1484. See "Great Schism," in *The Oxford Dictionary of the Christian Church*, 3rd ed., ed. F.L. Cross and E.A. Livingstone (Oxford and New York: Oxford University Press, 1997):702–703.

2 For background on the circumstances of the fall of the Roman Empire and on Augustine's production of *The City of God*, see biographical note (Random House, 1999) and introduction (Thomas Merton, 1950, renewed Random House, 1978) in *The City of God*, trans. Marcus Dods (New York: The Modern Library, 2000) and introduction in *The City of God against the*

Pagans, ed. and trans. R.W. Dyson (Cambridge, New York, and Melbourne, Australia: Cambridge University Press, 1998).

3   Cunningham, *The Meaning of Saints*, 18–19.
4   Ibid., 17–19.
5   Ibid., 45.
6   Kevin Donovan, "The Sanctoral," in *The Study of Liturgy*, rev. ed., ed. Cheslyn Jones, Geoffrey Wainwright, Edward Yarnold, and Paul Bradshaw (London: SPCK; New York: Oxford University Press, 1992), 480–481; "Martyrology," in *The Oxford Dictionary of the Christian Church*, 3ʳᵈ ed., ed. F.L. Cross and E.A. Livingstone (Oxford and New York: Oxford University Press, 1997):1047.
7   "Pilgrimages," *The Oxford Dictionary of the Christian Church*, 3ʳᵈ ed., ed. F.L. Cross and E.A. Livingstone (Oxford and New York: Oxford University Press, 1997):1288. Also, apart from quoted material in this paragraph, see William Melczer, *The Pilgrim's Guide to Santiago de Compostela* (New York: Italica Press, 1993), 40–41.
8   Melczer, *The Pilgrim's Guide to Santiago de Compostela*, 21–23, 35–63.
9   "Novena," *The HarperCollins Encyclopedia of Catholicism*, ed. Richard E. McBrien (New York: HarperCollins Publishers, 1995):922.
10   This biblical passage is cited in a section on "Holiness" in para. 2015 of *Catechism of the Catholic Church: With Modifications from the 'Editio Typica,'* trans. United States Catholic Conference (New York: Doubleday, 1997), original edition, [*Catechismus Ecclesiae Catholicae*], Città del Vaticano: Libreria Editrice Vaticana, 1994: "The way of perfection passes by way of the Cross. There is no holiness without renunciation and spiritual battle. Spiritual progress entails the ascesis and mortification that gradually lead to living in the peace and joy of the Beatitudes: . . . ."
11   See also parallels and related material: Mt. 10:37–39, 16:24–25; Lk. 9:23–24, 14:25–27, 17:33; and Jn. 12:25. For a study of the metaphor of the athlete that was popular in the New Testament and in early Christian literature, see Robert Paul Seesengood, *Competing Identities: The Athlete and the Gladiator in Early Christianity*, vol. 346, *Library of New Testament Studies*, ed. Mark Goodacre (New York and London: T & T Clark, 2006).
12   The entire periscope appears in Mt. 19:16–22. See parallels in Mk. 10:17–22 and Lk. 9:57–62.
13   For an overview of developments in ascetical life in the various ages of Christianity, see "Asceticism," *The Oxford Dictionary of the Christian Church*, 3ʳᵈ ed., ed. F.L. Cross and E.A. Livingstone (Oxford and New York: Oxford University Press, 1997):113–114.
14   John C. Cavadini, "Monasticism," *The HarperCollins Encyclopedia of Catholicism*, ed. Richard P. McBrien (New York: HarperCollins Publishers, 1995), 883, cf. 1 Tim. 5:3–16, Polycarp, *Philippians* c.4.
15   Cheslyn Jones, Geoffrey Wainwright, Edward Yarnold, and Paul Bradshaw, ed., *The Study of Liturgy*, rev. ed. (London: SPCK; New York: Oxford University Press, 1992), 87. The appointments of bishops, presbyters, and deacons also are covered in this document traditionally attributed to Hippolytus, along with those of confessors, readers, and sub-deacons. Frank

Hawkins, "The Tradition of Ordination in the Second Century to the Time of Hippolytus," *The Study of Liturgy*, rev. ed., ed. Cheslyn Jones, Geoffrey Wainwright, Edward Yarnold, and Paul Bradshaw (London: SPCK; New York: Oxford University Press, 1992), 354, emphasized distinctions in the *Apostolic Tradition*: widows (and readers) are appointed, not ordained (which is for clergy only because of their specific association with the liturgy); virgins (and sub-deacons) are named, not appointed.

16   Recent studies of the Desert Fathers and Mothers show these ascetics' impact upon Christianity: David G.R. Keller, *Oasis of Wisdom: The Worlds of the Desert Fathers and Mothers* (Collegeville, Minnesota: Liturgical Press, 2002); John Chryssavgis, *In the Heart of the Desert: The Spirituality of the Desert Fathers and Mothers,* rev. ed., with translation of Abba Zosimas' *Reflections* (Bloomington, Indiana: World Wisdom, 2008); and William Harmless, *Desert Christians: An Introduction to the Literature of Early Monasticism* (Oxford and New York: Oxford University Press, 2004).

17   St. Isaac of Nineveh, "First Discourse," *On Ascetical Life,* trans. Mary Hansbury (Crestwood, New York: St. Vladimir's Seminary Press, 1998), para. 5.

18   "Asceticism," 113–114.

19   "Stylite," *The Oxford Dictionary of the Christian Church*, 3rd ed., ed. F.L. Cross and E.A. Livingstone (Oxford and New York: Oxford University Press, 1997):1550.

20   "Anchorite, Anchoress," *The Oxford Dictionary of the Christian Church*, 3rd ed., ed. F.L. Cross and E.A. Livingstone (Oxford and New York: Oxford University Press, 1997):59, and "Anchorite, Anchoress," *The Harper Collins Encyclopedia of Catholicism*, ed. Richard E. McBrien (New York: HarperCollins Publishers, 1995):44–45.

21   "Asceticism," 113–114.

22   Saint Athanasius, *Saint Anthony of the Desert*, trans. Dom J.B. McLaughlin from Migne's Greek text (Rockford, Illinois: Tan Books and Publishers, 1995).

23   Cavadini, "Monasticism," 888.

24   Ware, *The Orthodox Church*, 37–38. For information on anchorites known as "Lavra," see that entry in *The Oxford Dictionary of the Christian Church*, 3rd ed., ed. F.L. Cross and E.A. Livingstone (Oxford and New York: Oxford University Press, 1997):959.

25   Hawkins, "The Tradition of Ordination in the Second Century to the Time of Hippolytus," 347–355. Hawkins offered an account of the influence of the battle against Gnosticism in this development in Christian clerical divisions that places the bishop in the role of "community-leader." Against the "Gnostic position on revelation," ". . . emphasis on the need to safeguard 'orthodox' teaching secured the connection of the bishop with the 'apostolic tradition', since he could be appealed to as a 'teaching authority'" (349). For New Testament references to "overseers" and "elders" and similar, see, for example, Acts 14:23; 20:17, 28; and Tit. 1:5, 7.

26   Paul F. Bradshaw, "Theology and Rite AD 200–400," in *The Study of Liturgy*, rev. ed., ed. Cheslyn Jones, Geoffrey Wainwright, Edward Yarnold,

and Paul Bradshaw (London: SPCK; New York: Oxford University Press, 1992), 355–356. Hawkins, "The Tradition of Ordination in the Second Century to the Time of Hippolytus," on 345–346, also dealt with the Jewish influence on Christian ministry.

27 Saint Bernard of Clairvaux, *On Loving God*, trans. from critical Latin ed. by Jean Leclercq and Henri Rochais (Kalamazoo, Michigan: Cistercian Publications, 1973), X.27, with analytical commentary by Emero Stiegman, 1995. Citations are to paragraph numbers.

28 Ibid., XII.34. The letter is written to the "Holy Brethren of Chartruse."

29 Augustine, *Confessions*, IX.x.24.

30 A helpful study of this focus in spirituality generally is that of Rachel Fulton, *From Judgment to Passion: Devotion to Christ and the Virgin Mary, 800–1200* (New York: Columbia University Press, 2002). In regard to mysticism in particular, see, for example, Bernard McGinn's summary of William of St. Thierry's mystical works, in *The Growth of Mysticism: Gregory the Great through the 12th Century*, vol. II of *The Presence of God: A History of Western Christian Mysticism* (New York: Crossroad Publishing, 1996), especially pages 245–250 on "Christ and the Economy of Salvation."

31 Brown, *The Cult of the Saints*, 60–61, cf. Augustine, *City of God*, 10.1, 3, 7, 16, 20, 8.27.

32 Ibid., 61. This new dynamic between earthbound men and women and their patron saints, for its advantages in terms of seemingly fostering the unity of all human beings and promoting the love of neighbor which exists between them, also brought with it a sense of precariousness that did not exist when earlier Christians depended upon the help of guardian angels. Brown explained, on 63: "The invisible companion may be as close to them [the men and women of late Antiquity and the Middle Ages] and as abiding as a guardian angel had once been; but the relationship itself no longer has the calm inevitability of ascending stages of the universe. It is tinged, now, with the sense of risk as with the warmth of a late-Roman relationship of friendship and patronage."

33 Ibid., 56.

34 Ibid., 58.

35 Cunningham, *The Meaning of Saints*, 18.

36 "Asceticism," 113–114.

37 For one of many discussions of miracles' demonstration of sanctity in one with whom they are linked, see Benedicta Ward, *Miracles and the Medieval Mind: Theory, Record and Event, 1000–1215* (Philadelphia: University of Pennsylvania Press, 1982), especially chapter 9. For extensive studies of the theology of miracles, two volumes dated in some respects but impressive and relevant still are René Latourelle, *The Miracles of Jesus and the Theology of Miracles*, trans. Matthew J. O'Connell (Mahwah, New Jersey: Paulist Press, 1988), original edition, *Miracles de Jésus et théologie du miracle*, Montreal: Les Éditions Bellarmin, [1986], and Louis Monden, *Signs and Wonders: A Study of the Miraculous Element in Religion* (New York: Desclee), 1966, original edition, *Het Wonder*, Antwerp: De Standaard, and Utrecht: Het Spectrum, [1958].

38   Luigi Gambero, *Mary and the Fathers of the Church: The Blessed Virgin Mary in Patristic Thought*, trans. Thomas Buffer (San Francisco: Ignatius Press, 1999), 83–85, original edition, *Maria nel pensiero del padri della Chiesa*, Milan: Edizione Paoline, 1991.

39   Ibid., 35–42.

40   See Gambero, *Mary and the Fathers of the Church*, for a sweeping survey of patristic thought on Mary.

41   See, for example, discussion of the Marian theology of Ambrose, in Gambero, *Mary and the Fathers of the Church*, 198, as well as of Aelred of Rievaulx and of Isaac of Stella in Luigi Gambero, *Mary in the Middle Ages: The Blessed Virgin Mary in the Thought of Medieval Latin Theologians*, trans. Thomas Buffer (San Francisco: Ignatius Press, 2005), 166 and 173, respectively, original edition, *Maria nel pensiero dei teologi latini medievali*, Milan: Edizioni San Paolo, 2000.

42   See, for examples, Jungmann, *The Early Liturgy*, 196; Gambero, *Mary and the Fathers of the Church*, 370–371, 477–478; Donovan, "The Sanctoral"; and Klauser, *A Short History of the Western Liturgy*, 90.

43   As with the focus on the humanity of Christ, for a detailed study of this medieval Marian spirituality, see Rachel Fulton, *From Judgment to Passion*.

44   For a brief history of the Angelus, see Michael O'Carroll, "Angelus, The," *Theotokos: A Theological Encyclopedia of the Blessed Virgin Mary* (Eugene, Oregon: Wipf and Stock Publishers, 1982), 379.

45   Gambero, *Mary in the Middle Ages*, 315–320. Fifteenth-century Dominican friar Alanus de Rupe was largely responsible for the development and popularization of the rosary.

46   See, for example, regarding monastic recitation of the Office of the BVM and Marian hymns, Gambero, *Mary and the Fathers of the Church*, 142–144, on the thought of Peter the Venerable.

47   Saint Thomas Aquinas, *Summa Theologica*, rev. ed., IIa IIae, q. 103, a. 4, trans. Fathers of the English Dominican Province (New York: Benziger Brothers, 1948), reprint edition, Allen, Texas: Christian Classics, 1981.

Five: Official and Universal Veneration of Saints: Liturgy and Canonization

1   The entry "Lex orandi, lex credendi" in *The HarperCollins Encyclopedia of Catholicism*, ed. Richard E. McBrien (New York: HarperCollins Publishers, 1995):767, summarizes succinctly the conditions that must be in place for this rule's application: "[F]irst, this worship must be connected to the presider's role in worship; second, it must be connected to the apostolic tradition; and third, it must be universally used."

2   E.J. Yarnold, "The Liturgy of the Faithful in the Fourth and Early Fifth Centuries," in *The Study of Liturgy*, rev. ed., ed. Cheslyn Jones, Geoffrey Wainwright, Edward Yarnold, and Paul Bradshaw (London: SPCK; New York: Oxford University Press, 1992), 232.

3   Jungmann, *The Early Liturgy*, 180, cf. Muratori, I, 311 f.

4 Ibid., cf. Muratori, I, 304 f.
5 In the early Church, and since Vatican II, the Preface was, and is, regarded as part of the Eucharistic Prayer.
6 Jungman, *The Early Liturgy*, 181.
7 Kennedy, in *The Saints of the Canon of the Mass*, 195–196, stated that the saints were inserted into the Roman Canon's *Communicantes* halfway through the fifth century and into its *Nobis quoque* likely by the end of the fifth century. Joseph A. Jungmann, in *The Mass of the Roman Rite: Its Origins and Development*, rev. and abr. ed., trans. Francis A. Brunner, rev. Charles K. Riepe (New York: Benziger Brothers, 1959), 42–43, stated that the *Communicantes* and the *Nobis quoque* do not exist in the Roman Canon in the early fifth century but appear in this Canon's earliest extant manuscripts "in a form that must at all events belong to the sixth century." For discussions of the *Communicantes* and the *Nobis quoque* in the Roman Canon, see pages 402–408 and 446–453, respectively.
8 Klauser, *A Short History of the Western Liturgy*, 50, 6.
9 Ibid., 50. Justin Martyr (d. ca. 165), in his *First Apology*, wrote of "prayers and thanksgivings" of the faithful offered after the Liturgy of the Word. Although his description has left room for interpretation, many scholars have understood his reference to be to intercessory prayers possibly offered extemporaneously. See Justin's passage and the editor's nt. in Justin Martyr, *First Apology*, in *The Apostolic Fathers with Justin Martyr and Irenaeus*, ed. Philip Schaff, vol. 1 of *Ante-Nicene Fathers*, ed. Alexander Roberts and James Donaldson, chapter LXVII, para.186 and nt. 1914, at Christian Classics Ethereal Library [online]; available from http://www.ccel.org/ccel/schaff/anf01.viii.ii.lxvii.html (accessed 31 January 2009). See also chapter LXV, para. 185, wherein Justin referred to "hearty prayers in common for ourselves and for the baptized [illuminated] person, and for all others in every place, . . ." occurring in the Mass after administration of the sacrament of Baptism and before the Offertory and the Eucharistic celebration. Such prayers—the only vernacular element in the Mass—existed still during the Middle Ages, thereafter virtually disappearing. In France, they were retained as "Les Prières de Prône"; during her trial, Saint Joan of Arc recited their conclusion. Prior to Vatican II, the tradition was reflected in the American churches' Sunday Mass custom of the priest making announcements and then leading the congregation in recitation of the "Our Father" and the "Hail Mary," offered for parishioners having died that week.
10 Klauser, *A Short History of the Western Liturgy*, 51.
11 Ibid.
12 Donovan, "The Sanctoral," 482.
13 Ibid., 476–477.
14 Ibid., 476–479.
15 In the Middle Ages his authority became civil as well as religious; the pope's presence afforded a stability to the West lacking after Constantine's physical relocation of his secular power to the East.

16   Donovan, "The Sanctoral," 483.
17   Klauser, *A Short History of the Western Liturgy*, 89.
18   Donovan, "The Sanctoral," 477–478; also Klauser, *A Short History of the Western Liturgy*, 85, 89–91. Donovan noted that impetus for the Nativity of Mary and the Assumption was the dedication to her of basilicas. Klauser noted, on 89–90, that the Annunciation and the Purification, or Presentation, have been regarded alternately as either Christological or Marian feasts in the history of the Church. Jungmann, in *The Early Liturgy*, on 197, referred to the Annunciation and Purification as "basically feasts of the Lord."
19   Klauser, *A Short History of the Western Liturgy*, 87.
20   Ibid., 91.
21   Ibid., 95. Klauser also remarked: "One has the impression that the Roman liturgical calendar was already lavishly filled with feasts around the year 800; and this moreover even before the onslaught of the innovations of the Middle Ages had begun" (91). In the eighth century, votive Masses for Our Lady for Saturdays were written by Alcuin, abbot at St. Martin's at Tours; see Michael O'Carroll, "Little Office of the Blessed Virgin Mary," *Theotokos: A Theological Encyclopedia of the Blessed Virgin Mary* (Eugene, Oregon: Wipf and Stock Publishers, 1982), 219–220.
22   Peter G. Cobb, "The History of the Christian Year," in *The Study of Liturgy*, rev. ed., ed. Cheslyn Jones, Geoffrey Wainwright, Edward Yarnold, and Paul Bradshaw (London: SPCK; New York: Oxford University Press, 1992), 480.
23   Johannes Quasten, in *Patrology*, vol. IV: The Golden Age of Latin Patristic Literature From the Council of Nicea to the Council of Chalcedon, ed. Angelo di Berardino, trans. Placid Solari (Allen, Texas: Christian Classics, n.d.), 191–192, reported that the expression first appeared in the West in an extant work of commentary on the Creed by Nicetas of Remesiana—in book V, *Explanatio symboli*, of his *Instructio ad competentes*. Some sources present the alternate spelling, "Niceta," for Nicetas of Remesiana.
24   J.N.D. Kelly, *Early Christian Creeds*, 3ʳᵈ ed. (New York: Longman, 1972), 388–390.
25   Stephen Benko, in *The Meaning of Sanctorum Communio* (Naperville, Illinois: Alec R. Allenson, 1964), 64.
26   Ibid. Benko traced the germ of the formulation of the phrase back to the period between Cyprian and Ambrose, in the third to the fourth century (34–47). With Cyprian and later Hilary, the notion arose that the Eucharist established communion with Christ. With Ambrose, both the Eucharist and Baptism were understood as salvific because through these sacraments the faithful receive "the benefits of Christ" (47). Augustine's coinage of the term "communio sacramentorum" brought to a completion the "two-sacrament doctrine" he followed out from Ambrose. Placed in the Creed precisely where we now find the term "communion of saints," the original sense of the phrase pertained to sacramental forgiveness. Therefore, Benko emphatically rejected any claim that the expression "sanctorum

communion" could be construed as originally denoting the personal, ecclesial dimension which later became its common interpretation (64–65).

27   Kelly, *Early Christian Creeds*, 391. The Church is "the congregation of all saints," Nicetas explained in his excursus, "[s]o you believe that in this Church you will attain to the communion of saints."

28   Ibid., cf. *Hom.* II in Caspari, *Quellen* II, 197. The latter, stricter understanding was that of a near-contemporary of Nicetas, Saint Faustus of Riez.

29   Augustine, *Confessions*, IX. xiii. 37.

30   Ibid., IX. xii. 32. Donovan, in "Communion of Saints," 339, noted that Augustine echoes Tertullian in these assertions.

31   Donovan, "Communion of Saints," 339, cf. Gregory I, *Dialogues*, 4.40.

32   Woodward, *Making Saints*, 59.

33   This period is outlined widely, for example in Woodward, *Making Saints*, 64–65, and in Cunningham, *The Meaning of Saints*, 45.

34   Pierre Delooz, "The Social Function of the Canonisation of Saints," in *Models of Holiness*, ed. Christian Duquoc and Casiano Floristán (New York: Seabury Press, 1979), 15.

35   Woodward, *Making Saints*, 67.

36   Ibid., 67–68.

37   Ibid., 68. According to Woodward, generally between 1200 and 1500, local cults and bishops determined their own "blesseds" for local veneration.

38   Ibid., 75, and Cunningham, *The Meaning of Saints*, 45.

39   P. Molinari and G.B. O'Donnell, "Canonization of Saints (History and Procedure)," in *New Catholic Encyclopedia*, vol. 3, 2nd ed. (Detroit, Michigan: Gale, 2006), 62–63.

40   Delooz, "The Social Function of the Canonisation of Saints," 15, and Woodward, *Making Saints*, 75. Woodward noted on 76 that "any unauthorized display of public cult toward a person prior to beatification or canonization [except those that already had existed for one hundred years or more at the time of the new decree] would automatically disqualify that candidate for canonization."

41   Molinari and O'Donnell, "Canonization of Saints (History and Procedure)," *New Catholic Encyclopedia*, 62–63.

42   Woodward, *Making Saints*, 76–77, and Cunningham, *The Meaning of Saints*, 45–46.

43   Woodward, *Making Saints*, 76.

44   The summarization of this process, which occurs over the next several pages, draws from numerous previous summaries: *Codex Juris Canonici*, cans. 1999–2141; Cunningham, *The Meaning of Saints*, 46–47; Paolo Molinari, "Canonization," in *New Catholic Encyclopedia*, vol. 3 (New York: McGraw Hill, 1967), 55–59; Paolo Molinari, "Canonization," *Sacramentum Mundi: An Encyclopedia of Theology*, vol. 5 (New York: Herder and Herder, 1970), 401–402; and Woodward, *Making Saints*, 79–86. The number of steps noted in any summary is not only based upon officially established stages but also is influenced by a given writer's logical grouping of activities aimed at canonization of an individual.

45   A matter of canon law, see chapter 7.

46   Cardinal José Saraiva Martins, in Congregation for the Causes of Saints, *New Procedures in the Rite of Beatification*, [29 September 2005], at the Vatican [online]; available from http://www.vatican.va/roman_curia/ congregations/csaints/documents/rc_con_csaints_doc_20050929_saraiva-martins-beatif_en.html (accessed 28 July 2008), noted that Pope John Paul II's novel tradition began with the beatification of Maximilian Kolbe (d. 1941) (para. IIc). Prior to this, from 1662 the procedure was for a Vatican representative other than the pope to preside at a morning Mass enacting the rite of beatification; in the afternoon the pope would venerate in Saint Peter's Basilica the newly beatified individual, gaining himself a plenary indulgence offered—by his grant—to all of the day's visitors to the Basilica (para. IIb).

47   See chapter 8, nt. 8, for exceptions in the pontificate of Benedict XVI.

48   Michael Pomazansky, "The Glorification of Saints," At *Holy Protection Russian Orthodox Church* [online]; available from http://www. fatheralexander.org/booklets/english/glorification_saints.htm (accessed 26 October 2008).

49   Timothy Ware, *The Orthodox Church*, new ed. (London: Penguin Books, 1997), 256.

Six: Historical Critiques of the Cult: Protestant and Catholic Reformations

1   The story is recounted widely, as in Martin Brecht, *Martin Luther: His Road to Reformation, 1483–1521*, trans. James L. Schaaf (Philadelphia: Fortress Press, 1985), 46–50, original edition, *Martin Luther: Sein Weg zur Reformation, 1483–1521*, Stuttgart, Germany: Calwer Verlag, 1981, and Peter Newman Brooks, "A Lily Ungilded?: Martin Luther, the Virgin Mary and the Saints," *The Journal of Religious History* 13 (1984):147.

2   Martin Luther, Preface to the 1535 Confession of Faith: Vorrede 1535, in *Weimer Ausgabe (WA)*, vol. 38, 313 f. Translations in this chapter from *WA* are accepted from Ewald M. Plass, comp., *What Luther Says: A Practical In-Home Anthology for the Active Christian* (Saint Louis, Missouri: Concordia Publishing House, 1959).

3   Martin Luther, Sermon on John 20:11–18 (from 1530): Johnnes 20, in *WA*, vol. 32, 92.

4   Martin Luther, Disputation on Romans 3:28 (from 1536): Disputatio de justificatione, in *WA*, vol. 39, part I, 85 f.

5   Martin Luther, Exposition of Psalm 45:6, *Lecture by Dr. Martin Luther on Psalm 45* (begun in 1532), trans. E.B. Koenker, in *Luther's Works*, vol. 12, part 1: Selected Psalms, ed. Jaroslav Pelikan (Saint Louis, Missouri: Concordia Publishing House, 1955), 239. Also see *WA*, vol. 40, 472–610 for Psalm 45 exposition.

6   Martin Luther, Sermon on Philippians 3:11–21 (from 1536): *Phil 3*, 17 ff, in *WA*, vol. 22, 370.

7   For studied accounts, including original documents in translation, of the
        Catholic Reformation and reform in the Catholic Church leading up to this,
        see two books by John C. Olin: *The Catholic Reformation: Savonarola to
        Ignatius Loyola* (New York: Fordham University Press, 1992) and *Catholic
        Reform: From Cardinal Ximenes to the Council of Trent 1495–1563: An
        Essay with Illustrative Documents and a Brief Study of St. Ignatius Loyola*
        (New York: Fordham University Press, 1990).

8   Steven Ozment, *The Age of Reform, 1250–1550: An Intellectual and
        Religious History of Late Medieval and Reformation Europe* (New Haven
        and London: Yale University Press, 1980), 216.

9   See Pope Benedict XVI's catechisms on Saint Paul's thought in "Saint Paul:
        The Doctrine of Justification: from Works to Faith," General Audience,
        Wednesday, 19 November 2008, at the Vatican [online]; available from
        http://www.vatican.va/holy_father/benedict/xvi/audiences/2008/documents/
        hf_ben-xvi_aud_20081119_en.html (accessed 19 December 2008) and in
        "The Doctrine of Justification: The Apostle's Teaching on Faith and
        Works," General Audience, Wednesday, 26 November 2008, at the Vatican
        [online]; available from http://www.vatican.va/holy_father/benedict/xvi/
        audiences/2008/documents/hf_ben-xvi_aud_20081126_en.html (accessed
        19 December 2008). The pope's comments addressed the difference in
        understanding that saint's teaching on justification on the part of Luther and
        Catholics. Luther interpreted Paul's words in Galatians about justification
        by faith and not by works of the law as meaning that we are justified by
        "faith alone." The works of the law to which Paul referred were those of
        Judaism; unity with God was not achieved by them after the Incarnation.
        Yet Catholics do not understand Paul to mean that "works" of charity—
        love of God and neighbor—are not required. If one truly is in Christ, one
        necessarily will be transformed in love (although complete conformity to
        Christ will not necessarily or usually be immediate). In Catholic theology,
        then, it can be said that we are justified by faith in Christ and by the works
        of charity that issue from this, for faith is given freely by God and is
        undeserved by us but this is a living faith that issues—in our freedom as
        aligned with God's unconstrained will—in love of God and neighbor. Faith
        and works are, for Catholics, intrinsically related not only on the part of
        God but on the part of human beings responding to God under the influence
        of his grace.

10   Martin Luther, *The Bondage of the Will*, in Erasmus-Luther, *Discourse on
        Free Will*, trans. and ed. Ernst F. Winter (New York: Continuum Publishing,
        1996), 137, para. 786.

11   Ibid., 121–122, para. 664.

12   This term is coined in Augustine's *Confessions*, V.ix.16, wherein Augustine
        writes to God that he had committed "sins both numerous and serious, in
        addition to the chain of original sin by which 'in Adam we die' (1Cor.
        15:22)." Nt. 13 offers: "This is the earliest occurrence of this phrase to
        describe inherent human egotism, the inner condition contrasted with overt
        actions." Description of the condition of original sin also occurs in this
        volume in VIII.ix.21, VIII.ix.22, and X.xx.29.

13   Steven Ozment, *The Age of Reform,* 236. Ozment concluded that Luther did see the difference between Ockhamist thought and that of other Scholastics, but that "[t]o the extent that his early writings already distinguish ethical activity and religious justification in principle—so that good works, whether done within or outside a state of grace, never contribute to one's salvation—the Thomist position squares as well with his definition of Scholastic theology [as Pelagianism] as does that of the Ockhamists." As a point of especial interest given Luther's own theological inclinations, Ozment remarked, on 236–237: "Although Ockhamists seem so boldly Pelagian, such was not, as Luther must also have known, the sum total of their teaching. If they glorified the will of man, they also exalted the will of God. They left little doubt that, when all things were considered, salvation hinged not on man's activity but on God's willingness to accept and value human effort so highly. It has been argued that Ockhamists inconsistently juxtaposed an Aristotelian concept of man with an Augustinian concept of God" (cf., Leif Grane, *Contra Gabrielem: Luthers Auseinandersetzung mit Gabriel Biel in der Disputatio contra Scholasticam Theologiam 1517,* Gyldendal, 1962, p. 217). Finally, on 234, Ozment noted that Nominalists meant to avoid Pelagianism; they thought it part of God's design and absolutely on his initiative that human beings "initiate their salvation" as a "semimerit within a state of nature." Cf. Heiko A. Oberman, *The Harvest of Medieval Theology* (Cambridge, Massachusetts, 1963), 175. Ozment's nt. remarks: "For a dissenting view, see Wilhelm Ernst, *Gott und Mensch am Vorabend der Reformation: Eine Untersuchung zur Moralphilosophie und Theologie bei Gabriel Biel* (Leipzig, 1972), 394."

14   Luther, *The Bondage of the Will,* 113, para. 638.

15   *Proslogium,* originally entitled "Faith Seeking Understanding," is the work containing Saint Anselm's famous ontological argument for God's existence. See Saint Anselm of Canterbury, *Proslogium,* at Medieval Sourcebook [online]; available from http://www.fordham.edu/halsall/basis/anselm-proslogium.html (accessed 5 August 2008).

16   Martin Luther, Sermons on the Second Article (from 1533): Sermo Jesu Christo, in *WA,* vol. 37, 39.

17   The typical medieval view of the Old Testament as law and the New Testament as gospel was transcended by Luther's view of the law and gospel as present in every biblical book. In Luther's thought, as the eternal testament of Christ, the New Testament precedes the Old Testament.

18   This point was underscored by Jared Wicks in an evaluative study of Luther's thought regarding justification by faith in "Justification and Faith in Luther's Theology," *Theological Studies* 44, no. 1 (1983):3–29, especially 21–24 and 27–29. Wicks also noted as important theological items of Luther's thought his denial—contra Catholic theology confirmed at the Council of Trent—of a role for human freedom in acceptance or refusal of grace, his stress of the necessity of God's agency in all of our movements toward good, and his focus upon soteriology as the unifying element of theological reflection. Passages noted by Wicks as particularly informative for Luther's theology include Rom. 1:17; 2:15; 3:4; 4:7; 5:15; 7:5, 7, 12; and 14:1.

19   The term "Evangelical" was used properly of Lutheran churches within the Protestant body in Luther's home of Germany. See "Evangelicalism," *The Oxford Dictionary of the Christian Church*, 3ʳᵈ ed., ed. F.L. Cross and E.A. Livingstone (Oxford and New York: Oxford University Press, 1997):579.

20   Accounts abound of Luther's life, theology, and theological influences, as well as of the beginnings of the Protestant Reformation and the events leading to it. Among sources drawn upon for this summary were the first two volumes of the three-volume study of Martin Brecht—*Martin Luther: His Road to Reformation, 1483–1521*, and *Martin Luther: Shaping and Defining the Reformation, 1521–1532*, trans. James L. Schaaf (Minneapolis: Fortress Press, 1990), original edition, *Martin Luther: Zweiter Band: Ordnung und Abgrenzung der Reformaton, 1521–1532*, Stuttgart, Germany: Calwer Verlag, 1986. Brief and accessible explanations of the basic history and theology offered here include textbooks and reference volumes: "Luther, Martin," *The Oxford Dictionary of the Christian Church*, 3ʳᵈ ed., ed. F.L. Cross and E.A. Livingstone (Oxford and New York: Oxford University Press, 1997):1007–1010; "Nominalism," *The Oxford Dictionary of the Christian Church*, 3ʳᵈ ed., ed. F.L. Cross and E.A. Livingstone (Oxford and New York: Oxford University Press, 1997):1158–1159; Thomas D. McGonigle and James F. Quigley, *A History of the Christian Tradition: From Its Jewish Origins to the Reformation* (New York and Mahwah, New Jersey: Paulist Press, 1988), chapters 21 through 24; *The Christian Theological Tradition*, ed. Catherine A. Cory and David T. Landry (Upper Saddle River, New Jersey: Prentice Hall, 2000), chapters 15 through 19; and Ozment, *The Age of Reform*.

21   Luther believed that in the Catholic Church elements of the gospel had been overshadowed by customs.

22   This summary of Luther's objections to Catholic traditions regarding the saints draws in part, with emendation recommended by colleagues, upon the topical collection of Luther's remarks compiled by Plass in *What Luther Says*, para. 3977–4009. In association with the charge of idolatry, on rare occasions Luther drew connections between practices of veneration of saints—such as belief in saintly patronage and placement of abundant statues and pictures of saints in churches—and customs of heathens and/or pagans (para. 4000–4001, cf. Luther writing in an A. Lauterbach collection and from Luther's March 1541 words of opposition to Duke Henry of Brunswick). Later, Zwingli was consistent in the charge of heathen or pagan foundation and form in veneration of saints. To address this, as was noted in chapter 3, even though there are similar practices that existed in Paganism, they existed in Judaism, too. The coincidence of their existence in these different settings probably owes both in part to custom and in part to a common human perception of God's work among us.

23   With the official promulgation of the dogma of the Immaculate Conception three centuries after the Council of Trent, Catholic theology may speak of a "guarantee" during earthly existence of Mary's salvation. Yet points made here hold about free will and one's certainty (lack thereof) of one's own salvation.

24 "Decree Concerning Justification," in *The Canons and Decrees of the Council of Trent*, Session 6, trans. H.J. Schroeder (Rockford, Illinois: Tan Books and Publishers, 1978), 38.

25 For a concise but illuminating account of the religious language of Scripture (on the resurrection of Christ, specifically, but containing general comments applicable to other matters), see Gerald O'Collins, *Christology: A Biblical, Historical, and Systematic Study of Jesus* (Oxford and New York: Oxford University Press, 1995), 83–90.

26 *Lumen Gentium*, 51.

Seven: The Corporate Life of the Church and Popular Piety: Theological Reflection and Traditional Practices

1 Most days commemorating the lives and deaths of saints have, in the Roman Catholic Church, the status of "memorial," but some for such as the Virgin Mary, the apostles, the evangelists, and martyrs, are properly "feasts." Feasts are greater than memorials, but they are less than "solemnities." Solemnities include Easter, Christmas, and Sundays, as well as commemorations of some events associated with the Blessed Mother and with a few other especially notable saints.

2 See sacramentary and lectionary *Collection of Masses of the Blessed Virgin Mary* (Collegeville, Minnesota: Liturgical Press, 1992).

3 Eucharistic Prayer II, at "Changes in the Parts of the Priest in the Order of Mass in the *Roman Missal, Third Edition*," United States Conference of Catholic Bishops [online]; available from http://old.usccb.org/romanmissal/priestsparts.pdf, accessed 20 August 2011.

4 *Lumen Gentium*, 50.

5 Canon 1188, *Code of Canon Law Annotated*.

6 *Sacrosanctum Concilium*, in *Vatican Council II: The Basic Sixteen Documents; Constitutions Decrees Declarations*, rev. trans., ed. Austin Flannery (Northport, New York: Costello Publishing, 1996), 60. Citations are to paragraph numbers.

7 The longstanding tradition of placing relics beneath fixed altars of churches is retained according to Canon 1237, para. 2, of the 1983 Code, although subsequent Church documents have given options for this requirement. See commentary on Canon 1237 in *New Commentary on the Code of Canon Law*, ed. John P. Beal, James A. Coriden, and Thomas J. Green (Mahwah, New Jersey: Paulist Press, 2000), cf. Sacred Congregation for Sacraments and Divine Worship, *Rite of Dedication of a Church and an Altar*, May 29, 1977, *Documents on the Liturgy 1963–1979, Conciliar, Papal and Curial Texts* (Collegeville: Liturgical Press, 1982), 547. See also *The General Instruction of the Roman Missal*, para. 302. Canon 1190, para. 1, corresponding to Canon 888 of *Code of Canons of the Eastern Churches*, Latin-English ed., trans. Canon Law Society of America (Washington, D.C.: Canon Law Society of America, 1992), forbids the sale of sacred relics.

So unique are the saints' relics that only under precise conditions may other bodies be buried in churches, according to Canon 1242, 1983 Code of Canon Law, *Code of Canon Law Annotated*: "Bodies are not to be buried in churches, unless it is a question of the Roman Pontiff or of Cardinals or, in their proper Churches, of diocesan Bishops even retired."

8   See commentary on Canon 1190, para. 2, in *New Commentary on the Code of Canon Law*, referencing Canon 1281, para. 2, the 1917 Code of Canon Law, *Codex Iuris Canonici*.

9   The three-class division is explained in standard popular Catholic references, such as Peter Klein, *The Catholic Source Book*, rev. ed. (Orlando, Florida: Harcourt Religion Publishers, 2007), 411. For information on particular famous Christian relics, see Joan Carroll Cruz, *Relics* (Huntington, Indiana: Our Sunday Visitor, 1984).

10   "Novena," in *The Oxford Dictionary of the Christian Church*, 3rd ed., ed. F.L. Cross and E.A. Livingstone (New York: Oxford University Press, 1997), 1165. This entry explains that novenas are "modeled on the nine days' preparation of the Apostles and the BVM [Blessed Virgin Mary] for the descent of the Spirit at Pentecost (Acts 1:13 f)."

11   Lawrence G. Lovasik, *Favorite Novenas to the Saints: Arranged for Private Prayer on the Feasts of the Saints* ([Totowa], New Jersey: Catholic Book Publishing, 2006), 3.

12   "Rosary," in *The Oxford Dictionary of the Christian Church*, 3rd ed., ed. F.L. Cross and E.A. Livingstone (New York: Oxford University Press, 1997), 1417. See this entry for a concise history of the rosary.

13   "Definition on Sacred Images," The Second General Council of Nicaea, in *The Christian Faith in the Doctrinal Documents of the Catholic Church*, 6th rev. and enlarged ed., ed. Jacques Dupuis (New York: Alba House, 1996), 1252, cf. Denz. 601. Citations are to paragraph numbers. Denzinger references are all to the 33rd edition, Denzinger-Schönmetzer, *Enchiridion Symbolorun, Definitionum et Declarationum de Rebus Fidei et Morum*, unless otherwise indicated.

14   "Definition on Sacred Images," 1251, cf. Denz. 600.

15   Canon 3, The Fourth General Council of Constantinople, in *The Christian Faith in the Doctrinal Documents of the Catholic Church*, 6th rev. and enlarged ed., ed. Jacques Dupuis (New York: Alba House, 1996), 1253, cf. Denz. 653.

16   Ibid., cf. Denz. 654.

17   Martin V, Bull *Inter Cunctas*, in *The Christian Faith in the Doctrinal Documents of the Catholic Church*, 6th rev. and enlarged ed., ed. Jacques Dupuis (New York: Alba House, 1996), 1254, cf. Denz. 1269.

18   See the entries "Basle, Council of," 169, and "Florence, Council of," 619–620, in *The Oxford Dictionary of the Christian Church*, 3rd ed., ed. F.L. Cross and E.A. Livingstone (New York: Oxford University Press, 1997). The Council of Florence is today often regarded as a continuation of a council that began at Basle in 1431, in which case the dating for the Council of Florence is 1431–1445. The Council at Basle was moved to Ferrara in 1438, to Florence in 1439, and to Rome in 1443.

19   The Eastern church had sought the assistance of the Western church in fending off the Turks.

20   *The Sources of Catholic Dogma*, trans. Roy J. Deferrari (Fitzwilliam, NH: Loreto Publications, n.d.), 693, original edition, *Enchiridion Symbolorum*, 30th ed., ed. Henry Denzinger, rev. Karl Rahner, Freiburg: Herder, 1954. Citations are to paragraph numbers.

21   Ibid., 740a.

22   "On the Invocation, Veneration, and Relics of Saints, and on Sacred Images," in *The Canons and Decrees of the Council of Trent*, Session 25, trans. H.J. Schroeder (Rockford, Illinois: Tan Books and Publishers, 1978), 215, Denz. 1821.

23   Ibid., Denz. 1822.

24   Ibid., 215–216, Denz. 1823.

25   Ibid., 216, Denz. 1823.

26   Ibid., 216.

27   Ibid., 216–217.

28   "Decree Concerning Purgatory," in *The Canons and Decrees of the Council of Trent*, Session 25, trans. H.J. Schroeder (Rockford, Illinois: Tan Books and Publishers, 1978), 214.

29   "Decree Concerning Indulgences," in *The Canons and Decrees of the Council of Trent*, Session 25, trans. H.J. Schroeder (Rockford, Illinois: Tan Books and Publishers, 1978), 254.

30   "The Sacrifice of the Mass is Propitiatory Both for the Living and the Dead," in *The Canons and Decrees of the Council of Trent*, Session 22, trans. H.J. Schroeder (Rockford, Illinois: Tan Books and Publishers, 1978), 146.

31   Ibid.

32   "Masses in Honor of the Saints," in *The Canons and Decrees of the Council of Trent*, Session 22, trans. H.J. Schroeder (Rockford, Illinois: Tan Books and Publishers, 1978), 146.

33   "The Tridentine Profession of Faith (1564)," in *The Teaching of the Catholic Church: As Contained in Her Documents*, ed. Karl Rahner (n.p.: Mercier Press, 1967), 854–856, original edition, *Der Glaube der Kirche*, Regensburg: Verlag Friedrich Pustet, 1965, cf. Denz. 1867. Citations are to paragraph numbers.

34   *Lumen Gentium*, 48.

35   Ibid., 49.

36   Ibid., 50.

37   Ibid.

38   Ibid.

39   Ibid.

40   Ibid., 49.

41   Ibid., 50.

42   Ibid., 51, according to nt. 23, from "The Mass, Preface of saints, granted to some dioceses."

43   Ibid., 49.

44   Ibid., 50.

45   Ibid., 52.

46 Ibid., 53.
47 Ibid., 55–57.
48 Ibid., 58.
49 Ibid., 59.
50 Ibid., 61.
51 Ibid., 60.
52 Ibid., 62. The document mentions various titles applied to Mary, including "advocate, helper, benefactress, and mediatrix," explaining, however, the correct meaning of these titles: "No creature could ever be counted along with the Incarnate Word and Redeemer; but just as the priesthood of Christ is shared in various ways both by his ministers and the faithful, and as the one goodness of God is radiated in different ways among his creatures, so also the unique mediation of the Redeemer does not exclude but rather gives rise to a manifold cooperation which is but a sharing in one source."
53 Ibid., 63.
54 Ibid., 65.
55 Ibid., 66.
56 Ibid., 68.
57 *Sacrosanctum Concilium*, 104.
58 Ibid., 111.
59 *Lumen Gentium*, 51.
60 Ibid., 67.
61 Ibid. The closing words to this section offer clarifying elaboration: "Let the faithful remember moreover that true devotion consists neither in sterile nor transitory feeling, nor in an empty credulity, but proceeds from true faith, by which we are led to recognize the excellence of the Mother of God, and we are moved to a filial love towards our mother and to the imitation of her virtues."
62 Paul VI, *Evangelii Nuntiandi*, in *The Christian Faith in the Doctrinal Documents of the Catholic Church*, 6th rev. and enlarged ed., ed. Jacques Dupuis (New York: Alba House, 1996), 1259. Citations are to paragraph numbers.
63 Ibid.
64 Canon 1187, *Code of Canon Law Annotated*.
65 Canon 885, *Code of Canons of the Eastern Churches*.
66 *Lumen Gentium*, 51. It is explained in the same section of the document that our faith is enriched by veneration of the saints, "[f]or if we continue to love one another and to join in praising the most holy Trinity—all of us who are children of God and form one family in Christ (see Heb. 3:6)—we will be faithful to the deepest vocation of the church and will share in a foretaste of the liturgy of perfect glory."
67 Paul VI, *Evangelii Nuntiandi*, 1259.
68 Ibid.
69 John Paul II, *Duodecimum Saeculum* (Washington, D.C.: United States Catholic Conference, 1987), 11. Citations are to paragraph numbers.
70 Ibid., 9.
71 Ibid., 11.

72   Canon 884, *Code of Canons of the Eastern Churches.*
73   Canon 1186, *Code of Canon Law Annotated*, 742. The difference in
language from the 1917 Code of Canon Law is worthy of note. Code 1276,
on "The Veneration, of Saints, Holy Images and Relics," represented in *The
Teaching of the Catholic Church: As Contained in Her Documents*, 403,
then read: "It is good and profitable to invoke the aid of the Servants of God
who reign together with Christ and to venerate their relics and images. All
the faithful should honour with childlike devotion the Blessed Virgin Mary
above all others."

Eight: Recovered Emphases and New Procedures: Vatican II and the 1983 Congregation for the Causes of Saints Reform

1   Pope John Paul II, Preface, *Divinus Perfectionis Magister*, 25 January 1983,
at the Vatican [online]; available from http://www.vatican.va/holy_father/
john_paul_ii/apost_constitutions/documents/hf_jp-ii_apc_25011983_
divinus-perfectionis-magister_en.html (accessed 28 July 2008).
2   Ibid.
3   Congregation for the Causes of Saints, *Normae Servandae in
inquisitionibus ab Episcopis faciendis in Causis Sanctorum* (New Laws for
the Causes of Saints: Norms to Be Observed in Inquiries Made by Bishops
in the Causes of Saints), 7 February 1983, at the Vatican [online];
available from http://www.vatican.va/roman_curia/congregations/csaints/
documents/rc_con_csaints_doc_07021983_norme_en.html (accessed 28
July 2008).
4   As previous chapters have explained, no public cult is permitted without the
ecclesiastical validation of beatification (which allows local cultic
veneration, as in a geographical area or of a particular religious order) or
canonization (which requires veneration throughout the universal Church),
so yet at this stage no liturgical activities or other events in churches may
celebrate a servant of God whose cause is in process.
5   The process thus far described follows three directives: John Paul II, *Divinus
Perfectionis Magister*; Congregation for the Causes of Saints, *Normae
Servandae*; and Holy See Press Office, *Canonization Process*, 12 September
1997, Vatican Information Service, accessible as reprint from catholic-
pages.com [online]; available from http://www.catholic-pages.com/saints/
process.asp (accessed 31 July 2008).
6   John Paul II, *Divinus Perfectionis Magister*, and Holy See Press Office,
Canonization Process.
7   "Address of His Holiness Benedict XVI to the Postulators of the
Congregation for the Causes of Saints," 17 December 2007, at the Vatican
[online]; available from http://www.vatican.va/holy_father/benedict_xvi/
speeches/2007/december/documents/hf_ben-xvi_spe_20071217_
postulatori_cause_en.html (accessed 1 August 2008).
8   Exceptions have been made to this rule, as in the cases of John Henry
Newman and Pope John Paul II.

9   Cardinal José Saraiva Martins and Archbishop Edward Nowak, *Communique by the Congregation for the Causes of Saints*, 29 September 2005, at the Vatican [online]; available from http:/www.vatican.va/roman_curia/congregations/csaints/documents/rc_con_csaints_doc_20050929_com mnicato_en.html (accessed 28 July 2008).

10   Cardinal Martins, Congregation for the Causes of Saints, *New Procedures in the Rite of Beatification.*

11   *Sanctorum Mater:* Instruction on the Procedure of Diocesan and Eparchial Inquires on the Causes of Saints. An English translation of the document is in process at Hagiography Circle: An Online Resource on Contemporary Hagiography [online]; available from http://newsaints.faithweb.com/index.htm (accessed 2 November 2008). Description of the document was widespread at the time of the document's presentation in the Holy See Press Office on 18 February 2008.

12   Pope Benedict XVI, *Letter of His Holiness Benedict XVI to the Participants of the Plenary Session of the Congregation for the Causes of Saints*, 24 April 2006, at the Vatican [online]; available from http://www.vatican.va/holy_father/benedict_xvi/letters/2006/documents/hf_ben-xvi_let_20060424_cause-santi_en.html (accessed 28 July 2008).

13   As described in the biography of Padre Pio da Pietrelcina (1887–1968), canonized 16 June 2002, at the Vatican [online]; available from http://www.vatican.va/news_services/liturgy/saints/ns_lit_doc_20020616_padre-pio_en.html (accessed 31 July 2008).

14   For a sense of the magnitude of the task for some processes, the Archbishop Fulton J. Sheen Foundation website reported that the cause of the popular religious writer, host of national radio broadcast "The Catholic Hour" and television series "Life is Worth Living," as well as professor, began officially on April 15, 2008, with the acceptance at the offices of the Congregation for the Causes of Saints of a crate of documentation including over sixty-five hundred pages, plus sixty-seven books of the Archbishop (1895–1979). See The Archbishop Fulton J. Sheen Foundation [online], especially for Jared Olar, "Sheen Cause Opens in Rome: Fr. Deptula to Direct Foundation," available from http://www.archbishopsheencause.org/, (accessed 31 July 2008), reprinted from *Catholic Post* [The Catholic Diocese of Peoria, http://www.cdop.org/pages/].

15   The "Chronology of the Cause for Canonization of Josemaria Escrivá de Balaguer," at the Vatican [online]; available from http://www.vatican.va/latest/documents/escriva_cronlogia-causa_en.html (accessed 31 July 2008), reports that the final *Positio* of the Opus Dei founder (1902–1975), canonized 6 October 2002, was over six thousand pages, divided into four volumes.

16   Woodward, from closer observation than most are granted, provides in chapter 6 of *Making Saints* a detailed account of the workings of the *Consulta Medica*, 191–220, that is obtained usually only piecemeal from a variety of other sources. The term "not scientifically explainable" is quoted from the report of the medical body in the biography of Fr. Charles of St. Andrew (1821–1893), in discussion of the miracle process that resulted in his canonization on 3 June 2007; see the Vatican [online]; available from http://www.vatican.va/news_services/liturgy/saints/ns_lit_doc_20070603_carlo-andrea_en.html (accessed 1 August 2008).

17 Holy See Press Office, *Canonization Process*, para. 6.

18 Ibid.

19 *Pastor Aeternus*, excerpted in *The Sources of Catholic Dogma*, trans. Roy J. Deferrari (Fitzwilliam, NH: Loreto Publications, n.d.), 1839, original edition, *Enchiridion Symbolorum*, 30ᵗʰ ed., ed. Henry Denzinger, rev. Karl Rahner, Freiburg: Herder, 1954. Vatican II's *Lumen Gentium*, para. 25, affirmed the teaching on papal infallibility, adding that "[t]he infallibility promised to the church is also present in the body of bishops when, together with Peter's successor, they exercise the supreme teaching office."

20 "Address of His Holiness Benedict XVI to the Postulators of the Congregation for the Causes of Saints."

Nine: The Christological Center: Catholic Doctrine and Ecumenical Conversation

1 Bernard J.F. Lonergan, in *Method in Theology* (Great Britain: Darton Longman & Todd, 1972; reprint, Toronto: University of Toronto Press, 1996), 105.

2 Karl Rahner and Herbert Vorgrimler, "Transcendence," *Theological Dictionary*, ed. Cornelius Ernst, trans. Richard Strachan (New York: Herder and Herder, 1965), 465, original edition, *Kleines Theologisches Wörterbuch*, Freiburg: Verlag Herder, [1961].

3 Lonergan, *Method in Theology*, 105. He explained: "That fulfilment brings a deep-set joy . . . brings a radical peace . . . bears fruit in a love of one's neighbor that strives mightily to bring about the kingdom of God on this earth." He noted that "the absence of that fulfilment opens the way to the trivialization of human life in the pursuit of fun, to the harshness of human life arising from the ruthless exercise of power, to despair about human welfare springing from the conviction that the universe is absurd."

4 Ibid., 106.

5 Ibid., 237–244.

6 Ibid., 241.

7 Ibid., 106. Lonergan noted that, named by other concepts, too, "[i]t corresponds to St. Ignatius Loyola's consolation that has no cause, as expounded by Karl Rahner." Cf. Rahner, *The Dynamic Element in the Church, Quaestiones disputatae 12*, Montreal: Palm Publishers, 1964, pp. 131ff.

8 Karl Rahner, in "Revelation: Concept of Revelation, Theological Interpretation," *Sacramentum Mundi: An Encyclopedia of Theology*, vol. 5, ed. Karl Rahner et al. (New York: Herder and Herder, 1970), 350, wrote of our ontological reality: "The formal definition and the material description of the end of man (or of the morally relevant finality of a particular element of his being) must always take man's 'intentionality' into account. . . . The 'end' of an essentially purposeful ('intentional') being can only be determined by the 'Whither' or goal of this intention. But if this intentionality is unlimited in knowledge and freedom, the intentional possession of reality as such (a possession which is very 'real') is the end of

this being, an end which is *quodammodo omnia*. The end is therefore the limitless fullness of reality, i.e., 'God' . . ."

9 Karl Rahner and Herbert Vorgrimler, "Formal Object, Supernatural," *Theological Dictionary*, ed. Cornelius Ernst, trans. Richard Strachan (New York: Herder and Herder, 1965), 178, original edition, *Kleines Theologisches Wörterbuch*, Freiburg: Verlag Herder, [1961]. In "Revelation: Concept of Revelation, Theological Interpretation," 350, Rahner stated more succinctly that "every human being is elevated by grace in his transcendental intellectuality in a non-explicit manner." Rahner, in "Church, Churches and Religions," *Theological Investigations*, vol. 10, trans. David Bourke (New York: Seabury Press, 1977), 35, original edition, *Schriften zur Theologie*, VIII, part II, Einsiedeln: Benziger, [1967], asserted that the fact of this elevated transcendentality "does not mean, and need not mean, that man must always have a conscious awareness of this 'supernatural existential' in his life, or that he must be able to create this awareness within him simply by a process of psychological introspection." On 36, he explained that a human being "develops to the full the supernaturally elevated transcendentality bestowed upon him, the 'supernatural existential'. . . . in and through his existence as engaged in human living in the concrete." All things in creation are potentially revelatory of God; some things—such as the Incarnation—have an objective meaning (and are a cause of the concrete constitution of human beings as those with an elevated cognitive intentionality), whether or not their full value and meaning is explicitly recognized by all human beings.

10 Karl Rahner, "Order: End of Man," *Sacramentum Mundi: An Encyclopedia of Theology*, vol. 4, ed. Karl Rahner et al. (New York: Herder and Herder, 1969), 302. Rahner's reference to the *finis qui* was to our "predetermined end"; his reference to our *finis quo* was to "the actual possession of God." As he explained, "The unlimited transcendence of man and God's self-communication in grace to man mean that God is the (intended) end of man, which therefore precedes his free realization of his goal. It is predetermined and not that which man sets himself and produces." God "takes this *finis quo* to himself as his own determination [in the Incarnation]."

11 Lonergan, *Method in* Theology, 107. Lonergan explained that this is "the gift of God's love," "sanctifying grace."

12 Bonaventure, *Breviloquium*, 2.12, as quoted and discussed in Denis Edwards, *Jesus the Wisdom of God: An Ecological Theology* (Maryknoll, New York: Orbis Books, 1995), 106, cf. *The Works of Bonaventure II: The Breviloquium*, trans. Jose de Vinck (Paterson, N.J.: St. Anthony Guild, 1963).

13 Karl Rahner, "The Theology of the Symbol," *Theological Investigations*, vol. 4, trans. Kevin Smyth (London: Darton, Longman & Todd; New York: Seabury Press, 1974), 224, original edition, *Schriften zur Theologie*, IV, Einsiedeln: Verlagsanstalt Benziger, [1960].

14 Karl Rahner, "Reflections on the Unity of the Love of Neighbour and the Love of God," *Theological Investigations*, vol. 6, trans. Karl-H. and Boniface Kruger (New York: Crossroad Publishing, 1982), 249, original edition, *Schriften zur Theologie*, VI, Einsiedeln: Verlagsanstalt Benziger, [1965].

15   Karl Rahner, "The One Christ and the Universality of Salvation," in *Theological Investigations*, vol. 16, trans. David Morland (New York: Crossroad Publishing, 1983), 212, original edition, *Schriften zur Theologie*, XII, part I, Einsiedeln: Verlagsanstalt Benziger, [1975].

16   The Lutheran World Federation and the Roman Catholic Church, *Joint Declaration on the Doctrine of Justification* (Grand Rapids, Michigan, and Cambridge, U.K.: William B. Eerdmans Publishing, 2000), 7, original edition, *Gemeinsame Erklärung zur Rechtfertigungslehre*, Frankfurt am Main: Verlag Otto Lembeck; Paderborn: Bonifatius-Verlag, 1999. Citations are to paragraph numbers.

17   Ibid., 16.

18   Ibid., 15.

19   Ibid., 19.

20   Ibid., 20.

21   Ibid., 21.

22   Ibid., 30.

23   Ibid.

24   Ibid., 29.

25   Ibid., 39.

26   Ibid., 38.

27   Pope John Paul II, *Novo Millennio Ineunte*, at the Vatican [online]; available from http://www.vatican.va/holy_father/john_paul_ii/apost_letters/documents/hf_jp-ii_apl_20010106_novo.millennio-ineunte_en.html (accessed 19 November 2008), 38. Citations are to paragraph numbers. The term is not exclusive to this document, occurring widely in Catholic theological works.

28   "Symbol of Chalcedon," The General Council of Chalcedon, in *The Christian Faith in the Doctrinal Documents of the Catholic Church*, 6th rev. and enlarged ed., ed. Jacques Dupuis (New York: Alba House, 1996), 615, cf. Denz. 302.

29   Bilateral Working Group of the German National Bishops' Conference and the Church Leadership of the United Evangelical Lutheran Church of Germany, *Communio Sanctorum: The Church as the Communion of Saints*, trans. Mark W. Jeske, Michael Root, and Daniel R. Smith (Collegeville, Minesota: Liturgical Press, 2004), 235, original edition, *Communio Sanctorum: Die Kirche als Gemeinschaft der Heiligen*, Paderborn: Bonifatius, 2000. Citations are to paragraph numbers.

30   Ibid., 236–237.

31   Ibid., 240.

32   Some Bible translations use the alternate terms "Comforter" and "Advocate."

33   See *Lumen Gentium*, chapter 5, "The Universal Call to Holiness," 39–42. ". . . [A]ll of the faithful are invited and obliged to try to achieve holiness and the perfection of their own state of life" (42).

34   *Lumen Gentium*, 40. See nt. 4 of this Dogmatic Constitution for a list of previous documents of the Catholic Church on this call to holiness for all Christians.

35 See Jn. 13:34–35: "'A new commandment I give to you, that you love one another; even as I have loved you, that you also love one another. By this all men will know that you are my disciples, if you have love for one another.'" See also Mt. 22:36–40 [where the Pharisees question Jesus and he replies]: "'Teacher, which is the great commandment in the law?' And he said to him, 'You shall love the Lord your God with all your heart, and with all your soul, and with all your mind. This is the great and first commandment. And a second is like it, You shall love your neighbor as yourself. On these two commandments depend all the law and the prophets.'" See Mk. 12:28–34 for Jesus' response to a scribe's question, "Which commandment is the first of all?": "Jesus answered, 'The first is "Hear O Israel: The Lord our God, the Lord is one; and you shall love the Lord your God with all your heart, and with all your soul, and with all your mind, and with all your strength." The second is this, "You shall love your neighbor as yourself." There is no other commandment greater than these.' And the scribe said to him, 'You are right, Teacher; you have truly said that he is one, and there is no other but he; and to love him with all the heart, and with all the understanding, and with all the strength, and to love one's neighbor as oneself, is much more than all whole burnt offerings and sacrifices.' And when Jesus saw that he answered wisely, he said to him, 'You are not far from the kingdom of God.' And after that no one dared to ask him any question." Finally, see Lk. 10:25–28: "And behold, a lawyer stood up to put him to the test, saying, 'Teacher, what shall I do to inherit eternal life?' He said to him, 'What is written in the law? How do you read?' And he answered, 'You shall love the Lord your God with all your heart, and with all your soul, and with all your strength, and with all your mind; and your neighbor as yourself.' And he said to him, 'You have answered right; do this, and you will live.'"

Note also Mt. 19:16–22 for Jesus' words about commandments to keep to have eternal life. Among them is loving one's neighbor as oneself (19). And the young man who fulfills all of the commandments that Jesus mentions, Jesus advises to "sell what you possess and give to the poor, and you will have treasure in heaven; and come, follow me" (21). Note Rom. 13:8–10 for Paul's words echoing the teaching of Christ: "Owe no one anything, except to love one another; for he who loves his neighbor has fulfilled the law. The commandments, 'You shall not commit adultery, You shall not kill, You shall not steal, You shall not covet,' and any other commandment, are summed up in this sentence, 'You shall love your neighbor as yourself.' Love does no wrong to a neighbor; therefore love is the fulfilling of the law." Paul's words in Gal. 5:14 confirm: "For the whole law is fulfilled in one word, 'You shall love your neighbor as yourself.'" Jas. 2:8 concurs: "If you really fulfil the royal law, according to the scripture, 'You shall love your neighbor as yourself,' you do well."

See, from the Old Testament, Dt. 6:4–5, where Moses delivers to Israel the commandments of the Lord, chief among them the first commandment, the *Shema*: "Hear, O Israel: The LORD our God is one LORD; and you shall love the LORD your God with all your heart, and with all your soul, and with all your might." See also Lev. 19:18 for the Lord's words to Moses:

"You shall not take vengeance or bear any grudge against the sons of your own people, but you shall love your neighbor as yourself: I am the LORD."

36   Karl Rahner, *The Love of Jesus and the Love of Neighbor* (New York, Crossroad Publishing, 1983), 71, original edition, *Was heist Jesus lieben?*, Freiburg im Breisgau: Verlag Herder, 1982, and *Wer ist dein Bruder?*, Freiburg im Breisgau: Verlag Herder, 1981.

37   Benedict XVI, *Deus Caritas Est*, 25 December 2006, at the Vatican [online]; available from http://www.vatican.va/holy_father/benedict_xvi/ encyclicals/documents/hf_ben-xvi_enc_20051225_deus-caritas-est_en.html (accessed 26 January 2006), 13–14, 7, and 20–42. Citations are to paragraph numbers. As a summary of the encyclical's explanation of love, *eros* love is understood as that which one might desire for the experience— a feeling of intoxication, of union with the divine—which encourages us to seek beyond ourselves, for ecstacy, for ourselves. *Agape* love desires to discover the other, to care for the other. It exists not just for itself but for the beloved, for whom it wants the good. *Eros* is an "ascending, possessive or covetous love," whereas *agape* is a "descending, oblative love" (7). The New Testament extols *agape* love. The pope points out that a cleansed notion of *eros*, such that this love can become less selfish and more for the other, plus a recognition that *agape* love must have sustenance if it is to survive (i.e., it must be received as well as given), can allow us to see how both types of love are operative in Christian love and the charitable works that must issue from this (7). God first loved us; Christ's sacrifice, in love, is the fuel of his disciples' love.

38   Leontius of Neapolis, quoted in *Introduction to Theology*, ed. John D. Laurance (Boston, Massachusetts: Pearson Custom Publishing, 2000), 86.

39   "Definition on Sacred Images (787)," 1252, cf. St. Basil, *De Spiritu Sancto*, 18, 45. See *Lumen Gentium*, 66, for affirmation of this teaching: "This cult [of Mary], as it has always existed in the church, while it is totally extraordinary, it yet differs essentially from the cult of adoration which is offered equally to the Incarnate Word and to the Father and the holy Spirit, and is most favorable to this adoration. The various forms of piety towards the Mother of God which, within the limits of sound and orthodox doctrine, the church has approved for various times and places according to the character and temperament of the faithful, ensure that while the mother is honored, the Son through whom all things have their being (see Col 1:15–16) and in whom it has pleased the Father that 'all fullness should dwell' (Col 1:19) is rightly known, loved and glorified and his commandments are observed."

40   "Definition on Sacred Images (787)," 1252.

41   *Lumen Gentium*, 62.

Ten: The Saints as Companions: A Contemporary Understanding

1   The intrinsic connections among the roles of the saints—companion, model, and intercessor—were discussed in my article "The Unity of Individual and

Ecclesial Graces in the Roles of the Saints," *Irish Theological Quarterly* 72, no. 4 (2007):371–390. Some of the ideas and text from that article appear in locations in this and the next two chapters dealing with the saintly roles.

2   *Lumen Gentium*, 50.

3   *Catechism of the Catholic Church*, para. 1.

4   Thomas L. Kinkead, *An Explanation of the Baltimore Catechism of Christian Doctrine for the Use of Sunday-School Teachers and Advanced Classes (Also known as Baltimore Catechism No. 4)* (Rockford, Illinois: Tan Books and Publishers, 1988), 29.

5   Augustine, *Confessions*, I.i.1.

6   A condemnation was delivered by Pope Pius XII in his encyclical *Humani Generis*, directed at those who "destroy the gratuity of the supernatural order, since God, they say, cannot create intellectual beings without ordering and calling them to the beatific vision." See Pius XII, *Humani Generis*, 12 August 1950, at the Vatican [online]; available from http://www.vatican.va/holy_father/pius_xii/encyclicals/documents/hf_p-xii_enc_12081950_humani-generis_en.html (accessed 19 June 2008), 26. Citations are to paragraph numbers.

7   In various contexts of reflection upon the saints, as already cited, I have summarized, as well as dissected, Rahner's theology of nature and grace, along with his theology of symbol: "A Reinterpretation of Invocation and Intercession of the Saints"; "The Unity of Individual and Ecclesial Graces in the Roles of the Saints"; and *The Unity of Dulia and Latria*. Ideas and some text from these works, plus from my "Mary's Virginity as 'the sign of her faith': A Study of the Nature-Grace Dynamic," *Marian Studies* 58 (2007):1–25, occasionally may be replicated or otherwise represented in this work, especially in the three chapters on the saints' roles.

8   The term appears throughout Rahner's writings, for example in Karl Rahner, *Foundations of Christian Faith: An Introduction to the Idea of Christianity*, trans. William V. Dych (New York: Crossroad Publishing, 1995), 44–89 (chapter II) and elsewhere, original edition, *Grundkurs des Glaubens: Einführung in den Begriff des Christentums*, Freiburg im Breisgau: Verlag Herder, 1976.

9   For a detailed exposition of the "uncreated grace" (i.e., communication of the divine persons) offered to human beings, see Karl Rahner, *The Trinity*, trans. Joseph Donceel (New York: Crossroad Publishing, 1997), original edition, *Der dreifaltige Gott als transzendeter Urgrund der Heilsgeschichte*, in *Die Heilsgeschichte vor Christus*, volume 2 of *Mysterium Salutis, Grundriss heilsgeschichtlicher Dogmatik*. Rahner wrote of the self-communication of God as an instance of "quasi-formal" causality rather than of "formal causality," to make it clear that our humanity does not become divinity (36 and 77, for example).

10   Rahner appropriated the notion of "obediential potency" from the thought of Thomas Aquinas, who wrote of the potency of human nature that exists because of its obedience to God's action. Cf. *Summa Theologiae*, IIIa, q. 1, art. 3 ad 3, and elsewhere. Citations are to part, question, article, and reply numbers.

11   Karl Rahner, "Concerning the Relationship Between Nature and Grace,"
     Theological Investigations, vol. 1, trans. Cornelius Ernst (London: Darton,
     Longman & Todd; New York: Seabury Press, 1974), 297–317, original
     edition, *Schriften zur Theologie*, I, Einsiedeln-Zürich-Köln: Verlangsanstalt
     Benziger, 1954.
12   Rahner, *Foundations of Christian Faith*, 128. This notion follows the
     teaching of the Second Council of Orange (529) condemning Semi-
     Pelagianism: grace is needed for us to accept grace. For example, as one
     conciliar canon states, "If anyone contends that God awaits our will before
     cleansing us from sin, but does not confess that even the desire to be
     cleansed is aroused in us by the infusion and action of the Holy Spirit, he
     opposes the Holy Spirit himself . . . ." See The Second Council of Orange,
     in *The Christian Faith in the Doctrinal Documents of the Catholic Church*,
     6th rev. and enlarged ed., ed. Jacques Dupuis (New York: Alba House, 1996),
     1916, cf. Denz. 374. See also 1915, 1917–1921, cf. Denz. 373, 375–396.
13   Rahner, *Foundations of Christian Faith*, 128, and elsewhere.
14   Karl Rahner, "Existence: 'The Existential,' Theological, Supernatural
     Existential," *Sacramentum Mundi: An Encyclopedia of Theology*, vol. 2, ed.
     Karl Rahner et al. (New York: Herder and Herder; London: Burns & Oates,
     1968), 306.
15   As evident in such as Karl Rahner, "Questions of Controversial Theology on
     Justification," *Theological Investigations*, vol. 4, trans. Kevin Smyth
     (London: Darton, Longman & Todd; New York: Seabury Press, 1974), 217,
     original edition, *Schriften zur Theologie* IV, Einsiedeln: Verlagsanstalt
     Benziger, [1960], Scholastic theology's notion of a "gradated grace" was
     accepted by Rahner as explanation of the distinction and the relationship
     between the graciousness of God and the grace for which it exists. Rahner
     explained that "[a] subject whose being or nature was grace in such a way
     as grace is just grace, would be, even as a subject, the pure affirmation of
     God, and could do nothing else but ratify the affirmation of God in Christ:
     it would have to believe. And since the subject is real and therefore very
     'objective', without this objective inclination in human nature, there would
     be no difference at all between objective and subjective redemption, there
     could be no possible contrast between the two dimensions which would be
     more than apparent. Not only are there grades of 'being in Christ', there are
     also essential gradations in the gratuitousness of grace itself. . . . The grace
     of the strictly supernatural procures for itself the grace of creation as its own
     presupposition on a lower level, maintains and animates it by virtue of the
     stronger will of God with regard to the higher grace: but it still leaves it as
     the lower grace. . . . Everything exists in Christ; there are degrees in this
     'everything'; . . . [T]he existence which the degrees have in Christ is of
     different kinds. The lower 'degree' only has its existence in Christ, the
     higher 'degree' consists essentially of the self-communication of God in
     Christ. . . ." (215–216).
16   See Rahner, *Foundations of Christian Faith*, 16, trans. nt : "'Existiential,' as
     in Rahner's phrase 'supernatural existential,' refers to an element in man's

ontological constitution precisely as human being, an element which is constitutive of his existence as man prior to his exercise of freedom. It is an aspect of concrete human nature precisely as human. 'Existentiell,' as in Rahner's phrase 'existentiell Christology,' refers to the free, personal and subjective appropriation and actualization of something which can also be spoken of in abstract theory or objective concepts without such a subjective and personal realization."

17 Ibid., 128. Also see Karl Rahner, "Why and How Can We Venerate the Saints?," 18.

18 Karl Rahner, in "Salvation: Theology, Redemption," *Sacramentum Mundi: An Encyclopedia of Theology*, vol. 5, ed. Karl Rahner et al. (New York: Herder and Herder; London: Burns & Oates, 1970), 431, wrote: "The radical acceptance of divinizing self-communication on the part of the creature occurs, however, by death. For death, as action, is the definitive acceptance of self by the free being, and, as undergone, it is the acceptance and endurance of the situation of guilt which is that of the free being."

19 Rahner, *Foundations of Christian Faith*, especially 195, and elsewhere, including Karl Rahner, "Questions of Controversial Theology on Justification," 213–214. Also Rahner, "Church, Churches, and Religions," 38. Also Karl Rahner, "Jesus Christ in the Non-Christian Religions," *Theological Investigations*, vol. 17, trans. Margaret Kohl (New York: Crossroad Publishing, 1981), 46–48, original edition, *Schriften zur Theologie*, XII, part II, Einsiedeln: Verlagsanstalt Benziger, [1975]. Also Karl Rahner, "The Theological Dimension of the Question About Man," *Theological Investigations*, vol. 17, trans. Margaret Kohl (New York: Crossroad Publishing, 1981), 68, original edition, *Schriften zur Theologie*, XII, part II, Einsiedeln: Verlagsanstalt Benziger, [1975].

20 Rahner, *Foundations of Christian Faith*, 195. See Karl Rahner, "On the Importance of Non-Christian Religions for Salvation," 292, for explanation of the "innermost entelechy of the history of the individual and of mankind as a whole" moving the world toward God as goal as "offer of salvation and revelation and a permanent existential of humanity and its history. . . ." In Jesus Christ, "God has irreversibly promised himself to the world in *historical* tangibility, . . ."

21 In Rahner, "Existence: 'The Existential,' Theological, Supernatural Existential," 306, the language of "objective justification" is used.

22 Rahner, "Order: End of Man," 301.

23 Rahner, in *Foundations of Christian Faith*, 118, wrote: "That the acceptance of God's self-communication must be based upon and is based upon God's offer itself, and hence that the acceptance of grace is once again an event of grace itself, this follows from the ultimate relationship between human transcendence as knowledge and freedom and the term and source by which this transcendence is opened and upon which it is based."

24 Ibid., 128.

25 Rahner, "Why and How Can We Venerate the Saints?," 19. Transcendental experience is "the *original* act of knowledge and freedom" which "bears

upon *the actual reality itself.*" Its categorial association with a particular object is "the *concept* of a given reality."

26   Ibid., 20.

27   Ibid.

28   Ibid., 21. Rahner explained, on 18, that "the exercise of love of neighbour (as charity) is *ipso facto* and in itself the love of God. But as true love it is a love that is supported by grace. In other words it is a love that is made open by God to attain to God."

29   Karl Rahner, in "Experience of the Spirit and Existential Commitment," *Theological Investigations*, vol. 16, trans. David Morland (New York: Crossroad Publishing, 1983), 28, original edition, *Schriften zur Theologie* XII, part I, Einsiedeln: Verlagsanstalt Benziger, [1975], explained: "Like any other experience, the transcendent experience of the radical nature of the Spirit is mediated through categorial objects, for the finite, spiritual essence of man only comes to self-expression in relationship to what is other." On 32, he explained that "the freely accepted transcendent experience of the Spirit is only possible here and now through concentration upon one distinct object of choice among others. . . . [T]his object does not in any way lessen or distort the experience of the Spirit but rather provides a concrete and practical means of expression for it."

30   Rahner, "Why and How Can We Venerate the Saints?," 19–21.

31   Ibid., 10. According to Rahner, on 21, such an act "derives its special value from that which the agent explicitly formulates to himself as its object, and is therefore higher in degree than an act in which the agent takes a creature as the object which he makes conceptually present to himself."

32   Ibid., 21. These words are the title of the final section of the essay.

33   Ibid.

34   Ibid., 21–22.

35   Ibid., 22.

36   Ibid., 18–21.

37   Ibid., 22.

38   Ibid., 20.

39   Ibid., 22. In yet more philosophical language describing this theological reality, Rahner wrote, in *Foundations of Christian Faith*, 133: "Man experiences himself . . . as a subject who actualizes the subjectivity of his gratuitously elevated transcendence in his a posteriori and historical encounter with his world of persons and of things, an encounter which is never completely at his disposal. And he actualizes it in his encounter with a human thou in whom history and transcendence find their one actualization together and in unity, and there he finds his encounter with God as the absolute Thou."

40   Karl Rahner, "One Mediator and Many Mediations," *Theological Investigations*, vol. 9, part 1, trans. Graham Harrison (London: Darton, Longman & Todd; New York: Seabury Press, [1972]), 169–184, original edition, [*Schriften zur Theologie*, VIII, part I, Einsiedeln: Benziger, 1968].

41   See Karl Rahner, "The Theology of the Symbol," *Theological Investigations*, vol. 4, trans. Kevin Smyth (London: Darton, Longman & Todd; New York: Seabury Press, 1974), 251, original edition, *Schriften zur Theologie* IV,

Einsiedeln: Verlagsanstalt Benziger, [1960]: "[A] symbol is not something separate from the symbolized (or different, but really or mentally united with the symbolized by a mere process of addition), which indicates the object but does not contain it. On the contrary, the symbol is the reality, constituted by the thing symbolized as an inner moment of itself, which reveals and proclaims the thing symbolized, and is itself full of the thing symbolized, being its concrete form of existence."

42 Karl Rahner, *The Dynamic Element in the Church*, trans. W.J. O'Hara (New York: Herder and Herder, 1964), 67, original edition, *Das Dynamische in der Kirche*, Freiburg: Herder KG, 1964.

43 Ibid., 55.

44 Ibid., 56, 58, 59, and elsewhere. Rahner remarked, on 61, that the Church is itself "of the charismata." The "official Church and hierarchy" have become "the institutional organizer and administrator of the gifts of the Spirit in the Church" where "*charismata*" have been judged authentic.

45 This summarizes part of my "The Unity of Individual and Ecclesial Graces in the Roles of the Saints."

46 See *Catechism of the Catholic Church*, para. 67, for a brief explanation about private revelations.

47 Sacred Congregation for the Doctrine of the Faith, *Recentiores episcoporum synodi*, in *Vatican Council II: More Postconciliar Documents*, ed. Austin Flannery (Collegeville, MN: Liturgical Press, 1982), 7. Citations are to paragraph numbers.

48 Ibid.

49 Ibid.

50 Ibid., 1–2.

51 Ibid., 3.

52 Ibid., 4.

53 Ibid., 5.

54 Ibid., 6.

55 Ibid., 7.

Eleven: The Saints as Models: A Contemporary Understanding

1 Saint Thérèse of Lisieux, *Story of a Soul: The Autobiography of Saint Thérèse of Lisieux*, 3rd ed., trans. John Clarke (Washington, D.C.: ICS Publications, 1996), 72.

2 Saint Augustine, *On Christian Doctrine*, trans. D.W. Robertson, Jr. (Upper Saddle River, New Jersey: Prentice-Hall, 1958), I.XXII.21. Citations are to book, chapter, and paragraph numbers.

3 Ibid., I.XXII.20.

4 Ibid., I.V.5.

5 Ibid., I.VI.4.

6 Ibid., I.III.3-XXIX.30.

7 *Lumen Gentium*, 50.

8 Ibid., 49.

9 Ibid., 50.

10   Irenaeus of Lyon, *Against Heresies*, in *The Christological Controversy*, trans. and ed. Richard A. Norris, Jr. (Philadelphia: Fortress Press, 1980), 58 (Book V, chap. 1, para. 1).

11   Rahner, "The Church of the Saints," 100. Emphasis mine.

12   Ibid.

13   Ibid., 97. The Church must do this so that she is not "holy merely in her objective institutions" which "unholy sinners might turn . . . into a weapon against God himself."

14   Ibid., 103, cf. Pius XII, *Mystici Corporis*, A.A.S. XXXV [1943], 200ff.; C.T.S. translation, *The Mystical Body of Jesus Christ* [London, 1948], 13–14; 23–24. Rahner contended that "[t]here is, therefore, a driving force for the further development of life in the Church which does not originate from the official element but directly from Christ himself, a law of life which goes out from 'Christ in a mysterious way in his own person' and embraces the saints who hold no office and through them affects the others *and* the official element." The Body of Christ has not only "the grace of the hierarchy" but "that of the 'charismatics'" (103–104).

15   Ibid., 99. He explained further: "The differences between Saints (which no one would deny) are not merely sublime accidents of a merely temporal kind, which are of no consequence for the holiness itself which they realize. No, precisely these unique accidents of history, the 'individual factor', the 'physiognomic element' of the Saints enters into eternity with them, into that eternity which is not something purely abstract but the genuine and permanent, individual product of history. Otherwise there would be a '*cultis sanctitatis*' in the Church but no '*cultus sanctorum*', and one would have to recommend moral theology books for reading and not the lives of the Saints."

16   *Lumen Gentium*, 50.

17   Ibid.

18   Ida Friederike Görres, *The Hidden Face: A Study of St. Thérèse of Lisieux*, trans. Richard and Clara Winston (San Francisco: Ignatius Press, [2003]), 97, original edition, *Das Senfkorn von Lisieux*, 8th rev. ed., *Idas Verborgene Antlitz Eine Studie über Therese von Lisieux*, Freiburg im Breisgau: Verlag Herder, 1959.

19   See "Explanatory Note: Letter of His Holiness Pope Benedict XVI to Chinese Catholics," para. A, 27 May 2007, at the Vatican [online]; available from http://www.vatican.va/holy_father/benedict_xvi/letters/2007/documents/hf_ben-xvi_let_20070527_china-note_en.html (accessed 21 July 2007), for a brief history of late religious persecution in China and reference to evidence there of "blood of the martyrs" which were "the seed of new Christians." See, for example, the listing and link to biographies for "Augustine Chao (+1815) and 119 companions, Martyrs of China," "Saints and Blessed: Table of Canonizations during the Pontificate of His Holiness John Paul II," Office of Papal Liturgical Celebrations, 1 October 2000, Saint Peter's Square, at the Vatican [online]; available from http://www.vatican.va/news_services/liturgy/saints/index_saints_en.html (accessed 21 July 2008).

20 See the listing for "103 Korean Martyrs," "Saints and Blessed: Table of Canonizations during the Pontificate of His Holiness John Paul II," Office of Papal Liturgical Celebrations, 6 May 1984, Seoul (Korea), at the Vatican [online]; available from http://www.vatican.va/news_services/liturgy/saints/index_saints_en.html (accessed 21 July 2008).

21 See, for example, the listing and link to biographies for "Daudi Okelo and Jildo Irwa (1902 ca.–1918) and Jildo Irwa (1906 ca.–1918)," "Saints and Blessed: Table of Beatifications during the Pontificate of His Holiness John Paul II," Office of Papal Liturgical Celebrations, Blesseds in the Year 2002, at the Vatican [online]; available from http://www.vatican.va/news_services/liturgy/saints/index_blessed_en.html (accessed 21 July 2008).

22 See the listing and link to biographies for "Martyrs of Vietnam (+1745–1862)," "Saints and Blessed: Table of Canonizations during the Pontificate of His Holiness John Paul II," Office of Papal Liturgical Celebrations, 19 June 1988, Saint Peter's Square, at the Vatican [online]; available from http://www.vatican.va/news_services/liturgy/saints/index_saints_en.html (accessed 21 July 2008).

23 See multiple listings and links to biographies at "Saints and Blessed: Table of Beatifications during the Pontificate of His Holiness John Paul II," Office of Papal Liturgical Celebrations, 20 November 2005, Guadalajara, at the Vatican [online]; available from http://www.vatican.va/news_services/liturgy/saints/index_blessed_en.html (accessed 21 July 2008).

24 For brief description of Romero's late life and death, see, for example, Richard P. McBrien, *Lives of the Saints: From Mary and St. Francis of Assisi to John XXIII and Mother Teresa* (San Francisco: HarperCollins Publishers, 2001), 143, or Mark Water, *The New Encyclopedia of Christian Martyrs*, comp. Mark Water (Grand Rapids, Michigan: Baker Books, 2001), 905. Romero, roundly respected for his defense of the poor, has been controversial for his theology of liberation that called upon the Church, particularly its leaders, to be actively engaged in the political and even military struggle of the poor.

25 McBrien, *Lives of the Saints*, 485–486.

26 Matthew Bunson, Margaret Bunson, and Stephen Bunson, "Maximilian Kolbe," *Our Sunday Visitor's Encyclopedia of Saints* (Huntington, Indiana: Our Sunday Visitor, 1998), 427.

27 Woodward, *Making Saints*, 147.

28 Bunson, "Maximilian Kolbe," 427.

29 Woodward, *Making Saints*, 147.

30 Matthew Bunson, Margaret Bunson, and Stephen Bunson, "Maria Goretti," *Our Sunday Visitor's Encyclopedia of Saints* (Huntington, Indiana: Our Sunday Visitor, 1998), 398.

31 Woodward, *Making Saints*, 150.

32 Saint Thomas Aquinas, *Summa Theologiae*, II-II, q. 124, art. 5 ad 3 and answer before replies, respectively. Translations in quotations are taken from Saint Thomas Aquinas, *Summa Theologica*, trans. Fathers of the English Dominican Province (New York: Benziger Brothers, 1948; reprint, Allen, Texas: Christian Classics, 1981).

33   "Saints and Blessed: Table of Beatifications during the Pontificate of His Holiness John Paul II," Office of Papal Liturgical Celebrations, at the Vatican [online]; available from http://www.vatican.va/news_services/ liturgy/saints/index_blessed_en.html (accessed 21 July 2008).

34   "Response of His Holiness Benedict XVI for the Examination of the Cause for Beatification and Canonization of the Servant of God John Paul II," at the Vatican [online]; available from http://www.vatican.va/roman_curia/ congregations/csaints/documents/rc_con_csaints_doc_20050509_rescritto_ gpii_en.html (accessed 21 July 2008).

35   Even secular media have reported widely on the potential beatification of Pope Pius XII, for its possible impact on relations between Jews and Catholics. See, for example, Justin Ewers, "Sainthood on Hold: The wartime record of Pope Pius XII roils Catholic-Jewish relations," *U.S. News & World Report*, 17–24 November 2008, 44–45.

36   These are explanations suggested by such as Woodward in chapter 12 of *Making Saints*, 353–373, updated according to recent developments.

37   Biography: "Teresa Benedict of the Cross Edith Stein (1891–1942): *nun, Discalced Carmelite, martyr,*" at the Vatican [online]; available from http://www.vatican.va/news_services/liturgy/saints/ns_lit_doc_19981011_ edith_stein_en.html (accessed 21 July 2008).

38   See "The Cause for the Canonisation of John Henry Cardinal Newman" [online]; available from http://www.newmancause.co.uk/ (accessed 19 November 2008).

39   McGinn, *The Growth of Mysticism,* and *The Flowering of Mysticism: Men and Women in the New Mysticism—1200–1350,* vol. III, in *The Presence of God: A History of Western Christian Mysticism* (New York: Crossroad Publishing, 1998).

40   Karl Rahner, "Experience of the Holy Spirit," *Theological Investigations,* vol. 18, trans. Edward Quinn (New York: Crossroad Publishing, 1983), 203, 205, original edition, *Schriften zur Theologie,* VIII, sections I–IV, Zürich-Einsiedeln-Köln: Benziger Verlag, 1978.

41   Karl Rahner, "Mysticism, Nature and History: Theological Interpretation," *Encyclopedia of Theology: The Concise 'Sacramentum Mundi,'* ed. Karl Rahner (New York: Seabury Press, 1975), 1011. From a Christian view, "theosophy" is another dangerous interpretation of mystical experience.

42   Karl Rahner and Herbert Vorgrimler, "Mysticism," *Theological Dictionary,* ed. Cornelius Ernst, trans. Richard Strachan (New York: Herder and Herder, 1965), 302, original edition, *Kleines Theologisches Wörterbuch,* Freiburg: Verlag Herder, 1965. "Monism" and "theopanism" are other wrong interpretations of mystical experience, from a Christian view.

43   See the listing and link to the biography for "Katharine Drexel (1858–1955)," "Saints and Blessed: Table of Canonizations during the Pontificate of His Holiness John Paul II," Office of Papal Liturgical Celebrations, 19 June 1988, Saint Peter's Square, at the Vatican [online]; available from http://

www.vatican.va/news_services/liturgy/saints/index_saints_en.html (accessed 19 November 2008).

44   "Luis Martin (1823–1894) and Zélia Guérin (1831–1877)," "Saints and Blessed: Blesseds," Office of Papal Liturgical Celebrations, Blesseds in the Year 2008, at the Vatican [online]; available from http://www.vatican.va/news_services/liturgy/saints/index_blessed_en.html (accessed 19 November 2008).

45   *Catechism of the Catholic Church*, 1604.

46   Ibid., 2204, cf. *Familiaris consortio*, 21, and *Lumen Gentium*, 11.

47   Ibid.

48   Ibid., 2208.

49   See, for such statistics for the United States, Mary E. Bendyna and Paul M. Perl, "Young Adult Catholics in the Context of Other Catholic Generations: Living with Diversity, Seeking Service, Waiting to Be Welcomed," CARA Working Paper 1 (June 2000), 12, at CARA: Center for Applied Research in the Apostolate at Georgetown University [online]; available from http://cara.georgetown.edu/pdfs/Young_Adult.pdf (accessed 15 March 2007), and Bryan T. Froehle and Mary L. Gautier, eds., *Catholicism USA: A Portrait of the Catholic Church in the United States*, CARA (Maryknoll, New York: Orbis Books, 2000), 12–14.

50   This description was coined for an exploration of the single state in my article "The Nonvowed Form of the Lay State in the Life of the Church," *Theological Studies* 68, no. 2 (2007):320–347.

51   *Catechism of the Catholic Church*, 2231.

52   *Lumen Gentium*, 51.

53   Ibid., 49.

54   Ibid., 48.

55   Ibid.

56   Ibid.

Twelve: The Saints as Intercessors: A Contemporary Understanding

1   *Lumen Gentium*, 50. Para. 51 explicitly appeals to "the decrees of the Second Council of Nicea, the Council of Florence, and the Council of Trent" as the tradition's long ratification of "the venerable faith of our ancestors in the living communion which exists between us and our sisters and brothers who are in the glory of heaven or who are yet being purified after their death." Per nt. 20, "[s]ee Second Council of Nicaea, session VII, Denz. 302 (600)." Per nt. 21, "[s]ee Council of Florence, Decree for the Greeks, Denz. 693 (1304)." Per nt. 22, "[s]ee Council of Trent, Session 25, On the invocation, veneration and relics of saints and on sacred images, Denz. 984–988 (1821–1824); Session 25, Decree on Purgatory, Denz. 983 (1820); Session 6, Decree on justification, canon 30, Denz. 840 (1580)."

2   Ibid. Nt. 16 attributes the phrase, "the crown of all the saints," to the
     Roman Breviary, Invitatory for the feast of All Saints. Nt. 17 directs readers
     to 2 Th. 1:10 for biblical reference to the glorification of God through the
     saints.
3   Karl Rahner, "The Life of the Dead," *Theological Investigations*, vol. 4,
     trans. Kevin Smyth (London: Darton, Longman & Todd; New York:
     Seabury Press, 1974), 353, original edition, *Schriften zur Theologie* IV,
     Einsiedeln: Verlagsanstalt Benziger, [1960].
4   *Lumen Gentium*, 49.
5   Rahner, "Why and How Can We Venerate the Saints?," 23.
6   Ibid., 21.
7   *Lumen Gentium*, 50–51.
8   Boethius, "God is Timeless," *Philosophy of Religion: Selected Readings*, ed.
     Michael Peterson et al. (New York, Oxford: Oxford University Press, 1996),
     123.
9   Ibid., 124.
10   Ibid., 123–124.
11   Ibid., 124.
12   Richard Swinburne, "God and Time," *Reasoned Faith: Essays in
     Philosophical Theology in Honor of Norman Kretzmann*, ed. Eleonore
     Stump (Ithaca, New York, and London: Cornell University Press, 1993),
     216. Swinburne's argument is premised on four principles. First, nothing
     happens in an "instant." All that happens in time happens over a period.
     The period provides the content of the happening since anything without
     duration cannot meaningfully be said to be a happening at all; lacking a
     comparative instant, nothing positive or verifiable can be said about a given
     instant (206–207). Second, it is because laws of nature provide a metric for
     time that statements can be made about lengths, or periods, of time, of
     which instants serve as boundaries. Between these boundaries, discernable
     or identifiable events constitute periods because they have beginnings and
     ends (208–211). Third, the boundary between the past and the future is the
     present instant, but Swinburne noted that when we refer to the "present" it
     is with the present instant and those close to it in mind—a period. The
     present period is separated from past and future by its causal relationships
     to them; events are past if we can no longer alter them and future if we
     might still effect or affect them. (Present periods—by virtue of the fact that
     they are periods—necessarily contain some past and future instants along
     with the present instant, however.) Causes and effects are events, therefore,
     and events have duration; they are marked by periods (211–215). In
     Swinburne's schema, then, backward and simultaneous causation are
     impossible, because "an effect must begin at an instant later than its cause
     begins" (214). Fourth, "there are truths about periods of time which can
     only be known at certain periods" and those which can only be known by
     certain persons. As an example of the first category of knowledge of periods,
     Swinburne offered "that something is happening now can only be known
     now, that something is going to happen can only be known before it
     happens." In the second category, "the knowledge that I am cold not being

the same item as the knowledge that Swinburne is cold" is an example. Knowledge that is not contingent upon its relationship to the knower can be possessed by anyone at any period (215–216).

13 Plato said that God is eternal whereas the universe is perpetual, Boethius reminded his contemporaries. See Boethius, "God is Timeless," 123.

14 Swinburne, "God and Time," 218.

15 Ibid., 221.

16 Ibid., 220.

17 Ibid., 218.

18 Ibid., 221, nt. 18, cf. Norman Kretzmann, "Omniscience and Immutability," *Journal of Philosophy* 63, no. 14 (1966):409–421.

19 Ibid., 216, nt. 14, cf., Eleonore Stump and Norman Kretzmann, "Eternity," *Journal of Philosophy* 78, no. 8 (August 1981):429–458. Stump and Kretzmann, in "Eternity, Awareness, and Action," *Faith and Philosophy* 9, no. 4 (October 1992), answered Brian Leftow, who argued that if atemporal existence does not have the dimensions of space and time, it is a point rather than a line—the apparent equivalent of Swinburne's "instant," cf. *op. cit.*, ch. V, sect. 5. They responded, on 471, that "this inference holds only if it exhausts the possibilities for any mode of existence to describe it either as linelike or as pointlike. . . ."

20 Ibid. Stump and Kretzmann, in "Eternity," 430, described the common misreadings of the eternality tradition: "Eternality . . . is misunderstood most often in either of two ways. Sometimes it is confused with limitless duration in time—semipiternality—and sometimes it is construed simply as atemporality, eternity being understood in that case as roughly analogous to an isolated, static instant. The second misunderstanding of eternality is not so far off the mark as the first, but a consideration of the views of the philosophers who contributed most to the development of the concept shows that atemporality alone does not exhaust eternality as they conceived of it, and that the picture of eternity as a frozen instant is a radical distortion of the classic concept."

21 Stump and Kretzmann, in "Eternity, Awareness, and Action," 457–460, recognized arguments proving "the incoherence of the concept of an omniscient, immutable, temporal entity." However, they emphasized that "that is not the concept of the perfect being that has been identified as God in orthodox Christian theology, which takes God to be eternal."

22 Ibid., 463.

23 In Stump and Kretzmann, "Eternity," on 430, "eternality" is defined as "the condition of having eternity as one's mode of existence." The term will be used here in reference to Stump and Kretzmann's work only. The more traditional term for God's mode of existence, "eternity," should be understood as a synonym. Stump and Kretzmann's explanation rebutted critiques of their notion of divine "eternality."

24 Stump and Kretzmann, "Eternity, Awareness, and Action," 466. The authors, on 468–469, emphasized that analogical speech predicates terms of God neither univocally nor equivocally.

25 Ibid., 468.

26   Thomas Mautner, ed., "Specious Present," *A Dictionary of Philosophy* (Cambridge, Massachusetts: Blackwell Publishers, 1996):403. Stump and Kretzmann, in "Eternity, Awareness, and Action," 468, offered the example of a mother hearing the sound of her son yell as he flies off a skateboard. Each of the moments of identifying and interpreting the cry are experienced as one, conceptually divisible only with respect to the duration of time involved, not with respect to the experience per se.

27   Eleonore Stump, in "Petitionary Prayer," *American Philosophical Quarterly* 16, no. 2 (April 1979):85–86, reviewed Aquinas's argument that God determines both effects in the world and their causes. Human actions are included among causes. Aquinas contended that Providence's ordination of human prayers and even *free* human actions as causes bringing about his plan does not constrain our free will, and that we therefore pray in order to bring about a cause that God has ordained to produce a particular effect rather than in hopes that God will change his mind. Cf. *Summa contra gentiles*, I.III.95–96; IV. *Sent.*, dist. XV, q. 4, a. 1. Stump recognized but set aside the apparent contradiction in Aquinas's assertion that God determines human free actions.

28   Stump and Kretzmann, "Eternity, Awareness, and Action," 475. The equivalent of a summary of their formula stating the "simultaneity relationship between eternity and time" (which they named "ET-simultaneity"), the authors explained that "from a temporal viewpoint the temporal present is ET-simultaneous with the infinite present of an eternal being's life. On the other hand, from the viewpoint of a being existing in the persisting eternal present, each temporal instant is ET-simultaneous with the eternal present, but only insofar as that instant is temporally present, so that from the eternal being's point of view the entire time line [of history] is lighted at once."

29   Stump and Kretamann, "Eternity," 453–454.

30   Karl Rahner, "Ideas for a Theology of Death," *Theological Investigations*, vol. 13, trans. David Bourke (New York: Seabury Press, 1975), 174, original edition, *Schriften zur Theologie*, X, part I, Einsiedeln: Verlagsanstalt Benziger, [1972].

31   Karl Rahner, "Theological Observations on the Concept of Time," *Theological Investigations*, vol. 11, trans. David Bourke (London: Darton, Longman & Todd; New York: Seabury Press, 1974), 307–308, original edition, *Schriften zur Theologie*, IX, part I, Einsiedeln: Verlagsanstalt Benziger, [1970]. Wrote Rahner: "With regard to the immutability, and therefore the non-temporal nature of God, . . , Christian theology must hold firm to the 'immutability' and 'eternal' timelessness of God 'in themselves'. At the same time, however, it will have to say that God *himself*, in the otherness of the world, undergoes history, change, and so too time; the time of the world is his own history. As the eternal he does not merely establish time by creating it, but freely assumes it as a specification of his own self. . . . He thereby causes his own eternity to be the true content of time. He creates his own time in order to impart to it his own eternity as the radical effectiveness of his own love. Temporal becoming is not merely the

distinguishing characteristic of that which is different from God, but that which, precisely as different from God in this way, and permanently maintaining itself as different, can become, and has become the distinguishing seal of God himself. Ultimately speaking this is possible because the difference between creaturely time and the eternity of God removes time from eternity but not, properly speaking, eternity from time."

32   Karl Rahner and Herbert Vorgrimler, "Creation," *Theological Dictionary*, ed. Cornelius Ernst, trans. Richard Strachan (New York: Herder and Herder, 1965), 105–107, original edition, *Kleines Theologisches Wörterbuch*, Freiburg: Verlag Herder, [1961].

33   Rahner, "Theological Observations on the Concept of Time," 308.

34   Ibid., 290.

35   Ibid., 297.

36   Rahner, "Why and How Can We Venerate the Saints?," 16.

37   Rahner, "The Life of the Dead," 348.

38   Ibid., 349.

39   Ibid., 350.

40   Ibid., 349–350.

41   Ibid., 351–352.

42   Rahner, "Ideas for a Theology of Death," 175.

43   Ibid., 174.

44   Rahner, "Existence: 'The Existential,' Theological, Supernatural Existential," 306.

45   Karl Rahner, "On the Importance of the Non-Christian Religions for Salvation," in *Theological Investigations*, vol. 18, trans. Edward Quinn (New York: Crossroad Publishing, 1983), 291, original edition, *Schriften zur Theologie*, XIII, Sections I–IV, Zürich, Einsiedeln, Köln: Benziger Verlag, [1978].

46   This is the subject of Rahner, "Concerning the Relationship Between Nature and Grace," 297–317.

47   Stump, "Petitionary Prayer," 86.

48   Ibid., 87.

49   Ibid., 88.

50   Ibid., 89.

51   Ibid., 85.

52   Rahner, "Questions of Controversial Theology on Justification," 217–218.

53   Karl Rahner, "A Fragmentary Aspect of a Theological Evaluation of the Concept of the Future," *Theological Investigations*, vol. 10, trans. David Bourke (New York: Herder and Herder, 1973), 240, original edition, *Schriften zur Theologie*, VIII, part II, Einsiedeln: Verlagsanstalt Benziger, [1967]. This future arrives from "God himself or the act of his absolute self-bestowal which has to be posited by him alone," as Rahner described in "The Question of the Future," *Theological Investigations*, vol. 12, trans. David Bourke (New York: Seabury Press, 1974), 185, original edition, *Schriften zur Theologie*, IX, part II, Einsiedeln: Verlagsanstalt Benziger, [1970]. Human beings are called to live in a "state of radical openness to the question of the mystery of the absolute future which is God" (189).

54 Ibid., 237.

55 Rahner, "The One Christ and the Universality of Salvation," 214. Rahner offered a concise explanation of the irreversible character of the offer of salvation to us in the Christ event: "The logical possibility is assured if the irreversible outcome, appearing within history, of the historical process of human and divine freedom is positive, i.e. signifies the salvation of the world which could not then be totally lost. This would be possible if God were to communicate himself to a man in such a unique manner that this man would become the definitive and irreversible self-gift of God to the world. He would also freely accept the divine self-gift in such a manner that this too would be irreversible, i.e. through his death as the definitive culmination of his free actions in history. If salvation history is irreversibly directed in this sense to salvation, and not to damnation, through a concrete event, then this historically tangible occurrence must be a sign of the salvation of the whole world in the sense of a 'real symbol', and so possesses a type of causality where salvation is concerned. To this we wish to apply a well known theological concept and call it 'sacramental'."

56 Rahner, "A Fragmentary Aspect of a Theological Evaluation of the Concept of the Future," 240–241.

57 Rahner, "The Question of the Future," 185.

58 Ibid., 185–186.

59 Karl Rahner and Herbert Vorgrimler, "Prayer," Theological Dictionary, ed. Cornelius Ernst, trans. Richard Strachan (New York: Herder and Herder, 1965), 371, original edition, Kleines Theologisches Wörterbuch, Freiburg: Verlag Herder, [1961].

60 Karl Rahner, "The Apostolate of Prayer," Theological Investigations, vol. 3, trans. Karl-H. and Boniface Kruger (New York: Crossroad Publishing, 1982), 210, original edition, Schriften zur Theologie, III, Einsiedeln: Verlagsanstalt Benziger, [1956].

61 Karl Rahner and Herbert Vorgrimler, "Prayer of Petition," Theological Dictionary, ed. Cornelius Ernst, trans. Richard Strachan (New York: Herder and Herder, 1965), 371, original edition, Kleines Theologisches Wörterbuch, Freiburg: Verlag Herder, [1961].

62 A parallel pericope appears in Lk. 12:22–31.

63 Rahner and Vorgrimler, "Prayer," 371.

64 Rahner and Vorgrimler, "Prayer of Petition," 371.

65 In Rahner, "The Apostolate of Prayer," 214, he stated that "prayer is still more important than the Sacraments. For many a soul has been saved without Sacraments, but never without prayer. And the grace of God can never be merited, neither in its beginning nor in its end. But if it gratuitously precedes our action, then the first reaction it arouses is that movement of the heart which can be described most simply and accurately as 'prayer'."

66 Ibid., 218–219.

67 Rahner, "Why and How Can We Venerate the Saints?," 23.

68 Ibid.

69 Lumen Gentium, 50.

70 Nicholas Ayo, *The Hail Mary: A Verbal Icon of Mary* (Notre Dame, Indiana: University of Notre Dame Press, 1994), 3.

Thirteen: Mariological Devotion: Catholic Doctrine and Ecumenical Conversation

1 Pope Benedict XVI, Homily of August 15, 2006, reprinted in *Marian Thoughts: Selection of Texts by Pope Benedict XVI*, ed. Lucio Coco, trans. supervised by Kate Marcellin-Rice, K.S. Giniger (New Jersey: Catholic Book Publishing, 2008), 13, original edition, *Pensieri Mariani*, Rome: Libreria Editrice Vaticana, 2007.

2 This assertion does not refute the patristic teaching about the *Ecclesia ab Abel*—the Church from Abel on—referring to the fact of God's grace as operative throughout human history as seen in those transformed by it. As stated in chapter 10 and as will be emphasized in chapter 15, the Incarnation is the means of God's offer of self-communication (his grace), and, although the Incarnation occurs in time, its effect upon human beings is not bound by time. As the vehicle of the Incarnation, Mary therefore can be viewed as the first to accept Christ.

3 *Lumen Gentium*, 62.

4 Ibid.

5 See, for example, his 1520–1521 exposition of the Magnificat, trans. A.T.W. Steinhaeuser, in *Luther's Works*, vol. 21: The Sermon on the Mount (Sermons) and The Magnificat, ed. Jaroslav Pelikan (Saint Louis, Missouri: Concordia Publishing, 1956), 295–355.

6 *Mary in the New Testament: A Collaborative Assessment by Protestant and Roman Catholic Scholars*, ed. Raymond E. Brown, Karl P. Donfried, Joseph A. Fitzmyer, and John Reumann (Philadelphia: Fortress Press; New York, Ramsey, and Toronto: Paulist Press, 1978), 294.

7 Winsome Munro, in "Mary, the Virgin," *The HarperCollins Bible Dictionary*, ed. Paul J. Achtemeier, and associate eds. Roger S. Boraas et al. with the Society of Biblical Literature (San Francisco: HarperCollins Publishers, 1996), 658–659, characterized Mary's portrayal as negative in Mark, "less so in Matthew," and positive in Luke. In this assessment, he followed, with regard to the gospels, the tradition noted in *Mary in the New Testament*, which also studied Mary in other biblical writings.

8 The notation for this pericope in *The New Oxford Annotated Bible*, 1242, offers: "The 'Magnificat' (so called from the first word of the Latin translation) is based largely on Hannah's prayer in 1 Sam.2.1–10. *Magnifies*, i.e. declares the greatness of."

9 This summary is indebted to some of the content of *Mary in the New Testament*, as well as Munro's "Mary, the Virgin." Regarding Gal. 4:4–5, the *Mary in the New Testament* scholars, on 41–45, pointed out that this is only an "indirect" reference to Mary; "'born of a woman,' is a frequently-used Jewish expression to designate a person's human condition" (42).

Other Pauline passages identified by these scholars as related to Mary in that they refer to Jesus' birth are Gal. 1:19; 4:28–29; Rom. 1:3–4; and Phil. 2:6–7.

10   *The Protoevangelium of James*, at New Advent: Church Fathers [online]; available from http:/www.newadvent.org/fathers/0847.htm (accessed 14 September 2008), cf. *Ante-Nicene Fathers*, vol. 8, ed. Alexander Roberts, James Donaldson, and A. Cleveland Coxe, trans. Alexander Walker (Buffalo, New York: Christian Literature Publishing, 1886).

11   Apocryphal Works on the Assumption of Mary (*Transitus Mariae*), at New Advent: Church Fathers [online]; available from http://www.newadvent.org/fathers/0832.htm (accessed 29 September 2008), cf. *Ante-Nicene Fathers*, vol. 8, ed. Alexander Roberts, James Donaldson, and A. Cleveland Coxe, trans. Alexander Walker (Buffalo, New York: Christian Literature Publishing, 1886).

12   Kennedy, *The Saints of the Canon of the Mass*, 98, cf. G. Wilpert, *Le pitture delle Catacombe Romane*, Testo (Roma, 1903), 187–197, and V. Lucius, *The Blessed Virgin in the Fathers of the First Six Centuries* (London, 1893).

13   Sally Cunneen, *In Search of Mary: The Woman and the Symbol* (New York: Ballantine Books, 1996), 63–69.

14   Kennedy, *The Saints of the Canon of the Mass*, 99.

15   Ibid., 99–100.

16   Ibid., 99, cf. L. Duchesne, *Les origins du culte chrétien* (Paris, 1925), 287. Kennedy postulated that even before then the nativity of Mary may have been celebrated on January 1, cf. Dom B. Botte, *La première fête mariale de la liturgie romaine: Ephemerides Liturgicae* 47 (1933), 425–430.

17   Cunneen, *In Search of Mary*, chapters 3 and 4, 59–140.

18   Ibid., 168–172. Cunneen noted, for example, the pagan influences upon Christian devotion to Mary in European agricultural centers in the later Middle Ages.

19   Ibid., chapters 5 and 6, particularly 149–158 and 185–194, and Fulton, *From Judgment to Passion*.

20   Anthony Buono, "Feasts of Mary," *Dictionary of Mary*, rev. and expanded (New Jersey: Catholic Book Publishing, 1997), 139–146, and Joseph N. Tylenda, *Saints and Feasts of the Liturgical Year* (Washington, D.C.: Georgetown University Press, 2003).

21   In addition to the Marian documents mentioned in this paragraph, other post-Vatican II papal writings involving Mary include Paul VI's *Signum Magnum* (1967) and John Paul II's *Mulieris Dignitatem* (1988), *Redemptoris Missio* (1990), *Veritatis Splendor* (1993), and *Rosarium Virginis Mariae* (2002).

22   Pope Paul VI, *Marialis Cultus*, at the Vatican [online]; available from http:/www.vatican.va/holy_father/paul_vi/apost_exhortations/documents/hf_p-vi_exh_19740202_marialis-cultus_en.html (accessed 15 October 2008), 34–37. Citations are to paragraph numbers.

23   Ibid., 35.

24   Ibid., 56.

25 Pope John Paul II, *Redemptoris Mater*, at the Vatican [online]; available from http://www.vatican.va/holy_father/john_paul_ii/encyclicals/documents/hf_jp-ii_enc_25031987_redemptoris-mater_en.html (accessed 15 October 2008), 2f. Citations are to paragraph numbers.

26 Ibid., 6.

27 Ibid., 52.

28 See examples of such varieties of scholarship: Elizabeth A. Johnson, *Truly Our Sister: A Theology of Mary in the Communion of Saints* (New York: Continuum International Publishing, 2004); Beverly Roberts Gaventa, *Mary: Glimpses of the Mother of Jesus* (Minneapolis: Fortress Press, 1999); and Marina Warner, *Alone of All Her Sex: The Myth and the Cult of the Virgin Mary* (New York: Alfred A Knopf, 1976).

29 Cunneen, *In Search of Mary*, 301. For explanation of the position, see Cunneen's chapter 8, "The Liberation of Mary," especially pages 301–306. For a psychological treatment of the history of Marian devotion tending to this strain, see Sarah Jane Boss, *Empress and Handmaid: On Nature and Gender in the Cult of the Virgin Mary* (London and New York: Cassell, 2000).

30 As an example of such a position, see Charlene Spretnak, *Missing Mary: The Queen of Heaven and Her Re-Emergence in the Modern Church* (New York: Palgrave Macmillan, 2004).

31 Albert Schweitzer famously presented scholarship noting and exploring this distinction. See *The Quest of the Historical Jesus: A Critical Study of Its Progress from Reimarus to Wrede*, trans. W. Montgomery (New York: MacMillan, 1968), original edition, *Von Reimarus zu Wrede*, 1906.

32 See *Mary in the New Testament*, especially 8–12 and 241–243. In the context of their discussion of the "Mary of history," these scholars note that the New Testament is a record of history understood "in faith" (8).

33 Edward Schillebeeckx, in Edward Schillebeeckx and Catharina Halkes, *Mary Yesterday, Today, Tomorrow*, trans. John Bowden (New York: Crossroad Publishing, 1993), 15–16, original edition, *Maria: Gisteren, Vandaag, Morgen*, Baarn: Uitgevirij H. Nelissen, 1992. Schillebeeckx did not use the terms "Mary of history" and "Mary of faith." Vatican II did not use the title "Mother of the Church." Schillebeeckx noted that, among Vatican II participants, the ecclesiological Mariology was favored by the majority. On 28–29, he remarked upon a tendency in the Catholic tradition to assign conceptually to Mary functions in the Church that belong properly to the Holy Spirit. He critiqued Mariologies such as those of Leonardo Boff that claim an integral relationship between Mary and the Holy Spirit.

34 Pope Pius IX, *Ineffabilis Deus*, 8 December 1854, at New Advent: Catholic Library [online]; available from http://www.newadvent.org/library/docs_pi09id.htm (accessed 11 September 2006).

35 Pope Pius XII, *Munificentissimus Deus*, 1 November 1950, at the Vatican [online]; available from http://www.vatican.va/holy_father/pius_xii/apost_

constitutions/documents/hf_p-xii_apc_19501101_munificentissimus-deus_en.html (accessed 11 September 2006).

36   See, for example, Catharina Halkes, in Edward Schillebeeckx and Catharina Halkes, *Mary Yesterday, Today, Tomorrow*, trans. John Bowden (New York: Crossroad Publishing, 1993), 61, original edition, *Maria: Gisteren, Vandaag, Morgen*, Baarn: Uitgevirij H. Nelissen, 1992. Halkes offered: "Theologically speaking it must be stated that three of the four dogmas have a Christological content and point to the Mystery of Christ: the fourth and last expresses the complete redemption of a human being."

37   *Lumen Gentium*, 62.

38   Ibid., 60.

39   Recent documents from popes and Catholic bishops have included the theme of Mary as a model of discipleship for all: Paul VI's *Marialis Cultus*; the National Conference of Catholic Bishops' *Behold Your Mother: Woman of Faith*; and John Paul II's *Redemptoris Mater*.

40   Origen, *On First Principles*, in *The Christological Controversy*, trans. and ed. Richard A. Norris, Jr. (Philadelphia: Fortress Press, 1980), 78–79 (Book II, chap. 6, para. 6).

41   Frederick M. Jelly, in "The Roman Catholic Dogma of Mary's Immaculate Conception," in *The One Mediator, the Saints, and Mary: Lutherans and Catholics in Dialogue VIII*, ed. H. George Anderson, J. Francis Stafford, and Joseph A. Burgess (Minneapolis, Minnesota: Augsburg Fortress, 1992), 271–272, noted that the use of these passages in *Ineffabilis Deus* relies upon the interpretive function of the tradition as regards Scripture.

42   Pius XII, *Munificentissimus Deus*, 44.

43   *Lumen Gentium*, 54.

44   Among those who have called for rewritten definitions of the Immaculate Conception and the Assumption are George H. Tavard, in *The Thousand Faces of the Virgin Mary* (Collegeville, Minnesota: Liturgical Press, 1996), 200, and Jelly, "The Roman Catholic Dogma of Mary's Immaculate Conception," 278.

45   Alain Blancy, Maurice Jourjon, and the Dombes Group, *Mary in the Plan of God and in the Communion of Saints*, trans. Matthew J. O'Connell (New York and Mahwah, New Jersey: Paulist Press, 2002), 132, original edition, *Marie dans le dessein de Dieu et la communion des saints*, [Paris]: Bayard Éditions, 1999.

46   Ibid., cf. *Lumen Gentium*, 56.

47   Ibid., 132–133. On the latter point and as regards the meaning of the dogma, the Dombes Group called to attention the distinction between the language used to describe Mary's Assumption and Christ's Ascension, the assertion of Mary's transformed state in her unity with her Son rather than any "change of place," and Vatican II's reference to the dogma which employed an even greater concentration upon Mary's unity with her Son as the Assumption's source and, if you will, reason.

48   "Decree Concerning Original Sin," in *The Canons and Decrees of the Council of Trent*, Session 5, trans. H.J. Schroeder (Rockford, Illinois: Tan Books and Publishers, 1978), para. 5. This paragraph affirms Pope Sixtus

IV's constitutions regarding Mary; he approved a feast for the Immaculate Conception, establishing a Mass. See "Constitution *Cum Praeexcelsa* (1477)" in *The Christian Faith in the Doctrinal Documents of the Catholic Church*, 6th rev. and enlarged ed., ed. Jacques Dupuis (New York: Alba House, 1996), 704, cf. Denz. 1400. As the commentators for this entry recalled, the Council of Basel had in 1439 declared Mary to be free of original sin and sinless in actuality—immaculate. As explained, however, this Council's decree was not universally binding, given that, at the time of its issue, communion with the pope has been severed.

49   "Decree Concerning Justification," can. 23.

50   Pius XII, *Munificentissimus Deus*, 2.

51   *The One Mediator, the Saints, and Mary: Lutherans and Catholics in Dialogue VIII*, ed. H. George Anderson, J. Francis Stafford, and Joseph A. Burgess (Minneapolis, Minnesota: Augsburg Fortress, 1992), 61–62, especially para. 104, along with the section of the volume in which this is situated, "The Problem Reexamined," as well as sections "Catholic Reflections" and "Lutheran Reflections." For a report of additional ecumenical conversation on this matter, see Bilateral Working Group, *Communio Sanctorum*, 262–268.

52   *Lumen Gentium*. 53.

53   Pius IX, *Ineffabilis Deus*.

54   Pius XII, *Munificentissimus Deus*, 5. The apostolic constitution explains that, although "Christ overcame sin and death by his own death, and one who through Baptism has been born again in a supernatural way has conquered sin and death through the same Christ. . . . according to the general rule, God does not will to grant to the just the full effect of the victory over death until the end of time has come. And so it is that the bodies of even the just are corrupted after death, and only on the last day will they be joined, each to its own glorious soul" (4). "Now God has willed that the Blessed Virgin Mary should be exempted from this general rule" (5).

55   *Lumen Gentium*, 56 and 59.

56   Ibid., 65.

57   Jungmann, *The Early Liturgy*, 196.

58   "Assumption of the Blessed Virgin Mary," *The Oxford Dictionary of the Christian Church*, 3rd ed., ed. F.L. Cross and E.A. Livingstone (Oxford and New York: Oxford University Press, 1997):117–118.

59   *Lumen Gentium*, 69.

60   Ibid.

61   Kyriaki Karidoyanes FitzGerald, "Mary the *Theotokos* and the Call to Holiness," *Mary, Mother of God*, ed. Carol E Braaten and Robert W. Jenson (Grand Rapids, Michigan, and Cambridge, U.K.: William B. Eerdmans Publishing, 2004). FitzGerald showed how, in Orthodox theology, these titles affirm certain long-held understandings of Mary. She had a "theocentric" orientation—absolute dependence upon God, acceptance of his love without reservation. Mary realized true freedom and the fullness of human personhood in responding positively to God and the plan that he willed to execute through her. She possessed the virtue of true humility—a

true sense of herself in relation to her creator and to other creatures. With and in God, she had "collaboration" or synergy"—"active cooperation between God and human persons." And she had an authentic relationship with Christ and with others in Christ, both living and dead.

62   Paul VI, *Marialis Cultus*, 32–33.

63   John Paul II, *Redemptoris Mater*, 29–37.

64   Hans Urs Von Balthasar and Joseph Cardinal Ratzinger, *Mary: The Church at the Source*, trans. Adrian Walker (San Fransisco: Ignatius Press, 2005), 125, original edition, *Maria: Kirche im Ursprung*, Einsiedeln, Freiburg: Johannes Verlag, 1997.

65   *Lumen Gentium*, 56.

66   Von Balthasar and Ratzinger, *Mary: The Church at the Source*, 117.

Fourteen: Concerns: The Mysterious, the Miraculous, and Miscellaneous

1   *The Holy Staircase: History and Devotion* (Roma: Arch-Confraternity of the Passion at *Scala Santa*, [2000?]), cf. A. Cempanari e T. Amodei, *La Scala Santa* (Marietti, Rome, 1963). This booklet admits of the late date (ninth century) of texts attesting to the authenticity of the staircase as a Passion relic, but it also notes that these sources "are confirmed by a series of undeniable historical facts, and make it possible to believe, with considerable probability, that at least a part of the *Scala Pilati* ['Pilate's Stairway'] was actually brought from Jerusalem to Rome." Booklet pages are not numbered.

2   Ibid.

3   Ibid.

4   Benedict T. Viviano, in "The Gospel According to Matthew," in *The New Jerome Biblical Commentary*, ed. Raymond E. Brown, Joseph A. Fitzmyer, and Roland E. Murphy (Englewood Cliffs, N.J.: Prentice Hall, 1990), 650, made the connection to the prayer shawl and followed M. Hutter, *Zeitschrift für die neutestamentlich Wissenschaft* 75 (1984), 133–136, in interpreting it as "a gesture of respect known from 1 Sam 15:27 and Zech 8:23 as well as Akkadian prayers." Daniel J. Harrington, in "The Gospel According to Mark," in *The New Jerome Biblical Commentary*, 608, following Lev. 15:25–30, attributed the "indirectness of her approach" to her ritual uncleanness and her reticence to transfer this by touch.

5   In connection with this Matthew passage, Viviano, on 658, noted that the ill are reaching for the fringe of Jesus' prayer shawl, "an implicit act of faith." This pericope serves to introduce the next on ritual purity, for, by touching the shawl, "from a Pharisaic point of view, they [the ill] in some cases communicated their ritual uncleanness to Jesus." Harrington, on 611, compared this passage to that of the hemorrhaging woman in 5:25–34, although here he noted that while physical healing is the focus, the use of the Greek verb *esozonto*—"saved"—"does set the healing in the context of the Christian kerygma."

6   As the relevant passages make clear, in these cases the power of Christ comes through the apostles. For example, of the pericope from Acts 3, Richard J. Dillon wrote, in "Acts of the Apostles," in *The New Jerome Biblical Commentary*, ed. Raymond E. Brown, Joseph A. Fitzmyer, and Roland E. Murphy (Englewood Cliffs, N.J.: Prentice Hall, 1990), 735: "The name [of Jesus Christ] is . . . the medium of the heavenly Christ's direct action, granted only upon confession of faith in him." Cf. 4:10; 3:16; G.W. MacRae, *Interpretation*, 27 (1973), 161–162; R.F. O'Toole, *Biblica*, 62 (1981), 488–90.

7   Dillon, "Acts of the Apostles," 738, cf. W. Dietrich, *Das Petrusbildder lukanischen Schriften* (Stuttgart, 1972), 238–239.

8   Fyodor Dostoevsky, *The Brothers Karamazov*, trans. Andrew H. MacAndrew (New York: Bantam Books, 1981), part III, book VII, chap. 1.

9   For a list of many Incorruptibles, pictures of some of these, the locations of their shrines, brief accounts of their lives, and stories of the discovery of their preserved remains, see Joan Carrol Cruz, *The Incorruptibles: A Study of the Incorruption of the Bodies of Various Catholic Saints and Beati* (Rockford, Illinois: Tan Books and Publishers, 1977).

10   *Catechism of the Catholic Church*, 977.

11   Ibid., 1263, cf. Council of Florence (1439): DS 1316.

12   Ibid., 985. See also 1265–1266.

13   Ibid., 1264. Also, "certain temporal consequences of sin remain in the baptized, such as suffering, illness, death, and such frailties inherent in life as weaknesses of character, and so on, . . ."

14   Ibid., 1427–1429.

15   Ibid., 1472.

16   Ibid., 1855. See also 1856–1861 and 1864 on mortal sin.

17   Ibid., 1863. See also 1862 on venial sin.

18   Ibid., 1472–1473.

19   Ibid., 1473.

20   Pope Clement VI, *Unigenitus Dei Filius*, in *The Christian Faith in the Doctrinal Documents of the Catholic Church*, 6th rev. and enlarged ed., ed. Jacques Dupuis (New York: Alba House, 1996), 643, cf. Denz. 1025.

21   Canon 992, *Code of Canon Law Annotated*. Provisions for indulgences are given in Canons 993–997.

22   Canon 996.1, *Code of Canon Law Annotated*, specifies that "[t]o be capable of gaining indulgences a person must be baptised, not excommunicated, and in the state of grace at least on the completion of the prescribed work." Canon 996.2 requires that such a person "must have at least the general intention of gaining them, and must fulfil the prescribed works at the time and in the manner determined by the terms of the grant." Canon 997 insists that "the other provisions contained in the special laws of the Church must also be observed."

23   *Manual of Indulgences: Norms and Grants*, approved by the Apostolic Penitentiary (Washington, D.C.: United States Conference of Catholic Bishops, 2006), original edition, *Enchiridion Indulgentiarum: Normae et Concessiones*, 4th ed., Città del Vaticana: Liberia Editrice Vaticana, 1999.

24   Ibid., 21–36.

25   Ibid., 37–102.

26   Canon 993, *Code of Canon Law Annotated.*

27   Norms 7 and 8, *Indulgentiarum Doctrna*, in *Manual of Indulgences: Norms and Grants,* approved by the Apostolic Penitentiary (Washington, D.C.: United States Conference of Catholic Bishops, 2006), 145, original edition, *Enchiridion Indulgentiarum: Normae et Concessiones,* 4th ed., Città del Vaticana: Liberia Editrice Vaticana, 1999.

28   Concerning those in the Church who have authority with regard to the granting of indulgences, Canon 995.1, *Code of Canon Law Annotated,* specifies that "[a]part from the supreme authority in the Church, only those can grant indulgences to whom this power is either acknowledged in the law, or given by the Roman Pontiff." Canon 995.2 mandates: "No authority below the Roman Pontiff can give to others the faculty of granting indulgences, unless this authority has been expressly given to the person by the Apostolic See."

29   See Canon 994 of *Code of Canon Law Annotated*: "All members of the faithful can gain indulgences, partial or plenary, for themselves, or they can apply them by way of suffrage to the dead."

30   *Catechism of the Catholic Church,* 1476.

31   Norms 5 and 6, *Indulgentiarum Doctrina.*

32   Norm 5, *Indulgentiarum Doctrina.*

33   Ibid.

34   Pope Pius XI, *Miserentissimus Redemptor,* in *The Christian Faith in the Doctrinal Documents of the Catholic Church,* 6th rev. and enlarged ed., ed. Jacques Dupuis (New York: Alba House, 1996), 658–659.

35   Karl Rahner, "Indulgences," *Sacramentum Mundi: An Encyclopedia of Theology,* vol. 3., ed. Karl Rahner et al. (New York: Herder and Herder; London: Burns & Oates, 1969), 128.

36   Pope Pius XII, *Mystici Corporis,* in *The Christian Faith in the Doctrinal Documents of the Catholic Church,* 6th rev. and enlarged ed., ed. Jacques Dupuis (New York: Alba House, 1996), 660.

37   James Martin, *My Life with the Saints* (Chicago, Illinois: Loyola Press, 2006), 379–380.

38   John Paul II, *Novo Millennio Ineunte,* 27.

39   Ibid., 26.

40   *Indulgentiarum Doctrina,* 5.

Fifteen: Veneration of Saints: Meaning and Value of the Tradition

1   C.S. Lewis, *Mere Christianity,* rev. and enlarged ed. (New York: MacMillan Publishing, 1984), 156.

2   Ibid.

3   Ibid.

4   Karl Rahner, *Spirit in the World,* trans. William Dych (New York: Continuum Publishing, 1994), original edition, *Geist in Welt,* Munich: Kösel-Verlag, 1957.

5   See *Nostra Aetate*, in *Vatican Council II: The Basic Sixteen Documents; Constitutions Decrees Declarations*, rev. trans., ed. Austin Flannery (Northport, New York: Costello Publishing, 1996). It has been said that the saints are the best apology for Christianity; saintly lives can convince of the truth of Christianity.

6   *The Martyrdom of Polycarp*, in *Early Christian Writings: The Apostolic Fathers*, trans. Maxwell Staniforth, rev. trans., ed. Andrew Louth (New York: Penguin Books, 1987), 13, original edition, n.p.: Penguin Books, 1968. Citations are to paragraph numbers.

7   *The Martyrdom of Perpetua*, 34, para. 15.

8   Benedict XVI, *Deus Caritas Est*, 42.

9   José Cardinal Saraiva Martins, "The Lives of the Saints Show the World 'the Divine in the Human, the Eternal in Time,'" at the Vatican [online]; available from http:/www.vatican.va/roman_curia/congregations/csaints/documents/rc_con_csaints_doc_20030315_martins_saints_en.html (accessed 19 November 2008), 4. Citations are to paragraph numbers.

10   *Lumen Gentium*, 50. The quotation within the quotation, per nt. 16, is from the "Roman Breviary, Invitatory for the feast of All Saints."

Appendix 2: Abstracts of Karl Rahner's Theologies of Symbol and Anamnesis

1   Rahner, "The Theology of the Symbol," 224.

2   Ibid., 226. Also important in the context of the discussion of symbol is the relationship between the Logos and the human nature of Christ, which Rahner called "essential and intrinsic." See Rahner, "Remarks on the Dogmatic Treatise 'De Trinitate,'" *Theological Investigations*, vol. 4, trans. Kevin Smyth (London: Darton, Longman & Todd; New York: Seabury Press, 1974), 91–94, original edition, *Schriften zur Theologie*, IV, Einsiedeln: Verlagsanstalt Benziger, [1960], for a detailed discussion of the following summary. The Word is essentially expressible and therefore may be communicated in divine or non-divine realities; when the Father expresses himself in the Word and this expression is "exteriorized," human nature results. Human nature, therefore, may be referred to as "real symbol," but in its case it is that of the Logos: "[Man] is possible because exteriorization of the Logos is possible. . . . What Jesus is and does as man, *is* the self-revealing existence of the Logos as our salvation among us" (94). "Universal human nature" (93) "displays" the Logos, because the revelation of the Logos is not only "the formal, abstract truth of his role as subject" (93) but a real communication of God through this divine person to humanity. Our sonship in grace is possible because of the relationship of the divine sonship of the Son to us, which occurs concretely—which is to say historically—in Jesus Christ (91–92). Rahner claimed that human nature generally is to be "*ultimately* explained on the basis of the self-exteriorizing self-expression of the Logos himself" (92), and the mission of this divine person connects us to the immanent life of the Trinity (91). The Logos and

the immanent life of the Trinity are, respectively, the means and the goal of our transcendence.

3   Rahner, "The Theology of the Symbol," 227.

4   Ibid., 228.

5   Ibid., 229.

6   Ibid., 225.

7   Ibid., 237.

8   Rahner, "The One Christ and the Universality of Salvation," 212. See 213–216 for elaboration.

9   Rahner, "The Theology of the Symbol," 237. Joseph Wong, in "Anonymous Christians: Karl Rahner's Pneuma-Christocentrism and an East-West Dialogue," *Theological Studies* 55, no. 4 (December 1994), 622, concisely explained why this is so for Rahner: "A revelation without the corresponding salvific reality being given would be the manifestation through an empty sign, not a sacramental sign. Hence, through the idea of sacramental symbol, revelation and salvation, sign and reality, norm and constituting cause all become one in Jesus Christ. Christ is the universal norm of salvation precisely because he is the constitutive cause of it."

10   Karl Rahner, "Jesus Christ in the Non-Christian Religions," 46. Rahner explained that the Incarnation and Cross are "the cause of the imparting of the Holy Spirit at all times and in all places in the world," since "[t]his Spirit is always, everywhere, and from the outset the entelechy, the determining principle, of the history of revelation and salvation. . . ." See David M. Coffey, "The Theandric Nature of Christ," *Theological Studies* 60, no. 3 (September 1999):405–431, and "The Spirit of Christ as Entelechy," *Philosophy and Theology* 13, no. 2 (2001):363–398, for a systematic presentation of the explicit relationship between the Holy Spirit and Christ with respect to the principle of the entelechy. Drawing upon 1 Pet. 1:10–11 in which the Holy Spirit—before the time of Christ—is called the "Spirit of Christ," Coffey married the evolutionary notion of the "Spirit" in the thought of Teilhard de Chardin with Rahner's notion of the entelechy to provide an explanation of the entelechy as the Spirit of Christ guiding the universe to and through the threshold of matter into spirit toward its end in God, with human beings at the apex of this development. The grounding for this thought is given in Coffey's "The Holy Spirit as the Mutual Love of the Father and the Son," *Theological Studies* 51, no. 2 (June 1990):193–229, in "The 'Incarnation' of the Holy Spirit in Christ," *Theological Studies* 45, no. 3 (September 1984):466–480, and in *Grace: The Gift of the Holy Spirit* (Sydney, Australia: Catholic Institute of Sydney, 1979). Here, following in but modifying the tradition of Augustine, Coffey presented a new model of the Incarnation and grace that understands the Holy Spirit as the mutual love of the Father and the Son who is bestowed by the Father beyond the Trinity itself, resulting in the humanity of Christ which is drawn into a unity with the Son of God. Through the love of Christ, the Son of God, for the Father, the Holy Spirit is "christified," which is to say that he becomes the Spirit of Christ. Through grace, we are drawn into union with Christ in the Spirit, into the life of the Trinity.

11   "Anamnesis," *A Dictionary of Philosophy*, ed. Thomas Maunter (Cambridge, Massachusetts: Blackwell Publishers, 1996):15.

12   Rahner, "Jesus Christ in the Non-Christian Religions," 47, cf. C. Huber, 'Anamnesis bei Plato', *Pullacher Philosophische Forschungen* VI (Munich 1964).

13   Rahner, "Why and How Can We Venerate the Saints?," 17.

14   Rahner, "Jesus Christ in the Non-Christian Religions," 48.

15   Ibid., 47.

16   Rahner, "Theological Observations on the Concept of Time," 291.

17   Rahner and Vorgrimler, "Anamnesis," 19–20.

18   Ibid., 20.

19   Rahner and Vorgrimler, "Formal Object, Supernatural," 178.

20   Rahner and Vorgrimler, "Anamnesis," 19–20.

21   Rahner and Vorgrimler, "Formal Object, Supernatural," 178.

22   Rahner and Vorgrimler, "Anamnesis," 20.

INDEX

About the Publisher

The Crossroad Publishing Company publishes Crossroad and Herder & Herder books. We offer a 200-year global family tradition of books on spiritual living and religious thought. We promote reading as a time-tested discipline for focus and understanding. We help authors shape, clarify, write, and effectively promote their ideas. We select, edit, and distribute books. With our expertise and passion, we provide wholesome spiritual nourishment for heart, mind, and soul through the written word.